LIBRARY OF NEW TESTAMENT STUDIES
646

Formerly the Journal for the Study of the New Testament Supplement Series

Editor
Chris Keith

Editorial Board
Dale C. Allison, John M. G. Barclay, Lynn H. Cohick, R. Alan Culpepper,
Craig A. Evans, Robert Fowler, Simon J. Gathercole, Juan Hernández Jr., John
S. Kloppenborg, Michael Labahn, Matthew V. Novenson, Love L. Sechrest,
Robert Wall, Catrin H. Williams, Brittany E. Wilson

The Dividing Wall

Ephesians and the Integrity of the Corpus Paulinum

Martin Wright

t&tclark
LONDON • NEW YORK • OXFORD • NEW DELHI • SYDNEY

T&T CLARK
Bloomsbury Publishing Plc
50 Bedford Square, London, WC1B 3DP, UK
1385 Broadway, New York, NY 10018, USA
29 Earlsfort Terrace, Dublin 2, Ireland

BLOOMSBURY, T&T CLARK and the T&T Clark logo are
trademarks of Bloomsbury Publishing Plc

First published in Great Britain 2021
This paperback edition published in 2023

Copyright © Martin Wright, 2021

Martin Wright has asserted his right under the Copyright, Designs and Patents Act, 1988, to be identified as Author of this work.

For legal purposes the Acknowledgements on p. xi constitute an extension of this copyright page.

Cover design: Charlotte James

All rights reserved. No part of this publication may be reproduced or transmitted in any form or by any means, electronic or mechanical, including photocopying, recording, or any information storage or retrieval system, without prior permission in writing from the publishers.

Bloomsbury Publishing Plc does not have any control over, or responsibility for, any third-party websites referred to or in this book. All internet addresses given in this book were correct at the time of going to press. The author and publisher regret any inconvenience caused if addresses have changed or sites have ceased to exist, but can accept no responsibility for any such changes.

A catalogue record for this book is available from the British Library.

Library of Congress Cataloging-in-Publication Data
Names: Wright, Martin, 1981– author.
Title: The dividing wall : Ephesians and the integrity of the Corpus Paulinum / Martin Wright.
Description: London ; New York : T&T Clark, 2021. |
Series: The library of New Testament studies, 2513–8790 ; 646 |
Includes bibliographical references and index. | Summary: "This volume critiques preoccupation with the authorship of the Pauline letters, and argues for more integrative and interpretive readings of the Pauline Corpus"– Provided by publisher.
Identifiers: LCCN 2020051494 (print) | LCCN 2020051495 (ebook) |
ISBN 9780567698452 (hardback) | ISBN 9780567698469 (pdf) |
ISBN 9780567698483 (epub)
Subjects: LCSH: Bible. Epistles of Paul–Criticism, interpretation, etc.
Classification: LCC BS2650.52 .W748 2021 (print) |
LCC BS2650.52 (ebook) | DDC 227/.506–dc23
LC record available at https://lccn.loc.gov/2020051494
LC ebook record available at https://lccn.loc.gov/2020051495

ISBN: HB: 978-0-5676-9845-2
PB: 978-0-5676-9849-0
ePDF: 978-0-5676-9846-9
ePUB: 978-0-5676-9848-3

Series: Library of New Testament Studies, ISSN 2513–8790, volume 646
ISSN 2513–8790

Typeset by Newgen KnowledgeWorks Pvt. Ltd., Chennai, India

To find out more about our authors and books visit www.bloomsbury.com and sign up for our newsletters.

Contents

List of Tables	ix
Acknowledgements	xi
List of Abbreviations	xiii
Introduction: The dividing wall	1
Part One Canon and countercanon	13
1 The formation of the Corpus Paulinum	15
1. Theories	16
1.1. A single, early collection	16
1.2. A gradual collection	17
1.3. Ephesians as dam buster	18
1.4. Paul or a Pauline school?	19
1.5. Coalescence of multiple collections	20
2. Evidence	22
2.1. Manuscripts	22
2.1.1. $\mathfrak{P}^{46}$	23
2.1.2. $\mathfrak{P}^{126}$	25
2.1.3. Other papyri from collections	26
2.1.4. Distribution of single-letter papyri	28
2.1.5. Uncials	30
2.1.6. Minuscules	31
2.1.7. Stichometry	31
2.1.8. Summary	31
2.2. Traces of early variation	32
2.2.1. Attested orders	32
2.2.2. Textual character in minuscules	33
2.3. Textual variation in addresses	35
2.3.1. Romans	35

2.3.2. Ephesians	35
2.3.3. 1 Corinthians	37
2.4. Patristic references	38
2.4.1. Lists	38
2.4.2. Frequency of citation	40
2.5. Marcion	42
2.6. The Latin prologues	47
2.7. The Muratorian Fragment	49
3. Conclusions	53
2 The dissolution of the Corpus Paulinum	**57**
1. The hermeneutics of decadence	58
1.1. From doubt to disjunction: F. C. Baur	58
1.2. Canon and catholicity: Käsemann and his heirs	65
1.2.1. Ernst Käsemann and *Frühkatholizismus*	65
1.2.2. Criticism of Käsemann's model	67
1.2.3. The persistence of the decadence model: James Dunn	69
2. Alternative profiles of Paul	72
2.1. In search of a better model	72
2.1.1. Reassertion of traditional authorship	73
2.1.2. Modified trajectories	73
2.1.3. Reframing the Corpus: Douglas Campbell	76
2.1.4. Indifference to authorship	79
2.2. The promise of canonical interpretation: Brevard Childs	82
3. The Corpus Paulinum as interpretative dialogue	88
Part Two Reading Paul in Ephesians	**93**
3 From estrangement to reconciliation	**95**
1. Introduction	95
2. Exegesis	96
2.1. What kind of works? (Eph. 2.8-10)	96
2.2. Learning to remember (Eph. 2.11)	102
2.3. No Israel, no Christ (Eph. 2.12)	108

	2.4. Reconciliation, human and divine (Eph. 2.13-18)	114
	2.5. Foundation and capstone (Eph. 2.19-22)	129
3.	Conclusions	134

4 The body and the Corpus — 137

1. Introduction — 137
2. Interpretations of the body of Christ — 139
   - 2.1. Decadence: Ernst Käsemann — 139
   - 2.2. Metaphor: Gregory Dawes — 143
   - 2.3. Ideology: Dale Martin — 147
   - 2.4. Ontology: Robert Jenson — 151
3. Exegesis — 156
   - 3.1. 1 Corinthians — 156
   - 3.2. Romans — 164
   - 3.3. Colossians — 166
   - 3.4. Ephesians — 168
4. Conclusions — 183

Conclusion: *Corpus conpactum et conexum* — 185

Bibliography — 191
Index of Authors — 205
Index of Biblical References — 208
Index of Subjects — 212

Tables

1 Distribution of Pauline Papyri   29
2 Distribution of Citations   41
3 Aspects of Σῶμα Χριστοῦ in 1 Corinthians and Romans   156

Acknowledgements

This study was made possible by the generous support of the Florence and Alexander Yule Memorial Scholarship. I offer my sincere thanks to the trustees and to the nominating faculty at Pilgrim Theological College, Melbourne.

I am deeply indebted to Francis Watson for his wonderful supervision of the doctoral research which has led to this book. From his erudite counsel, sagacious in direction and shrewd in critique, and from the example of his work, I have learnt a tremendous amount about the practice of biblical interpretation, and return my heartiest thanks.

Many others have contributed to the formation of this project. Michael Champion and Kylie Crabbe, faithful friends both, generously read an earlier draft and helped to strengthen it considerably. I also benefited greatly from the judicious and stimulating critiques of my doctoral examiners, John Barclay and Eddie Adams, and of T. J. Lang, who kindly discussed the typescript with me. I was immensely fortunate in the friends I found at Durham University, through St Chad's College, the Department of Theology and Religion, Durham Cathedral and St Cuthbert's Catholic Church; in the fen-steeped bohemian comradeship of Matthew Champion, Miranda Stanyon and Miriam; in the love and support of my family, unwavering despite a hemisphere's separation; and most fortunate of all in the steadfast companionship of Harriet. Sincere thanks to you all.

Abbreviations

General

AV	Authorized Version
BADG	Baur, Arndt, Danker and Gingrich *Lexicon*
CP	Corpus Paulinum
ESV	English Standard Version
LXX	Septuagint
MS(s)	Manuscript(s)
NA^{28}	Nestle–Aland *Novum Testamentum Graece*, 28th edn
NIV	New International Version
NT	New Testament
OT	Old Testament
RSV	Revised Standard Version

Patristic works

Cyprian	*Fort.*	*Ad Fortunatum*
	Quir.	*Ad Quirinum*
Epiphanius	*Pan.*	*Panarion*
Eusebius	*Hist. Eccl.*	*Historia Ecclesiastica*
Origen	*Cels.*	*Contra Celsum*
	Hom. Num.	*Homilies on Numbers*
	Princip.	*De Principiis*
Tertullian	*Bapt.*	*De Baptismo*
	Marc.	*Adversus Marcionem*
	Prasec.	*De Praescriptione Haereticorum*
Victorinus	*Fabr.*	*De Fabricatione Mundi*

Bibliographical

AB	Anchor Bible
ACT	Ancient Christian Texts
AnBib	Analecta biblica
ANF	Ante-Nicene Fathers
ANTC	Abingdon New Testament Commentaries

ANTF	Arbeiten zur neutestamentlichen Textforschung
BBR	*Bulletin of Biblical Research*
BECNT	Baker Exegetical Commentary on the New Testament
BETL	Bibliotheca ephemeridum theologicarum lovaniensium
BEVT	Beiträge zur evangelischen Theologie
BGBE	Beiträge zur Geschichte der biblischen Exegese
BJRL	*Bulletin of the John Rylands Library*
BNTC	Black's New Testament Commentaries
BTCB	Brazos Theological Commentary on the Bible
BZNW	Beihefte zur *Zeitschrift für die neutestamentliche Wissenschaft*
CBQ	*Catholic Biblical Quarterly*
CBQMS	*Catholic Biblical Quarterly* Monograph Series
CCSL	Corpus Christianorum series latina
EKKNT	Evangelisch-katholischer Kommentar zum Neuen Testament
FRLANT	Forschungen zur Religion und Literatur des Alten und Neuen Testaments
GCS	Die Griechischen christlichen Schriftsteller
GNS	Good News Studies
HNT	Handbuch zum Neuen Testament
HTR	*Harvard Theological Review*
HUT	Hermeneutische Untersuchungen zur Theologie
ICC	International Critical Commentary
JBL	*Journal of Biblical Literature*
JR	*Journal of Religion*
JSNT	*Journal for the Study of the New Testament*
JTS	*Journal of Theological Studies*
KEK	Kritisch-exegetischer Kommentar über das Neue Testament
LNTS	Library of New Testament Studies
NET	Neutestamentliche Entwürfe zur Theologie
NHS	Nag Hammadi and Manichaean Studies
NICNT	New International Commentary on the New Testament
NIGTC	New International Greek Testament Commentary
NovT	*Novum Testamentum*
NovTSup	Supplements to *Novum Testamentum*
NTD	Das Neue Testament Deutsch
NTL	New Testament Library
NTM	New Testament Monographs
NTOA	Novum Testamentum et orbis antiquus
NTS	*New Testament Studies*
PaSt	Pauline Studies
PNTC	Pillar New Testament Commentary
PTS	Patristische Texte und Studien
QD	Quaestiones disputatae
RBL	*Review of Biblical Literature*
SBLBSNA	Society of Biblical Literature Biblical Scholarship in North America

SBLWGRW	Society of Biblical Literature Writings from the Greco-Roman World
SBR	Studies of the Bible and Its Reception
SC	Sources chrétiennes
SD	Studies and Documents
SJT	*Scottish Journal of Theology*
SNT	Studien zum Neuen Testament
SNTSMS	Society for New Testament Studies Monograph Series
SP	Sacra pagina
SR	*Studies in Religion/Sciences Religieuses*
TF	Theologische Forschung
THKNT	Theologischer Handkommentar zum Neuen Testament
TLZ	*Theologische Literaturzeitung*
TS	*Theological Studies*
TUGAL	Texte und Untersuchungen zur Geschichte der altchristlichen Literatur
TZ	*Theologische Zeitschrift*
VC	*Vigilae christianae*
VF	*Verkündigung und Forschung*
WBC	Word Biblical Commentary
WTJ	*Westminster Theological Journal*
WUNT	Wissenschaftliche Untersuchungen zum Neuen Testament
ZAC	*Zeitschrift für Antikes Christentum*
ZTK	*Zeitschrift für Theologie und Kirche*

Introduction: The dividing wall

Ephesians, that epistle of the apostle which stands in the middle in concepts as well as order. Now I say middle not because it comes after the first epistles and is longer than the final ones, but in the sense that the heart of an animal is in its mid-section, so that you might understand from this the magnitude of the difficulties and the profundity of the questions it contains.

Origen apud Jerome[1]

For Origen, the Corpus Paulinum is not just a collection but a body. The letters can even be compared to an animal's physiology, so organically are they connected. Ephesians has a place of great honour, at the heart; but if the whole body were heart, where would be the sight? Origen's analogy depends on a positive, creative view of the differences within the Corpus. Each letter has its own character, and poses distinctive questions for the interpreter, but each also contributes uniquely to the coherence of the whole. In the interplay of the several members is incorporated the legacy of Paul the apostle.

Times have changed; we have no longer one Pauline Corpus, but two. For current biblical scholarship, the functional corpus comprises the seven letters universally ascribed to the apostle. They are read as a body, one letter elucidating another; collectively they characterize their author, Paul, and delineate his thought. The seven other letters stand under various degrees of suspicion, their apostolic authorship doubted or dismissed; they are read apart, and represent not Paul himself but the church that remembered him. While the received Corpus of fourteen letters is still normative for most Christians, in the practice of interpretation, it is bisected by a dividing wall.

From the beginnings of the Christian canon, the authenticity of Pauline texts was a subject of debate. Tertullian lambasts Marcion for 'mutilating' the Corpus by omitting the Pastoral letters (*Marc.* 5) and is scarcely kinder to the unnamed presbyter who sought to supplement it with the *Acta Pauli* (*Bapt.* 17). Eusebius counts Paul's fourteen letters among the 'accepted' texts of the New Testament (ὁμολογούμενα), as

---

[1] Origen and Jerome, *The Commentaries of Origen and Jerome on St. Paul's Epistle to the Ephesians*, ed. and trans. Ronald E. Heine (Oxford: OUP, 2002), 77. This introductory part of the commentary survives only in Jerome's version, but Heine attributes much of it, including the quoted passage, to Origen.

distinct from the 'disputed' (ἀντιλεγόμενα) or 'spurious' (νόθα) (*Hist. Eccl.* 3.25.1–4; cf. 3.3.5). The Muratorian Fragment condemns Pauline forgeries to the Laodiceans and Alexandrians (ll. 63–68), but seems unaware of Hebrews. These are among the surviving traces of the gradual, piecemeal, contested process by which the canonical boundary was drawn, including or excluding texts on the basis of communal usage. Biblical scholarship of the last two centuries has reopened the question and recapitulated the debates, sometimes even in the same terms, as when F. C. Baur reprised Eusebius to divide the Pauline letters into homologoumena, antilegomena and notha.[2] The new division cuts across the old: church and academy now have, for practical purposes, rival canons.

This is a study of the Corpus Paulinum (CP), how it has been received by readers both ancient and modern, and in that light, how we might interpret it more fruitfully today. My basic thesis is that a partition based on 'authenticity' distorts the interpretation of the Corpus. Exegetical scholarship, whether liberal or conservative, has become preoccupied with authorship: it is widely assumed that 'authentic' and 'pseudonymous' writings must be read in fundamentally different ways, and so correctly classifying a disputed letter becomes a primary object in its interpretation. Depending on their view of authorship, exegetes develop a keener eye for either continuity or discontinuity with other Pauline texts. But this approach disregards the way in which the letters were in fact received and transmitted. I will argue for renewed attention to the canonical shaping that constitutes the Corpus as a complex, composite text, a dialogue of several interrelated voices which – precisely in their interaction – transmit Paul's legacy to the church. This historical and hermeneutical discussion forms Part One of the study.

My second focus is the letter to the Ephesians, which will serve as a case study for this approach to the CP. It is a text especially well suited to the purpose, partly for the sheer richness of its intertextuality: if we may extend Origen's analogy, from its place at the heart of the Corpus, Ephesians draws together many vital threads that flow through the whole body. It is also among the antilegomena of the modern canon and exemplifies how the authorship question dominates the interpretation of this group. In the two exegetical studies which comprise Part Two, I will try to show that when that matter is set aside, and the interplay between different letters is read with an unprejudiced eye, a richer interpretation is possible not only of Ephesians but also of the undisputed letters on which it draws. Throughout, I make full use of modern critical methods, but without admitting all their claims to hermeneutical hegemony; rather, I will draw attention to the theological partiality that often lies beneath the profession of historical neutrality.

Biblical scholars are not unanimous as to where exactly the dividing wall of authorship lies. For some among the more conservative, it coincides exactly with the canonical boundary, and so there is no conflict between the critical and ecclesial

---

[2] F. C. Baur, *Paulus, der Apostel Jesu Christi: Sein Leben und Wirken, seine Briefe und seine Lehre*, 2nd edn, vol. 1 (Leipzig: Fues, 1866), 275–7. The notha, at least in Baur's usage, are a subset of the antilegomena. I will continue to refer to 'antilegomena' and 'homologoumena' as a convenient shorthand for the seven disputed and seven undisputed letters of modern scholarship. The only true 'notha' now, in the sense of texts universally rejected, would be the likes of *3 Corinthians*, recognized by neither church nor academy.

corpora. A larger number would locate the division within the received CP, and so distinguish two or more bodies of texts for interpretation. There are any number of variations, qualifications and intermediate positions on the spectrum of opinion, but for the most part, they share a common logic. Texts belong together, are fundamentally coherent, are the same *kind* of text, when they stem from a single author. This criterion works both ways: difference too strained implies pseudonymity, and pseudonymity invites contrastive interpretation. 'Authentic' and 'inauthentic' texts tend to be read *against* one another. A corollary is that the received Christian canon is vulnerable to the critique of authorship: a decision that some biblical texts are pseudonymous will at least destabilize, at worst invalidate, the canonical boundary. Those sympathetic and those unsympathetic to the canon share the assumption of its fragility. I will illustrate this claim briefly from the work of two quite different scholars, Bart Ehrman and Stanley Porter. Despite occupying roughly opposite extremes in their orientation towards the Christian canon, I suggest that their underlying logic is not so dissimilar.

Bart Ehrman stakes out his rhetorical ground patently enough in the title of his recent study, *Forgery and Counterforgery: The Use of Literary Deceit in Early Christian Polemics*.[3] His subject is the phenomenon of early Christian pseudepigraphy across a large number of texts, without regard for the canonical boundary, and in relation to comparable Greco-Roman practice. Ehrman dismisses various conciliatory or mediating positions, for example, that pseudepigraphy was a 'transparent fiction', not intended to deceive (129–32), or that some letters were composed indirectly through a third party (218–22). He characterizes such arguments as 'wishful thinking' (222) on the part of theologically compromised scholars. Instead, he opts throughout for abrasive terminology – 'forgery', 'deceit', 'lie' – which, however, he insists is value-neutral:

> When I call a text forged I am making a literary-historical claim about its author; I do not mean to imply any kind of value judgment concerning its content or merit as a literary text. ... My ultimate concerns do not lie (at least in this study) with theological or ontological questions of ultimate truth, but in historical questions about how Christianity developed as a religion. (7)

This separation of history from theology is a constant of Ehrman's approach. The canon is a theological concern, which should not be allowed to 'skew' the historical investigation into pseudepigraphy more generally (2). David Meade's positive view of NT pseudepigrapha as *Vergegenwärtigung*, for example, 'requires either a set of

---

[3] Bart Ehrman, *Forgery and Counterforgery: The Use of Literary Deceit in Early Christian Polemics* (New York: OUP, 2013). Ostentatiously brusque language for pseudepigraphy seems to be becoming a fashion, extended *ad absurdum* in David Brakke's sympathetic review of Ehrman, 'Early Christian Lies and the Lying Liars Who Wrote Them', *JR* 96 (2016): 378–90. Ehrman claims that his is the first monograph on the subject of early Christian pseudepigraphy in general since Speyer's in 1971 (2), but David Aune's bibliography notes a number of others ('Reconceptualizing the Phenomenon of Ancient Pseudepigraphy: An Epilogue', in *Pseudepigraphie und Verfasserfiktion in frühchristlichen Briefen*, ed. Jörg Frey et al., WUNT 246 (Tübingen: Mohr Siebeck, 2009), 789–824 (792–3)).

theological (not historical) norms or a pair of canonical blinders' (42).[4] The canon is regarded as a non-historical, even an anti-historical phenomenon which is accordingly vulnerable to critique from more rigorously disciplined research.

Ehrman's rhetoric of scientific neutrality sets up a conflict between the compromised, ecclesial hermeneutic of the canon and the impartial, transparent hermeneutic of the critical historian. The modern reconstruction of authorship determines the kind of text we are dealing with; canonical recognition does not. So Ephesians, *3 Corinthians* and the letters of Paul and Seneca belong together on one side of the divide, Romans and 1–2 Corinthians on the other. Ehrman does not discuss how texts are gathered and reshaped by reading communities; his concern is with origins, not reception, even though both are historical processes that contribute to a text's formation.

A *locus classicus* of Pauline intertextuality, Eph. 2.1-10, can illustrate Ehrman's interpretative approach. He notes the obvious resonance with the discussion of faith, works and justification in earlier letters, but gives it little credit: 'Once the patina of Pauline phrases is scratched … the alien character of the passage is clearly shown' (186). The apparent continuity with the genuine Paul is entirely specious:

> How could the historical Paul speak of being saved by faith, and not by 'good works'? Good works? … Paul's own insistence that Gentiles do not need to keep the 'works' of Jewish Law has somehow become transmuted into a claim that no one can be 'good enough' to merit salvation. For Paul the issue was not moral probity; it was Jewish Law. This author has either very much misunderstood Paul's language or has rewritten it for a new situation, in which the words may sound similar but in fact mean something very different. (187)

I will offer an alternative reading of this passage in due course (see Chapter 3, §2.1). For now, I simply note that Eph. 2 does not contrast faith with 'good works' but simply with 'works', as in the earlier letters (the antithesis is in 2.8-9; the adjective does not occur until v. 10, when things have moved on). A detail, perhaps, but characteristic: Ehrman's focus on the authorship divide leads him to exaggerate the discontinuity between texts. This approach, with the accompanying claim that the author of Ephesians misunderstands Paul, is hardly unique;[5] Ehrman's reading of Eph. 2, though expressed with unusual bluntness, is in substance wholly conventional. In fact, despite his reputation as an iconoclast, I would suggest that his approach to interpretation is anything but radical. He states his hermeneutical principles starkly and follows them strictly, but in themselves they are entirely characteristic of post-Enlightenment exegesis: for example, the opposition between theology and history, the focus on individual texts rather than collections, the exclusive privileging of origins over reception. His pejorative account of the canon and its (possibly) pseudonymous

---

[4] See David G. Meade, *Pseudonymity and Canon: An Investigation into the Relationship of Authorship and Authority in Jewish and Earliest Christian Tradition*, WUNT 39 (Tübingen: Mohr, 1986).

[5] We will see other examples of similar rhetoric, e.g. from F. C. Baur (see the quotation on p. 64 below), or, on a different topic, Albert Schweitzer (p. 138 below).

members usefully illustrates the working out of these principles to their logical conclusion.

If Ehrman is quick to detect biblical pseudepigraphy, Stanley Porter is correspondingly sceptical; still he has a similar view of the phenomenon itself.[6] Porter gives equally short shrift to theories of indirect authorship and dismisses the idea of 'transparent fiction' altogether. If some letters are in fact pseudonymous, that is deceit, plain and simple, which if detected would have kept them out of the canon. While some might argue this no longer matters, Porter asks, 'Why should the successfully deceptive document be privileged over [noncanonical pseudepigrapha], simply by tradition, lack of perception, or historical precedent?' The conclusion follows inevitably:

> It may well be necessary to conclude that even though the early church failed to detect the non-Pauline nature of the [Pastoral] letters one must now decide to exclude them from their place as canonical writings. Or, it may be necessary (even if begrudgingly) to accept them as Pauline, because the alternative demands that we give up too much that we are unwilling to sacrifice.[7]

For Porter as for Ehrman, it is the origin of a text, and not its reception, that counts in determining its status. The formation of Paul's letters into a Corpus is not relevant to their interpretation, except insofar as it provides evidence for their authenticity. Also like Ehrman, Porter criticizes the introduction of theological argument into historical discussion.[8] He insists that the formation of the canon is a historical process which must be investigated as such, but he does not apparently regard the process as having any value in itself. The canon's validity lies not in its actual social function, but only as an expression of the criteria of apostolicity and orthodoxy, and thus it is open in principle to revision on those grounds.

In fact, Porter does not want to revise the canon, as he believes the letters included to be authentic.[9] But despite this opposite conclusion, his interpretative logic is closely parallel to Ehrman's. The two are equally scathing towards theological special pleading which evades a properly impartial historical investigation. And they both fail to realize that, in pressing this distinction, they make a choice for one historical criterion

---

[6] For the following see Stanley E. Porter, 'Pauline Authorship and the Pastoral Epistles: Implications for Canon', *BBR* 5 (1995): 105–23, and the ensuing exchange, Robert W. Wall, 'Pauline Authorship and the Pastoral Epistles: A Response to S. E. Porter', *BBR* 5 (1995): 125–8; and Stanley E. Porter, 'Pauline Authorship and the Pastoral Epistles: A Response to R. W. Wall's Response', *BBR* 6 (1996): 133–8; also Stanley E. Porter and Kent D. Clarke, 'Canonical-Critical Perspective and the Relationship of Colossians and Ephesians', *Biblica* 78 (1997): 57–86; and a more recent, but essentially unchanged, restatement of his views in Stanley E. Porter, *The Apostle Paul: His Life, Thought, and Letters* (Grand Rapids, MI: Eerdmans, 2016), esp. ch. 6, 'Pseudonymity and the Formation of the Pauline Canon'.
[7] Porter, 'Pauline Authorship', 122–3. He and Clarke offer a similarly stark alternative for Colossians and Ephesians: the 'canonical critic' who is persuaded of non-Pauline authorship must either 'be faithful to the function of the canonical process and reject the letters from the canon' or else 'reject the findings of higher criticism regarding authorship in the light of canonical formation' ('Canonical-Critical Perspective', 72). They argue for Pauline authorship (82).
[8] Most clearly in his 'Response to Wall'.
[9] Porter, 'Response to Wall', 138, n. 13.

(authorship) over another (reception), which is itself a value judgement, and arguably a theological one.

It may seem unfair to focus on two interpreters who treat canonical pseudepigraphy in such stark terms, when many biblical scholars would take a more moderate position. I do so to illustrate the logical outworking of an orientation I take to be widespread, if not always so well developed: a selective historicism where origin but not reception, authorship but not canonical shaping, is hermeneutically decisive. Even among those who do not take a negative view of pseudepigraphy, there remains a division between 'authentic' and 'inauthentic' texts which is foundational for interpretation. Studies of the undisputed letters, or of Pauline theology generally, neglect the later parts of the CP, while exegesis of the disputed letters is usually shaped by the question of authorship one way or another. The latter tendency is epitomized in these remarks of James Dunn:

> The question of whether Ephesians should also be categorized as early catholic depends on the interpretation of one or two key passages, that is to say it depends on whether Ephesians is regarded as Pauline or post-Pauline in origin: if Pauline, then the passages are better interpreted as a development of the Pauline understanding of the Church which does not significantly depart from his vision of the Church as charismatic community; if post-Pauline, then they could be interpreted as a movement ... towards the early catholicism of the Pastorals.[10]

Few mainstream interpreters are so blatantly oppositional as this. A more typical position is represented by Andrew Lincoln's commentary on Ephesians. In the Introduction, Lincoln reviews the authorship question and judges that the letter is pseudonymous. He concludes, though, with the assurance that this fact does not compromise its validity or authority; to suppose otherwise is to commit 'the "authorial fallacy", that is, to set more store by who wrote a document than by what it says'.[11] Yet, as Porter responds, if authorship really does make no difference, 'then perhaps even asking the question of authorship at all is unnecessary or committing the "authorial fallacy"'.[12] For Lincoln as for so many others, authorship becomes a preoccupation which influences the sorts of questions put to the individual text, while the canonical reception of the Corpus has no corresponding significance.

Over recent years, a number of studies have proposed new angles on the question of Pauline pseudepigraphy. I will briefly mention three. Annette Merz draws on intertextual theory to critique the interpretation of pseudo-Pauline letters, which she believes have too long controlled how the authentic letters are read.[13] Throughout, she takes a deeply critical view of the content of the Pastorals (her main focus), of the canon

---

[10] James D. G. Dunn, *Unity and Diversity in the New Testament: An Inquiry into the Character of Earliest Christianity*, 3rd edn (London: SCM, 2006), 397.
[11] Andrew T. Lincoln, *Ephesians*, WBC 42 (Dallas: Word, 1990), lxxiii.
[12] Porter, 'Pauline Authorship', 120.
[13] Annette Merz, 'The Fictitious Self-Exposition of Paul: How Might Intertextual Theory Suggest a Reformulation of the Hermeneutics of Pseudepigraphy?', in *The Intertextuality of the Epistles*, ed. Thomas L. Brodie, Dennis R. MacDonald and Stanley E. Porter, NTM 16 (Sheffield: Sheffield Phoenix, 2006), 113–32.

that legitimized them and of the history that has validated that canon. The 'fundamental error' of pre-critical interpretation was the failure to distinguish Pauline from pseudo-Pauline theology (114), and subsequent scholarship has insufficiently reformed this mistake: by claiming the status of self-interpretation, the Pastorals attempt to change the meaning of Paul's genuine letters, and such *'intentional reference-text-oriented effects'* have not been attended to (125; her emphasis). For Merz, then, the authorship division within the CP should be entrenched still more deeply. Her commentary is a critique of contemporary Pauline scholarship opposite to my own: she believes we have not yet done enough to extricate the letters from their canonical enmeshment, and to recontextualize them according to the circumstances of their composition.

Eve-Marie Becker, noting that 'pseudo-Pauline' texts are often themselves directed against 'pseudo-apostolic' teaching, suggests that such pseudepigraphy be understood as a literary strategy, a continuation of the 'Gegnerpolemik' in the undisputed letters, rather than evaluated for theological correctness or ethical integrity.[14] The contrast with the pejorative terminology of Ehrman, Porter and Merz is plain. *Substantial* authenticity can be distinguished from *literary* authenticity; the assessment of how a letter represents Paul's theology should not be confused with the question of its authorship. Already within the CP we see a contest over 'genuine' Pauline theology (384–5). Becker concludes,

> So gesehen, beginnt die Hermeneutik paulinischer Briefe textintern in den Paulusbriefen selbst und setzt sich textextern in den Deutero- und Tritopaulinen und/oder anderen frühchristlichen Schriften (z.B. 2Petr) fort. Dieser textexterne hermeneutische Deutungsprozess dauert bis in die Gegenwart an und ist bleibend unabgeschlossen. (386)

Pauline interpretation begins within the CP itself, and extends outside it: this is a promising approach, to which we will return in due course (Chapter 2, §3). Here I note that Becker still presupposes a single division, between the authentic letters, on the one hand, and their external interpreters – from ancient pseudepigrapher to modern exegete – on the other. Although she treats the division more sympathetically, it still represents a redrawing of the boundaries of the received Corpus.[15]

Finally, Gregory Fewster argues for an entirely different conceptualization of the author in reading canonical pseudepigrapha.[16] Conventional historical approaches associate a text's truthfulness with its authenticity (whatever the value of Ephesians, it does not represent *truly* Pauline thought); canonically oriented alternatives simply

---

[14] Eve-Marie Becker, 'Von Paulus zu "Paulus": Paulinische Pseudepigraphie-Forschung als literaturgeschichtliche Aufgabe', in *Pseudepigraphie und Verfasserfiktion in frühchristlichen Briefen*, ed. Jörg Frey et al., WUNT 246 (Tübingen: Mohr Siebeck, 2009), 363–86 (382).

[15] I appreciate that the 'textextern/textintern' distinction is a technical one which I am unable to unpack here. For discussion see Eve-Marie Becker, 'Text und Hermeneutik am Beispiel einer textinternen Hermeneutik', in *Die Bibel als Text: Beiträge zu einer textbezogenen Bibelhermeneutik*, ed. Oda Wischmeyer and Stefan Scholz, NET 14 (Tübingen: Francke, 2008), 193–215.

[16] Gregory P. Fewster, 'Hermeneutical Issues in Canonical Pseudepigrapha: The Head/Body Motif in the Pauline Corpus as a Test Case', in *Paul and Pseudepigraphy*, ed. Stanley E. Porter and Gregory P. Fewster, PaSt 8 (Leiden: Brill, 2013), 89–111.

focus on a later point in the text's history, and tend to harmonize differences.[17] Instead, following Foucault, Fewster redefines Paul's authorship 'functionally': the author-signature implies a corpus, and so creates a context for the letters' interpretation. Whereas a 'canon' makes a claim to interpretative authority – an ethical problem, in Fewster's view – a 'corpus' so understood does not:

> The functional author perspective avoids interpretive hegemony by appeals to an historic author or community of reception for meaning. Religious truth is a feature of texts themselves and creative interaction with them. For canonical pseudepigrapha, this assertion can be stated more specifically; the meaning of canonical pseudepigrapha can be ascertained vis-à-vis a dialogical relationship between those texts circumscribed by the author-signature. (103)

Fewster's approach has certain advantages. Because he treats a corpus as defined by an author-signature, he is able in exegesis to move freely across the 'authenticity' divide.[18] His location of meaning in the dialogue of different Pauline texts is promising, and (like Becker) has some common ground with the approach I will suggest in Chapter 2. Fewster is also right that a canonically focused reading is, in its own way, a historical reading; however, I cannot agree that this is a weakness. What is lacking is an appreciation of the canon's social embeddedness. Fewster acknowledges the communal element in the CP's formation, but not thereafter; that a community shaped by the canon has a legitimate, enduring interest in its interpretation, that it might indeed regulate its interpretation in certain normative ways, is a possibility he will not entertain. *Any* claim of interpretative hegemony is to be resisted.

The foregoing survey, I hope, indicates the potential value of this study. There is a need to revisit the assumptions associated with canonical pseudepigraphy. Individual texts are changed when they are shaped into a canon, and a new whole is created with its own stability and coherence. The phenomenon occurs within a particular reading community, and has its enduring validity in relation to that community, but is no less legitimate on that account: the historical contingency of a canon is not a liability, it is the condition of its intelligibility. This observation has important implications for how we approach a composite text like the CP. To read it sympathetically, we must appreciate the *kind* of text it is, and so understand its formation as a Corpus. Whatever sense it makes, it makes from that particular history. To reorganize the letters by new criteria is to form a new corpus, to change the text that has been transmitted to us and seek a different sort of coherence. That approach may have its own validity, but it comes at a cost: to change the canon is to change the reading community. If an interpretation is to speak meaningfully to the community receiving

---

[17] 'A hermeneutics of canon is about similarity not difference' (99, following Aichele) – perhaps an understandable response to some examples of the genre, but a caricature nonetheless.
[18] Although his exegetical illustration, focusing on the body of Christ, is not altogether successful (see n. 37, p. 152 below). Note also that Fewster's definition still excludes Hebrews from the CP.

and transmitting the Christian canon, it must engage with the coherence implicit in the canon's shaping.

So this study attempts to reengage with the CP as a body, reading it congruently with its reception and transmission, as a composite text with its own integrity. Using the particular example of Ephesians, I aim to show that this hermeneutic has a felicity lacking in the modern division by authorship, for disputed and undisputed letters alike. Part One appraises the contrast between the original formation of the CP and its recalibration over the last two centuries. Chapter 1 reviews several theories for how the CP was formed, and examines the surviving body of evidence, including the manuscripts. The sources are too scarce and obscure to admit much certainty, but point to the familiar CP emerging surprisingly quickly. In particular, the evidence that the Pastorals were a late inclusion is weaker than generally supposed; the place of Hebrews, however, is clearly ambiguous.

Chapter 2 turns to the modern redrawing of canonical boundaries. I argue that the philological interrogation of authorship, pioneered by Schleiermacher and others, was radicalized by F. C. Baur into a 'hermeneutics of decadence', a declining trajectory from the authentic Pauline gospel into the *Frühkatholizismus* of the later letters. This position was most notably advanced in the twentieth century by Ernst Käsemann, and continues to exercise influence. After briefly examining a number of other approaches to the CP, none wholly satisfactory, I turn to the more promising work of Brevard Childs. Although welcoming his canonical orientation, I identify significant weaknesses in his actual exegesis of the CP. The final part of Chapter 2 sets out my own approach. Drawing on the work of Margaret Mitchell on the Corinthian correspondence, I propose an understanding of the CP as an interpretative dialogue, in which the question of authorship is secondary to the ongoing reception and reinterpretation of earlier texts throughout the whole.

Part Two moves from these broad hermeneutical questions to the interpretation of particular texts, and is intended both to illustrate and to test the approach proposed in Part One. It comprises two distinct exegetical studies. Chapter 3 focuses on a particular passage, Eph. 2.8-22, in relation to a number of earlier Pauline texts, from Romans, 1-2 Corinthians, Galatians and Colossians. Chapter 4 takes a thematic approach and considers the body of Christ throughout the CP. A number of different contemporary interpretations of this theologoumenon are surveyed, before exegesis of the relevant passages from 1 Corinthians, Romans, Colossians and Ephesians. These two chapters show that Ephesians is deeply embedded in the CP, that its continuity with earlier Pauline letters is generally underestimated, that it serves an integrating function within the Corpus and, above all, that patterns of reception and reinterpretation across the Corpus are far more complex than the bifurcation between 'authentic' and 'spurious' letters can admit. I believe this second part of the study offers fruitful new readings of familiar texts – in fact occasionally addresses widespread misreadings – and so vindicates the hermeneutical position adopted in the first part.

A few points of clarification. Throughout this study, I remain deliberately agnostic about the authorship of Ephesians and the other antilegomena. I intend no historical judgement when I use terms like 'deuteropauline'; nor, conversely, when I sometimes refer to their author as 'Paul', by which I simply mean the implied author, the Paul of the canon. I think it probable, but not certain, that among the thirteen letters attributed to Paul there are some that do not stem directly from his hand. The present study claims no more than this, but not because I consider authorship always and altogether irrelevant to interpretation. Rather, at the present time, we have so monstrously inflated both the importance of authorship and the certainty with which it can be known that we would do better simply to forget this matter for a while, in the hope of eventually seeing it with fresh eyes.

However, a moratorium on the authorship question does not mean historical incuriosity. It will be apparent that I do not approach the CP only in its 'final form', but as the product of a complicated history which affects its interpretation; in fact, treating the 'final' text apart from its formation seems to me dangerously close to separating theological meaning from history. It makes a difference to the meaning of Ephesians whether it is an earlier or a later text than Romans, for example; and as I argue in response to Campbell (Chapter 2, §2.1.3), although novel reconstructions of the letters' 'framing' are possible, they must be shown to make better *exegetical* sense if they are to persuade. Hence the studies in my Part Two, which presuppose the relative order Gal.–1 Cor.–2 Cor.–Rom.–Col.–Eph., contribute to the defence of this conventional chronology. Similarly, I accept a literary relationship between Colossians and Ephesians, and assume Colossian priority; but whereas much modern exegesis focuses on this two-way relationship to the neglect of others, I will address it in the context of broader Pauline intertextuality. We will see that, despite the linguistic closeness of these two letters, they sometimes diverge quite markedly.

Another corollary is that the literary order of the letters within the Corpus, as distinct from their historical order, has not played a major role in the exegesis offered here, at least not overtly. In this I may seem to differ from some other canonically oriented interpreters, but if so I think it is mainly in emphasis. Of course the order in which the letters are transmitted affects how they are read in relation to one another (Origen would never have called Ephesians the 'heart' if it had not been placed in the middle). Nevertheless, the final literary arrangement of the letters does not simply replace their historical sequence. The two kinds of order are often in tension, a fact which works against the unilateral subordination of some texts to others. I will have more to say about historical than literary ordering, but I am ultimately advocating a dialectical approach which can recognize more than one sort of directionality across the Corpus.

Finally, my thesis is that a preoccupation with authorship distorts exegesis at *all* points on the ecclesial and critical spectrum. An interpreter who wants to demonstrate pseudonymity will tend to emphasize difference and minimize continuity; another, persuaded of a letter's authenticity, will do the reverse. I will give examples of both kinds in what follows, but my critique focuses principally on those who exaggerate difference. That is simply because they are in the ascendant (in the academy, at least): it is far more usual than not to divide the CP in the practice of interpretation. As a corrective, therefore, this study at times places more weight upon continuity than discontinuity within the Corpus. This emphasis should not be misconstrued as harmonization. As I hope my exegetical chapters will show, it is not in mere similarity, but in the *transformation* of Pauline texts – the creative reworking of earlier strands in later letters – that this interpretative approach finds its most fertile ground. After all, the proper functioning of the body depends upon the distinctive role of each particular member, no less than upon the connectedness of the whole.

Part One

Canon and countercanon

1

The formation of the Corpus Paulinum

How did fourteen distinct letters become a single book? Was there a particular moment when the collection was formed, a particular codex that established its scope, or did the letters coalesce together more gradually? Did a single collection prevail throughout the Christian world, or was there variation from place to place? Did some letters gain earlier or wider acceptance than others? Were all fourteen treated in the same way, or was there differentiation between them? These questions are fundamental to how we understand the Corpus Paulinum as a composite text. Its history plays into its interpretation, just as the history of Paul and the Corinthians, for example, plays into the interpretation of their correspondence. And as with the individual letters, the background to the Corpus is shrouded, but not completely opaque.

This chapter investigates the earliest reception and collection of the Pauline letters, reviewing the main theories for the Corpus's formation and reconsidering the available evidence. Our familiar CP is well attested from the fourth century: for example, Eusebius, as we have noted, acknowledges fourteen letters as Paul's, and they are all listed in Athanasius's famous Festal Letter of 367.[1] But it is disputed how early this collection was in widespread use, and what process brought it about. Some reconstructions we will find to be overly speculative, but although the sources are sparse, we will see at least the outline of a picture emerging. There is evidence of considerable variation through the second century, with a number of proto-collections probably in circulation, but the situation is not totally chaotic, and a relatively stable Corpus develops surprisingly soon. Throughout, we will be particularly attentive to the place of what are now the antilegomena; for this study, it is especially important to understand whether the modern dividing wall has any foundation, or any parallel, in the history of the CP's formation.

This complex topic can easily occupy a monograph in its own right. Our discussion is necessarily selective, and draws particularly upon two such longer treatments, namely the doctoral dissertations of Lovering and Trobisch.[2] First, the main reconstructions

---

[1] See the full translation in David Brakke, 'A New Fragment of Athanasius's Thirty-Ninth Festal Letter: Heresy, Apocrypha, and the Canon', HTR 103 (2010): 47–66 (§18, pp. 60–1, for the Pauline letters).
[2] Eugene H. Lovering, 'The Collection, Redaction and Early Circulation of the Corpus Paulinum' (PhD, Southern Methodist University, 1988); David Trobisch, *Die Entstehung der Paulusbriefsammlung: Studien zu den Anfängen christlicher Publizistik*, NTOA 10 (Freiburg (Schweiz): Universitätsverlag, 1989). Other summary discussions, of varying usefulness, include: Harry Y. Gamble, *The New Testament Canon: Its Making and Meaning* (Philadelphia,

of the CP's history will be sketched in outline, before we proceed to an analysis of the relevant evidence, and finally an assessment of the competing theories and the implications for the present study.

1. Theories

1.1. A single, early collection

The first systematic investigations of the CP's origins concluded that, apart from Hebrews, it reached its canonical form in the first century. This was Theodor Zahn's view: from Pauline citations in the Apostolic Fathers, and from lists in Tertullian, the Muratorian Fragment and elsewhere, he infers that a thirteen-letter collection was extant before the time of *1 Clement*, and that it originally began with 1 Corinthians and ended with Romans. Letters were undoubtedly exchanged before this, as suggested by Col. 4.16 and 2 Pet. 3.15-16, and so would have been occasionally found in small collections, but the production of the thirteen-letter corpus was a deliberate act of authoritative selection independent of any such earlier private collections. This CP's suitability for liturgical reading led to its widespread acceptance, displacing any alternatives, which in any case could not have been very well established. It is therefore to be dated very early, not long after Paul's death; the question of when Hebrews was added remains open.[3]

Adolf von Harnack's position does not depart far from Zahn's. He refuses to speculate about smaller collections that may have predated the surviving MSS, with the exception of the ten-letter canon attested in Marcion. This is as far back as we can trace, and represents a collection formed in the last quarter of the first century, to which the Pastorals were added before 100.[4] Although Paul's letters were therefore known as a corpus from very early on, they were not weighted equally alongside the gospels and

---

PA: Fortress, 1985), 36–41; Jerome Murphy-O'Connor, *Paul the Letter-Writer: His World, His Options, His Skills*, GNS 41 (Collegeville, MN: Liturgical, 1995), 114–30; Robert M. Price, 'The Evolution of the Pauline Canon', *Hervormde Teologiese Studies* 53 (1997): 36–67; Andreas Lindemann, 'Die Sammlung der Paulusbriefe im 1. und 2. Jahrhundert', in *The Biblical Canons*, ed. Jean-Marie Auwers and H. J. de Jonge, BETL 163 (Leuven: Leuven University & Peeters, 2003), 321–51; Stanley E. Porter, 'When and How Was the Pauline Canon Complied? An Assessment of Theories', in *The Pauline Canon*, ed. Stanley E. Porter, PaSt 1 (Leiden: Brill, 2004), 95–127; Porter, 'Paul and the Process of Canonization', in *Exploring the Origins of the Bible: Canon Formation in Historical, Literary, and Theological Perspective*, ed. Craig A. Evans and Emanuel Tov (Grand Rapids, MI: Baker, 2008), 173–202; Porter, 'Paul and the Pauline Letter Collection', in *Paul and the Second Century*, ed. Michael F. Bird and Joseph R. Dodson, LNTS 412 (London: Clark, 2011), 19–36 (there is considerable overlap between these three chapters from Porter).

[3] Theodor Zahn, *Geschichte des neutestamentlichen Kanons*, vol. 1, part 2 (Erlangen: Deichert, 1889), 811–39; Theodor Zahn, *Grundriß der Geschichte des neutestamentlichen Kanons: Eine Ergänzung zu der Einleitung in das Neue Testament*, 2nd edn (Leipzig: Deichert, 1904), 35–7. Porter mistakenly attributes to Zahn the view that this original CP excluded the Pastorals, and on this basis distinguishes him from Harnack ('When and How', 100, and similarly elsewhere).

[4] Adolf von Harnack, *Die Briefsammlung des Apostels Paulus und die anderen vorkonstantinischen christlichen Briefsammlungen* (Leipzig: Hinrichs, 1926), 6–7. Polycarp's *Philippians* is cited as the earliest evidence for a thirteen-letter collection, available in both Smyrna and Philippi, though this allows for a slightly later date than Harnack suggests.

OT until after Marcion. The formal canonization of a (admittedly edited) CP and gospel was his innovation, to which the church was obliged to respond, albeit hesitantly; he forced the church fathers into Paulinism, and so led indirectly to the CP's eventual enshrinement as canonical scripture. The Muratorian Fragment shows that by *ca.* 200, this push was succeeding.[5]

A scheme of an early and comprehensive collection can accommodate the possibility that Ephesians, Colossians or 2 Thessalonians were written after Paul's death, but allows no distinction in their canonical reception. Any special place they may have had in the earliest circulation is no longer traceable; so far as can be determined, they have always been received in the middle of a Pauline Corpus. The case with respect to the Pastorals is less clear in this model, and Hebrews is treated as distinctive.

1.2. A gradual collection

A number of later scholars have been more confident than Zahn or Harnack of the pre-canonical circulation of various small letter collections. In their view, the shaping of the CP owes less to its final redactor than to the gradual process of accretion by which these collections were exchanged and gathered together. This model places greater weight upon variation in the attested forms of the CP, seeing there traces of an originally more fluid state, while still postulating a decisive redaction at some point. A representative exponent is Günther Zuntz, who traces subsequent tradition back to an archetypal CP around 100, but believes that smaller collections were made and circulated before this point.[6]

Kurt Aland adopts a similar view after a survey of varying text character in Pauline minuscule MSS, which leads him to reject a single *Ursammlung* in favour of multiple early corpora; this study will be discussed in §2.2.2 below.[7] The completest and most sober survey of our question in recent times, Eugene Lovering's doctoral dissertation, also reaches a conclusion of this kind, adopting Zuntz's image of a 'river' into which flow various streams at different points.[8] Lovering also emphasizes that if this model is correct, it causes difficulties for many historical critics who presuppose not only the pseudonymity of Ephesians, Colossians, 2 Thessalonians and the Pastorals but also partition theories in many of the undisputed letters. Where authorship or redaction really does postdate Paul, it must have occurred at a very early stage to have been so widely accepted across different collections, and such theories need to plausibly account for how and why this could be.[9]

Inasmuch as there is a twentieth-century scholarly 'mainstream' on the formation of the CP, it can be plotted on a rough continuum from (e.g.) Harnack, emphasizing

---

[5] Ibid., 17–22.
[6] Günther Zuntz, *The Text of the Epistles: A Disquisition upon the* Corpus Paulinum (London: OUP, 1953), 278–9.
[7] Kurt Aland, 'Die Entstehung des Corpus Paulinum', in *Neutestamentliche Entwürfe* (München: Kaiser, 1979), 302–50.
[8] Lovering, 'Corpus Paulinum', 327–8, 346. As well as Zuntz and Aland, Lovering mentions Lake, Lietzmann and Harrison as representing this kind of position.
[9] Ibid., esp. 346–8 and chs. 1 and 4.

uniformity in the sources and postulating a single early edition, to (e.g.) Aland, emphasizing diversity and postulating multiple early collections. Within this framework, a spectrum of basically commensurable views have been debated. But there have also been proposals that sit altogether outside the square.

1.3. Ephesians as dam buster

The first and most influential such radical alternative was proposed by Edgar J. Goodspeed.[10] His account of the CP begins from the observation that the synoptic gospels and Acts do not appear to refer to Paul's letters, suggesting that their collection and dissemination was yet to occur.[11] The publication of Acts provided the stimulus for an admirer of Paul's to collect letters which had been individually preserved by their recipients. This person then wrote a meditative digest drawn from all the letters, the text we now know as Ephesians. In this he most closely follows the text he knows best, Colossians; Colossae being the one church to which Acts would not have led him, it is likely that his prior acquaintance with this letter led to the idea of seeking out the others. He probably also had Philemon, which was addressed to much the same community as Colossians, and which is 'doubtless' the original letter to the Laodiceans (Col. 4.16).[12] Around this nucleus, the letters to the Romans, Corinthians, Galatians, Philippians and Thessalonians are gathered, and to the whole Ephesians is prefaced (lacking the words 'in Ephesus', 1.1), part-rhapsody, part-commentary, introducing the newly arranged Corpus as a unified testimony to the catholic faith in all its varied particularity:

> It is as though the letters of Paul had been gathering, dammed up behind the obstacle of their private-letter style, until Ephesians breaks a way through for them, and forms the cascade by which their refreshing waters reach the churches.[13]

Foremost among Goodspeed's followers was John Knox, who was particularly concerned with Marcion's witness to the putative ten-letter collection, and its compatibility with early references to Paul's 'seven churches'.[14] Knox believed not only that Corinthians and Thessalonians were treated in this corpus as single letters but also that Philemon was attached to Colossians, as being addressed to the same community. This he infers partly from the 'Marcionite' prologues to the letters, which appear in the Latin textual tradition, and partly from the order of Marcion's canon.[15] Knox also identifies the collector of the CP and author of Ephesians as Onesimus, bishop of

---

[10] Edgar J. Goodspeed, *New Solutions of New Testament Problems* (Chicago: University of Chicago, 1927); Goodspeed, *The Meaning of Ephesians* (Chicago: University of Chicago, 1933); and in various other publications.
[11] Zahn had in fact made the same observation, at least regarding Acts, and took this as a *terminus a quo* for the collection of the letters, which he dated around 80–85 (*Geschichte*, 1889, 1.833–5). Clearly he did not draw Goodspeed's other conclusions from the silence of Acts.
[12] Goodspeed, *Meaning*, 6.
[13] Ibid., 10–11.
[14] John Knox, *Marcion and the New Testament: An Essay in the Early History of the Canon* (Chicago: University of Chicago, 1942), 53–60.
[15] Ibid., 40–6.

Ephesus and the subject of Paul's letter to Philemon, a suggestion first introduced by Goodspeed as 'mere conjecture' in a later restatement of his theory.[16]

The Goodspeed theory has been widely influential, though much more so among English- than German-speaking scholars.[17] It has an attractive completeness and satisfying narrative, especially as developed by Knox, but we will find that it fails as an interpretation of the evidence. For one thing, it is by no means certain that the author of Acts did not know the Pauline letters,[18] and the assumption that they did not circulate before the formation of the Corpus is highly dubious. Yet these points cannot be conceded without the loss of the whole theory. Goodspeed is more convincing on the close intertextual relationship between Ephesians and the rest of the Corpus, a theme to be further developed in the second part of this study.[19]

1.4. Paul or a Pauline school?

Hans-Martin Schenke shares with Goodspeed the view that Paul's letters were not widely known until after the publication of Acts, and agrees with him that the production of pseudepigraphal letters and the collection of the CP must be considered together.[20] But unlike Goodspeed, he attributes this process not to an individual but to a school of Paul's disciples, who were also responsible for the redaction of the authentic letters from fragments. This allows for considerable diversity in what counts as 'deuteropauline', a term that Schenke takes to include Ephesians, Colossians, 2 Thessalonians, the Pastorals and even 1 Peter. Many subsequent students of these letters presumed some such thesis, although what is actually meant by a 'Pauline school' varies considerably,[21] and the whole idea has more recently come in for strong criticism.[22]

---

[16] John Knox, *Philemon among the Letters of Paul*, 2nd edn, 1935 (London: Collins, 1960), 92; Edgar J. Goodspeed, *The Key to Ephesians* (Chicago: University of Chicago, 1956), xiv–xv. Of course, the identification of the two figures as the same Onesimus is itself uncertain.

[17] Others who developed it further include Albert E. Barnett, *Paul Becomes a Literary Influence* (Chicago: University of Chicago, 1941); Lucetta Mowry, 'The Early Circulation of Paul's Letters', *JBL* 63 (1944): 73–86; Kenneth L. Carroll, 'The Expansion of the Pauline Corpus', *JBL* 72 (1953): 230–7; and C. Leslie Mitton, *The Formation of the Pauline Corpus of Letters* (London: Epworth, 1955).

[18] See William O. Walker, 'Acts and the Pauline Corpus Reconsidered', *JSNT* 24 (1985): 3–23.

[19] Another 'sudden collection' theory is advanced by Schmithals, who argues that the earliest CP ran 1–2 Corinthians, Galatians, Philippians, 1–2 Thessalonians, Romans; that these seven letters were compiled from sixteen fragments; and that the purpose was to combat gnosticism. For the theory, see Walter Schmithals, 'Zur Abfassung und ältesten Sammlung der paulinischen Hauptbriefe', in *Paulus und die Gnostiker*, TF 35 (Hamburg–Bergstedt: Reich, 1965), 175–200; for convincing rebuttal, principally Harry Y. Gamble, 'The Redaction of the Pauline Letters and the Formation of the Pauline Corpus', *JBL* 94 (1975): 403–18; also Lovering, 'Corpus Paulinum', 301–5, and Porter, 'When and How', 107–9.

[20] Hans-Martin Schenke, 'Das Weiterwirken des Paulus und die Pflege seines Erbes durch die Paulus-Schule', *NTS* 21 (1975): 505–18. The idea of a 'Pauline school' exemplified by the later Pauline letters was first suggested by Hans Conzelmann, 'Paulus und die Weisheit', *NTS* 12 (1966): 231–44.

[21] On this point see Angela Standhartinger, 'Colossians and the Pauline School', *NTS* 50 (2004): 572–93 (572–3). One modification of Schenke's thesis is proposed by Alexander Sand, 'Überlieferung und Sammlung der Paulusbriefe', in *Paulus in den neutestamentlichen Spätschriften: Zur Paulusrezeption im Neuen Testament*, ed. Karl Kertelge, QD 89 (Freiburg: Herder, 1981), 11–24. Sand does not admit the necessity of partition theories, and limits the 'school' to Paul's immediate co-workers and, later, their disciples.

[22] Bart D. Ehrman, *Forgery and Counterforgery: The Use of Literary Deceit in Early Christian Polemics* (Oxford: OUP), 172–4. Among other things, the conflict over Paul's teaching even within his lifetime makes the idea of a *single* enduring Pauline school implausible.

That some such group of Paul's disciples was responsible for preserving, editing, collecting and sometimes writing the Pauline letters is also the view of Harry Gamble.[23] To this extent he follows Schenke, but goes beyond him at a number of points: for example, suggesting that Paul himself may well have kept copies of some of his own letters (not an unusual practice), and these were later edited by his associates; or, on the basis of textual evidence, concluding that some letters were already being circulated during Paul's lifetime.[24] Gamble also postulates three early editions of the CP, namely one used by Marcion, another lying behind early MSS and a third, the oldest, reflected in references to Paul's 'seven churches'; in this last point he follows Knox.[25] Gamble does not so much advance a new theory as integrate elements of a number of others, which are themselves of varying strength. Accordingly, some of his conclusions are sounder than others.

Unlike some of the other approaches discussed here, the theory of a Pauline school requires a division of the CP by authorship. The letters classed as deuteropauline are interpreted with reference not to Paul himself, but to later tradition; the hermeneutic is of course not unique to this historical hypothesis, but does necessarily accompany it.

A theory essentially opposite to the 'Pauline school', advocated in recent years by E. Randolph Richards and Stanley Porter, is that Paul himself was personally involved in the collection not just of a few letters but of the whole CP.[26] This builds upon the high degree of consistency in the attested corpora, apart from the position of Hebrews. Whether such a theory seems plausible depends partly on how much weight is attached to such variations as do exist – Porter downplays them where many others make much of them – and partly on the willingness to accept as authentic all thirteen letters bearing Paul's name, usually a corollary of this position.[27] Clearly, this approach does not admit any deuteropauline texts within the CP, but Hebrews must be marginal, and individual letters could arguably still play hermeneutically distinctive roles by virtue of position or content.

1.5. Coalescence of multiple collections

The suggestion that the canonical CP represents the coalescence of two or more earlier letter collections has been advanced in a number of different ways. The first theory of this kind was proposed by H. J. Frede, who surveyed every available example of or

---

[23] Gamble, *New Testament Canon*, 39–41. See also Harry Y. Gamble, 'Pseudonymity and the New Testament Canon', in *Pseudepigraphie und Verfasserfiktion in frühchristlichen Briefen*, ed. Jörg Frey et al., WUNT 246 (Tübingen: Mohr Siebeck, 2009), 333–62 (334–9).

[24] Harry Y. Gamble, *Books and Readers in the Early Church: A History of Early Christian Texts* (New Haven, CT: Yale University Press, 1995), 97–101.

[25] Ibid., 59–62.

[26] E. Randolph Richards, 'The Codex and the Early Collection of Paul's Letters', BBR 8 (1998): 151–66; Richards, *Paul and First-Century Letter Writing: Secretaries, Composition and Collection* (Downers Grove, IL: InterVarsity, 2004), ch. 14; and see Porter's chapters cited in n. 2, p. 16 above, esp. 'Process of Canonization', 191–202. Richards suggests that the CP arose from Paul's notebook copies of his own letters, and that this led unintentionally to the Christian adoption of the codex.

[27] Richards allows for the possibility that the Pastorals are pseudonymous, and that only a ten-letter CP originated with Paul's notebook, but his case is stronger if the Pastorals are authentic.

reference to the CP, and by comparing the different orders in which the letters were there attested, reconstructed two primitive corpora, 'Western' and 'general'; the gradual accommodation of the former to the latter explains the attested variations.[28] This study, which will be discussed in §2.2.1 below, has been widely influential, and later multi-source theories have generally followed Frede's lead in focusing on canon order. One example is that of Jerome Murphy-O'Connor, who proposes two proto-collections: 'A' (Rom.–Gal.) and 'B' (Eph.–Thess.), a division derived from the capitulation of Codex Vaticanus.[29]

The most thoroughly worked-out such hypothesis is that of David Trobisch.[30] From his survey of the evidence, Trobisch concludes that only nine significant orders of the CP are attested. He subjects this data to a comparative analysis to reconstruct the archetypal order or orders (the method is based upon Hans von Soden's analysis of Cyprian's letters).[31] This results in two proposed proto-collections (56–62). The first comprises thirteen letters in the familiar canonical order, but lacking Hebrews; they are ordered by addressee (communities then individuals), and then by length (descending). However, because Ephesians is longer than Galatians, which it follows, Trobisch believes that it begins a new sequence of letters ordered by length, signalling that an early appendix begins at this point.[32] Rom.–Gal., then, is the earliest kernel of this collection. The second proto-collection comprises Romans, Hebrews, 1 Corinthians and Ephesians. In a separate analysis, Trobisch finds evidence for common redaction in these four letters to make their address less particular, and takes this as independent confirmation of his earlier findings (79–83). So his proposal is that *two* early four-letter corpora were later absorbed into the canonical CP.

Finally Trobisch compares the CP with other ancient letter collections, reconstructing the stages of their growth and placing his proposed Pauline sources within the same framework, proceeding from later to earlier stages with increasingly hypothetical results. Two major conclusions follow. First, a proto-collection of Romans, Corinthians and Galatians became the kernel of the later thirteen-letter collection; Rom. 16 was

---

[28] Hermann Josef Frede, 'Die Ordnung der Paulusbriefe und der Platz des Kolosserbriefs im Corpus Paulinum', in *Epistulae ad Philippenses et ad Colossenses*, Vetus Latina 24 (Freiburg: Herder, 1969), 290–303. A third, 'chronological' order accounts for some exceptions. Nils A. Dahl, 'The Origin of the Earliest Prologues to the Pauline Letters', *Semeia* 12 (1978): 233–77 (263), also advocates a modified version of Frede's thesis.

[29] Murphy-O'Connor, *Paul the Letter-Writer*, 120–30. Hebrews is placed between Galatians and Ephesians in this numbered capitulation only, not in the codex's main text, as Murphy-O'Connor implies (124); see §2.1.5 below. For another two-source theory, postulating distinct private and church letter collections, see Jerome D. Quinn, 'P46 – The Pauline Canon?', *CBQ* 36 (1974): 379–85; and Lovering, 'Corpus Paulinum', 326.

[30] Above all in his doctoral thesis, *Die Entstehung*; this analysis underlies his later books *Paul's Letter Collection: Tracing the Origins* (Minneapolis, MN: Fortress, 1994) and *The First Edition of the New Testament* (Oxford: OUP, 2000), which add little new for our purposes.

[31] Trobisch, *Die Entstehung*, 46–56.

[32] This argument has a family resemblance with F. C. Baur's analysis of Marcion's canon. He argues that Marcion's order, beginning Gal.–Cor.–Rom., can only be chronological; when the Thessalonian letters follow next, it must indicate the beginning of a second proto-collection. Happily these two collections tally exactly with Baur's division between homologoumena and antilegomena. (F. C. Baur, *Paulus, der Apostel Jesu Christi: Sein Leben und Wirken, seine Briefe und seine Lehre*, 2nd edn, vol. 2 (Leipzig: Fues, 1867), 278.)

added as a 'cover note' when this collection was sent to the congregation at Ephesus. Second, Paul was personally involved at the earliest stage of editing his letters for circulation. 2 Corinthians is an exemplary instance of authorial recension, but almost all the undisputed Pauline letters bear some trace of this process (123–31). In *Paul's Letter Collection*, Trobisch goes further and claims that 'it is highly probable that this old collection [i.e. Rom.–Gal.] was edited and prepared for publication by Paul himself'.[33]

Trobisch's theory is elaborate and, to say the least, controversial, but it is a thoroughgoing attempt to account for the data, and not without continuing influence. Among other things, it implies that different kinds of theological significance attach to the 'catholic' Pauline letters, and again to those edited by Paul himself. Either or both of these subgroups may be hermeneutically privileged if Trobisch's hypothesis is accepted.

Each of these accounts of the CP's formation has its own implications for interpreting both the individual letters and the collection as a whole. If Goodspeed is correct, for example, then clearly Ephesians plays a unique role within the Corpus, but Hebrews, the Pastorals, Philemon and even Colossians also contribute in distinctive ways. A position like Gamble's gives a certain priority to the church letters over the personal ones, which is harder to maintain if we follow Zahn, and impossible in Porter's case. For Trobisch, 2 Corinthians and Galatians constitute a particular link with Paul himself, Ephesians and Hebrews especially represent the wider reception of his letters, Romans and 1 Corinthians belong to both these groups and the remaining letters have a more secondary status. Almost all the more recent scholars surveyed above make some claim for the distinctiveness of the Pastoral letters within the Corpus; in the case of Ephesians, Colossians and 2 Thessalonians, opinions vary more widely, while everyone agrees that Hebrews is in some way unique. We will now turn to consider the MSS and other relevant evidence, with a view to evaluating these various accounts and seeing what we can confidently conclude about the CP's shaping.

2. Evidence

2.1. Manuscripts

The relative significance of the various MS sources is discussed by Trobisch,[34] and there is no need to replicate the detail of his work. What follows gives only an overview, with more attention to some papyri that have come to light since the time of his study. Useful information is also available in Aland's indices,[35] though these too lack the most recent discoveries. Apart from the various editions cited below, I have

---

[33] Trobisch, *Paul's Letter Collection*, 54.
[34] Trobisch, *Die Entstehung*, 14–29. See also the useful overview in D. C. Parker, *An Introduction to the New Testament Manuscripts and Their Texts* (Cambridge: CUP, 2008), 249–56.
[35] Kurt Aland, ed., *Repertorium der griechischen christlichen Papyri*, vol. 1: Biblische Papyri, PTS 18 (Berlin: de Gruyter, 1976); Aland, ed., *Kurzgefasste Liste der griechischen Handschriften des Neuen Testaments*, 2nd edn, ANTF 1 (Berlin: de Gruyter, 1994).

examined online images of many MSS through the invaluable website of the Institut für Neutestamentliche Textforschung, Münster (ntvmr.uni-muenster.de), which also provides details of findings more recently catalogued.[36]

With the exception of Hebrews, which moves about within the Corpus and is sometimes omitted altogether, we will see that the MS evidence attests a relatively stable CP. Occasional instances of variation are the more noticeable because of the widespread consistency. In particular, we will find no evidence that Ephesians, Colossians or 2 Thessalonians had an independent reception outside the context of the CP, and only rare variation in their placement. It should be noted, though, that apart from $\mathfrak{P}^{46}$ the MSS are not the earliest evidence we have, and a more complex picture will emerge when other sources are considered.

What follows focuses on papyri which attest a collection of more than one Pauline letter.[37] Briefer consideration is given to the distribution of papyri attesting only a single letter, and to Greek uncials and minuscules. The significance of variation in later sources, especially minuscules, and in translations, is discussed in §2.2 below.

2.1.1. $\mathfrak{P}^{46}$

(*ca.* 200) Rom. (5.17–) Heb. 1–2 Cor. Eph. Gal. Phil. Col. 1 Thess. (–5.28)[38]
Dublin, Chester Beatty Library, P. Chester Beatty II
Ann Arbor, University of Michigan, P. Michigan Inv. 6238

This is one of the two earliest surviving Pauline MSS, usually being dated around 200 (although earlier dates have been proposed),[39] and is the oldest CP for which we have direct evidence. But it is incomplete, and its original scope is unclear. The surviving leaves belong to a single quire, the size of which can be determined from pagination. Nine double sheets, that is, eighteen leaves or thirty-six pages, are missing from an original fifty-two sheets (208 pages); this includes fourteen missing pages each at the beginning and end. It has generally been assumed that this quire would have formed a complete codex itself, a view which is however not unchallenged (see below).

The reconstruction of the amount of text missing from the quire is unusually difficult, because the script becomes more dense (in lines per page and characters per line) as it proceeds. It seems that the scribe became increasingly concerned about lack

---

[36] Still more MSS have been catalogued since the following survey was completed.
[37] Throughout, references to 'Pauline' letters include Hebrews, since as this chapter will show, it is received as part of the CP, however ambivalently.
[38] Frederic G. Kenyon, *The Chester Beatty Biblical Papyri*, vol. 3, Supp.: Pauline Epistles (Text) (London: Walker, 1936).
[39] For an overview of the dating debate, see Don Barker, 'The Dating of New Testament Papyri', *NTS* 57 (2011): 571–82. The late first-century date proposed by Young K. Kim has been much criticized; Barker settles tentatively on a range of 150–250. The other Pauline MS to be dated *ca.* 200 is $\mathfrak{P}^{32}$, a fragment of Titus (Arthur S. Hunt, ed., *Catalogue of the Greek Papyri in the John Rylands Library Manchester*, vol. 1: Literary Texts (Nos. 1–61) (Manchester: Quaritch, Sherratt & Hughes, 1911), 10–11, dates this to the third century; Kurt Aland and Barbara Aland, *The Text of the New Testament: An Introduction to the Critical Editions and to the Theory and Practice of Modern Textual Criticism*, trans. Erroll F. Rhodes (German 1981; Grand Rapids, MI: Eerdmans, 1987), 98 and NA[28] give *ca.* 200).

of space. The last surviving leaf breaks off before the very end of 1 Thess. 5.28; it is virtually certain that 2 Thessalonians would have followed, as it invariably does in other collections and canon lists, but beyond that point is less clear. The missing seven leaves would have been too many for 2 Thessalonians alone, or 2 Thess.–Phlm.,[40] but too few for these letters and the Pastorals as well. Trobisch is justified to conclude that there has probably been some sort of scribal error, and that this makes any reconstruction highly fraught.[41]

Jeremy Duff calculates that if the 2 Thessalonians + Philemon hypothesis is correct, the final ten pages or so of the quire would have been left blank, making a nonsense of the increasing compression of the script.[42] Instead, he argues that 𝔓46 may well have included the Pastorals, with the lacking space supplied by the addition of some extra leaves or a small extra quire, which is consistent with known scribal practice from other surviving codices.[43] This is possible, but if such was in fact the scribe's intention, the compression would seem unnecessary. Duff's proposal has been critiqued by Eldon Jay Epp,[44] who refines his calculations and tries out some alternative hypotheses, such as the inclusion of one or more noncanonical texts after 2 Thessalonians, but nothing fits satisfactorily. As Epp acknowledges in the end, the arguments both that 𝔓46 included the Pastorals and that it did not proceed from silence.[45] Accordingly, this MS cannot be taken as evidence for a Pauline canon lacking the Pastorals; it neither excludes nor corroborates that possibility.

Apart from the question of the missing pages, the canonical order of 𝔓46 is remarkable for (1) the unusual position of Hebrews and (2) the placement of Ephesians before Galatians. The MS also includes counts of stichoi at the end of some but not all letters; it has been suggested on the basis of the handwriting that these are copied from another source.[46] The figures are quite inaccurate, and Trobisch suggests that this may explain the scribe's miscalculation of the available space,[47] but the fact that they are added in a different hand makes this unlikely.

---

[40] Suggested by, among others, Jack Finegan, 'The Original Form of the Pauline Collection', HTR 49 (1956): 85–104.

[41] Trobisch, *Die Entstehung*, 27–8.

[42] Jeremy Duff, '𝔓46 and the Pastorals: A Misleading Consensus?', NTS 44 (1998): 578–90.

[43] This suggestion had also been made in passing by Ellwood Mearle Schofield, 'The Papyrus Fragments of the Greek New Testament' (PhD, Southern Baptist Theological Seminary, 1936), 312–13.

[44] Eldon Jay Epp, 'Issues in the Interrelation of New Testament Textual Criticism and Canon', in *The Canon Debate*, ed. Lee Martin McDonald and James A. Sanders (Peabody, MA: Hendrickson, 2002), 485–515 (495–502).

[45] Epp suggests that Duff wants to include the Pastorals in the early CP by 'any framework possible', but counters that their 'character and role' should be determined in other ways. He then lists some of the conventional criteria by which the Pastorals are reckoned pseudonymous, including their purported lack of 'eschatological motivation' (502). These criteria are in themselves questionable (see Chapter 2, §1.2.2), but at any rate concern date and authorship, not how the letters were received into the early CP, for which the MS evidence is entirely relevant, though in this case inconclusive. If, as Epp believes, the Pastorals stem from 'an early to mid-second-century period', they may still have been part of the earliest relatively complete collections, for which the *terminus ante quem* is Marcion.

[46] Finegan, 'Original Form', 99; see also Kenyon, *Papyri*, xii.

[47] Trobisch, *Die Entstehung*, 27, n. 65.

2.1.2. 𝔓¹²⁶

(IV) Heb.[48]
Florence, Papyrological Institute, 'G. Vitelli', PSI 1497 (PSI Inv. 2176)

As this papyrus had not been discovered at the time of Trobisch's survey, and has been claimed to attest a unique order of the CP, it deserves individual consideration here. The single surviving leaf contains text from Hebrews, together with page numbers. The recto is headed ΡΞΑ (161) with text from Heb. 13.12-13, the verso ΡΞΒ (162) with Heb. 13.19-20.

As we have the beginning of these two consecutive pages, we can reconstruct the number of characters to be expected per page from the presumed text of p. 161, and therefore how much the codex contained before Hebrews. The available space comes to roughly 70,700 characters.[49] This is too little for Rom.–Gal., which total 100,548 characters by Trobisch's count, and too much for Romans alone at 34,410. The orders of 𝔓⁴⁶ (Hebrews second) and the capitulation in Codex Vaticanus (Hebrews fifth; see §2.1.5 below) are therefore excluded.

Clivaz observes that Romans and 1 Corinthians would fit in this space, but that this order is nowhere else attested.[50] That is true, but such an order would have a certain logic, since it would reflect a strict declension according to length: Hebrews is shorter than 1 Corinthians but longer than 2 Corinthians. Length was an important criterion in ordering the Corpus, but even where Hebrews is placed early, the two Corinthian letters are kept together in all other sources.[51] So this order in 𝔓¹²⁶ would not be inexplicable, but it would certainly be odd.

There is a simpler explanation, however. 𝔓¹²⁶ may perhaps come from the second of two volumes containing the complete CP in the familiar canonical order, with the pages numbered separately in each codex. In that case, a first volume might have comprised Rom.–2 Cor. (89,457 characters), and a second Gal.–Heb. (97,584), with our Hebrews preceded by Gal.–Phlm. (71,202). This explanation is clearly compatible with the evidence and, given the widespread attestation of the familiar order, should be preferred to the supposition of an arrangement unique to this MS.[52]

---

[48] The original edition is Guido Bastianini et al., eds, *Papiri Greci e Latini*, vol. 15: ni. 1453–1574 (Firenze: Istituto Papirologico, G. Vitelli, 2008); see also Claire Clivaz, 'A New NT Papyrus: 𝔓¹²⁶ (PSI 1497)', *Early Christianity* 1 (2010): 158–62.

[49] Following the text of NA²⁸, p. 161 would contain 606 characters, which agrees with the estimate of 20 lines × 30 characters per page in Bastianini et al., *Papiri*, 15.171. By this count, the preceding 160 pages would have included 96,000 characters. Hebrews will have occupied roughly 25,300 of these, leaving 70,700 for whatever preceded. The figures are indicative only; no allowance has been made for *nomina sacra*, textual variants, variation in column width, *inscriptiones*/*subscriptiones*, etc. The remaining length of Hebrews is taken from Trobisch's count (*Die Entstehung*, 138); the total figure is 26,382, minus the 1,113 characters from the beginning of p. 161 to the end of the letter, as per NA²⁸.

[50] Clivaz, 'A New NT Papyrus', 159, n. 12. She and Bastianini et al. give figures for pages rather than characters; by Trobisch's count, Romans and 1 Corinthians total 67,177, which is compatible with the available space.

[51] Apart from 𝔓⁴⁶, there are a few later sources that place Hebrews second, and some minuscules and Sahidic witnesses that place it fourth; see William H. P. Hatch, 'The Position of Hebrews in the Canon of the New Testament', *HTR* 29 (1936): 133–51.

[52] 𝔓⁷⁵, an early third-century codex containing only Luke and John, may attest a two-volume format for the four-gospel collection; on the other hand, Skeat argues that this MS is the second of two

2.1.3. Other papyri from collections

There are six further papyri from which at least partial collections can be inferred. Dates and references are taken from NA[28].

𝔓[13] (III/IV) Heb.[53]
London, British Library, Inv. 1532v; P. Oxy. 657; Cairo, Egyptian Museum, PSI 1292

This MS is an opisthograph, a reused roll with the Epitome of Livy still legible on the recto. It contains large portions of Hebrews, between 2.14 and 12.17, in fragments of eleven columns. The columns are numbered, the first of them MZ (47), showing that something else must have preceded this letter; the space would be far too small for either the Pauline church letters or the whole CP, but could well accommodate Romans, making this MS compatible with the order of 𝔓[46].[54] 𝔓[13] also has several distinctive readings which agree with 𝔓[46],[55] increasing the probability of a connection between the two MSS.

An alternative possibility, advocated by Schofield, is that Eph.–Thess. in the usual canonical order preceded Hebrews in this roll, which by his calculation fits better than Romans alone.[56] This would presumably make it the second of a two-part collection, as suggested above for 𝔓[126].

Hurtado observes, apropos of this MS and other opisthographs, that when writing materials were reused, it was usually 'for personal study of literary texts or for documentary texts'.[57] Most of the MSS examined here are codices, typically of early Christian usage; the distinctive form of 𝔓[13] makes it likelier that it was privately owned and used, which raises the further possibility of an eccentric collection of texts.

𝔓[30] (III) 1–2 Thess.[58]
Ghent, Central Library, Rijksuniversiteit, Inv. 61; P. Oxy. 1598

Odd verses of the last two chapters of 1 Thessalonians, and the first two verses only of 2 Thessalonians, with traces of a *subscriptio* and *inscriptio* between the two letters. Two leaves survive, of which the first is numbered recto ΣΖ (207) and verso ΣΗ (208); Grenfell and Hunt calculate that the usual preceding sequence Rom.–Col. would fit this pagination.[59] After further calculations, Trobisch agrees, excluding the possibility that Hebrews was also included before 1 Thessalonians.[60]

---

quires that would have been bound together in a single four-gospel codex (T. C. Skeat, 'The Origin of the Christian Codex', *Zeitschrift für Papyrologie und Epigraphik* 102 (1994): 263–8 (264)).
[53] Bernard P. Grenfell and Arthur S. Hunt, eds, *The Oxyrhynchus Papyri*, vol. 4 (London: Egypt Exploration Fund, 1904), 36–48.
[54] See the calculations in Trobisch, *Die Entstehung*, 24–5.
[55] Aland and Aland, *Text of the New Testament*, 97, 102.
[56] Schofield, 'Papyrus Fragments', 156.
[57] Larry W. Hurtado, *The Earliest Christian Artifacts: Manuscripts and Christian Origins* (Grand Rapids, MI: Eerdmans, 2006), 57, n. 49.
[58] Bernard P. Grenfell and Arthur S. Hunt, eds, *The Oxyrhynchus Papyri*, vol. 13 (London: Egypt Exploration Fund, 1919), 12–14.
[59] Ibid., 12; so also Schofield, 'Papyrus Fragments', 229.
[60] Trobisch, *Die Entstehung*, 25–6.

𝔓³⁴ (VII) 1–2 Cor.⁶¹
Vienna, Österreichische Nationalbibliothek, Pap. G. 39784

Verses from 1 Cor. 16 and 2 Cor. 5, 10 and 11 preserved on two fragments of a double sheet from a four-column codex. The two sides of the first leaf preserve discontinuous text, suggesting that this MS contained only selections. The recto concludes with 1 Cor. 16.10, an odd but not impossible place to stop; the verso would have begun with 2 Cor. 5.17. Schofield, who makes this calculation, objects that this is not the beginning of a sense unit, but in fact it is a plausible place to begin a lection; on the other hand, there are no traces of any titles or directions for lectionary use. It could be that this MS derives from private rather than public use, a personal and idiosyncratic selection of Pauline texts. Schofield's alternative suggestions of a defective exemplar or scribal error are also possible.⁶² There is no pagination preserved.

𝔓⁶¹ (ca. 700) Rom. 1 Cor. Phil. Col. 1 Thess. Tit. Phlm.
New York, Pierpont Morgan Library, P. Colt 5

The few surviving fragments accord with the familiar canonical order, in that on opposite sides of the same leaves, Rom. 16 is found with 1 Cor. 1, Phil. 3 with Col. 1, Col. 4 with 1 Thess. 1, Tit. 3 with Phlm.

𝔓⁹² (III/IV) Eph. 2 Thess. (order unclear)⁶³
Cairo, Egyptian Museum, P. Narmuthis 69.39a.229a

Trobisch considered only the eighty-eight papyri already catalogued by the Alands at the time, thus stopping short of this MS, which is in any case of little use for our purposes. It comprises two separate fragments with discontiguous text from Eph. 1 and 2 Thess. 1. No pagination or other indications have survived to tell us anything about the extent or order of the original collection.⁶⁴

𝔓⁹⁹ (ca. 400) 2 Cor. Gal. Rom. Eph. (order varies)⁶⁵
Dublin, Chester Beatty Library, P. Chester Beatty Ac. 1499, fol. 11–14

This curious codex includes a Greek grammar, a Greek-to-Latin gloss of selected words from a few Pauline letters, and for good measure a Latin alphabet. The words glossed are taken mostly from 2 Corinthians, Galatians and Ephesians, with some movement back and forth between different passages and indeed different letters, and with the single word quoted from Romans (ἀφωρισμένος, 1.1) appearing between the

---

⁶¹ The text is transcribed in Karl Wessely, ed., *Studien zur Palaeographie und Papyruskunde*, vol. 12: Griechische und koptische Texte theologischen Inhalts III (Leipzig: Haessel, 1912), 246.
⁶² Schofield, 'Papyrus Fragments', 247.
⁶³ Claudio Gallazzi, 'Frammenti di un codice con le epistole di Paolo', *Zeitschrift für Papyrologie und Epigraphik* 46 (1982): 117–22.
⁶⁴ Ibid., 118.
⁶⁵ Alfons Wouters, ed., *The Chester Beatty Codex Ac 1499: A Graeco-Latin Lexicon on the Pauline Epistles and a Greek Grammar*, Chester Beatty Monographs 12 (Leuven: Peeters, 1988).

end of Galatians and the beginning of Ephesians. Elsewhere, a selection from the end of Ephesians is followed by more from the beginning of Galatians. This MS obviously does not give a complete or ordered text, and Wouters is right that there is little to be confidently deduced about the order of its *Vorlage*.[66]

2.1.4. Distribution of single-letter papyri

Table 1 sets out the attestation of Pauline letters in papyri according to NA[28]. Those MSS described above, which either contain more than one letter or give evidence that they originally did, are listed as 'collections'; the rest as 'single papyri', though of course it is impossible to know whether or not these too come from collections. Within this latter group of twenty-seven papyri, the percentage of times that each letter is attested is given at the foot of the table, together with its length in characters and as a percentage of the whole CP.[67] The subscript numbers for 𝔓[46] show how the letters are ordered in that codex; as discussed above, no other papyrus collection preserves a non-standard sequence.

If Paul's letters circulated only in complete collections, it would be reasonable to expect that papyrus fragments would survive from individual letters roughly in proportion to their relative lengths; that is, the two percentage figures in each column of Table 1 would be similar. In fact, there is noticeable discrepancy in the case of Romans and Hebrews, which suggests that at least these two letters did circulate individually (or in smaller collections). The sample size of twenty-seven papyri is admittedly small, but this inference is supported by other data: textual history in the case of Romans (§2.3.1 below) and varying placement in the case of Hebrews (§§2.1.5, 2.2.1 below, and elsewhere).[68] The individual circulation of Romans, in particular, presents a major problem for Goodspeed's theory of lapsed interest followed by sudden collection.[69]

For the remaining letters, the figures are very small, but the overall pattern of distribution approximately resembles the respective lengths. The hypothesis of a relatively stable collection, suggested by the papyri from collections, is coherent with this distribution.[70]

---

[66] Ibid., 149–50.
[67] The count again following Trobisch, *Die Entstehung*, 138.
[68] Cf. the distribution of gospel papyri, where the sample is larger and the discrepancy far starker, showing conclusively that Matthew and John circulated more widely than Luke and, especially, Mark. See the table of distribution in Aland and Aland, *Text of the New Testament*, 85; the trend applies both to 'early' papyri (IV and earlier) and to the overall total, and continues to hold for those discovered after this publication.
[69] So Gamble can tellingly criticize Goodspeed, and others with like theories, on the basis of this letter (Harry Y. Gamble, *The Textual History of the Letter to the Romans: A Study in Textual and Literary Criticism*, SD 42 (Grand Rapids, MI: Eerdmans, 1977), 120). Hebrews is not such a problem for Goodspeed, who does not regard it as part of the original CP. But Claire Rothschild's argument that Hebrews did not circulate individually, because no Pauline letter can be shown to have done so, is questionable in the light of this evidence (*Hebrews as Pseudepigraphon: The History and Significance of the Pauline Attribution of Hebrews*, WUNT 235 (Tübingen: Mohr Siebeck, 2009), 145, n. 2). Her main thesis that Hebrews was from the beginning associated with the CP does not necessarily require this, however. See also Charles P. Anderson, 'The Epistle to the Hebrews and the Pauline Letter Collection', *HTR* 59 (1966): 429–38, who similarly argues that Hebrews was initially part of the CP and subsequently excluded, rather than being a late addition.
[70] Hurtado notes proposals that 𝔓[15] and 𝔓[16] derive from one common codex, and 𝔓[49] and 𝔓[65] from another (*Earliest Christian Artifacts*, 68). If this is correct it would leave only nine 'single' papyri apart from Romans and Hebrews.

Table 1 Distribution of Pauline Papyri

	Rom.	1 Cor.	2 Cor.	Gal.	Eph.	Phil.	Col.	1 Th.	2 Th.	1 Tim.	2 Tim.	Tit.	Phlm.	Heb.
Collections								$\mathfrak{P}^{30}$	$\mathfrak{P}^{30}$					$\mathfrak{P}^{13}$
	$\mathfrak{P}^{46}_1$	$\mathfrak{P}^{34}$ $\mathfrak{P}^{46}_3$ $\mathfrak{P}^{61}$	$\mathfrak{P}^{34}$ $\mathfrak{P}^{46}_4$	$\mathfrak{P}^{46}_6$	$\mathfrak{P}^{46}_5$	$\mathfrak{P}^{46}_7$ $\mathfrak{P}^{61}$	$\mathfrak{P}^{46}_8$ $\mathfrak{P}^{61}$	$\mathfrak{P}^{46}_9$ $\mathfrak{P}^{61}$				$\mathfrak{P}^{61}$		$\mathfrak{P}^{46}_2$
	$\mathfrak{P}^{61}$				$\mathfrak{P}^{92}$				$\mathfrak{P}^{92}$					
	$\mathfrak{P}^{99}$	$\mathfrak{P}^{99}$	$\mathfrak{P}^{99}$	$\mathfrak{P}^{99}$	$\mathfrak{P}^{99}$									$\mathfrak{P}^{126}$
Single Papyri	$\mathfrak{P}^{10}$	$\mathfrak{P}^{11}$	$\mathfrak{P}^{117}$	$\mathfrak{P}^{51}$	$\mathfrak{P}^{49}$	$\mathfrak{P}^{16}$		$\mathfrak{P}^{65}$				$\mathfrak{P}^{32}$	$\mathfrak{P}^{87}$	$\mathfrak{P}^{12}$
	$\mathfrak{P}^{26}$	$\mathfrak{P}^{14}$	$\mathfrak{P}^{124}$											$\mathfrak{P}^{17}$
	$\mathfrak{P}^{27}$	$\mathfrak{P}^{15}$												$\mathfrak{P}^{79}$
	$\mathfrak{P}^{31}$	$\mathfrak{P}^{68}$												$\mathfrak{P}^{89}$
	$\mathfrak{P}^{40}$	$\mathfrak{P}^{123}$												$\mathfrak{P}^{114}$
	$\mathfrak{P}^{94}$													$\mathfrak{P}^{116}$
	$\mathfrak{P}^{113}$													
	$\mathfrak{P}^{118}$													
Length	34410	32767	22280	11091	12012	8009	7897	7423	4055	8869	6538	3733	1575	26382
% Length	18.4	17.5	11.9	5.9	6.4	4.3	4.2	4.0	2.2	4.7	3.5	2.0	0.8	14.1
Single Papyri	8	5	2	1	1	1	0	1	0	0	0	1	1	6
% Single Papyri	29.6	18.5	7.4	3.7	3.7	3.7	0.0	3.7	0.0	0.0	0.0	3.7	3.7	22.2

2.1.5. Uncials

Trobisch examined all available uncials containing Pauline text, as far as the publication of his study in 1989, and here it will suffice to summarize his findings.[71] After excluding a number of MSS too fragmentary to be useful for the purpose, he identifies four orders of the CP attested in the uncials:

(a) Rom.–Phlm. Heb.
   (i.e. the familiar canonical order)
(b) Rom.–Thess. Heb. Tim.–Phlm.
   (i.e. the familiar order, but with Heb. following the church letters rather than the personal letters)
(c) Rom.–Phlm.
   (i.e. the familiar order, lacking Heb.)
(d) Rom.–Eph. Col. Phil. Thess.–Phlm. Heb.
   (i.e. the familiar order, but with Col. and Phil. reversed)

Of these, (b) is the best attested, including by ℵ, A and B (until it breaks off partway through Hebrews). The only variable in (a)–(c) is obviously the presence and position of Hebrews. The order (c), lacking Hebrews altogether, is found only in F and G, though in D this letter follows three originally empty sheets, subsequently filled with a catalogue of the letters. Following Frede,[72] Trobisch concludes that these three codices derive from an original in which Hebrews was not to be found.[73] The order (d), inverting Colossians and Philippians, is attested only in D (and its very precise transcription, D^{abs1}).

To the orders listed above should also be added one more implied in B. Here, chapters are numbered consecutively through the whole CP, but the numbering differs from the actual sequence of letters in the codex, though only in the placement of Hebrews. The underlying order implied by the numbering, which presumably reflects a *Vorlage* so arranged, is:

(e) Rom.–Gal. Heb. Eph.–Thess. (remaining leaves lost)

The evidence of the uncials is of a relatively stable corpus with the exception of Hebrews. The inversion of Colossians and Philippians in D is the only other significant variation, resembling the inversion of Ephesians and Galatians in 𝔓^{46}. Both of these exceptions to the usual order concern letters of very similar length, and neither removes any letter far from its usual context.

---

[71] Trobisch, *Die Entstehung*, 17–23. Many more uncials have since been catalogued and some include Pauline texts: see Aland, *Liste*, 42–4, for 0275–0306, and ntvmr.uni-muenster.de/liste for 0307 onward. Of these, at the time of writing there were no critical editions available for MSS with multiple Pauline texts, where a partial order might be reconstructed.

[72] Hermann Josef Frede, *Altlateinische Paulus-Handschriften*, vol. 4, Vetus Latina (Freiburg: Herder, 1964), 81–97.

[73] Trobisch, *Die Entstehung*, 23.

2.1.6. Minuscules

In the minuscules, Trobisch finds the orders (a) and (b) widely attested, with only two singular exceptions: 5 has Rom.–Eph. Col. Phil. Thess. Heb. Tim.–Phlm., that is, (b) with Col. and Phil. inverted, and 794 includes Hebrews twice, effectively conflating (a) and (b) to the order Rom.–Thess. Heb. Tim.–Phlm. Heb.[74]

The late date of the minuscules and many of the uncials limits their usefulness for our purposes of reconstructing the CP's earliest history. It is possible that odd variations represent distant traces of much earlier diversity: on the arguments of Frede and Aland to this effect, see §2.2 below. However, even if this is admitted, the degree of uniformity is still relatively high.

2.1.7. Stichometry

Various differing accounts of the length of Pauline letters by *stichoi* are preserved in MSS.[75] A few odd figures were added to $\mathfrak{P}^{46}$ by a later hand (see §2.1.1 above). The *Catalogus Claromontanus*, a canon list with stichometry placed between Phlm. and Heb. in D, is likewise incomplete and wild (e.g. 2 Tim. is counted as longer than 1 Tim., four letters are omitted (Phil., 1–2 Thess. and Heb.) and Col. follows the Pastorals). A count at the end of most Pauline letters in ℵ also contains some obvious errors, and probably derives from a different source than the main text of the codex. A more widespread stichometry, sometimes attributed to 'Euthalius' (an otherwise obscure figure), appears in various later MSS such as L.

These numbers become important when considering the order of letters in the CP, particularly the relative positions of Galatians and Ephesians, and of Philippians and Colossians. Gal. is counted as longer than Eph. in $\mathfrak{P}^{46}$ (which however uniquely places Eph. earlier), Eph. is counted as longer in D and 'Euthalius' and the count is identical in ℵ. The count for Phil. and Col. is identical in 'Euthalius', and perhaps also in the exemplar of ℵ, if its obviously mistaken figure of 300 for Col. was originally 200, as for Phil. (Neither D nor $\mathfrak{P}^{46}$ has a count for both of these letters.) The important point is that in *stichoi*, the measurement most relevant for ancient scribes (as distinct from modern counts of characters, lines or pages), the relative length of each of these letter pairs was ambiguous. This may partly account for the exceptional inversions of their usual placement that we have observed above.

2.1.8. Summary

The majority of MS evidence is compatible with the familiar canonical order of the CP. Among the papyri that certainly derive from collections, only $\mathfrak{P}^{46}$ gives definite evidence of another form, with Hebrews second and Ephesians before Galatians. $\mathfrak{P}^{13}$ may have matched this order, but (like $\mathfrak{P}^{126}$) it can also be interpreted as the second

---

[74] Ibid., 14–17.
[75] For the following see Finegan, 'Original Form', 96–9. He also lists some modern reconstructions of stichometry, which may be more accurate, but are not attested in the MSS and so not considered here.

half of a two-part collection in the familiar order. The remaining Pauline papyri suggest that Romans and Hebrews circulated individually.

There is no MS which definitely attests a CP smaller than thirteen letters. The compression in the script of $\mathfrak{P}^{46}$ does not allow any conclusion to be reached on this point. Hebrews is lacking in F and G, and perhaps in a *Vorlage* lying behind these MSS and D. Both this fact and the extensive variation in its placement in other sources show that the place of Hebrews in the Corpus was contested. But the same cannot be said of the Pastoral letters (on the basis of MSS, at any rate).

The organizing principle of the familiar canonical order is clear: letters addressed to churches precede those addressed to individuals, and within each group, letters are ordered from longest to shortest. Hebrews is usually placed at the end of either the church letters or the whole collection, and therefore rather as an appendix than as an entirely integrated part of the CP. The main exceptions to this are $\mathfrak{P}^{46}$ (Heb. second), the capitulation of B (Heb. fourth) and possibly (but dubiously), if it represents a self-contained codex, $\mathfrak{P}^{126}$ (Heb. third). These orders integrate Hebrews fully among the church letters, while differently solving the problem that its length lies between that of the two Corinthian letters.[76]

Apart from the placement of Hebrews, the most significant departures from the familiar order are the inversion of Galatians and Ephesians in $\mathfrak{P}^{46}$ and of Philippians and Colossians in D. These pairs of letters are each very close in length, and varying stichometric counts show an ambiguity here which may account for the different placements.[77] Hebrews is the only letter for which there is clear evidence of distinctive treatment; there is no division corresponding to the modern category of the 'deuteropauline'.

2.2. Traces of early variation

Some decades ago, the relative stability attested by the MS tradition was called into question by two influential studies: Frede's 1969 survey of attested orders of the CP and Aland's 1979 examination of textual variation in minuscules.[78] Each argued in its own way that the diversity present in later sources reflects a much more chaotic beginning for the CP.

2.2.1. Attested orders

Frede surveyed every attested CP order he could find, including not only Greek MSS but also Old Latin, Vulgate and other translations, as well as catalogues and commentaries from the patristic era. He found twenty variations in three groupings: general (A), western (W) and chronological (C).[79] The predominant

---

[76] For a more exhaustive catalogue of attested orders, including translations and minuscules, see the work of Frede discussed in §2.2.1 below.
[77] Other explanations have been proposed; in particular, Trobisch places great weight upon the order of Galatians and Ephesians, but without sufficient attention to their variable stichometry.
[78] See nn. 28 and 7 above, respectively.
[79] For an expanded tabulation of Frede's results, see Lovering, 'Corpus Paulinum', 259–62. Lovering lists thirty-seven orders with a further fifteen sub-variations. Frede regards the C grouping as secondary, dependent on the W order ('Die Ordnung', 292).

A and W groups order the letters according to length, their prototypes differing in whether Corinthians and Thessalonians were counted as single or double letters. Frede assumes that the earliest collection would have included letters to seven churches, though for him this does not imply the exclusion of the personal letters. His basic thesis is that the earlier W order was gradually accommodated to the A order, this process producing most of the attested variations.[80] The proposed primitive orders are as follows:

A1	Rom.	Cor.	[Heb.]	Eph.	Gal.	Phil.	Col.	Thess.	Tim.	Tit.	Phlm.
W1	Cor.	Rom.	—	Eph.	Thess.	Gal.	Phil.	Col.		Tim.	Tit.	Phlm.

Not all of Frede's evidence is of equal value; it cannot be assumed that commentaries, for instance, reproduce an existing canonical order.[81] Some of the orders are scantily attested, and the proposed foundational W1 not at all. His assumption that the earliest collection was organized around seven churches is questionable, as we shall see (§§2.6 and 2.7 below), but if it is correct, the inclusion of the Pastorals at this point is unlikely. For these reasons, Frede's two-source reconstruction may be doubted. Nevertheless, even if some of his proposed orders are excluded, his study does demonstrate more variability in the CP than is evident from the papyri and uncials; how far this should be read back into the earliest collection(s) is less sure.

2.2.2. Textual character in minuscules

As already noted, the minuscules are in general too late to be immediately useful for reconstructing the CP's origins. Aland, however, argues that they testify indirectly to a diversity of early MS sources, based on an analysis of variation in textual character.[82] He selected 256 representative loci from across the CP (including Hebrews), and compared the readings of 634 minuscules for each one, recording the extent of their variation from the Byzantine text as a percentage and tabulating the figures by letter. The results were surprising to Aland: in about a quarter of cases (164), the text character varies significantly between letters within the same MS, some conforming closely to the majority text, others departing widely. Different letters show a non-standard character in different MSS. A 'control' survey of the same kind was undertaken for twenty-three relevant uncials, which showed a similar albeit less stark pattern, so far as their incomplete text permitted.

---

[80] 'In der fortschreitenden Angleichung der W-Ordnung an die A-Ordnung besteht zum wesentlichen Teil die Geschichte des Kanons der Paulusbriefe' (ibid., 292).
[81] See Trobisch, *Die Entstehung*, 29–45, for a critique of several non-manuscript sources. Trobisch perhaps tends to the opposite extreme, defining too narrowly the scope of attested orders he will consider. This selectivity is criticized by Eugene H. Lovering, 'Review of David Trobisch, *Die Entstehung der Paulusbriefsammlung*', JBL 110 (1991): 736–8.
[82] Aland, 'Die Entstehung'. The study is limited to Greek MSS.

Aland cannot square this sort of variation with theories of a single unified prototype for the CP. On the contrary, the extent of attested variation implies the existence of different *Vorlagen* for different letters at an early stage:

> Jede der 164 Handschriften weist Schwankungen im Textcharakter auf, die sich nicht daraus erklären lassen, daß der Schreiber jeweils nur seine Vorlage gewechselt habe. Es ist jenseits jeder Wahrscheinlichkeit, daß im Verlauf der späteren Tradition ein derart häufiger und allem Anschein nach willkürlicher Wechsel der Vorlagen erfolgte, vielmehr wurde damals eine Handschrift vollständig aus einer vorhandenen Musterhandschrift abgeschrieben.[83]

On these grounds, as well as Frede's analysis of varying corpus order, Aland concludes that the idea of a single *Urcorpus*, to which all subsequent textual tradition can be traced, is a myth; rather, we should assume a number of smaller early *Urcorpora*. The fact that some letters – namely, 1–2 Corinthians, Hebrews, Romans, Galatians, Ephesians, Philippians – show noticeably less departure from MSS' text character than the others may suggest that they were among the earliest so collected. Many of these letters, though not Galatians and Philippians, are also the best attested in patristic sources.[84] The variety within second-century sources, among which Aland counts Tertullian (*Praesc.* 36.1, *Marc.* 4.5.1) and the Muratorian Fragment as sequential canon lists alongside Marcion and $\mathfrak{P}^{46}$, gives only a glimpse of the variety that in fact then prevailed, and that tenaciously survived in individual MSS despite the increasing standardization of a canonical edition. One example among many is the nine minuscules, dating from between the eleventh and sixteenth centuries, that preserve the order (1) Romans (2) Hebrews otherwise found only in $\mathfrak{P}^{46}$.[85]

This impressive study has been influential in challenging the thesis of a single decisive CP redaction, whether in the traditional shape of Zahn/Harnack or the more radical alternatives of Goodspeed and others. Nevertheless, it is questionable whether such late MSS can bear the evidential weight Aland places upon them. Over the course of many centuries, the opportunities for interference in the textual tradition are manifold, and to trace all such variation back to original second-century diversity is an insecure proceeding. The high degree of consistency in the papyri must also be accounted for. Aland may well be right in at least some cases, but even if the minuscules do show traces of some 'non-standard' collections in the second century, that does not diminish the likelihood of a more 'standard' CP circulating widely at the same time. If the situation were as chaotic as Aland describes, we would expect to find much less consistency in the early sources than is in fact the case.

---

[83] Ibid., 309.
[84] Ibid., 335.
[85] Ibid., 348.

2.3. Textual variation in addresses

2.3.1. Romans

Gamble has shown that Romans circulated in at least three different recensions, comprising fourteen, fifteen and sixteen chapters.[86] This has important implications for the origins of the CP. For one thing, it disproves the most extreme accounts of a single *Ursammlung*, which do not allow for any separate circulation of individual letters before canonical redaction. Gamble critiques Schmithals on this basis, as well as more mainstream exponents of a decisive early edition,[87] and it is just as much a problem for Goodspeed and his followers. On the other hand, Gamble considers Romans 'the exception that proves the rule: when textual revisions have taken place they have left their marks in the evidence'.[88] The lack of further such variation tells against a long period of chaotic circulation, and some sort of stabilizing collection is still probable relatively early. In fact Gamble believes there were three such collections (see p. 20 above), but that is not a necessary corollary of these observations.

There is another important detail in his findings. Some sources omit the words ἐν Ῥώμῃ from Rom. 1.7 and 1.15, thus making the letter general in its address. Textually, this variant belongs with the fourteen-chapter recension, where the closing greetings are also lacking, with the result that the letter's historical context is entirely obscured.[89] Gamble's quite reasonable conclusion is that this short version of Romans was deliberately edited to departicularize or 'catholicize' the letter. Such adaptation is easily intelligible at an early stage of its history; it is less likely to have coincided with the formation of the Corpus, since the problem of particularity arises more acutely for a letter circulating individually. Inclusion in a collection alongside other church letters makes a particular address more rather than less appropriate.[90] Whenever the collection is finally dated, though, the shortest form of Romans must have been in circulation in the mid-second century, since it appears to have been used by Marcion.[91]

2.3.2. Ephesians

A similar textual issue occurs in Eph. 1.1, where the words ἐν Ἐφέσῳ are lacking in several weighty MS sources (including 𝔓⁴⁶, ℵ*, B* and 1739), certainly in Marcion's text and probably also in Tertullian's. Tertullian notes that Marcion has the wrong title for this letter, calling it Laodiceans rather than Ephesians, but does not seem terribly

---

[86] Gamble, *Textual History*. There is no need to rehearse his argument, which is widely accepted. Evidence for the shortest form includes Vulgate *capitula*, the Latin prologues, Tertullian's *Marc.* and MS variation in the placement of the doxology (16–29). The fifteen-chapter recension is uniquely attested by the doxology's appearance after ch. 15 in 𝔓⁴⁶, though external evidence had prompted similar speculation before the discovery of this MS (33–4).
[87] Gamble, 'Redaction'; Lietzmann is cited as an example of the latter 'widely held' view (415, n. 31).
[88] Ibid., 418.
[89] Gamble, *Textual History*, 32–3. The fifteen-chapter recension may also have lacked the particular addresses in ch. 1, but as the opening leaves of 𝔓⁴⁶ are lost, there is no evidence for this.
[90] Ibid., 115–18, with support from Lovering, 'Corpus Paulinum', 144–7.
[91] Gamble, *Textual History*, 113, having rejected the argument that Marcion created this recension.

worried: 'There is no importance in titles, since when the apostle wrote to some, he wrote to all' (*Marc.* 5.17.1).[92] He is not so relaxed when Marcion deletes words from the apostle himself, and his unconcern here suggests it is only the title, and not the text, in which he sees a discrepancy.[93]

There has been various speculation about the original form of this opening verse; Lovering gives a useful survey, with possibilities including the loss or deletion of one or more original addresses, or the deliberate provision of a blank space for different addresses to be filled in later on.[94] Common to many of these theories is the view of Ephesians as a sort of encyclical, and as Gamble emphasizes, different considerations apply to this letter by virtue of its content: there is little obvious particularity outside the greeting, without which it reads easily as a 'catholic' letter, whether this was the original intent or a subsequent emendation.[95]

Apart from Tertullian's text, the *inscriptio* ΠΡΟΣ ΕΦΕΣΙΟΥΣ is present in all MS sources, with a corresponding *subscriptio* in virtually all except 𝔓[46]. The inclusion of Ephesians in a corpus alongside other church letters is unimaginable without some such title, which could easily have been added to a text lacking any address. The shorter text, τοῖς ἁγίοις τοῖς οὖσιν καὶ πιστοῖς, is syntactically extremely awkward, but cannot be logically accounted for by the deletion of the two words specifying the location.[96]

Perhaps the best guess is that neither of the attested variants, the awkward sentence or ἐν Ἐφέσῳ, represents the original text, from which something else has been deleted or lost. Marcion's identification of this letter as 'Laodiceans' would in that case be the clue. Ephesus was a far more important centre for postapostolic Christianity than Laodicea, and also emerges much better from the competing assessments of Rev. 2–3. It is not inconceivable that a letter originally directed to the Laodiceans, but scarcely identifiable with their particular congregation, could have been rebadged to augment its prestige, or to provide apostolic patronage to an important congregation. Alternatively, the opposite change may have been made to supply the missing letter of Col. 4.16; or again, if the short text is the original, its awkwardness may have independently prompted two similar 'completions' by the addition of placenames. Any of these scenarios would result in two competing addresses circulating simultaneously in the letter's early history, which would account for both the MS variation and Marcion's text.[97]

---

[92] 'nihil autem de titulis interest, cum ad omnes apostolus scripserit dum ad quosdam.'
[93] So Judith M. Lieu: 'The question for both Tertullian and Marcion was of the superscription and hence one of interpretation' (*Marcion and the Making of a Heretic: God and Scripture in the Second Century* (New York: CUP, 2015), 237). The claim to apostolicity is, of course, established by Paul's name in the text itself. It is otherwise when Tertullian criticizes the lack of a title for Marcion's gospel, which should by rights be attributed to Luke (4.2.3).
[94] Lovering, 'Corpus Paulinum', 147–53.
[95] Gamble, *Textual History*, 119. Goodspeed of course finds support in the textual variation for his own 'encyclical' theory, but only by the implausible translation of τοῖς ἁγίοις τοῖς οὖσιν καὶ πιστοῖς ἐν Χριστῷ Ἰησοῦ as 'to God's people who are steadfast in Christ Jesus' (*Meaning*, 18).
[96] 'Anyone wanting to expel the mention of an addressee – supposing that the text contained one from the first – would surely have had the sense to delete also τοῖς οὖσιν and thus to produce an understandable phrase' (Zuntz, *Text of the Epistles*, 228, n. 1). There is also no reason to delete the address from a letter already bearing the title ΠΡΟΣ ΕΦΕΣΙΟΥΣ.
[97] The received text can of course be interpreted meaningfully, however odd its syntax may appear. Origen reads it as 'to the saints *who are*, and the faithful in Christ Jesus', relating τοῖς οὖσιν to Ex.

2.3.3. 1 Corinthians

In 1900, Johannes Weiss first suggested that the received text of 1 Cor. 1.2 includes a catholicizing insertion: τῇ ἐκκλησίᾳ τοῦ θεοῦ τῇ οὔσῃ ἐν Κορίνθῳ, ἡγιασμένοις ἐν Χριστοῦ Ἰησοῦ, κλητοῖς ἁγίοις, *σὺν πᾶσιν τοῖς ἐπικαλουμένοις τὸ ὄνομα τοῦ κυρίου ἡμῶν Ἰησοῦ Χριστοῦ ἐν παντὶ τόπῳ, αὐτῶν καὶ ἡμῶν*.[98] As recently as NA[27], the italicized words were marked as disputed on the basis of Weiss's conjecture alone, but this indication has been removed along with other conjectures from the newest Nestle-Aland apparatus.[99]

Weiss finds it 'unthinkable' that Paul could have meant his letter not only for the Corinthians but for all Christians in the world, and accordingly attributes these words to the collector of the CP. His premise is coloured by undisguised reservations about the process of 'catholicization' itself,[100] and in fact the opposite conclusion is not only possible, but in the absence of any textual evidence to the contrary, preferable: 1 Cor. 1.2 strengthens the case that letters were circulated even within Paul's own lifetime, and indeed that some measure of 'catholicization' was anticipated by Paul himself. 2 Cor. 1.1 also implies this – if the audience is somewhat more restricted (τῇ ἐκκλησίᾳ τοῦ θεοῦ οὔσῃ ἐν Κορίνθῳ σὺν τοῖς ἁγίοις πᾶσιν τοῖς οὖσιν ἐν ὅλῃ τῇ Ἀχαΐᾳ), that is understandable in view of the letter's content – and Gal. 1.2, addressed to the churches (plural) of Galatia, also presupposes at least local circulation.[101]

An unrelated argument is made by Nils Dahl, who notes the widespread textual variant in 1.2 where the words τῇ οὔσῃ ἐν Κορίνθῳ follow, rather than precede, ἡγιασμένοις ἐν Χριστῷ Ἰησοῦ, and from this infers that a form of the text existed without reference to Corinth. As this could hardly be original, it would represent a 'catholicizing' edition of the letter, comparable with what has been postulated of Romans and Ephesians, and suggesting the individual circulation of at least these three letters. The same three are those most frequently cited by patristic authors (see §2.4.2 below), which would be consistent with this thesis.[102] That is a lot to infer from one small textual variant, but Dahl's argument is more plausible than Weiss's, and fits with what has been observed about Romans and Ephesians.

3.14 and 1 Cor. 1.28-29 (Origen and Jerome, *The Commentaries of Origen and Jerome on Ephesians*, ed. and trans. Ronald E. Heine (Oxford: OUP, 2002), 80; my emphasis).

[98] Johannes Weiss, 'Der Eingang des ersten Korintherbriefs', *Theologische Studien und Kritiken* 73 (1900): 126-30. See also Weiss, *Der erste Korintherbrief*, KEK (Göttingen: Vandenhoeck & Ruprecht, 1910), 3-4.

[99] NA[28], 4* (English: 49*).

[100] 'Diese "Katholisierung" ist und bleibt ein ungeschichtliches und gewaltthätiges Verfahren, das nur durch eine ausgebildete Methode des Umdeutens und Allegorisierens durchzuführen war' (Weiss, 'Eingang', 129). On the negative evaluation of 'catholicization', see further the discussion of Baur and Käsemann in Chapter 2, §1.

[101] Also in favour of this verse's authenticity are the Pauline parallels of Rom. 10.12 (Christians are 'those who call on the Lord', cf. Joel 2.32 and Acts 2.21) and, more distantly, 1 Thess. 1.8 (the Thessalonians' faith has gone out 'in every place').

[102] Nils A. Dahl, 'The Particularity of the Pauline Epistles as a Problem in the Ancient Church', in *Neotestamentica et Patristica*, ed. Oscar Cullmann, NovTSup 6 (Leiden: Brill, 1962), 270-1.

2.4. Patristic references

2.4.1. Lists

In a few early patristic works, reference is made to some of Paul's letters in a list-like fashion that may, or may not, preserve the order of a collection known to the author. Some scholars attach a lot of weight to this evidence, but it is of dubious value. The earliest examples are from Tertullian:

> Go then, you [sg.] who want to better engage your curiosity in the business of your salvation. Run through the apostolic churches, where the very thrones of the apostles still preside in their places, where their own authentic letters [*ipsae authenticae litterae eorum*] are read, sounding the voice and representing the face of each one. **2.** Nearest to you is Achaia – you have Corinth. If you are not far from Macedonia, you have Philippi; <you have the Thessalonians>.[103] If you can cross to Asia, you have Ephesus. If you lie near Italy, you have Rome, from which (this) authority presents itself even to us [*unde nobis quoque auctoritas praesto est*]. (*Praesc.* 36.1–2)[104]

Dahl takes this to be a geographical order without any relevance to the letter sequence known to Tertullian,[105] but in fact the arrangement seems to be, geographically speaking, arbitrary. A later text may provide corroboration that some other principle of order is concerned:

> Let us see what milk the Corinthians drank from Paul, to what rule the Galatians were reformed, what the Philippians, Thessalonians, Ephesians read, and most recently [*de proximo*] what even the Romans speak, to whom both Peter and Paul bequeathed the gospel, sealed too in their own blood. (*Marc.* 4.5.1)[106]

Tertullian's two lists, if they are to be regarded as such, generally match, but with one or two significant exceptions: the omission of Galatia in *Praesc.*, which may reflect the demise of the apostolic church in that region,[107] and the textually doubtful mention of the Thessalonians, which has the ring of later harmonization.[108] The absence of any

---

[103] This phrase is lacking in some sources and not included in the main text of either the *Sources Chrétiennes* or the *Corpus Christianorum* edition.
[104] Latin text in Tertullian, 'De Praescriptione Haereticorum', in *Opera*, ed. R. F. Refoulé, CCSL 1 (Turnhout: Brepols, 1954), 185–224 (216).
[105] Nils A. Dahl, 'Welche Ordnung der Paulusbriefe wird vom Muratorischen Kanon vorausgesetzt?', ZNTW 52 (1961): 39–53 (41). Dahl is supported by Gamble, *Textual History*, 117–19.
[106] Latin text in Tertullian, *Adversus Marcionem*, ed. and trans. Ernest Evans, 2 vols (Oxford: Clarendon, 1972) (my translation). 'De proximo' may be either geographical or chronological in reference: Evans translates 'our near neighbours the Romans' (271); Holmes, 'so very near (to the apostles)' (Tertullian, 'The Five Books against Marcion', trans. Peter Holmes, ANF 3, 1885 (Peabody, MA: Hendrickson, 1994), 269–475 (350)). But it may also mean last in the historical sequence of letters.
[107] Aland, 'Die Entstehung', 328.
[108] It is also, dubiously, the only place listed in *Praesc.* by the name of the inhabitants.

reference to the personal letters is not especially surprising in the context of these passages, but the omission of Colossians is less easily explained. *Marc.* 5.19 shows that this letter was certainly part of Tertullian's CP, and its absence from these quotations means they can hardly reproduce the letter sequence he knew.

This passage from Origen is similarly inconclusive:

> Paul says: 'We speak wisdom among them that are perfect ...' [quotes 1 Cor. 2.6-8] 20. And we say to those who hold similar opinions to those of Celsus: 'Paul then, we are to suppose, had before his mind the idea of no pre-eminent wisdom when he professed to speak wisdom among them that are perfect?' Now, as he spoke with his customary boldness when in making such a profession he said that he was possessed of no wisdom, we shall say in reply: first of all examine the Epistles of him who utters these words, and look carefully at the meaning of each expression in them – say [φέρ' εἰπεῖν], in those to the Ephesians, and Colossians, and Thessalonians, and Philippians, and Romans, – and show two things, both that you understand Paul's words, and that you can demonstrate any of them to be silly or foolish. (*Cels.* 3.19–20)[109]

Zahn compares the omission of Galatians here with Tertullian's in *Praesc.* – though in fact the reference here is to letters rather than churches, so the context does not explain the omission – and takes the quotation from 1 Cor. 2 as the beginning of the sequence. An order thus emerges beginning with Corinthians and ending with Romans, like the supposed 'lists' in Tertullian and the Muratorian Fragment (see §2.7 below), but otherwise quite different from them.[110] Although many others have been willing to follow this reconstruction,[111] it must be regarded as tendentious: there is no good reason to put Corinthians at the head of Origen's sequence, and the remaining letters may simply reflect a geographical organization, Asia–Macedonia–Rome.

The evidence of these passages is not strong. It is not clear that they are meant as ordered rehearsals of letter collections at all, though the existence of such collections is obviously presupposed. It is possible, as Zahn, Frede and others have concluded, that primitive variant orders of the CP are reflected here, but on the present evidence this is little more than speculation.[112]

---

[109] Origen, 'Against Celsus', trans. Frederick Crombie, ANF 4, 1885 (Peabody, MA: Hendrickson, 1994), 395–669 (471). Greek text in Origen, *Contre Celse*, ed. and trans. Marcel Borret, vol. 2, 3 vols, SC 136 (Paris: Cerf, 1968).

[110] Zahn, *Geschichte*, 1890, 2.353. Zahn also takes *1 Clement* 47 to show conclusively that 1 Corinthians was the first Pauline letter in Clement's CP (*Geschichte*, 1889, 1.811-14), but the relevant words can be differently interpreted: ἀναλάβετε τὴν ἐπιστολὴν τοῦ μακαρίου Παύλου τοῦ ἀποστόλου. τί πρῶτον ὑμῖν ἐν ἀρχῇ τοῦ εὐαγγελίου ἔγραψεν; this could well refer to the beginning of either Paul's preaching or his correspondence with the Corinthians, rather than the beginning of a letter sequence.

[111] E.g. Frede, 'Die Ordnung', 295.

[112] Where a number of Paul's letters are quoted in the course of a separate discussion, no real weight can be attached to the sequence of quotations. There is no reason to suppose that canonical order would be followed in such cases, *pace* Zahn and Frede; Trobisch is right to exclude this data from consideration (*Die Entstehung*, 31–2). An example of typical value is the sequence Cor. Eph.

2.4.2. Frequency of citation

A proper investigation of Pauline citations among patristic authors is beyond the scope of this project. Happily, is it a subject receiving increasing attention, and the relevant resources are becoming more readily accessible.[113] Here I will do no more than suggest how this evidence bears upon our question – that is, how patterns of the letters' use may reveal something about their distribution. As an illustration, I have taken the total number of citations recorded in the first volume of *Biblia Patristica*, which goes as far as Tertullian and Clement of Alexandria; this is a wonderful starting point, but as a simple index without attention to context, or distinction between different sorts of reference, its value is limited.[114] Nevertheless, a blunt comparison of the relative length of the letters (see Table 1, p. 29 above) with the proportion of citations recorded is not without interest (see Table 2, opposite).

The most striking figures here are the relatively frequent use of 1 Corinthians and Ephesians, and the relatively rare use of 2 Corinthians and Hebrews. The Pastoral letters, though largely absent from the papyri, are attested in citations more or less proportionately to length. Various explanations are possible for this data: for example, one would expect the Corinthian correspondence to be cited with especial frequency by *1 Clement*, a letter addressed to the church at Corinth.[115] Or some letters may simply be more interesting or relevant than others. Still, the very high figure for 1 Corinthians – nearly a third of all citations noted – lends weight to the suggestion that it circulated to some extent individually. The same could be said in reverse for Hebrews: its scarcity here implies that some collections circulated without it, which is consistent with the MS evidence. The frequent reference to Ephesians is a clear illustration of the authority ascribed to this letter from the earliest postapostolic years, which on this showing is no less than for the undisputed letters. But such results remain only indicative at this stage.[116]

Cor. Rom. Cor. Thess. Cor. Eph. Rom. Col. Cor. Phil. Thess., which Frede finds in Tertullian's *De Resurrectione Mortuorum*, and which he bewilderingly construes as evidence for an order beginning with Corinthians and ending with Romans ('Die Ordnung', 295).

[113] See especially Jennifer R. Strawbridge's 'Paul and Patristics Database' at paulandpatristics. web.ox.ac.uk; and cf. Strawbridge, *The Pauline Effect: The Use of the Pauline Epistles by Early Christian Writers*, SBR 5 (Berlin: De Gruyter, 2015). See also the database of Pauline quotations from the COMPAUL Project (University of Birmingham) at epistulae.org/citations, and the digital continuation of *Biblia Patristica* as 'BiblIndex' (Sources Chrétiennes – HiSoMA) at biblindex. mom.fr.

[114] J. Allenbach et al., eds, *Biblia Patristica: Index des citations et allusions bibliques dans la littérature patristique*, vol. 1: Des origines à Clément d'Alexandrie et Tertullien (Paris: Centre National de la Recherche Scientifique, 1975). Although Strawbridge's more differentiated database does include the Pastorals and Hebrews (*Pauline Effect*, 1, n. 2), at the time of writing the online version does not extend to these letters, and therefore I take vol. 1 of *Biblia Patristica* as my indicative sample. In fact, for the ten letters currently accessible, Strawbridge's data for the first two centuries does show a pattern of distribution broadly similar to Table 2, except for Colossians, which has a significantly higher citation rate in Strawbridge's database.

[115] On Bornkamm's suggestion that Clement knew only 1 Corinthians, which he takes as evidence that 2 Corinthians was of a later date, see Lovering, 'Corpus Paulinum', 232–3.

[116] A more thorough analysis would need to look at the particular use of different letters by different authors. To take just one example, again remaining with blunt figures, the letters of Ignatius

Table 2 Distribution of Citations

	Rom.	1 Cor.	2 Cor.	Gal.	Eph.	Phil.	Col.	1 Th.	2 Th.	1 Tim.	2 Tim.	Tit.	Phlm.	Heb.
Length	34410	32767	22280	11091	12012	8009	7897	7423	4055	8869	6538	3733	1575	26382
% Length	18.4	17.5	11.9	5.9	6.4	4.3	4.2	4.0	2.2	4.7	3.5	2.0	0.8	14.1
Citations	902	1622	400	424	537	182	256	110	55	249	125	69	11	287
% Citations	17.2	31.0	7.6	8.1	10.3	3.5	4.9	2.1	1.1	4.8	2.4	1.3	0.2	5.5

2.5. Marcion

Marcion's collection of the Pauline letters is the earliest we have definitely attested, though like all that pertains to him, it survives only via polemical commentary, principally Tertullian and Epiphanius.[117] Tertullian devotes the fifth book of his *Adversus Marcionem* to refuting Marcion's claim to the theological legacy of Paul. Although the surviving work dates from the first decade of the third century, it is possible that the portion on Paul already existed in an earlier edition.[118] Tertullian works with the biblical text as Marcion presents it, claiming that even this defective canon provides enough ammunition to defeat him.[119] This does not prevent various protests against the heretic's shameful 'eraser', most notably for our purposes his omission of the Pastoral letters (the absence of Hebrews is not mentioned),[120] but his claim to adhere to Marcion's text makes Tertullian a very informative source for its reconstruction.[121]

---

show a very strong preference for 1 Corinthians. Of forty-two Pauline allusions noted in Lake's apparatus, seventeen are from this letter; Romans is in second place with seven (Kirsopp Lake, ed. and trans., *The Apostolic Fathers*, vol. 1, 2 vols, Loeb 24 (London: Heinemann, 1912)). Ehrman's more conservative apparatus notes only eighteen Pauline allusions, half from 1 Corinthians (Bart D. Ehrman, ed. and trans., *The Apostolic Fathers*, vol. 1, 2 vols, Loeb 24 (Cambridge, MA: Harvard University, 2003)). If Ignatius was especially familiar with 1 Corinthians, it is likely he had earlier or better access to it than to the whole CP, which supports the hypothesis of individual circulation. The tendency is too marked to be coincidental, but requires closer investigation.

[117] The other source for Marcion's scripture, the *Dialogues of Adamantius*, does not delineate its scope, though including various quotations from Paul.

[118] Markus Vinzent, *Marcion and the Dating of the Synoptic Gospels*, Studia Patristica, Sup. 2 (Leuven: Peeters, 2014), 90. Lieu, on the other hand, argues that this part was written last, and that Tertullian did not have access to Marcion's Paul earlier (*Marcion*, 235).

[119] 'It is enough that I receive those things which he did not think it equally necessary to erase as instances of his neglect and blindness' (*Marc.* 5.13.4); this is apropos of Romans but can be taken as a general principle. Cf., apropos of his Gospel,

> He erased whatever was against his own opinion ... but kept what agreed with it. These things we shall address and discuss, in case they turn out rather in our favour, and strike a blow against Marcion's audacity. Then it will be clear that the parts erased fell victim to the same vice of heretical blindness by which the other parts were retained. Thus runs the design and outline of our little work, on terms undoubtedly agreeable to both parties [*sub illa utique condicione quae ex utraque parte condicta sit*]. (4.6.2-3)

On the question of whether Tertullian was working from a Latin translation of Marcion or was newly translating from his original Greek, see T. J. Lang, 'Did Tertullian Read Marcion in Latin? Grammatical Evidence from the Greek of Ephesians 3.9 in Marcion's *Apostolikon* as Presented in the Latin of Tertullian's *Adversus Marcionem*', ZAC 21 (2017): 63-72.

[120] *Marc.* 5.21.1. The letters have been 'mutilated even in number' (5.1.9).

[121] Jason David BeDuhn, *The First New Testament: Marcion's Scriptural Canon* (Salem, OR: Polebridge, 2013), 30-1, deplores the 'uncritical adoption of polemic as history' by modern scholars who assume that Marcion did indeed edit Paul and Luke, as Tertullian claims, without considering whether Marcion's text could be the earlier. But this possibility would require the longer canonical texts, attested by all extant MSS as well as Tertullian, to stem from a post-Marcionite redaction: a premise unlikely per se, and even less probable in view of the existence of a CP before Marcion, which BeDuhn accepts (206-7). He agrees with Gamble ('The New Testament Canon: Recent Research and the Status Quaestionis', in *The Canon Debate*, ed. Lee Martin McDonald and James A. Sanders (Peabody, MA: Hendrickson, 2002), 267-94 (283-4)) that many distinctively 'Marcionite' readings derive from a pre-Marcion text, but this does not apply to his omissions.

Epiphanius, writing perhaps 150 years later, devotes a large section of his comprehensive anti-heretical 'medicine chest' to Marcion.[122] This incorporates a treatise he had composed some years earlier, in which various citations are assembled against Marcion from his own scripture (*Pan.* 42.10.2). Some modern scholars have questioned the veracity of the original source, but not compellingly;[123] the oddities in his selection can be otherwise explained. Harnack may well be right that Epiphanius fails to quote from 1 and 2 Thessalonians, Philippians and Philemon not because he really believes in his assertion that Marcion has distorted them beyond usefulness (according to Tertullian, Philemon alone escaped his editing),[124] but simply because his earlier treatise did not draw on them, for reasons he had since forgotten.[125] That the *Panarion*'s citations come at one additional remove is cause for caution, and the imperfect state of the text limits its usefulness for reconstructing the Marcionite scriptures.[126] Still Epiphanius, writing independently, is explicitly concerned with the order of Paul's letters in a way that Tertullian is not, so his evidence should not be dismissed.

The CP is attested by the two authors as follows:

Tertullian: Gal. 1–2 Cor. Rom. 1–2 Thess. Laod. Col. Phil. Phlm.
                                                    = Eph.
Epiphanius: Gal. 1–2 Cor. Rom. 1–2 Thess. Eph. Col. Phlm. Phil. Laod.

Significant differences are: (1) the order of Philippians and Philemon, (2) the status of Laodiceans and (3) whether the order of the canon is explicit (Epiphanius) or implicit (Tertullian).

To begin with the last of these points, Tertullian does not seem particularly concerned with the order of the letters. He discusses them in the sequence given above, but does not say directly that he is following Marcion's bible in this; however, the extensive agreement with Epiphanius, as well as his general strategy of using Marcion's own text against him, makes this almost certain. Epiphanius, on the other hand, repeatedly draws attention to the difference between the Marcionite and orthodox

---

[122] Epiphanius, *Panarion haer.* 34–64, ed. Karl Holl, 2nd edn, 1922, GCS, Epiphanius II (Berlin: Akademie, 1980), 93–186. Translations quoted from Epiphanius, *The Panarion of Epiphanius of Salamis: Book I (Sects 1–46)*, trans. Frank Williams, NHS 63 (Leiden: Brill, 2009).
[123] See Ulrich Schmid, *Marcion und sein Apostolos: Rekonstruktion und historische Einordnung der marcionitischen Paulusbriefausgabe*, ANTF 25 (Berlin: de Gruyter, 1995), 153–5.
[124] *Marc.* 5.21.1.
[125] Adolf von Harnack, *Marcion: Das Evangelium vom fremden Gott. Eine Monographie zur Geschichte der Grundlegung der katholischen Kirche*, TUGAL 45 (Leipzig: Hinrichs, 1921), 63*. Or, perhaps these letters are lacking because Epiphanius's 'treatise' is in fact a compilation made from assorted anti-Marcionite works (the view of John J. Clabeaux, *A Lost Edition of the Letters of Paul: A Reassessment of the Text of the Pauline Corpus Attested by Marcion*, CBQMS 21 (Washington, DC: Catholic Biblical Association of America, 1989), 14). Epiphanius's more precise treatment of Marcion's gospel, compared with his CP, may imply that he had immediate access to the former but not the latter (BeDuhn, *First New Testament*, 37).
[126] Judith M. Lieu, 'Marcion and the New Testament', in *Method and Meaning*, FS Harold W. Attridge, ed. Andrew B. McGowan and Kent Harold Richards (Atlanta, GA: SBL, 2011), 399–416 (401).

canonical orders, though interestingly he derives hardly any actual polemic from this, in contrast to the excisions from and changes to the text itself.[127] That neither author makes the sequence a point of serious contention suggests it was not a theologically weighted issue, and this probably reflects an assumption that the collection of letters postdated Paul; his apostolic authority is at stake in the texts themselves, but not in their relative positioning, so that while omissions are a major problem, rearrangement is not.[128]

The one place where Tertullian does seem to comment obliquely on Marcion's order is the beginning of his discussion of Galatians: 'principalem adversus Iudaismum epistulam nos quoque confitemur quae Galatas docet' (*Marc.* 5.2.1).[129] 'Principalem' here undoubtedly denotes the letter's theological relevance or power, but could it also refer to the sequential priority that Marcion gives it? Tertullian does sometimes use the word 'principalis' in this sense of the first in a series.[130] In fact, presuming there was no commentary in Marcion's *Apostolikon* (we would expect a refutation had there been any), only the position of Galatians could have signified its primacy. Tertullian flags this as potentially contentious ground while choosing not to contest it ('nos quoque confitemur'), but carefully limits his concession to the theological priority of the letter *vis-à-vis* Judaism rather than its canonical priority in general.[131] The implication is that Marcion's order, if not actually heretical, was idiosyncratic.

Unlike Tertullian, Epiphanius regards Laodiceans as a distinct eleventh letter in Marcion's canon, one which is not authentically Pauline. He includes only one citation from it – 'one Lord, one faith, one baptism, one God and Father of all, who is above all, and through all, and in all' (42.11.8 schol. Laod. 1; Eph. 4.5-6) – stating that Marcion perversely chose to quote this from Laodiceans rather than Ephesians (42.13.4).[132] The 'Laodiceans' that made its way into the Latin MS tradition does not include this verse, corroborating J. K. Elliott's view that the reference to such a letter in Col. 4.16 would have prompted more than one apocryphal composition.[133] It is

---

[127] For example, 'I have put <the> [texts] from the Epistle to the Galatians first, and keep that order throughout, for in Marcion's canon Galatians stands first. At the time I did not make my selection <in> his <order> but in the order of the Apostolic Canon, and put Romans first. But here I cite in accordance with Marcion's canon' (*Pan.* 42.12.2–3). Cf., 'However all sound, accurate copies have Romans first, Marcion, and do not place Galatians first as you do' (42.12.3 refut. Phlm.). Even here, Epiphanius does not draw any substantive conclusion from the order; it is the difference itself that is suspicious.

[128] The addition of uniform titles clearly belongs to the stage of collecting letters, so Tertullian's relatively relaxed response to the title 'Laodiceans' for Ephesians (see §2.3.2 above) is further evidence that he considers this postapostolic.

[129] Holmes translates, 'The epistle which we also allow to be the most decisive against Judaism, is that wherein the apostle instructs the Galatians'; Evans, 'We too claim that the primary epistle against Judaism is that addressed to the Galatians.'

[130] See references in *Thesaurus Linguae Latinae* (www.degruyter.com/db/tll) s.v. 'principalis' III.a.

[131] Cf. also the decisive theological role attributed to Galatians in *Marc.* 4.3.2.

[132] Tertullian does not quote this verse in discussing Laodiceans/Ephesians (*Marc.* 5.17–18), but appears to refer to it elsewhere: 'habemus illum alicubi unius baptismi definitorem' (*Marc.* 5.10.2). So this verse was probably part of the Marcionite scriptures known to Tertullian.

[133] J. K. Elliott, *The Apocryphal New Testament: A Collection of Apocryphal Christian Literature in an English Translation* (Oxford: OUP, 1993), 544. The allegedly Marcionite 'Laodiceans' mentioned in the Muratorian Fragment may be another letter again.

difficult to explain Epiphanius's attribution of this verse to Laodiceans, while others are quoted from Ephesians, without concluding that he had a different version of the Marcionite scriptures from that known to Tertullian;[134] given the long survival and broad geographic spread of Marcionite Christianity, this is not unlikely.

The relative placement of Philippians and Philemon may also reflect distinct sources. Knox argues that Epiphanius's placement of Philemon first is likelier to be original for the following reasons: Epiphanius is more interested in the order of the letters; Philippians would have made a stronger conclusion to the collection than Philemon; it is easier to explain the subsequent demotion of Philemon on grounds of length, rather than the reverse; and Colossians and Philemon taken together are longer than Philippians, relevant if the collection is ordered according to length.[135] This fits with Knox's theory of a close association between Philemon and Colossians from the earliest days of a Pauline collection, for which he also finds evidence in the Latin prologues.[136]

Apart from the proposed connection between Philemon and Colossians, which may indeed be supported by the prologues (see §2.6 below), Knox's arguments are weak. We have seen that Tertullian is aware of Marcion's order, though he does not foreground it; and neither length nor an emphatic conclusion are particularly relevant criteria for this edition of Paul. If, however, Tertullian's is the better account of Marcion's canon order, as we must assume prima facie, it is not difficult to imagine Philemon being later 'reunited' with Colossians on thematic grounds, either in fact or in Epiphanius's imagination. The discrepancy remains puzzling, but this is the less unsatisfactory explanation.

There remain various peculiarities in the arrangement of Marcion's CP, relative to our familiar canon, attested by both Tertullian and Epiphanius: the placement of Galatians at the head, Corinthians before Romans, the Thessalonian letters in fifth and sixth places and Colossians before Philippians. The promotion of Galatians is usually taken to be a doctrinal decision, favouring the letter most amenable to his theology; we have seen that this is implied by Tertullian (*Marc.* 5.2.1). Colossians and Philippians are nearly identical in length, actually identical by some stichometric counts (see §2.1.7 above), and we have seen that Codex Claromontanus (D) and minuscule 5 share this atypical ordering. In Tertullian's account of Marcion the inversion makes good sense, since 'Laodiceans' is then followed by Colossians, which makes reference to it (4.16).[137]

If the Corinthian and Thessalonian letters are counted as single entities, a possibility arguably supported by the Latin prologues (see §2.6 below), Marcion may have arranged the letters after Galatians in descending order of length. By this count, though, Ephesians should precede the combined Thessalonians.[138] Harnack explains this by the

---

[134] *Pace* Harnack (see n. 125 above), Epiphanius's faulty memory or incomplete notes are not enough to explain this difference from Tertullian.
[135] Knox, *Philemon*, 72–5.
[136] Knox, *Marcion and the New Testament*, 45. Knox is followed in this by Gamble, *Books and Readers*, 61; 273, n. 83.
[137] If correct, this interpretation would support Tertullian's account over Epiphanius's, but it is obviously speculative.
[138] Finegan, 'Original Form', 101–2, makes this suggestion, and resolves the discrepancy by counting the number of lines each letter occupies in Codex Vaticanus: by this measure, 1–2 Thessalonians

extra space required for two titles and subscriptions,[139] but it would be strange for the letters to be counted together but titled separately. Knox, following Goodspeed's theory of Ephesians as an introductory letter, thinks Marcion has simply swapped Galatians and Ephesians from an exemplar in which the other letters were arranged by length, that is, Eph. Cor. Rom. Thess. Gal. Col–Phlm. Phil.[140] This is ingenious, and has the additional attraction of accounting for the promotion of Colossians; but the hypothesis of Ephesians as an introduction to the canon is without any solid basis, and this postulated edition too is highly speculative.

An alternative explanation, advanced by Ulrich Schmid and Markus Vinzent, is that the letters stand in a supposed chronological order, conforming to the locations of writing given in the Latin prologues.[141] The prologues do seem to read the order chronologically, though this may reflect either an original rationale or a retrospective interpretation. Schmid takes the sequence to be pre-Marcionite, following the arguments of Nils Dahl against the Marcionite origin of the prologues, which we will find reason to doubt; Vinzent takes the collection (and prologues) to be Marcion's own. It would be at least a convenient coincidence for Marcion if the letter he received as chronologically earliest also happened to be that best adapted to his theological purposes; still, this is Vinzent's view.[142] Against its apparent improbability must be set the inexplicable position of Thessalonians in a schema that, apart from Galatians, follows length. There is no obvious solution to this conundrum, but on balance I incline towards Vinzent and think the Galatians-first order is likeliest to have been Marcion's innovation, whether motivated by doctrine, chronology or both.[143]

Finally, the absence of the Pastorals and Hebrews from Marcion's collection is obviously significant; Tertullian only mentions the former,[144] but Epiphanius also laments the omission of the latter.[145] Marcion is the strongest evidence we have that a ten-letter collection lacking these letters did circulate at some early stage, although not too long after his time the Pastorals were part of the collection for Tertullian, and Hebrews for 𝔓[46]. F. C. Baur appealed to Marcion when categorizing the Pastorals

---

is two lines longer than Ephesians. It is shorter, though, by the 'Euthalian' stichometry as well as the count of characters he cites from Graux (96).

[139] Harnack, *Marcion*, 149*. He also gives a character count for these letters, differing slightly from Trobisch's computer-generated count (Trobisch, *Die Entstehung*, 138) but without changing the order of length by this reckoning. But as Harnack observes, a character count is of much less relevance than contemporary stichometry, a fact Trobisch does not take properly into account.

[140] Knox, *Marcion and the New Testament*, 60-1. This would mean Corinthians, Thessalonians and Colossians–Philemon were each divided into two letters by or before Marcion, or at least by the version of his canon known to Tertullian.

[141] Schmid, *Marcion und sein Apostolos*, 294–6; Vinzent, *Marcion*, 125–6.

[142] 'The organization of the Pauline letters followed *not only* a theological agenda, as indicated by Tertullian, *but also* a geographical-historical one' (Vinzent, *Marcion*, 126; my emphasis).

[143] Frede too believes that Marcion's order is chronological, but representative of an 'Old Syriac' tradition also attested in Ephrem, the *Catalogus Sinaiticus* and the Latin Prologues ('Die Ordnung', 295–7). However, the evidence for a Galatians-first tradition independent of Marcion is not convincing. The Muratorian Fragment is probably not reproducing an existing canon order (see §2.7), and Marcion may well have influenced the Syrian sources (Vinzent, *Marcion*, 114; against Dahl, 'Welche Ordnung?', 254) and Prologues (see §2.6).

[144] *Marc.* 5.21.1.

[145] *Pan.* 42.11.11. He notes elsewhere that Hebrews is placed tenth in some copies of the collection, fourteenth in others, which reflects the variation already noted in MSS (42.12.3 refut. Phlm.).

as a third-class group within the CP, not just disputed (antilegomena) but positively spurious (notha).¹⁴⁶ Despite Baur's assurance, though, it cannot be definitely known whether Marcion chose to excise the Pastorals and so created this shorter collection (as Tertullian claims), or whether it was the form of the CP he received.¹⁴⁷

Marcion further attests the integration of the now-disputed letters within the earliest traceable history of the CP. The title 'Laodiceans' for Ephesians and the promotion of Colossians to follow it establish a strong connection between the two which accords with Col. 4.16; in a similar way, the promotion of Philemon in Epiphanius's account emphasizes its links with Colossians. The antilegomena which we do find in Maricon's collection are, if anything, even more embedded there than in the canonical CP.

2.6. The Latin prologues

These short prologues to Paul's letters (not Hebrews) survive in a number of medieval Latin MSS, and are first attested in the fourth century.¹⁴⁸ Their supposed Marcionite character and origin has been debated since the work early last century of de Bruyne and Corssen, who each independently proposed this connection.¹⁴⁹ From internal textual evidence they reconstructed the original sequence of the prologues, and concluded that some are later imitations, while the remainder follow Marcion's corpus order.¹⁵⁰

Nils Dahl, reviewing the evidence for the prologues' origin, concludes on textual grounds that some are indeed of later date – namely, 2 Corinthians, Ephesians, 2 Thessalonians, Philemon and the Pastorals – and that the remainder do correspond to an edition of Paul's letters that looks like Marcion's. Corinthians and Thessalonians would be treated as single letters, and Philemon attached to Colossians, as suggested by Knox. However, Dahl does not in fact consider these earlier prologues Marcion's own, but argues that they attest an edition of 'Paul's letters to seven churches' preceding him and circulating more widely, an edition eventually supplanted by the thirteen- or

---

[146] Baur, *Paulus*, 1867, 2.277–8.
[147] Contrast BeDuhn's surprising assertion: 'We know for a fact that ... there was no larger Pauline corpus from which Marcion excised the Pastorals' (*First New Testament*, 31). There is no decisive proof that such a thirteen-letter corpus *did* exist before Marcion, but obviously such silence does not prove its non-existence, and as we are finding, there is considerable evidence suggesting the reverse. BeDuhn also assumes that 𝔓⁴⁶ excluded the Pastorals (357, n. 20), and appears unaware of Duff's work on this point (see p. 24 above).
[148] By Marius Victorinus. See Dahl, 'Earliest Prologues', 237.
[149] Donatien de Bruyne, 'Prologues bibliques d'origine Marcionite', *Revue Bénédictine* 24 (1907): 1–16; Peter Corssen, 'Zur Überlieferungsgeschichte des Römerbriefs', ZNTW 10 (1909): 1–45, 97–102. Reviews of subsequent scholarship are found in Karl Theodor Schäfer, 'Marcion und die ältesten Prologe zu den Paulusbriefen', in *Kyriakon*, ed. Patrick Granfield and Johnannes Jungmann, vol. 1, 2 vols (Münster: Aschendorff, 1970), 135–50 (135–6); Dahl, 'Earliest Prologues', 234–6; and Vinzent, *Marcion*, 111, n. 423.
[150] Schäfer, 'Marcion', 137–9, summarizes the textual evidence for the inferred order and its correspondence to Marcion. He reports that he repeatedly gave the prologue texts to students unaware of the related scholarship, who without further prompting would reliably make the same observations.

fourteen-letter collection. The simultaneous circulation of two such collections could account for much of the variation in the surviving attested orders.[151]

Renewed arguments for the Marcionite origin of the prologues have recently been made by Markus Vinzent and Eric W. Scherbenske.[152] Scherbenske gives a thorough critique of Dahl's reasoning and concludes, correctly in my view, that although doubt can be cast on discrete points, 'cumulatively and cohesively' the evidence points to 'Marcion or his followers' as the simplest explanation for the prologues' origin.[153] In particular:

> The only known edition of the *Corpus Paulinum* that transmits this order opening with Galatians, contains Ephesians under the title Laodiceans, lacks the Pastoral epistles, lacks Hebrews, and stresses the distinction between Paul and the false apostles, the gospel truth and Jewish error, is Marcion's. Other hypothetical alternatives do not warrant the dismissal of the concrete evidence pointing to a Marcionite origin.[154]

Vinzent does not accept Dahl's supposition that the prologues are too widely attested to have been Marcionite in origin. This, he argues, rests upon an anachronistic distinction between heresy and orthodoxy, whereas in the second century the situation was fluid enough for a Marcionite collection of Paul's letters to have circulated widely, accompanied by the prologues.[155] Vinzent draws a number of parallels between *Adversus Marcionem* and the prologues, concluding that Tertullian may well have known them and allowed his response to be shaped by them.[156] This is certainly possible, but the connections are mostly thematic and can be otherwise explained. For example, Vinzent attributes Tertullian's reluctant foregrounding of the law in *Marc.* 5.13 to its prominence in the prologue to Romans, when various other aspects of the epistle could easily have been thematized instead. But equally Tertullian may have found the law unavoidably central to the logic of Romans, which would hardly be unusual. Tertullian may well have known the prologues, but the case is not proven.

Vinzent also questions whether the prologues to 2 Corinthians and 2 Thessalonians are later additions, explaining their differences from the others by the superfluity of repeating information about the addressees.[157] This does not address the fact that the prologue to 1 Corinthians introduces the content of both Corinthian letters, and the arguments of Dahl and Schäfer remain convincing on this point.[158]

---

[151] Dahl, 'Earliest Prologues', 252–7.
[152] Vinzent, *Marcion*, 111–31; Eric W. Scherbenske, *Canonizing Paul: Ancient Editorial Practice and the Corpus Paulinum* (New York: OUP, 2013), 88–93, 237–42.
[153] Scherbenske, *Canonizing Paul*, 242.
[154] Ibid., 92.
[155] Vinzent, *Marcion*, 116.
[156] Ibid., 127–30. See also Scherbenske, *Canonizing Paul*, 94–115, for the independent argument that some of Tertullian's attacks on Marcion's text reflect the influence of Marcionite 'paratexts', namely the *Antitheses* and on occasion the prologues (105).
[157] Vinzent, *Marcion*, 114. He agrees that the Pastorals and their prologues were added later to Marcion's collection, and takes this as evidence 'that the collecting of Pauline letters and prefacing them carried on after Marcion's death' (131).
[158] Dahl, 'Earliest Prologues', 247–8; Schäfer, 'Marcion', 142–3.

If we accept a reconstruction of the prologues along the lines described, they attest powerfully to the reading of the CP as a 'seven church' collection. It should be emphasized that this is an *interpretation* of the collection's catholicity, and does not necessarily reflect a distinct *edition*. The CP so described may quite probably exclude the Pastorals and Hebrews, and could attach Philemon to Colossians; if Epiphanius's order is correct, Marcion may have shaped such a collection himself, but he could just as well have inherited it. Whether the prologues derive from Marcion himself or a later Marcionite, they should not be regarded as a separate tradition, independently attesting to a CP without the Pastorals. It remains uncertain whether any corpus other than the Marcionite excluded these letters.

2.7. The Muratorian Fragment

This partial list and discussion of the books of the New Testament, found by Lodovico Antonio Muratori in a codex of the Ambrosian Library of Milan and published by him in 1740,[159] has long been regarded as the church's earliest recorded canon.[160] It has usually been dated to the late second century, largely on the basis of its reference to the *Shepherd of Hermas* as being written while the author's brother Pius was bishop of Rome, that is, in the mid-second century, 'most recently, in our times' (ll. 74–77).[161] This consensus has been challenged by Albert C. Sundberg and more recently Geoffrey Mark Hahneman, who propose a fourth-century origin.[162] They argue that the phrase 'nuperrime temboribus nostris' is more accurately interpreted 'most recently [of the books here listed], in our own [as distinct from apostolic] times'.

This reading is sound, but a fourth-century dating does not follow. Parallels have long been noted between the Fragment and Gaius of Rome, an antagonist of Hippolytus

---

[159] Lodovico Antonio Muratori, 'De literarum statu, neglectu et cultura in Italia', in *Antiquitates Italicae medii aevi*, vol. 3, 6 vols (Milan: Societas Palatina, 1740), 809–80; the Fragment and commentary is found in coll. 853–6.

[160] For the uncorrected text and extensive discussion, see Geoffrey Mark Hahneman, *The Muratorian Fragment and the Development of the Canon* (Oxford: Clarendon, 1992).

[161] The dreadful Latin in which the Fragment has survived can hardly be its original form. A Greek source has been postulated and occasionally reconstructed, even in verse. There are excerpts of a better Latin text embedded in a medieval prologue to Paul's letters: on this see Adolf von Harnack, 'Excerpte aus dem Muratorischen Fragment (saec. XI. et XII.)', *TLZ* 23 (1898): 131–4. Hahneman (9–10) assumes that this preserves an earlier source, but does not acknowledge Harnack's persuasive argument that it is a later correction of Muratori's text. Nevertheless, since the text we have is almost certainly a corruption of *some* better original, Everett Ferguson is right to observe against Hahneman that its orthography cannot prove a late date, and if the original is Greek, neither can its vocabulary ('Review of Geoffrey Mark Hahneman, *The Muratorian Fragment and the Development of the Canon*', *JTS* 44 (1993): 691–7 (691); so also Christoph Johannes Markschies, *Christian Theology and Its Institutions in the Early Roman Empire*, trans. Wayne Coppins (German 2009; Waco, TX: Baylor University, 2015), 206–7).

[162] Albert C. Sundberg, 'Canon Muratori: A Fourth-Century List', *HTR* 66 (1973): 1–41; see also Albert C. Sundberg, 'Towards a Revised History of the New Testament Canon', in *Studia Evangelica*, ed. F. L. Cross, vol. 4/1, TUGAL 102 (Berlin: Akademie, 1968), 452–61, esp. 458–9. See n. 162 above for Hahneman.

attested in Eusebius and elsewhere.¹⁶³ Gaius seems to have rejected both the Gospel and Revelation of John; the Fragment is clearly at pains to justify the former, while the latter, Sundberg argues, is treated ambiguously, 'on the very fringe of canonicity'.¹⁶⁴ He finds this compatible only with an eastern provenance, but as Francis Watson argues, the third-century west, with the Gaius–Hippolytus controversy in the background, is a better fit.¹⁶⁵

Hahneman considers the earliest dating anachronistic in the history of canon formation. Because the Old Testament canon was not finally settled until the fourth century, he finds the idea of a second-century New Testament canon unlikely;¹⁶⁶ but the two processes are not entirely analogous. The Fragment is not simply a canon *list*, but a discussion of the inspiration and authority of allegedly apostolic texts.¹⁶⁷ Its evidently contested defence of some texts, and rejection of others, is entirely plausible for the late second or early third century. As Ferguson notes in his critical review of Hahneman, the Fragment seems to represent an 'open canon' stage in the history of scripture, where the principle of an exclusive canon is accepted, but there is still some debate about its exact parameters.¹⁶⁸ Indeed, the controversy around Gaius is a case in point.¹⁶⁹

Hahneman is also unjustified to claim that 'with the exception of the Fragment as traditionally dated, there is no evidence of a Pauline canon until the fourth century'.¹⁷⁰ The present review is finding considerable evidence for a CP before this point, with ten letters always present, some ambiguity around the Pastorals and more around Hebrews. This hardly constitutes 'ample attestation of a continually expanding Pauline collection', Hahneman's description of the situation before the fourth century;¹⁷¹ it looks more like an 'open canon', with some borderline cases remaining.¹⁷²

The actual CP attested in the Fragment is notable in a few respects. Most striking is its complete silence about Hebrews, which cannot be explained by doubt about authorship, since a Laodiceans and an otherwise unknown letter to the Alexandrians

---

163 Muratori's own suggestion is that Gaius was the author, but in view of subsequent scholarship on Gaius this can no longer be considered plausible (Muratori, 'De literarum statu', 853–4).
164 Sundberg, 'Canon Muratori', 21.
165 Francis Watson, *Gospel Writing: A Canonical Perspective* (Grand Rapids, MI: Eerdmans, 2013), 477–91, esp. 490, n. 161.
166 Hahneman, *Muratorian Fragment*, 83.
167 It has been variously categorized, including as 'Einleitung' (Graham N. Stanton, 'The Fourfold Gospel', NTS 43 (1997): 317–46 (323)), but is really too fragmentary and unusual to be assigned to any ancient literary genre (Markschies, *Christian Theology*, 203).
168 Ferguson, 'Review of Hahneman', 693.
169 Watson, *Gospel Writing*, 479, n. 119.
170 Hahneman, *Muratorian Fragment*, 111.
171 Ibid.
172 On this question, see also C. E. Hill, 'The Debate over the Muratorian Fragment and the Development of the Canon', WTJ 57 (1995): 437–52, who disagrees that authors before the fourth century showed no interest in a canon (as distinct from scripture), and cites various counterexamples (447–51). The Sundberg–Hahneman dating has also been extensively critiqued by Joseph Verheyden, 'The Canon Muratori: A Matter of Dispute', in *The Biblical Canons*, ed. Jean-Marie Auwers and H. J. de Jonge, BETL 163 (Leuven: Leuven University & Peeters, 2003), 487–556, who observes, among other things, that the features of this canon that appear anomalous in the second-century West are even stranger if it belongs to the fourth-century East.

are explicitly excluded as pseudo-Pauline forgeries (ll. 63–68).¹⁷³ In a document that discusses the ambiguous authority of the *Apocalypse of Peter* and the *Shepherd of Hermas*, it is surprising that Hebrews should not warrant even a mention, positive or negative. This fades somewhat in the light of the Fragment's other peculiarities. The letters of Peter and James are lacking, while Jude and perhaps only two letters of John are known (ll. 68–69), a configuration of the Catholic epistles not elsewhere attested.¹⁷⁴ The incomplete preservation of the Fragment and the poor quality of its transcription have sufficed for many to account for at least some of these omissions. But other oddities, such as the order of the Pastorals, with Titus mentioned before Timothy (l. 60), not to mention the inclusion of the Wisdom of Solomon (ll. 69–71), are not so easily explained.

The Fragment is also unusual in mentioning some of Paul's letters twice. We are told that Paul wrote first of all to the Corinthians, then to the Galatians, and to the Romans (ll. 42–44); then, within the framework of 'seven churches', Paul is reported to have written 'in this order' to the Corinthians, Ephesians, Philippians, Colossians, Galatians, Thessalonians and Romans, respectively, enumerated from first to seventh (ll. 50–54).¹⁷⁵ 2 Corinthians, 2 Thessalonians and the personal letters are appended to this list. This has led to various speculation, including Nils Dahl's ingenious suggestion that the Fragment's author knew the letters in their now familiar canonical order, but moved Romans and Galatians in the interests of chronology, then underlined the relative dating of Corinthians, Galatians and Romans in a prefatory comment to justify this alteration.¹⁷⁶ Dahl's solution shows that it is not necessary to postulate some other form of the CP lying behind the Fragment. But this is in many ways an eccentric document, and there is little chance that any explanation of its unusual ordering will prove definitively satisfactory.¹⁷⁷

Most significant in the Fragment for our purposes is the claim that Paul writes to 'seven churches'. In this he follows the example of his 'predecessor' John (ll. 47–50), who in Revelation 'writes to seven churches, but nevertheless speaks to all' (ll. 57–59),¹⁷⁸ while the Fragment refers to 2 Corinthians, 2 Thessalonians and the personal letters in

---

¹⁷³ The inevitable suggestion that this 'Alexandrians' is in fact Hebrews will not hold water. There is no other reference that would support this identification, and the Fragment claims that Alexandrians is both Marcionite and forged in Paul's name (ll. 64–65), neither of which applies to Hebrews (Bruce M. Metzger, *The Canon of the New Testament: Its Origin, Development and Significance* (Oxford: Clarendon, 1987), 197).

¹⁷⁴ See the tables in David R. Nienhuis, *Not by Paul Alone: The Formation of the Catholic Epistle Collection and the Christian Canon* (Waco, TX: Baylor University, 2007), 91–5. Nienhuis rejects the Sundberg–Hahneman provenance because 'one would expect to see a more fully developed [Catholic Epistle] collection in a fourth-century Eastern list' (76).

¹⁷⁵ Along with the omission of Hebrews, the fact that the letters are specifically enumerated is another point of resemblance with Gaius (Watson, *Gospel Writing*, 478).

¹⁷⁶ Dahl, 'Welche Ordnung?'. He suggests that among the personal letters, 2 Timothy was put last as a 'farewell letter', and Philemon brought forward because of its association with Colossians (48).

¹⁷⁷ According to Frede, reporting a private communication, Dahl no longer held this view in 1968 (Frede, 'Die Ordnung', 297, n. 2). Frede himself groups the Fragment's unique order under C ('Chronological'), suggesting that the author inferred a chronological sequence from the length-based order he had received (297).

¹⁷⁸ Cf. Tertullian: 'ad omnes apostolus scripserit dum ad quosdam' (*Marc.* 5.17). He makes no mention of seven churches, however.

almost apologetic terms, apparently needing to justify their inclusion separately. The catholicity of such obviously particular texts as Paul's letters is *prima facie* questionable, a potential problem for their canonization; a symbolically complete corpus of seven churches is a solution to this problem, one that we have already seen implied in the Latin prologues.[179]

Various other third-century authors refer to Paul's 'seven churches'.[180] The earliest is Hippolytus, as attested in Dionysius Bar Salibi's *Commentary on Revelation*: 'Hippolytus says that in writing to seven Churches, [John] writes just as Paul wrote thirteen letters, but wrote them to seven Churches.'[181] If this is accurately preserved, it is distinctive in reckoning the Pastoral letters within the seven-church schema; Hippolytus's rationale for this accounting is not reported.

Later, Cyprian (*Quir.* 1.20; *Fort.* 11) and Victorinus of Pettau (*Fabr.* 8)[182] both cite the Pauline letters among other illustrations of the fullness of the number seven. On another occasion, Victorinus offers a more extensive defence of Paul's catholicity:

> Whether in Asia or in the whole world, Paul taught that all of the seven churches that are named are one catholic church. And therefore, that he might preserve this understanding, he did not exceed the number of seven churches, but he wrote to the Romans, to the Corinthians, to the Ephesians, to the Thessalonians, to the Galatians, to the Philippians and to the Colossians. Later he wrote to individual persons, lest he exceed the number of seven churches.[183]

An apology is required for the personal letters to account for their disturbing the seven-church scheme; this closely resembles the Muratorian Fragment, and in fact Victorinus has been suggested as a candidate for its authorship.[184]

This reading of Paul's letters as a seven-church collection clearly had some currency in the third century, but to reiterate, such an *interpretation* can circulate without necessarily accompanying a distinctive *edition* of the CP. Gamble, for instance, too readily concludes from this evidence that the most primitive Corpus, now lost, was a seven-church collection.[185] While this is not impossible, there are no solid grounds to

---

[179] On this, see Krister Stendahl, 'The Apocalypse of John and the Epistles of Paul in the Muratorian Fragment', in *Current Issues in New Testament Interpretation*, ed. William Klassen and Graydon F. Snyder (London: SCM, 1962), 239–45; and Dahl, 'Particularity'.

[180] Hahneman, *Muratorian Fragment*, 117, n. 97, mentions the following as well as later references (Jerome and Isidore).

[181] Quoted in Theodore H. Robinson, 'The Authorship of the Muratorian Canon', *Expositor* 7 (1906): 481–95 (488). According to Bar Salibi, Hippolytus did not consider Hebrews to be Paul's.

[182] Hahneman cites *Fabr.* 11, but the division in the *Sources Chrétiennes* edition extends only to §10.

[183] Victorinus, 'Commentary on the Apocalypse', in *Latin Commentaries on Revelation*, ed. and trans. William C. Weinrich, ACT (Downers Grove, IL: IVP Academic, 2011), 1–22 (3). There are four MS variants of the letter sequence here, so little can be made of that (Jonathan Armstrong, 'Victorinus of Pettau as the Author of the Canon Muratori', *VC* 62 (2008): 1–34 (16, n. 49)).

[184] Armstrong, 'Victorinus', for this reason among others. Armstrong also notes the earlier proposal of J. B. Lightfoot that Hippolytus wrote the Fragment, rebutted by Harnack.

[185] Gamble, *Books and Readers*, 59–61, and similarly in other publications. He believes that this corpus led to the widespread adoption of the codex among Christians (see Harry Y. Gamble, 'The Pauline Corpus and the Early Christian Book', in *Paul and the Legacies of Paul*, ed. William S. Babcock (Dallas, TX: Southern Methodist University, 1990), 265–80).

suppose that such a construal of the letters' catholicity preceded Marcion, and indeed it may reflect the influence of his ten-letter CP.

3. Conclusions

Does anything emerge with certainty from this perplexing array of data and hypotheses? Within the scope of a single chapter, it is not possible to construct a new and comprehensive synthesis, or even to adjudicate thoroughly between the various proposals outlined above. Such a project requires a monograph, and the reader is referred to Lovering's doctoral thesis for the best treatment currently available. The broad outline of his conclusion – that a certain amount of early variation in letter circulation eventually gave way to a uniform CP – is in my view correct, but within that framework, I believe he inclines too far to the side of initial diversity and multiplicity of sources.

The reason for this disagreement is the relative weight placed upon different sorts of evidence: on the one hand, late traces of early variation, and on the other, the relative stability of the papyri and uncials. In my view, the studies of Frede and Aland (§2.2) are less conclusive than Lovering allows, because there are too many other possible explanations for how difference could have crept into the CP's transmission history. To infer early chaos from late chaos is an unreliable strategy. Frede is also too quick to detect canon lists in dubious places; some of the orders he cites are not lists at all, and others may simply be idiosyncratic or regional variants of a common source. On the other hand, if there were indeed multiple primitive corpora in general circulation, we would expect more divergence within the MSS than is actually attested.

For these reasons, I am more confident than Lovering of a *relatively* stable CP in the second century. None of the sources most usually quoted to disprove this are in fact decisive. The Muratorian Fragment and the 'canon lists' in Tertullian and Origen do not actually seem to transcribe existing canon orders. Marcion's sequence is unique, but since he almost certainly edited the text of the letters (and Luke), differences in his canon are also explicable by his innovation. The peculiarities of $\mathfrak{P}^{46}$ arise from fully integrating Hebrews among the church letters, and from promoting Ephesians, possibly to reflect its length more accurately. This shows that the canon had not yet reached a settled state, and some variation was still possible; it need not imply multiple, widely differing sources.

It should also be emphasized that the only strong evidence for a CP without the Pastorals is Marcion, who may of course have excised them as Tertullian alleges. The Latin prologues, which also imply their absence, are probably dependent on him. The theory of Paul's seven churches, as attested in the Muratorian Fragment and elsewhere, is capable of accommodating the Pastorals, albeit at a stretch: this defence of Paul's catholicity does not necessarily imply an edition of the CP that included only community letters, *pace* Gamble. The surviving portion of $\mathfrak{P}^{46}$ does not show whether the codex originally included the Pastorals or not.

The strongest supporting evidence for an original ten-letter collection is the scarcity of the Pastorals among the surviving papyri, apart from the extremely early $\mathfrak{P}^{32}$, but the sample size is too small to be very useful. The strongest counterargument is found in the allusions to these letters in the Apostolic Fathers alongside other Pauline texts. There remains some doubt about when the Pastorals were added to the Corpus, and their secondary status is far from proven. Hebrews, on the other hand, very clearly occupies a contested place in the CP, suggesting either that it was a latecomer to the Corpus or that it was once excluded and later re-included; this doubt is reflected in ongoing patristic debates about the letter's authorship.

If these considerations imply greater and earlier stability than is admitted by Lovering, we can still confidently exclude the extreme position represented by Porter, namely that Paul personally edited the thirteen-letter CP. From the textual history of Romans and Ephesians, and to a lesser extent 1 Corinthians, it is clear that at least these letters circulated for a time independently. (The pattern of Pauline allusions in early patristic sources may corroborate this, on closer examination.) Even limited circulation of individual, variant texts is difficult to square with the theory of a personally authorized apostolic corpus. The use of the fourteen-chapter Romans as late as Marcion's time and the problematic address of Ephesians that leaves its autograph form obscure are particular stumbling blocks for this theory. And although variation in the MS tradition should not be overstated, it is more than would be consistent with a single apostolic exemplar.

Some circulation of individual letters is *prima facie* to be expected, particularly in light of Col. 4.16; nothing could be more natural than for communicating congregations to exchange copies of Paul's treasured legacy. The surprise, if anything, is that this is not more widely attested. Individual circulation poses no difficulty for the thesis of a relatively early collection, only for Paul's personal authorization of the Corpus.

What then of Trobisch's theory? He sees authorial redaction in all the 'authentic' Pauline letters, and believes that Paul himself arranged a small collection comprising Romans, 1–2 Corinthians and Galatians; that this was expanded in the early second century to a thirteen-letter corpus; and that it was finally consolidated with a variant 'catholic' edition of Romans, 1 Corinthians, Ephesians and Hebrews. Trobisch acknowledges that aspects of his reconstruction are rather imaginative, but has great confidence in his comparative method to unearth primitive proto-corpora. This method is highly unreliable for two reasons: the data set of attested canon orders is contestable, as a comparison with Frede's study makes clear, and the corpus size is too small. The method may work well for the much larger collection of Cyprian's letters (Trobisch models his approach on a study of the Corpus Cyprianum), but where only fourteen letters are concerned, slight and potentially arbitrary variation can skew results considerably. Trobisch builds reconstruction upon reconstruction, so these small differences vastly alter the shape of the whole theoretical edifice.

A case in point is the weight placed upon the relative order of Ephesians and Galatians. Galatians, the slightly shorter letter, is usually placed first, and this is critical for Trobisch's inference of a primitive Romans–Corinthians–Galatians collection. But as we have seen, when ancient stichometric measurements are followed rather than a modern computer-aided count, the relative length of the two letters is more ambiguous; so it is unsurprising that the MSS vary somewhat in this order. Exactly the same is true of Philippians and Colossians, yet that variation is dismissed by Trobisch as unimportant. His account is highly speculative and depends upon the over-interpretation of selected evidence, and it cannot be considered a realistic option, notwithstanding his stimulating engagement with the sources.

Goodspeed's theory is still less accountable to the evidence. MS variation and the clear signs of independent circulation are problems as substantial for him as for Porter. Moreover, the claim that Paul's legacy fell into obscurity after his death, only to be redeemed by the publication of Acts, is inherently implausible, and requires a tendentious reading of that book. Goodspeed's following must be largely attributed to the considerable power of his narrative – largely, but perhaps not exclusively. His account builds not only on his speculative history but also on an analysis of manifold intertextual links between Ephesians and the other nine letters he considers genuinely Pauline. It is this literary relationship, together with the lack of obvious particularity in the letter's contents, and the problem of its address, that prompts him to classify it as an integrating digest, deliberately crafted as an introduction to the Corpus. That there is no single trace of a CP with Ephesians first (Knox's artful convolutions notwithstanding) must be added to the case against Goodspeed. But his insistence that 'the problem of Ephesians is inextricably intertwined with that of the Pauline corpus'[186] is more judicious than his particular solution to the problem, as I hope this study will go on to show.

To return to the questions with which this chapter began, it seems clear that the CP was formed gradually rather than instantly, with some initial independent circulation of single letters, and some variation in the scope and order of early collections. This conclusion will not come as a surprise to any student of early Christianity; in fact, we may well have expected more extensive variation. I myself had not anticipated the degree of consistency that is in fact attested, especially but not only in the MSS. The indications are of a surprisingly stable Corpus surprisingly early.

The one letter that has a definitely marginal place in the CP – Hebrews – is received in a way that corresponds to its literary distinctiveness, its anonymity and ambiguous genre. As we have seen, it is much harder to say the same for the Pastorals, though they were clearly a theological fault line for Marcion and his opponents, as they are for many readers today. The case that they were latecomers to the Corpus is not baseless, but it is fairly weak and to my mind often overstated, perhaps reflecting more the modern perception of these texts than the ancient. Among the remaining letters, the sources know no separation: Ephesians, Colossians and 2 Thessalonians are always fully integrated into the attested collections. Apart from Galatians in Marcion's account, the arrangement of the CP does not seem to have prioritized particular texts except by length, though there is a clear distinction between church and personal letters. This mirrors the widespread 'seven-church' gloss of the Corpus, which however it may seem to marginalize the personal letters, does not exclude them.

---

[186] Goodspeed, *Meaning*, 9.

In summary, the CP that emerges from the evidence surveyed here is a composite text of remarkable integrity and consistency. It gives little grounds for a hierarchy of letters, and apart from the marginal Hebrews (still ultimately included), none at all for the dividing wall of modern scholarship. The separation of 'genuine' from 'spurious' elements works against the grain of this canonical history; in fact, it constructs a new corpus in place of the old. There must inevitably arise a contest for hermeneutical normativity.

2

The dissolution of the Corpus Paulinum

Until we begin to treat the seven-letter 'genuine' Paul versus the 'pseudepigraphical' Paul discourse as part of a much later era of Pauline reception, yet still driven by the same kinds of ideological concerns as were already present in the second century (i.e., Who was the 'real' Paul?), the early history of the Pauline tradition will continue to be narrated in our own image.[1]

One salient lesson from Benjamin White's *Remembering Paul* is that the quest for the historical Paul is not unique to the modern age. Contests over the image of Paul ran along similar lines in the second century and in the nineteenth: for F. C. Baur no less than for Marcion or Tertullian, defining the authentic canon of letters, and therefore discovering the apostle's true identity, involves theological as well as historical argument. Their claims to the 'real Paul', in contrast to the 'false Pauls' of rival traditions, follow similar strategies, such as the exclusion of some texts as inauthentic. In our own time, when the bifurcation of the CP is so widely taken for granted, it is worth reviewing the context in which this hermeneutic was developed, and the kinds of theological agenda that have tended to accompany it. For Baur, the iconoclastic, 'radical' Paul of the *Hauptbriefe* was pitted against the tamer, institutionalized, 'ecclesial' Paul of the Pastorals, Ephesians and even Philippians. Although Baur's historiographical model, along with his narrow selection of letters, was highly controversial, this essentially Protestant, oppositional *outline* of the CP has been widely accepted ever since. Even the New Perspective, otherwise so critical of 'Lutheran' exegesis, inhabits the same basic framework.[2]

We are in White's debt for reminding us how fraught any claim to the 'real Paul' must be. Still, despite the many merits of his study, I cannot unreservedly second his approach. The history of the divided CP is not, in my opinion, wholly one of ideological conflict; when Schleiermacher first questioned the authenticity of 1 Timothy, it was on narrowly philological grounds, and although his mode of enquiry was eventually radicalized by Baur, that step was not inevitable. The phenomenon of biblical

---

[1] Benjamin L. White, *Remembering Paul: Ancient and Modern Contests over the Image of the Apostle* (Oxford: OUP, 2014), 65.
[2] The New Perspective 'has failed to recognize that a largely Lutheran image of Paul persists in the very selection of the texts in the first place' (ibid., 40).

pseudonymity per se need not lead to an antithetical, disjunctive hermeneutic, even though such an approach has in fact become common. This chapter examines some aspects of the interpretative history that have contributed to this situation. When I am critical of the theological partisanship involved, I do not mean to suggest that exegesis can or should be entirely disinterested. But neither do I believe that naked ideological sparring is the only alternative. As things stand, philological analysis and theological contention have become bewilderingly muddled; perhaps the distinction between them will always be somewhat blurred, but it could be a good deal clearer than it is, to the benefit of both.

Since it is obviously beyond our scope here to trace the whole trajectory of Pauline interpretation for the last two centuries, what follows is grouped around a few significant nodes in the story. The first part is concerned with the prevailing disjunctive hermeneutic of the CP, which tends to favour the 'authentic' letters over the later 'deuteropaulines', and – explicitly or implicitly – the Protestant over the Catholic 'Paul'. At root here is what I call a 'decadence' model of the CP's gradual decline.[3] This part focuses mainly on the two scholars I consider most influential in propagating this schema, F. C. Baur and Ernst Käsemann, with some discussion of their more recent legacy. The second part gives some examples of alternative interpretative strategies, touching on a few that seem to me more or less unsatisfactory, before focusing on the promising but only partially successful model of Brevard Childs. Finally I set out my own suggested approach, which will inform the remaining chapters. Throughout, particular attention is given to Ephesians, and the role assigned to it within the CP by various interpreters.

1. The hermeneutics of decadence

1.1. From doubt to disjunction: F. C. Baur

Our modern divided Pauline Corpus can look to F. C. Baur not exactly as a direct progenitor, but certainly as a godfather. He represents a sort of high-water mark for the scepticism more cautiously advanced by Schleiermacher, Eichhorn and de Wette, among others; famously, only the four so-called *Hauptbriefe* (Romans, 1–2 Corinthians and Galatians) counted for him as authentic. But Baur's more significant innovation was in kind, not degree: he shifted the discussion from the philological to the theological plane, from the analytical to the evaluative. From the fissure appearing between authentic and pseudonymous texts, he developed a hermeneutic of disjunction, opposing the intrepid Paul of the genuine letters to the wan avatar of his imitators. The one he lionizes, the other he laments. The distinction within the Corpus now

---

[3] Borrowing from Udo Schnelle, who uses the term *Dekadenztheorie* for this trajectory: 'Am Anfang steht Paulus, dann folgen der Kolosser- und Epheserbrief (und der 2Thess), bis schließlich die Pastoralbriefe die Paulinische Theologie vollständig in zeitgenössische Moral und Bürgerlichkeit auflösen' (*Theologie des Neuen Testaments* (Stuttgart: Vandenhoeck & Ruprecht, 2007), 562). Throughout, I use the word 'decadence' in this older sense of cultural/intellectual decay, and not with the now usual connotation of glamour and indulgence.

represents a fault line in Christian history, with the authentic apostolic gospel found on the far side. Baur was an extreme and controversial figure, but it is a remarkable fact that for all his detractors in later scholarship, this evaluative hermeneutic has survived quite tenaciously.

The philological 'higher criticism' was first seriously applied to the New Testament by Friedrich Schleiermacher, building on his similar experience with the Platonic corpus, in an 1807 study hypothesizing that 1 Timothy is pseudonymous.[4] His arguments still have a familiar ring two centuries later: the number of *hapax legomena* and formulations unusual for Paul, the disjointed style and the literary relationship with the other two Pastoral letters, from which Schleiermacher argued 1 Timothy was compiled. But although radical at the time, in retrospect this seems a relatively tentative foray. Five years later, when J. G. Eichhorn argued that the three Pastoral letters belonged together and were all pseudonymous, Schleiermacher remained unpersuaded: although later hailed as a pioneer, he was himself unhappy with the way in which succeeding NT criticism developed his methods.[5]

Among those bolder successors was W. M. L. de Wette, the first to pronounce against the Pauline authorship of Ephesians. The evolution of his views on this matter gives one glimpse of a shift that was occurring more widely.[6] In the 1826 first edition of his NT *Einleitung*,[7] he comments on the authorship of each of the Pauline letters: all three Pastorals are most likely pseudonymous; Colossians is certainly authentic,

---

[4] Friedrich Schleiermacher, *Ueber den sogenannten ersten Brief des Paulos an den Timotheos: Ein kritisches Sendschreiben an J. C. Gass* (Berlin: Realschulbuchhandlung, 1807). There were some partial precedents, more on grounds of content than strict philology: e.g. J. E. C. Schmidt, who raised the question of 2 Thessalonians's authenticity, though concluding that only one passage (2.1-12) was a spurious insertion ('Vermuthungen über die beyden Briefe an die Thessalonicher', in *Bibliothek für Kritik und Exegese des neuen Testaments und älteste Christengeschichte*, vol. 2.3 (Habamer: Gelehrtenbuchhandlung, 1801), 380-6); or the exceptionally heterodox Edward Evanson, who rejected the vast majority of the NT (*The Dissonance of the Four Generally Received Evangelists, and the Evidence of Their Respective Authenticity, Examined; with That of Some Other Scriptures, Deemed Canonical*, 2nd edn (Gloucester: Walker, 1805)). A somewhat different case was the provenance of Hebrews, long disputed in the ancient church, and controversial again from the Renaissance; Erasmus, Luther and Cajetan, among others, rejected Pauline authorship (see Kenneth Hagen, *Hebrews Commenting from Erasmus to Bèze, 1516-1598*, Beiträge zur Geschichte der Biblischen Exegese 23 (Tübingen: Mohr Siebeck, 1981)). This too partially anticipated the wider-ranging interrogation of authorship in the nineteenth century. But, as we have seen, Hebrews is an exceptional case within the CP. Apart from anything else, since it lacks explicit attribution to Paul, to doubt its authorship is not exactly to doubt its *authenticity*; there is theologically less at stake.

[5] See Hermann Patsch, 'Die Angst vor dem Deuteropaulinismus: Die Rezeption des "kritischen Sendschreibens" Friedrich Schleiermachers über den 1. Timotheusbrief im ersten Jahrfünft', ZTK 88 (1991): 451-77 (470-1). In a recent reappraisal of the *status quaestionis*, Jens Herzer has put forward a position similar to Schleiermacher's ('Zwischen Mythos und Wahrheit: Neue Perspektiven auf die sogenannten Pastoralbriefe', NTS 63 (2017): 428-50). He argues that, while 1 Timothy is demonstrably pseudonymous, 2 Timothy and Titus are part of the Pauline tradition received in that letter, and can plausibly be interpreted as authentic.

[6] The comparison is suggested by Baur, who notes that de Wette's doubts were made firm only in the 1843 *Kurze Erklärung* (F. C. Baur, *Paulus, der Apostel Jesu Christi: Sein Leben und Wirken, seine Briefe und seine Lehre*, 2nd edn, vol. 2 (Leipzig: Fues, 1867), 3). De Wette had earlier been the first reviewer to respond positively to Schleiermacher's critique of 1 Timothy (Patsch, 'Die Angst', 459).

[7] W. M. L. de Wette, *Lehrbuch der historisch kritischen Einleitung in die kanonischen Bücher des Neuen Testaments* (Berlin: Reimer, 1826).

as is Philippians, though not a unity, and Galatians, which bears the unmistakeable stamp of the apostle despite relatively late attestation; when it comes to Ephesians, the question is doubtful. Echoing Schleiermacher on 1 Timothy, de Wette cites both the literary relationship between this letter and Colossians, 'disconcerting' (*befremdend*) in itself, and much theology and diction unlike or unworthy of the apostle. On the other hand, plenty *is* worthy of him, and the letter was universally attributed to Paul from earliest days (263–4). This criterion could still carry the day in 1826, but by 1843 it no longer seemed to matter, and de Wette's doubts had become overwhelming. The letter's historical situation and seemingly incongruous address would pose a problem, but only if it is was authentic:

> Hierbei müsste man nun als bei einem geschichtlichen Räthsel stehen bleiben, wenn der Brief jenes ächte Gepräge paulinischen Geistes trüge, welches man ihm allgemein zuschreibt. … Ich aber muss es ihm absagen.[8]

The critic's discernment of spirits contributes materially to his assessment of authenticity: where the genuine Pauline character is lacking, other objections are magnified. The same standard had applied in reverse to Galatians:

> Dieser Brief stimmt so sehr mit der Geschichte des Apostels zusammen (gewisse Abweichungen der Nachrichten in der Apostelgeschichte abgerechnet) *und trägt so sehr das Gepräge seines Geistes*, daß sich gegen die kirchliche Ueberlieferung, welche ihm denselben zuschreibt, auch nicht der geringste Zweifel erheben läßt, obgleich diese Ueberlieferung erst durch die Kirchenväter, welche zu Ende des zweyten und zu Anfang des dritten Jahrhunderts gelebt haben, bezeugt ist.[9]

On historical criteria alone de Wette finds reason to doubt the letter, but such misgivings shrink in light of its palpable paulinity. Clearly there is a circularity to the argument, between the character of the author inferred from the texts and the selection of the texts that represent the author. That is not necessarily a flaw; it is in fact essential, in Schleiermacher's hermeneutical tradition, to move dialectically between the objective/grammatical and divinatory/psychological modes of interpretation, and that in effect is what de Wette is doing.[10] But this procedure has its vulnerabilities, not least that a different image of the author can easily emerge from, and in turn reinforce, a different choice of texts. Much depends on the disposition of the interpreter, and it may be

---

[8] W. M. L. de Wette, *Kurze Erklärung der Briefe an die Colosser, an Philemon, an die Ephesier und Philipper*, Kurzgefasstes exegetisches Handbuch zum Neuen Testament, 2.4 (Leipzig: Weidmann'sche Buchhandlung, 1843), 79.
[9] de Wette, *Einleitung*, 232–3; my emphasis. The question of Galatians's authenticity does not even arise in de Wette's later treatment of that letter (*Kurze Erklärung des Briefes an die Galater und der Briefe an die Thessalonicher*, Kurzgefasstes exegetisches Handbuch zum Neuen Testament, 2.3 (Leipzig: Weidmann'sche Buchhandlung, 1841)).
[10] See e.g. the 'General Hermeneutics', §§13–20 (Friedrich Schleiermacher, *Hermeneutics and Criticism and Other Writings*, ed. and trans. Andrew Bowie, Cambridge Texts in the History of Philosophy (Cambridge: CUP, 1998), 229–30).

that for de Wette et al., the pre-eminence of Galatians in Luther's reading of Paul still exercises significant if subterranean influence.

So it would be unfair to F. C. Baur to suggest that his theological partiality arose precipitously *ex nihilo*. But it did represent a sharp radicalization of his philologist predecessors, both in the ruthlessness of his critical judgements and in the value with which they were charged. Baur understood the early history of Christianity as a dialectical conflict between 'Pauline' universalism and 'Jewish' particularism, which eventually, in the postapostolic age, resolved into a 'Catholic' synthesis. He locates each text within this schema, and accordingly divides the CP not only by authorship but also by theological faction. Thus he moves beyond textual scepticism into an antithetical hermeneutic, in which for the first time authentic and pseudonymous letters are read systematically *against* one another. At the same time, the circularity already noticeable in de Wette becomes more pronounced in Baur, in proportion to his more elaborate historical speculation. The kinds of difference he finds in Colossians, Philippians or the Thessalonian letters are used to buttress the hypothesis that classed them as pseudonymous in the first place.[11]

Ephesians is an illustrative example. Other than the Pastorals, Baur considered the case against its authenticity to be the strongest.[12] His main arguments are (1) its literary relationship with Colossians, (2) its dependence on the thought of gnostic and other heretical groups and (3) the character of its theology, unlike Paul but signally apt to the early postapostolic age. If the relationship between Ephesians and Colossians was 'disconcerting' for de Wette, for Baur it told decisively against the authenticity of at least one letter, and (as had already occurred with the Pastorals) severely damaged the claim of the other. Baur sees here not just a literary dependency, but two letters which are identical in substance,[13] and which therefore stand or fall together. Paul simply would not copy himself so closely as does the author of Ephesians; but then he would not write like the author of Colossians in the first place. The long discussion Baur devotes to his alternative provenance, locating the letters in the controversies with the Valentinians (both letters, 8–25), Montanists (Ephesians, 25–30) and Ebionites (Colossians, 30–6), reads now as the weakest part of his argument. That these schools

---

[11] One reason this circularity is more problematic in Baur is the greater role played by confessional predispositions in his criticism. According to White,

> the 'objective' and 'secure' data about apostolic conflict in the *Hauptbriefe* were the starting point for Baur's work. He never questioned, though, whether or not they were actually *representative* of a nearly three-decade apostolate, such that other letters were necessarily *unrepresentative* of Paul. Why? 'Opposition' between Spirit and Law, Protestantism and Catholicism, and Christianity and Judaism was the ideological frame through which he already read Paul. (White, *Remembering Paul*, 26; his emphasis)

> This comment seems fair to me, but White is too quick to tar nineteenth-century biblical scholarship generally with the same brush. He blurs Baur's untypically schematic approach with the 'positivist historiography' that, on his account, marred *all* contemporary claims about the 'historical Paul'.

[12] Baur, *Paulus*, 1867, 2.3.

[13] 'Bei der wesentlichen Identität [kann] der Inhalt des einen von dem des andern nicht getrennt werden' (ibid., 2.8). Baur will nevertheless go on to distinguish between the controversies reflected in each letter.

might depend upon the biblical texts, rather than the other way around, is a possibility he dismisses out of hand, along with Tertullian's testimony to that effect:

> Was kann ... Tertullian für eine Meinung beweisen, die durch die ganze Beschaffenheit der gnostischen Systeme widerlegt wird, namentlich des valentinianischen Systems, das seiner innern Anlage nach zu originell ist, als dass sein Ursprung nur daraus zu erklären wäre, dass Valentin, wie Tertullian sagt, *materiam ad scripturas excogitavit*.[14]

This is more rhetorical appeal than argument: Valentinus is simply too original to be derived from biblical texts, so the dependency *must* run the other way. Later scholarship would go against Baur here. Still, as we shall see, a similar move became common after Bultmann, with an earlier, 'proto-Gnostic' religious worldview postulated to lie behind both later NT texts and the emerging heresies of the second century.[15]

More lastingly significant was Baur's location of the letters within his broader dialectical schema. The deuteropaulines belong to the postapostolic age, when the rival Pauline and Jewish factions were integrated into a united front against the rising tide of heresy. Ephesians and Colossians represent the movement of Pauline Christianity towards bridging the gulf (whereas Hebrews approaches the same point from the Jewish Christian side). That is the significance of their emphasis on reconciliation: the universal reunion of all things divided is the dominant idea and basis of both letters.[16] The postapostolic synthesis is designated by Baur the 'catholic' church, and here we find the origin of the view that Ephesians, among other texts, is an example of 'early catholicism'. The letter occupies a transitional place, both temporally and doctrinally standing between the genuine Paul and the Pastorals, Acts and the Apostolic Fathers.[17] As we shall see, this trajectory would prove remarkably resilient in subsequent scholarship, long after Baur's wider schema was abandoned.

In the positioning of the various letters within his narrative, it becomes clear how theologically charged the question of authenticity is for Baur, and how starkly evaluative his analysis. He never conceals his sympathies, frankly calling Ephesians and Colossians 'deeply inferior' to Romans.[18] Paulinism is the superior principle of

---

[14] Ibid., 2.25. The reference is to *Praesc.* 38: unlike Marcion, who cut the scriptures to fit his argument, 'Valentinus autem pepercit quoniam non ad materiam scripturas sed materiam ad scripturas excogitavit'.

[15] See Chapter 4, §2.1. In passing we might note that, on the score of 'gnosticism', Baur found Philippians just as tainted as Ephesians and Colossians ('Die Verwandtschaft des Inhalts mit der Gnosis ist der Hauptberührungspunkt des Philipperbriefs mit den Briefen an die Epheser und Colosser', ibid., 2.59).

[16] 'Allgemeine Versöhnung, Vereinigung des Getrennten und Entzweiten ist die höchste durch den ganzen Inhalt der beiden Briefe hindurchgehende Idee, auf welche sich alles bezieht, und deren höchster Ausdruck die Christologie dieser Briefe ist' (F. C. Baur, *Kirchengeschichte der drei ersten Jahrhunderte*, 3rd edn, Geschichte der christlichen Kirche 1 (Tübingen: Fues, 1863), 116).

[17] Ibid., 116–35. Baur does align some of the Apostolic Fathers, notably 1 Clement and Polycarp, more on the Pauline side of his antithesis, though he finds elements of catholicism in them all.

[18] Against the possibility that Paul would have written extensively to churches where he was not well known: 'Auf den Römerbrief kann man in dieser Hinsicht so wenig berufen, als sich überhaupt der Inhalt des Römerbriefs mit *dem so tief unter ihm stehenden Inhalt* dieser beiden Briefe [sc. Eph. und Col.] zusammenstellen lässt' (Baur, *Paulus*, 1867, 2.49; my emphasis). Similarly, Baur

the apostolic gospel, and whatever is amiss in the emerging church can be attributed to the Jewish-Christian faction. By converting the Gentiles, for example, Paulinism had 'conquered the ground' upon which Jewish Christianity would erect the church's 'hierarchical edifice', assimilating the institutionalism of the Old Testament. Typically, such regression on the part of ancient (small-c) catholicism is writ large in the later (capital-C) Catholic church. So the medieval papacy is descended in a direct line from 'theocratic institutions and aristocratic forms' of Judaism.[19]

The trajectory from the *Hauptbriefe* into 'early catholicism', then, is unambiguously a deterioration. This is I think the earliest example of a decadence model of the CP's formation, in which the genuine Paul recedes gradually from view, and is increasingly eclipsed by the institutional church. It is worth quoting at length Baur's own description of the historical archetype at work here:

> Wie [der Paulinismus] zuerst den christlichen Universalismus für das allgemein christliche Bewusstsein principiell dadurch begründete, dass er die aristokratischen Ansprüche des jüdischen Particularismus widerlegte und in ihrer tiefsten Wurzel vernichtete, so blieb ihm auch für alle Zukunft der Kirche vorbehalten, immer wieder mit derselben Schärfe und Entschiedenheit einzugreifen, so oft der hierarchische Katholicismus das evangelische Christenthum überwucherte und das urchristliche Bewusstsein in seinem innersten Grunde verletzte.[20]

The perennially calcifying (Catholic, *quasi* Jewish) church must periodically be shattered and re-formed by the resurgent spirit of the primeval (Protestant) Paul. The pattern – at least in part – is instantiated within the CP itself, for the first but not the last time. This metanarrative of Christian history is another aspect of Baur's work with lasting echoes.

Although Baur's Protestant partiality is undisguised, he is also critical of Martin Luther's reading of Paul, particularly its preoccupation with 'earning' salvation. As the last quotation illustrates, he considers Paul's main concern to be Christian universalism *vis-à-vis* Jewish particularism, and he interprets the faith/works opposition accordingly.[21] But in his willingness to excise biblical texts which do not represent the authentic gospel, Baur stands directly in Luther's tradition. Admittedly, the Reformer's translation of the NT did not quite venture to remove texts altogether (the OT 'apocrypha' were less fortunate), but he relegated Hebrews, James, Jude and Revelation to what amounts to an appendix at the end of the canon. Luther's prefaces, and in the 1522 edition his introduction to the whole NT, make it clear that these four books are of decidedly inferior status – in the case of James, almost an anti-gospel.

---

comments generally on the 'shorter letters' (i.e. all but the *Hauptbriefe*): 'Sie charakterisieren sich vielmehr durch eine gewisse Dürftigkeit des Inhalts, durch Farblosigkeit der Darstellung, Mangel an Motivirung, Monotonie, Wiederholungen, Abhängigkeit theils von einander, theils von den Briefen der ersten Klasse' (ibid., 2.116–7).

[19] Baur, *Kirchengeschichte der drei ersten Jahrhunderte*, 107.
[20] Ibid., 107–8.
[21] See Francis Watson, *Paul, Judaism, and the Gentiles: Beyond the New Perspective* (Grand Rapids, MI: Eerdmans, 2007), 40–3.

Although Luther does not dispute the Pauline authorship of any letter apart from the anonymous Hebrews, his subdivision of the canon provides the most respectable precedent imaginable for a German Protestant like Baur. Calvin did not accept Luther's opposition between scripture and gospel, and if nineteenth-century Anglophone scholars were more conservative on authorship and canonical integrity than their German counterparts, perhaps this confessional difference was partly responsible.[22]

For an example of Baur's hermeneutic in practice, consider his treatment of justification by faith in Eph. 2. The author of Ephesians, he argues, dutifully puts forward the Pauline position in vv. 8-9, albeit with artificial emphasis. However, he is no true Paulinist, and so cannot refrain from mentioning works as well; to this end he borrows the teaching of James (the archetypal Jewish Christian) for v. 10.[23] The two factions are synthesized in Ephesians, but this is not a welcome development. There is a stark gulf between Paul and the deuteropaulinist, who simply does not understand the apostle:

> Der tiefere Grund dieser Differenz ist, dass diesen Briefen [sc. Eph. und Col.] der eigentlich paulinische Begriff des Glaubens völlig fremd geblieben ist. Von dem Glauben, als einem innern Process des Bewusstseins, dessen wesentliches Moment die eigene Erfahrung und Überzeugung von der Unmöglichkeit der Rechtfertigung durch das Gesetz ist, wissen sie im Grunde nichts.[24]

Faith as 'personal experience' is central to Paul (again echoing Luther) – this conception is 'entirely foreign' to Ephesians and Colossians, and that evidence tells decisively against the two letters' authenticity. The question of authorship is, for Baur, subsumed into a wider antithetical hermeneutic that opposes apostolic and postapostolic, universal and particular, radical and reactionary, Paul and Peter, Protestant and Catholic. What began with Schleiermacher as a philological enquiry has transmuted into a fierce and sometimes polemical rupturing of the CP.[25]

---

[22] On Luther's NT, and the different approach of Calvin, see Francis Watson, '"Every Perfect Gift": James, Paul and the Created Order', in *Muted Voices of the New Testament: Readings in the Catholic Epistles and Hebrews*, ed. Katherine M. Hockey, Madison N. Pierce and Francis Watson, LNTS 565 (London: Clark, 2017), 121–37. As Klaus Haacker notes, Baur also echoes Luther when he takes the anti-Judaic Paul for the 'true' Paul. On this measure, Galatians is the gold standard, whereas a more irenic view of Judaism is counted against Ephesians and even Philippians ('Rezeptionsgeschichte und Literarkritik: Anfragen an die Communis Opinio zum Corpus Paulinum', TZ 65 (2009): 209–28 (212–13)).

[23] Baur, *Paulus*, 1867, 2.44.

[24] Ibid., 2.45–6.

[25] Glib dismissals of Baur come easily today, since in the light of later research, and after the passing of the fashion for Hegel, his dialectical schema appears so foreign. But this fact should not overshadow his significant contribution to scholarship. In particular, he was seminal in interpreting the Pauline letters historically, as situated theology directed at real conflicts – now common wisdom, but controversial in his day. See e.g. Hans Rollmann, 'From Baur to Wrede: The Quest for a Historical Method', SR 17 (1988): 443–54, who argues that in this respect, Baur advances significantly beyond the empiricism of his predecessors: 'Baur was aware of the mediate character of all knowledge, including historical knowledge, and called for cognitive categories appropriate to comprehend these data' (445).

1.2. Canon and catholicity: Käsemann and his heirs

1.2.1. *Ernst Käsemann and* Frühkatholizismus

Baur was certainly untypical and met plenty of opposition. His four-letter corpus was never widely accepted, and his dialectical account of Christian origins soon fell from favour. But his view of the postapostolic period as an 'early catholic' compromise survived the loss of his wider framework, as did the trajectory of gradual decline along which early Christian literature, including the Pauline letters, could be located. To trace the development of this idea continuously from Baur is beyond my scope, so I now leap forward a century to the scholar upon whom his mantle most manifestly fell.

A couple of generations ago, confessional politics remained quite overt within the academy, and the term *Frühkatholizismus* was still regularly and opprobriously bandied about in NT studies. On this theme no one discoursed more sonorously than Ernst Käsemann, a scholar whose ecclesial partisanship was at any rate unconcealed. He is Baur's direct descendant; his work crystallizes and further propagates an approach to the CP essentially similar to his Tübingen forebear's. Käsemann's exposition of decadence within the CP has had lasting influence. In the more genteel ecumenical climate of recent decades, his polemics have come in for some criticism, and we are no longer so likely to label a text like Ephesians 'early catholic'. But I suggest this represents for the discipline less a seismic shift than an alluvial slide: our language has become smoother, but the contours of the same underlying ecclesial bias persist. Here I will review Käsemann's account of *Frühkatholizismus* in the CP and especially in Ephesians, which he saw as exemplifying the trend.[26]

Käsemann defines *Frühkatholizismus* thus:

> Frühkatholizismus meint jenen Übergang aus dem Urchristentum in die sogenannte alte Kirche, der mit dem Erlöschen der Naherwartung sich vollzieht, keineswegs überall gleichzeitig oder mit den gleichen Symptomen und Konsequenzen, aber in den verschiedenen Strombetten doch mit einem charakteristischen Gefälle hin zu der sich als Una Sancta Apostolica verstehenden Großkirche.[27]

Käsemann proposes a fundamental shift from 'early Christianity' to the 'ancient Church', and discerns it already within the NT. By opposing Paul to this movement, he openly acknowledges that he is following the contemporary Protestant view; the implication is that he aligns his own confession with Paul against both big- and small-c Catholicism. He argues that Paul has throughout Christian history, beginning with Luke, repeatedly been domesticated (247). But the misunderstood apostle remains

---

[26] For an earlier survey of some of these areas, see Charles D. Dennison, 'Ernst Käsemann's Theory of Early Catholicism: An Inquiry into the Success of the "Lutheran Gospel"' (MA, Duquesne University, 1984). This covers some ground I have not tackled here, in particular the earlier history of the term (which seems to have originated with Troeltsch, though obviously drawing on Baur's historical schema) (5–29) and Käsemann's philosophical context (58–68).

[27] Ernst Käsemann, 'Paulus und der Frühkatholizismus', 1963, in *Exegetische Versuche und Besinnungen*, vol. 2, 2 vols (Göttingen: Vandenhoeck & Ruprecht, 1964), 239–52 (240).

preserved in his seven authentic letters, to be periodically rediscovered at times of ecclesial crisis. At such moments, the unalloyed gospel of justification breaks forth anew, shattering piety, cult and the authority of tradition – but only ever temporarily, for even Protestants cannot escape the snare of *Frühkatholizismus* (251–2).

The echo of Baur could hardly be clearer. It will be evident that this is not a simple case of confessional politics, validating the Lutheran at the expense of the Roman Catholic church, but represents a deeper intellectual fissure between competing construals of history. For Käsemann as for Baur, the movement from apostolic to postapostolic Christianity means a decline from the purity of the original gospel into the ecclesial settlement. Gospel and church are not merely separable but antagonistic *in principle*. Needless to say, this is an axiom that could hardly command ecumenical assent. It represents a fault line in the hermeneutics of church history underlying the more visible controversies in Käsemann's exegesis.

One consequence is that the NT canon is presumed not to be coherent: it testifies both to the true gospel and to the compromises made by the young church. On this basis, Käsemann develops an ambivalent view of the ecumenical movement. In his view, the diversity of modern Christian parties reflects, indeed is grounded in, the diversity of NT texts and the parties that produced them. The church attested by the NT was 'at best an early ecumenical confederation', which should be a consolation to its fragmented posterity.[28] Of course, not all parties are equal in Käsemann's eyes, then or now, but he does not envisage the unity of the church in the ascendancy of any particular faction. Rather, it is to be found only in the free action of Christ, over against the diversity both of ecclesial bodies *and* of the texts they produced. The canon of scripture is a testament to *dis*unity, and will not resolve the ecumenical conundrum.[29]

Inter-confessional controversy appears most patently in Käsemann's debate with Heinrich Schlier, where the ecclesial stakes were never concealed. His critical review essay of Schlier's 1957 commentary on Ephesians is even couched in the metaphor of a battle between two opposing fronts.[30] The Catholic interpreter errs fundamentally by taking Ephesians for genuine, seeing in the elevated doctrine of the church a natural development of earlier Pauline theology, but the wish is father to the thought. If the letter is authentic, why is no more space given to apocalyptic? Or anthropology? Or justification, the law and the eschatological priority of Jewish Christians? Ephesians neglects these key areas, and 'damit wird ... Entscheidendes in der ursprünglichen

---

[28] Ernst Käsemann, 'Unity and Diversity in New Testament Ecclesiology', *NovT* 6 (1963): 290–7 (295); the lecture was apparently given first in English, though later published also in German. On this topic see also Käsemann, 'Begründet der neutestamentliche Kanon die Einheit der Kirche?', 1951, in *Exegetische Versuche und Besinnungen*, vol. 1, 2 vols (Göttingen: Vandenhoeck & Ruprecht, 1960), 214–23, and the interaction with Küng in Käsemann, *Das Neue Testament als Kanon* (Göttingen: Vandenhoeck & Ruprecht, 1970).

[29] For a more optimistic view, cf. the lecture given by Raymond Brown alongside Käsemann's of the same name, on the same occasion (the World Council of Churches 1963 Faith and Order Conference), 'The Unity and Diversity in New Testament Ecclesiology', *NovT* 6 (1963): 298–308.

[30] Ernst Käsemann, 'Das Interpretationsproblem des Epheserbriefes', 1961, in *Exegetische Versuche und Besinnungen*, vol. 2, 2 vols (Göttingen: Vandenhoeck & Ruprecht, 1964), 253–61. For example, '[Schlier] wird schon merken, daß wir unsererseits noch nicht alles Pulver verschossen haben und den Qualm des Kampfesplatzes zur Erbauung oder zum Leidwesen der Nichtkombattanten nicht bloß aus einer Windrichtung wehen lassen können' (256); and so throughout the review.

Botschaft und Theologie des Paulus verkürzt und bagatellisiert' (256). It is not only changing ecclesiology that casts doubt upon the letter's authenticity but also its relative uninterest in certain key theological battlefields of the Reformation.

In summary, Käsemann's hermeneutic of decadence sees Ephesians as an early misreading of Paul, and a first step towards the *Frühkatholizismus* more completely formulated in the Pastorals and elsewhere. This trend continues with Paul's subsequent reception throughout church history – interrupted only occasionally by the apostle's true voice, when the gospel is heard with fleeting clarity – and still shapes present-day interpretation. As in Baur, the literary thesis of pseudonymity is sublimated into an antithetical and theologically evaluative hermeneutic. Even while noting elements of continuity, Käsemann sees the second generation of Christian texts as reactive against the first, which means the CP is fundamentally ruptured rather than fundamentally coherent. Such is in fact his view of the NT canon as a whole: diversity in principle means discontinuity and the separation of parties, and unity is found not in a canon or a community but only in the free action of Christ independently of either. It is this confessionally charged view of Christian history, and not merely a confessionally charged exegesis of the text, that lies behind Käsemann's depreciation of Ephesians.[31]

1.2.2. Criticism of Käsemann's model

Käsemann was a more mainstream and widely accepted figure than Baur; still, his analysis of *Frühkatholizismus* has been extensively debated. Catholic contemporaries like Raymond Brown and Hans Küng engaged more immediately with Käsemann himself,[32] and in the following decades a number of studies appeared, mainly in German, on both sides of the ecumenical divide.[33] I will mention just a few examples of more general discussion that has followed subsequently.

C. Clifton Black was relatively early in doubting whether the term 'early catholicism' is useful at all. Examining its relevance to the Johannine letters, he concludes that the category is not only unhelpfully pejorative but also 'intrinsically ill-defined':

> If one were to leave intact the sociological concepts essential to the criteria (i.e., tradition, shared beliefs, hierarchical organization, rites, and so forth), divesting them only of their superficial Catholic *theologoumena*, one could probably discover

---

[31] This overview of Käsemann's approach to Ephesians and the CP has been necessarily general. In Chapter 4, however, it will be amplified with some exegetical particularity as we consider the 'Body of Christ' in various Pauline texts. This was the subject on which Käsemann thought Schlier most gravely mistaken, and which affords the clearest explication of his interpretative method.

[32] E.g. Brown, 'Unity and Diversity'; and Hans Küng, 'Der Frühkatholizismus im Neuen Testament als kontroverstheologisches Problem', in *Das Neue Testament als Kanon*, ed. Ernst Käsemann (Göttingen: Vandenhoeck & Ruprecht, 1970), 175–204.

[33] E.g. Ulrich Luz, 'Erwägungen zur Entstehung des "Frühkatholizismus": Eine Skizze', ZNTW 65 (1974): 88–111; Hans-Josef Schmitz, *Frühkatholizismus bei Adolf von Harnack, Rudolph Sohm und Ernst Käsemann* (Düsseldorf: Patmos, 1977); Joachim Rogge and Gottfried Schille, eds, *Frühkatholizismus im ökumenischen Gespräch* (Berlin: Evangelische Verlagsanstalt, 1983); Heinz Schürmann, 'Frühkatholizismus im Neuen Testament: Neun fragende Thesen', *Catholica* 51 (1997): 163–8.

'nascent Catholic' tendencies, not only in the letters of John, but also at Qumran, among the Rabbis, in Islam, and even in one's local Rotary Club.[34]

In fact, *Frühkatholizismus* denotes nothing particularly Catholic at all. There is some truth in this; but Black takes insufficient account of the contrast always implied in the term. It means not only a set of 'sociological tendencies' but, more particularly, the movement away from an earlier, more pristine, more 'apocalyptic' Christianity. The change is the problem; the church begins to go astray, so the story goes, precisely as it begins to look more like Rotary and the Rabbis. The observation that 'early catholic' characteristics are not uniquely Christian, though broadly true, is therefore an insufficient response.

More recently, David J. Downs has questioned one of the basic assumptions underpinning the account of *Frühkatholizismus* in Käsemann and his heirs: the 'truism' that in the postapostolic church, increasingly institutionalized order corresponded to decreasing fervour of eschatological expectation.[35] After noting from the example of Qumran that ancient religious societies certainly could combine highly developed institutionalization with vivid apocalyptic expectation (648–51), he critiques the widespread claim that the Pastoral letters show a decided movement away from the latter. He accepts that they do indeed show some characteristics generally called 'early Catholic', which 'represent real developments within the Pauline corpus, even if they are developments of degree and not of kind' (661). However, their eschatological outlook remains closer to the undisputed letters than has often been asserted. 'Apocalypticism' and 'early Catholicism' are not mutually exclusive categories, and since this assumption has been fundamental to the sense of the latter term in NT studies, its usefulness may be doubted. This is an important study because in Käsemann's seminal account, the failure of *Naherwartung* is the single decisive cause of *Frühkatholizismus*; other associated characteristics (institutionalization, sacramentality, etc.) are mere symptoms. If Downs is correct, Käsemann's diagnosis is fundamentally wrong.

Finally, and in accord with my own analysis, Klaus Haacker locates Käsemann within a longer tradition of confessionally weighted Pauline interpretation, stemming from Baur.[36] Luther's reading of Paul continues to influence outwardly historical-critical judgements, for example, where a supposed deficit in the area of 'justification' is reason to doubt a letter; Haacker finds this tendency even in some Roman Catholic scholars (e.g. Schnackenburg), and still in quite recent work (Schnelle, Maisch) despite a generation and more of New Perspective critique. The problem is clearest in the case of *Frühkatholizismus*, discussed chiefly with respect to Käsemann. His rejection

---

[34] C. Clifton Black, 'The Johannine Epistles and the Question of Early Catholicism', *NovT* 28 (1986): 131–58 (157).

[35] David J. Downs, '"Early Catholicism" and Apocalypticism in the Pastoral Epistles', *CBQ* 67 (2005): 641–61. Downs is partly anticipated by P. H. Towner, 'The Present Age in the Eschatology of the Pastoral Epistles', *NTS* 32 (1986): 427–48, who critiques the reductionist view of the Pastorals' eschatology in Dibelius and Conzelmann, and notes how imminent expectation is still vivid in the letters' focus on the present age. Their eschatology is more consistent with Paul and other NT authors than is often recognized.

[36] Haacker, 'Rezeptionsgeschichte und Literarkritik'.

of later letters is no disinterested judgement, but reflects his underlying paradigm of 'origin and degeneration' (*Ursprung und Entartung*). Haacker concludes,

> Die mehr oder weniger auffälliger Unterschiede zu den anerkannten Paulusbriefen werden aus theologischen Gründen für so gravierend gehalten, dass eine identische Verfasserschaft ausgeschlossen und zugleich eine zeitliche Abstand zu Paulus postuliert wird. Mein Eindruck ist, dass auch auf dieser Linie die negative *konfessionelle* Wertung bestimmter Unterschiede wesentlich zu Annahme der Pseudonymität bestimmter Briefe beigetragen hat. (219)

Theological criteria determine the evaluation of difference within the CP, and reflect a prejudice against catholicism both 'early' and modern.

On the basis of these critiques, should we then reject the category of *Frühkatholizismus* altogether? For practical purposes, yes; it is irreversibly associated with a polemical historiography that is no longer defensible. But that does not mean there is no truth in it. Although one could argue with Black that the word 'catholic' is anachronistic in this context, in fact I think Käsemann is right that something confessionally significant is at stake here. There is undoubtedly material variation in ecclesiology across the NT, and the particular trajectories labelled as 'early catholic' are in some cases really discernible, even if they have been crudely delineated. Although we should resist the oversimplification of a single, constant continuum, the opposite extreme is no better, namely rejecting any generalization at all about the tendencies of early Christian development. The supposed 'fading of eschatological expectation' has been at least exaggerated, but on the other hand, later texts generally do show the church as a body increasingly ordered in faith, sacraments and ministry, and more conscious of its continuity through time as well as space. The church's emerging self-understanding as Catholic in the patristic age does indeed build upon and extend these tendencies, and how they are evaluated remains critical to confessional identity today. In this sense, the label 'early catholicism' does not seem to me inherently inept. Other language will be needed, though, if we are to move beyond the association of Catholicism with degeneration.

1.2.3. *The persistence of the decadence model: James Dunn*

The last section gives only a sample of a much wider discussion. In view of such criticism, it is unsurprising that the language of *Frühkatholizismus* has receded somewhat, but it has not disappeared;[37] and even when the openly confessional label is dropped, the

---

[37] In addition to what follows, see the discussion in Reinhart Staats, 'Ignatius und der Frühkatholizismus: Neues zu einem alten Thema', VF 48 (2003): 80–92, showing the persistence of this language in German-language studies into the twenty-first century. Specialized treatments are now rarer, but the topic recurs in general studies: e.g. Delbert Burkett, *An Introduction to the New Testament and the Origins of Christianity* (Cambridge: CUP, 2002), ch. 31, preferring the term 'Proto-Orthodox Christianity' but identifying it with 'Early Catholicism'; or Graham H. Twelftree, *People of the Spirit: Exploring Luke's View of the Church* (Grand Rapids, MI: SPCK & Baker, 2009), ch. 12, asking whether Luke is 'Early Catholic, Protestant or Charismatic', and (unsurprisingly when the question is so framed) finding in him elements of each.

underlying decadence theory may persist. No interpreter more perfectly demonstrates its resilience than James Dunn. In 1977, Dunn devoted a chapter of *Unity and Diversity in the New Testament* to 'early catholicism', and despite criticism left it substantially unaltered in the second (1990) and third (2006) editions.[38] More recently, his three-volume account of 'Christianity in the Making' repristinates some of the same claims.[39] The continuity is unmistakeable, but the label has disappeared.

Even the first edition of *Unity and Diversity* provoked a critical response on the subject of 'early catholicism'. In his foreword to the second edition, Dunn admits that the language is becoming outmoded, but sticks with it all the same. He rejects charges of anti-Catholicism, and denies any implication that the movement he describes was a departure from authentic Christianity; rather, such 'early catholicism' as is to be found in the NT is one element among many and should not be allowed hegemony. His critique is of '*a catholicism which is not catholic enough*':

> [The danger is that] 'catholic' becomes a party name or factional claim which excludes others who have a legitimate right to the title 'Christian'. The problem of early catholicism is precisely that of the majority seeking to draw boundaries which both include and exclude round the whole body of Christian believers. (xlviii–xlviv; his emphasis)

Despite this protest against exclusive boundaries, Dunn will presently speak approvingly of the need to distinguish between 'acceptable and unacceptable diversity', and the canon's role in doing so (l). So, we must conclude, the problem is the particular character of 'early catholic' exclusivity, rather than the drawing of boundaries per se. Similarly, the second edition's one concession to the critics is to drop the capital letters from 'early catholicism', partly in order to avoid 'possible confusion' with Roman Catholicism:

> But also with the hope that the ambiguity embodied in the title might serve as a constant reminder of the historical problem of retaining the full sweep of legitimate diversity within the recognized forms of the church universal. (xlix)

There are two boundaries, then: one separating legitimate from illegitimate diversity and a narrower, unacceptable 'catholic' boundary. In this light, the alignment of 'early' and Roman Catholicism would seem not to be 'confusion' at all, but that very 'ambiguity' that Dunn openly wishes to exploit. The loss of a capital letter may slightly obscure the confessional critique, but does not substantially alter it.[40]

---

[38] Citations here are taken from the third edition (see n. 10, p. 6 above).
[39] Only the latter two volumes concern us here: James D. G. Dunn, *Beginning from Jerusalem*, Christianity in the Making 2 (Grand Rapids, MI: Eerdmans, 2009); and Dunn, *Neither Jew nor Greek*, Christianity in the Making 3 (Grand Rapids, MI: Eerdmans, 2015).
[40] The foreword to the third edition essentially repeats the same defence, claiming that the book requires a chapter, 'whatever heading it goes under', questioning whether the 'institutionalization and credalization of Christianity' produced an excessively narrow unity (xxvi–xxvii). The language remains unchanged.

Dunn lacks the polemical frankness of Käsemann, but otherwise in this discussion he is his direct descendant, as his definition of 'early catholicism' clearly shows. He names three characteristics: 'the fading of the parousia hope', 'increasing institutionalization' and 'crystallization of the faith into set forms' (376). While the Pastorals display all three of these, the position of Ephesians is more ambiguous:

> The question of whether Ephesians should also be categorized as early catholic depends on the interpretation of one or two key passages, that is to say it depends on whether Ephesians is regarded as Pauline or post-Pauline in origin: if Pauline, then the passages are better interpreted as a development of the Pauline understanding of the Church which does not significantly depart from his vision of the Church as charismatic community; if post-Pauline, then they could be interpreted as a movement ... towards the early catholicism of the Pastorals. (397)

As we noted in the Introduction, this is a remarkably explicit instance where alternative views of authorship yield opposite interpretations.[41] But leaving that to one side, the important point here is the location of Ephesians on a theological and chronological continuum between Paul and the Pastorals.[42] As we have seen in Baur and Käsemann, the development of the early Christian mainstream is plotted along a single broad trajectory, represented in stages within the NT and continuing into the apostolic fathers.

The hardy half-life of this conceptual framework is conspicuous in Dunn's recent, three-volume study of 'Christianity in the Making'. The 'early catholic' label appears only tangentially; but when it comes to introducing the Pastorals, the arguments for their pseudonymity include, with eerie familiarity, 'increasing institutionalization' and 'crystallization of the faith into set forms'.[43] Notably, though, 'the fading of the parousia hope' is no longer attributed to the Pastorals, a marked contrast with *Unity and Diversity* (378–9, 396) that perhaps registers the forceful critique of Downs. The same general continuum of development is presupposed:

> The date [of the Pastorals] depends primarily on how soon the developed ecclesiology of the letters can be dated. On a rough estimate the date seems to fall somewhere between the ecclesiology of Ephesians and that of Ignatius, and to match that of Acts.[44]

This course corresponds exactly to the old theory of progressive 'catholicization'. So although Dunn evaluates Ephesians itself positively – even endorsing Mitton's epithet,

---

[41] In this conditionality, too, Dunn echoes Käsemann: 'Was besagt die thematische Reduktion des Briefes jedoch, *wenn man ihn als unecht zu behandeln hat*, anders, als daß auch von der paulinischen Gemeinde wie von den Pastoralen und vom lukanischen Werk aus ein Weg in den Frühkatholizismus führt?' (Käsemann, 'Interpretationsproblem', 256; my emphasis). Käsemann is, of course, in no real doubt about the letter's inauthenticity.
[42] This is spelled out in more detail with regard to 'fading expectation' (377–9).
[43] Dunn, *Neither Jew nor Greek*, 87–8, 678–82.
[44] Ibid., 91.

the 'quintessence of Paulinism'[45] – it is implicitly compromised by its movement towards the negatively evaluated Pastorals. This continuum, which is still widely presupposed in the interpretation of later Pauline texts, derives ultimately from the Baur–Käsemann hermeneutic of decadence, and represents the persistent but veiled legacy of a once vivid polemic.[46]

2. Alternative profiles of Paul

The Baur–Käsemann approach has been highly influential in Pauline studies, but it hardly represents the only or even the principal option now available for organizing the CP. The various alternatives, ranging from incremental modifications to wholesale rejection of the decadence model, are the subject of this second part of the chapter. First I survey some which do not seem to me ultimately satisfactory (§2.1), before turning to the canonically oriented approach of Brevard Childs, which I argue holds greater promise, albeit only imperfectly realized (§2.2).

2.1. In search of a better model

This section may seem something of a detour, but it has two important aims. First, to show that the hermeneutics of decadence, nowadays only occasionally appearing with the clarity we observed in Dunn, has a more subtle and widespread legacy. The presumption for a simple, linear trajectory of institutionalization in the CP remains common, even when the trend is not negatively assessed. And second, to acknowledge some other interpretative approaches that really do dispense with this schema, but which in my view do not offer satisfactory alternatives. The discussion is highly selective and mostly very brief; the aim, once again, is not to summarize the whole recent history of interpreting Paul, but simply to give an indication of the wider situation through some characteristic examples.

---

[45] Dunn, *Beginning from Jerusalem*, 1122. Dunn attributes this phrase to Bruce (1106), but see C. Leslie Mitton, *The Epistle to the Ephesians: Its Authorship, Origin and Purpose* (Oxford: OUP, 1951), 269, for an earlier use.

[46] The same legacy is sometimes perceptible in a binary opposition:

> Catholicism can convincingly appeal to Ephesians, but Protestantism draws its ecclesiology and much of its practice from the *real* Paul reflected in his *authentic* epistles. Defining the church in terms of the word being preached and the (gospel) sacraments being celebrated, desacralizing the ministry, valuing the secular, and insisting that all believers have their vocation (*Beruf*) and ministry are all *genuine* Pauline emphases, even if national churches are not. (Robert Morgan, 'Paul's Enduring Legacy', in *The Cambridge Companion to St. Paul*, ed. James D. G. Dunn (Cambridge: CUP, 2003), 242–55 (252); my emphasis)

> Although the ecclesiological developments of the later letters are not without confessional significance, this stark opposition between the 'real' Paul of the Reformation and the Catholic Paul of Ephesians perceptibly echoes the polemical Baur–Käsemann schema.

2.1.1. Reassertion of traditional authorship

Some conservative scholars remain unconvinced by the critical case for pseudonymity in biblical texts. The extreme position, rejecting the possibility altogether as incompatible with literal inspiration and inerrancy, is not usually argued within mainstream academe. Nevertheless, scholars sympathetic to these doctrinal convictions are generally more reluctant to categorize texts as pseudonymous, and among those who accept the legitimacy of historical criticism are many who defend the authenticity of all thirteen letters bearing Paul's name (and others who defend most of them).[47] Of the alternatives to the decadence model of the CP, this rebuttal of the case against traditional authorship is perhaps the most straightforward, and need not be discussed at length. It is a position with obvious attractions for those who value the coherence and authority of the Corpus. Unfortunately, in my view, it tends to underrate the strength of the arguments it dismisses, and more importantly, to diminish difference between texts. Throughout this study, I argue that a preoccupation with authorship distorts the interpretation of the CP; this applies equally whether authenticity or pseudonymity is being asserted (although my critique is directed mainly against the latter). It is no less distorting to harmonize the Corpus than to amplify its tensions to breaking point, and we will see examples of both in the following chapters.

2.1.2. Modified trajectories

For Baur and Käsemann, and their more direct heirs like Dunn, the direction of inner development within the CP is single and ultimately negative. But some other interpreters, while not dispensing with a generally teleological framework, depart somewhat from the decadence model, either by modulating its evaluative language or by proposing a more complex and multifaceted development. An example of the former kind is Margaret MacDonald, whose social-scientific work on the late Pauline letters eschews the pejorative category of 'early catholicism', and instead focuses on progressive 'institutionalization' in Pauline churches.[48] Paul himself represents a first

---

[47] Any number could be cited. Porter, as discussed in the Introduction (pp. 5–6 above), is one example of a scholar defending thirteen letters as authentic; one other example among many is Thomas R. Schreiner, *Paul: Apostle of God's Glory in Christ* (Downers Grove, IL: InterVarsity & Apollos, 2001). N. T. Wright, if more qualified in his actual position, is less moderate in rhetoric:

> Colossians is certainly Pauline, and to be used without excuse or apology. … Ephesians and 2 Thessalonians are highly likely to be Pauline, even if (a concession to the weaker siblings; I do not myself find this plausible) they were written by someone close to Paul and doing their best to imitate him. … 2 Timothy may well be by Paul, writing in a different mood and context, and may be drawn on similarly, though again with due caution. 1 Timothy and Titus come in a different category, and will be used … for illumination rather than support. (N. T. Wright, *Paul and the Faithfulness of God*, vol. 1 (London: SPCK, 2013), 61)

In the particular case of Ephesians, recent commentaries defending authenticity include Peter T. O'Brien, *The Letter to the Ephesians*, PNTC (Grand Rapids, MI: Eerdmans, 1999); Harold E. Hoehner, *Ephesians: An Exegetical Commentary* (Grand Rapids, MI: Baker Academic, 2002); and Frank Thielman, *Ephesians*, BECNT (Grand Rapids, MI: Baker, 2010).

[48] Margaret Y. MacDonald, *The Pauline Churches: A Socio-Historical Study of Institutionalization in the Pauline and Deutero-Pauline Writings*, SNTSMS 60 (Cambridge: CUP, 1988) (her doctoral monograph, building on the sociological work of Berger, Luckmann and

level of 'community-building institutionalization', followed in turn by 'community-stabilizing' (Eph./Col.) and 'community-protecting' (Pastorals) levels.

The description is of a single historical process, not undifferentiated but broadly continuous, and also occurring in the non-Pauline church. So for instance, in the development of ministerial office, the line from Ephesians to the Pastorals is analogous with that from Matthew to Ignatius (136); Acts and 1 Peter are also aligned with Colossians and Ephesians in between Paul and the Pastorals (217–18). Overall, in the movement from 'sect' to church, 'Colossians and Ephesians represent an intermediate step' (237). MacDonald's commentary on these two letters further develops this argument, focusing on the transfer of Pauline Christianity to a new generation, which seems to have occurred by the time of the latter but not the former text.[49] For example, Eph. 4.1-16 shows a 'transitional period' between the charismatic leadership of Paul and other apostles to the hierarchical ordering represented by Ignatius (298–9); or from 4.30, it is evident that 'despite some tendencies in the direction of "realized eschatology" Ephesians continues to assign a future dimension to salvation that is in keeping with the undisputed letters of Paul' (309).

Although MacDonald avoids evaluative comment, the individuality of Colossians and Ephesians is ultimately subsumed into their 'intermediate' role in her broader narrative. And while it is not self-evident that Matthew, Acts, Colossians, Ephesians, the Pastorals, 1 Peter and Ignatius must all be located along a single trajectory at all – the various texts could equally represent divergent, even independent trends – MacDonald prefers a single, unidirectional continuum of ecclesial development. In this way she continues to reflect the Baur–Käsemann legacy. Even though institutionalization is per se neutral, or even socially necessary, this linear account of the CP is still influenced by the decadence paradigm, and can easily be invested with its pejorative connotations by interpreters less careful than MacDonald.

Another alternative is represented by Petr Pokorný, who regards Ephesians and Colossians not as an intermediate stage between Paul and the Pastorals, but as a separate stream of the Pauline tradition in competition with the Pastorals. Pokorný finds the contradictions between these two *Briefgruppen* too difficult to explain otherwise: they represent two independent Pauline schools, each developing the apostle's inheritance in a relatively logical way, but not consistently with one another.[50] The implication is that the CP cannot be read as a coherent whole; or at least, the question of how to negotiate its theological diversity is left open. But in this scheme, the distinctiveness of both Ephesians and Colossians is given greater acknowledgement.

A related suggestion is made by Nils Dahl, in the last published essay of a lifetime's work on Ephesians.[51] Like Pokorný, Dahl sees two competing trajectories, in this case rival readings of Ephesians itself. A 'catholic' line of interpretation runs through

---

Weber). See also her ambivalent entry on 'Early Catholicism', in *The SCM Dictionary of Biblical Interpretation* (London: SCM, 1990), 182–3.

[49] Margaret Y. MacDonald, *Colossians and Ephesians*, SP 17 (Collegeville, MN: Liturgical, 2000), 3, 18.
[50] Petr Pokorný, *Der Brief des Paulus an die Kolosser*, THKNT, 10/I (Berlin: Evangelische Verlagsanstalt, 1987), 5–6.
[51] Nils A. Dahl, 'Interpreting Ephesians: Then and Now', in *Studies in Ephesians*, WUNT 131 (Tübingen: Mohr Siebeck, 2000), 461–73. This reworks earlier, previously unpublished material.

Polycarp and Ignatius on to Irenaeus, against an 'enthusiastic' line from the *Odes of Solomon*, also touching Ignatius, through to the Valentinian Gnostics. The Pastorals and 1 Peter are associated with the former group, but Dahl leaves open the question of their literary connection with Ephesians. Where 'catholicism' is defined in relief against 'enthusiasm', the inheritance of Käsemann is unmistakable; the difference for Dahl is that Ephesians is a volatile text that can be claimed by either side. This account at least does not limit the letter's interpretative potential to a single trajectory, though in fact only one of the two alternative streams is represented within the canon.[52]

Finally, in a book focusing on the Pastoral letters, James Aageson laments that the history of early Pauline reception is frequently oversimplified, when it was in fact 'exceedingly complex, diverse and uneven', with 'rarely a straight-line to be drawn'.[53] That sounds like a clear repudiation of a straightforward, single trajectory. Yet when it comes to the relationship of the Pastorals with Ephesians and Colossians, the position is less clear:

> To the extent that we can clearly see the institutional development of the church, the movement is clearly from 1 Corinthians, to Ephesians, and on to 1 Timothy and Titus. Once again, putting the issue in this way suggests a straight line of development that may not be sustainable historically, but it is helpful in positioning the respective ecclesiological patterns.[54]

This position does not make sense to me. If a 'straight line of development' is historically unsound, then it should not be used as an interpretative key. That does not mean excluding every possible generalization about the growth of the early church. But if Ephesians (for example) is plotted simply as an intermediate point on a line, its own unique voice will be compromised; the kind of distinctiveness perceived by Pokorný, for example, would be excluded *a priori*. Aageson's re-evaluation of the canonical role of the Pastorals is generally positive, but falters when it comes to the deuteropauline letters. We will see something similar in Childs. This difficulty, I suggest, shows the inadequacy of any simple linear model for the CP, even one which attempts to redress the bias of the decadence model.

These interpreters have in common a broad acceptance of the conventional chronological sequence of Pauline letters, however they may qualify either the details

---

[52] In sketching the history of the scholarship, Dahl notes the competing views of Fischer and Merklein, who in a sense continued the debate between Käsemann and Schlier into a later generation. Fischer sees Ephesians not as the endorsement of ecclesial office but as a 'utopian attempt' to restore Paul's charismatic organization of the church; Merklein, on the other hand, accepts a linear view of developing ecclesiology, through Ephesians and on to the Pastorals, but evaluates this positively (ibid., 464–5).

[53] James W. Aageson, *Paul, the Pastorals and the Early Church* (Peabody, MA: Hendrickson, 2008), 2. Part of Aageson's complaint is that the Pastorals should not be treated as an undifferentiated block; on this see also Jens Herzer (n. 5, p. 59 above). They are right, and I admit the present study may leave something wanting in this regard. That is perhaps excusable given my focus on Ephesians as a test case of Pauline interpretation, but a fuller exploration of relationships within the CP would require more careful differentiation.

[54] Aageson, *Paul, the Pastorals*, 121.

2.1.3. Reframing the Corpus: Douglas Campbell

Douglas Campbell's recent 'epistolary biography' *Framing Paul* affronts a host of orthodoxies about the authenticity and chronology of the Pauline letters.[55] But quite apart from its particular historical claims, the study is significant in its call for a total reformation of interpretative method. Campbell's critique focuses on the 'framing' of the Corpus:

> The way we frame the object of our investigation inevitably controls what we see, but the biases and interpretative acts involved with this framing tend to be hidden unless we name them explicitly.[56] (xxi–xxii)

The 'frame' of the CP, the historical context we reconstruct for it, is critical to its interpretation, but the way we reach it is 'often corrupt in methodological terms' (xxii). This objection applies, first, to appeals to Acts in constructing Paul's biography, and second, to the adjudication of authorship on theological, confessionally influenced grounds.[57] Instead, Campbell proposes a new history of Paul's letters, excluding Acts in the first instance, and making no prior assumptions about authenticity, integrity or chronology; each canonical letter is 'innocent until proven guilty' (25). He rejects circular, 'question begging' arguments that would exclude certain letters as stylistically or substantively 'different', since without first establishing our sample of genuine Pauline writing, there is no meaningful measure of what they are different *from*. Stylometric analysis is open to the same objection, especially the highly selective data sets that are sometimes quoted by biblical scholars unschooled in statistics.[58] Instead of reinforcing

---

[55] Douglas Campbell, *Framing Paul: An Epistolary Biography* (Grand Rapids, MI: Eerdmans, 2014).
[56] Campbell bases his account of framing on Derrida, although his study as a whole is not particularly Derridean.
[57] As an example of the latter problem he cites Schnelle, who in *Paulus: Leben und Denken* (2003) limits the corpus to the usual seven letters on familiar theological grounds, including the diminishing importance of justification, apocalyptic Christology, etc. (Campbell, *Framing Paul*, 14).
[58] '"Cherry-picked" data reads impressively to the statistically uninformed but establishes nothing' (404). Bart Ehrman comes in for particular criticism here for uncritical dependence on Daryl Schmidt (apropos 2 Thessalonians, 204–16) and Walter Bujard (apropos Colossians, 286–92). Other examples of the continuing positive use of these analyses include Andrew T. Lincoln, 'The Letter to the Colossians', in *New Interpreter's Bible*, vol. 11, 12 vols (Nashville, TN: Abingdon, 2000), 551–669 (578); Outi Leppä, *The Making of Colossians: A Study on the Formation and Purpose of a Deutero-Pauline Letter*, Publications of the Finnish Exegetical Society 86 (Göttingen: Vandenhoeck & Ruprecht, 2003), 9–10; Victor Paul Furnish, *1 Thessalonians, 2 Thessalonians*, ANTC (Nashville, TN: Abingdon, 2007), 132–7; and Christina M. Kreinecker, 'The Imitation Hypothesis: Pseudepigraphic Remarks on 2 Thessalonians with Help from Documentary Papyri', in *Paul and Pseudepigraphy*, ed. Stanley E. Porter and Gregory P. Fewster, PaSt 8 (Leiden: Brill, 2013), 197–219 (217) (Lincoln and Leppä follow Bujard; Furnish and Kreinecker follow Schmidt). Campbell makes positive use of more comprehensive analyses (Anthony Kenny, Kenneth Neumann, David Mealand and Gerard Ledger), and expects that as a result of maturing method and technology, more useful stylometric results will emerge in the future.

existing hypotheses of pseudonymity, we should 'treat the differences in style apparent between Pauline texts in the first instance as possible evidence of spread within the authentic Pauline sample' (289).

The resulting 'frame' gives us a startlingly unfamiliar CP. Both Thessalonian letters are authentic, and date from as early as 40; Colossians and Ephesians are also authentic, the latter is really the 'Laodiceans' of Col. 4.16, and together with Philemon these letters constitute a 'single epistolary event', dating from an imprisonment in Asia Minor in 50;[59] they therefore precede 1-2 Corinthians, Galatians, Philippians and Romans, which follow in that order in 51-52; all these letters are whole, though Phil. 3.2-4.3 quotes an earlier letter of the same year; the Pastorals alone are pseudonymous, a mid-second-century response to Marcion. These conclusions are provisional, and could be revised as new data is brought into consideration, including an appropriately cautious consideration of Acts, but Campbell insists that the pure framing task takes precedence; and, accordingly, that he has established a new burden of proof against the interpreter who wishes to argue for, for example, the authenticity of 2 Timothy, the pseudonymity of Colossians, the partition of 2 Corinthians, the late date of Ephesians and so on.

As yet there is little sign of a groundswell among Pauline scholars eager to subscribe to Campbell's new playbook. That is hardly surprising; if he is right, then pretty well everyone else has been wrong all along, since at least Tertullian. Few are likely to agree that the burden of proof has shifted so entirely, so suddenly. But this should not blind us to the perspicacity of much of Campbell's criticism. On confessional bias in judging authenticity, I have already voiced similar concerns. His critique of the less expert kinds of stylometrics is acute, and calls into question the authority with which such analysis is still often credited. In my view, his initial presumption in favour of each canonical letter's authenticity is methodologically quite correct, and it is refreshing to read a discussion of these questions unburdened by traditional assumptions about 'genuine' Pauline theology.

The place of Ephesians ('Laodiceans') in Campbell's schema is intriguing. In his view it is not prompted by any particular crisis, but gives 'an account of pagan Christian identity' to a Gentile congregation not founded by Paul (314). Whether or not one accepts his judgement of authenticity, and his identification of the letter as 'Laodiceans', this seems to me as probable a description of its purpose as any proposed (it could also hold, more or less, for a pseudonymous author). But as a result, and because Campbell locates the letter *before* 1-2 Corinthians, Galatians, Philippians and Romans, its role in the CP is transformed. Ephesians becomes a distinctively 'unconditioned' statement of Paul's gospel, more so even than Romans; its echoes throughout the Corpus reflect its closeness to the heart of his theology, with motifs first articulated here to be developed later on, perhaps transformed in the crucible of conflict and schism. This is of course

---

[59] As Campbell acknowledges, the assignment of these three letters to an early Asian imprisonment resembles the chronology of George S. Duncan, *St. Paul's Ephesian Ministry: A Reconstruction with Special Reference to the Ephesian Origin of the Imprisonment Epistles* (London: Hodder & Stoughton, 1929). In other respects, though, and particularly in the exclusion of Acts material, Campbell's reconstruction is quite different.

the opposite of the usual modern position, that Ephesians is a late text drawing together strands from various earlier Pauline letters (though it sits well with Origen's view quoted at the beginning of this study). As Campbell realizes, if his frame is accepted, one consequence will be 'a more "Ephesiocentric" account of Paul's thought' (326).

In this connection I must raise a caveat about Campbell's approach. In his desire for methodological regularity, he excludes any sort of circular reasoning between the selection and ordering of the texts, and the theological integrity of their contents. The one must precede the other wholesale; the contents cannot be substantively compared until the frame is complete. Campbell sticks to his policy, and there is no exegesis to be found in *Framing Paul*. As we have noted, though, he allows that the frame is provisional; it could later be revised on substantive grounds, but only from exegesis undertaken *within* the frame. In other words, Campbell does reserve a certain sort of hermeneutical circularity, but on so broad a scale that his more than four hundred pages cannot broach it. Given the prohibition against future 'circular appeals to Paul's theology, development and biography' (404), I find it hard to imagine how Campbell's frame could be exegetically undermined from within; and to judge by the confidence of his conclusions, so does he.

The problem here is that Campbell admits the need for some circularity, but defers it until it is too late to be useful. I argued above (§1.1) that there is a difference, albeit a muddy one, between the examples we saw in de Wette and Baur. Both move to some extent dialectically between their image of Paul the apostle and the selection of texts that genuinely represent him, but in Baur's case the role of prior theological commitments is more pronounced. Circularity can become vicious in such circumstances, but it can also be practised more carefully. It seems to me that, if any proposed frame is to prove finally persuasive, it must work as a reading of the texts themselves at every step of the way. The emerging view of the whole must constantly be referred to the particularities of the parts. Even incremental, provisional framing judgements must be shown to make exegetical sense; this cannot be reserved to the end without creating a purported 'burden of proof' that is effectively unassailable.

This observation brings us back to the place of Ephesians, or 'Laodiceans', within the CP. I find Campbell's hypothesis appealing, but unfortunately cannot persuade myself that it makes better *exegetical* sense than the alternative he rejects. The deep intertextual embeddedness of Ephesians within the Corpus means either that several other Pauline letters draw upon it or that it draws upon them. The present study remains purposefully agnostic about authorship, which in any case is not settled by any number of textual echoes.[60] But the direction of dependence between the letters, and so their chronology, cannot in my view be determined apart from their actual interpretation; and my own exegetical work on Ephesians persuades me that it is more plausibly explained as the later, 'receiving' text.

One example will have to suffice to illustrate this for now, though it is perhaps the most transparent one. In Eph. 2.5 and 8–9, we find compressed statements that the

---

[60] Campbell rightly rejects the assumption that literary dependence must entail pseudonymity, especially since both Paul and his recipients probably kept copies of his letters, and knew them well (200–3).

readers are saved by grace through faith, and not by works. In Chapter 3, §2.1, I will argue at length that this whole passage is closely modelled on Rom. 3. But deferring those particulars for now, we should consider the implications if Campbell's hypothesis is correct. He believes that the crisis instituted by a rival Jewish-Christian Teacher, the spur for the extensive discussion of law, grace, faith and justification/righteousness in Galatians, Philippians and Romans, does not begin until after Ephesians is written. If so, what appears to us now as an abbreviated recollection of these themes in Eph. 2 is in fact an anticipation, a short statement of a more marginal part of Paul's gospel; it would later become centrally important, but he could not foresee that at the time.

This seems to me highly improbable. The three words χάριτί ἐστε σεσῳσμένοι in 2.5 are syntactically parenthetical, and can only make sense in context as a reference to a theme more fully developed elsewhere; similarly, the discussion of faith and works in 2.8-10 is at first sight puzzlingly tangential. If this is simply one motif of Paul's gospel, mentioned in passing, it is extremely obscure. Recall that in Campbell's model, the purpose of the letter is to introduce Paul's theology to a congregation he has never met: in that context, these verses would be clumsily baffling. The problem evaporates, however, if we suppose that the readers are familiar with the discussion elsewhere, particularly in Rom. 3. The gnomic statements of Eph. 2 then become immediately intelligible as a precis of earlier texts, and their relevance in context begins to make sense.

The full discussion in Chapter 3 will flesh out this argument. But the point here is that when Campbell excludes this sort of exegetical data from the framing task, he leaves his hypothesis only half-formed and accordingly vulnerable. He provides an appealing narrative of the composition of Paul's letters; in this he resembles his forebear Knox, and Knox's forebear Goodspeed. But to be persuasive, he must give not only a plausible 'epistolary biography' but also a plausible reading of the actual letters, and as the two tasks are interdependent, there must be some careful and controlled circularity between them. Instead, he offers a precariously linear hypothesis, one claim building upon another without exegetical support.[61] So his case remains unproven. Generations of fruitful exegesis of Ephesians (to stay with this example) have assumed its dependence on most of the other Pauline letters; until Campbell can show that his reversal makes better sense of the text, it will continue to seem improbable.

2.1.4. Indifference to authorship

All the interpreters discussed so far share a common assumption: that correctly identifying the provenance of each Pauline letter is a necessary step in its interpretation. Campbell takes this to an extreme by insisting that his 'framing' prolegomena wholly precede exegesis, but an overwhelming majority of modern interpreters would agree

---

[61] As one reviewer has it, 'Campbell's procedure of establishing one possibility at a time, each one resting upon the last, sometimes tempts one to diminishing confidence in the emerging composite picture' (Matthew V. Novenson, 'Review of Douglas A. Campbell, *Framing Paul: An Epistolary Biography*', RBL, October 2016).

that authorship, date and context have at least some relevance to meaning. Concluding this survey, though, we should acknowledge some exceptions.

Unconcern about historical authorship is in fact axiomatic for the more zealously reader-oriented models of interpretation. Dale Martin's recent manifesto *Biblical Truths* may serve as an example.[62] The book is a thoroughgoing repudiation of 'biblical theology', which he describes as 'a genre of historical studies that ascertains the primary meaning of the text as foundational in order then to be used or applied by modern theologians or everyday Christians' (30). Instead, he advocates an entirely reader-response model of theological interpretation:

> The 'meaning' of a text is not some property inherent in the text itself but is generated by the interpretive activities of readers. Texts do not 'mean'; people 'mean' with texts. This is not a proposal for how people *ought* to interpret texts. This is not a suggestion for an interpretive agenda. It is first and foremost an empirical observation of how human beings actually do read texts and 'get meaning' from them. (96)

This assertion of empirical transparency is, of course, rhetorical; there do exist other hermeneutical models with rational advocates. Martin censures as naïve the identification of meaning with the original author's intention, but to exclude the author from meaning-making altogether might well seem equally simplistic. I do not wish to fight this battle here; suffice it to say that Martin's 'empirical observation' of the practice of interpretation is in fact a particular and contestable ideological choice.

A corollary of an exclusively reader-oriented approach should be that historical authorship does not govern, indeed has nothing to do with, a text's interpretation. Such a model, whatever its limitations, would presumably be unencumbered by the strictures of the decadence model. In fact, Martin's readings do not always bear out this expectation. For example, he places the undisputed Paul's views on marriage and family in opposition to the *Haustafeln* of Ephesians and Colossians, and to the Pastorals' view of the church as household of God (317–19). The authorship division allows him to read these groups of texts against one another, without pausing over the extent and significance of the continuity between them; and unsurprisingly, it is the deutero- and tritopauline letters that he depreciates. The case is similar with the body of Christ, where the most distinctive aspect of Ephesians's interpretation – the interlaced reflection on marriage and church – is dismissed as 'sexism and misogyny' (321), or the real Paul of 1 Corinthians is praised for *not* calling Christ the head of the body, which 'better enabled him to turn the more conservative "social body" upside down' (337). As a reader making his own meaning from the texts, Martin is of course at liberty to prefer 1 Corinthians to Ephesians or 1 Timothy. Nevertheless, his interpretations are sometimes buttressed with an authorship rhetoric that is entirely conventional.

---

[62] Dale B. Martin, *Biblical Truths: The Meaning of Scripture in the Twenty-First Century* (New Haven, CT: Yale University, 2017).

Benjamin White's *Remembering Paul*, quoted at the beginning of this chapter, can also be considered in this category.[63] The book's focus is 'history-telling', how the 'real Paul' is variously constructed by his interpreters, rather than who he in fact was. This is a worthwhile project, and I have already acknowledged its merits as a critique, but I have also registered reservations about what seems to me an exaggerated concern with ideology. So intent is White to repudiate empiricist history that one is left doubting whether Paul himself, as distinct from ideologically loaded Pauline traditions, can ever be a realistic object of study. White does finally suggest that, with a properly reformed historiography, we might 'approach the kind of deconstructive position necessary for developing more transparent methodologies for reconstructing the "real" or the "historical" Paul' (177), but his proposals are tentative almost to the point of stasis:

> Rather than working to establish certain letters or smaller portions of letters as authentically Pauline (like the so-called authentic sayings of Jesus), we *may* be on firmer ground to speak of 'broad impressions' across the entire early Pauline literature. (180–1)

It is easy to overestimate what we can really know about Paul, and throughout this study I criticize the readiness with which the prevailing account is so widely accepted. But by this critique I do not mean to endorse the opposite extreme of absolute agnosticism. I assume that qualified and provisional empirical historical knowledge is possible, even though in the case of Paul and his letters, the nature of our sources means it is very limited. I also assume that both readers and authors participate in making meaning with texts, together with the communities to which they belong. This study proceeds on that basis, and so whatever convergence there may be with the critical observations of White or Martin or others similarly minded, our ultimate aims are quite different.

None of the alternative profiles of the CP surveyed so far has afforded a sufficient riposte to the decadence model of Baur and Käsemann. Those confidently reasserting authenticity tend to dismiss too quickly both the critical objections they face and the depth of difference within the Corpus. Various modifications to the negative trajectory of decadence offer some improvements, but generally without escaping its overly narrow, linear directionality. Douglas Campbell's reframing of the Corpus is beguiling but, without exegetical support, excessively speculative; it also continues to bifurcate the CP by authorship, although he draws the line in a different place. And the more decidedly postmodern interpreters, despite their critical merits, are epistemologically antagonistic to the idea of authorial meaning. I turn now to the one model that I think does offer a real, constructive alternative, the canonically oriented approach associated principally with Brevard Childs.

---

[63] See n. 1, p. 57 above.

2.2. The promise of canonical interpretation: Brevard Childs

From the 1970s until his death in 2007, Brevard Childs was a sedulous critic of the assumptions governing mainstream biblical scholarship. Rejecting any separation between the Bible's significance for faith and its historical contingency, Childs called for a renewed appreciation of both testaments as Christian scripture, in the academy as well as the church. In particular, he insisted that the canonical shaping of the biblical texts is hermeneutically decisive. For Childs, this canonical orientation does not mean abandoning historical-critical methods, but it does relativize some of their claims. In a 1978 essay, he described the two sides of his alternative approach:

> On the one hand, its negative role ... strongly resists the assumption that every biblical text must first be filtered through an established historical-critical mesh before one can even start the task of interpretation. On the other hand, its positive role seeks to challenge the interpreter to look closely at the text in its received form, and then critically to discern its function for a community of faith.[64]

Here Childs is responding to the classification of his work as 'canonical criticism', a label which misses the extent of his critique; it sounds like just another method for the scholar's toolbox, akin to source criticism, form criticism and so on. Against this 'mischievous misunderstanding', still common, Leander Keck comments,

> 'Method' (i.e., the appropriate procedure for studying a particular phenomenon) is not at issue. What *is* at issue is precisely the 'approach', the assumptions that determine one's stance towards the phenomenon; an 'approach' is hospitable to a range of methods. Actually, then, the nonaggressive phrase 'canonical approach' signals a clash of approaches.[65]

These initial observations help to orient Childs's work in relation to the other models described throughout this chapter. He attempts not just to contribute to the existing discussion, but to shift its ground by asking new questions, while continuing to engage constructively with more conventional scholarship. To take the example of authorship, authenticity may reasonably be questioned, and this judgement will affect how some texts are read. But a reconstructed 'genuine' oeuvre, chronology and *Sitz im Leben* – a 'frame' in Campbell's sense – cannot replace the canonical shaping as the primary context for interpretation. In my view, Childs is persuasive both in critiquing prevailing trends in scholarship and in situating critical enquiry within a canonical framework. His approach promises much. However, as we consider it more concretely in relation to the CP, some reservations will emerge. I will argue that these do not arise of necessity from his hermeneutical model, but are simply flaws in its application. It will be possible

---

[64] Brevard S. Childs, 'The Canonical Shape of the Prophetic Literature', *Union Seminary Review* 32 (1978): 46–55 (54–5).

[65] Leander E. Keck, 'Faith Seeking Canonical Understanding: Childs's Guide to the Pauline Letters', in *The Bible as Christian Scripture: The Work of Brevard S. Childs*, ed. Christopher R. Seitz and Kent Harold Richards, SBLBSNA 25 (Atlanta, GA: SBL, 2013), 103–17 (105).

to build upon Childs's work towards a better account of the CP, but it will require some departures from what he himself proposes.

Childs first turned his canonical approach, honed on the OT, to the Pauline letters in his 1984 NT *Introduction*.[66] After this work he returned mainly to OT studies until his last, posthumously published work, an analysis of the canonical shaping of the CP.[67] The lapse of a quarter of a century saw Childs's approach refined, but not essentially changed, and we will begin with the groundwork set out in his *Introduction*. The crucial hermeneutical question occupying him is the relationship between the Paul of history and the Paul of the canon. The two are to be distinguished but not separated; authorship is relevant for interpretation, but cannot abrogate the coherence which the canonical form claims for the Corpus. 'A profile of Paul has been shaped by the canon which transcends that of the historical apostle' (426–7), and there is tension between the two. Whereas both liberal and conservative scholars resolve the tension (by dividing canon from history or collapsing them together, respectively), Childs seeks to maintain it.

This is an excellent principle, but difficult to implement. 2 Thessalonians offers a good illustration (358–72). Within the Corpus, Childs argues, the letter serves as a commentary on 1 Thessalonians, not replacing its eschatology but modifying or 'extending' it. However, this ultimate canonical function may well differ from the letter's original occasion; there are real problems with assuming Pauline authorship. This text poses the hermeneutical problem of pseudonymity in its most acute form – more so than Ephesians, Colossians or the Pastorals – because it so explicitly asserts its Pauline authenticity against the forgeries of impostors (2.2, 15, 3.17). Did it attain its place in the canon by 'a literary ploy designed to deceive its readers' (369)?

Childs's response to this question is instructive. He does not believe the historical data is sufficient for a decisive answer, but instead concentrates on the different *kinds* of post-Pauline authorship which might be possible for 2 Thessalonians. The extreme position, that the letter was written *against* 1 Thessalonians, Childs cannot square with what we know about the formation of the canon more broadly. On this theory, the letter would have successfully corrupted the original Pauline gospel, precisely what the early church was scrupulously careful to avoid, for example, in the exclusion of the *Acts of Paul and Thecla*. 'The dividing line was a narrow one between a process of extending Paul's apostolic witness which was considered legitimate and a process of pseudepigraphical composition which was rejected as deceptive by the church' (370). In other words, not all kinds of pseudonymity are equal. To treat 2 Thessalonians as in principle equivalent to *Paul and Thecla* is not scholarly impartiality, it is an arbitrary disregard of highly relevant canonical data.

Allowing that Paul may not have personally written the letter, Childs suggests some kind of indirect Pauline provenance, for example, composition through an associate. He offers no categorical defence of this particular option; rather, the point

---

[66] Brevard S. Childs, *The New Testament as Canon: An Introduction* (London: SCM, 1984).
[67] Brevard S. Childs, *The Church's Guide for Reading Paul: The Canonical Shaping of the Pauline Corpus* (Grand Rapids, MI: Eerdmans, 2008). He remarks that the silence which greeted his *Introduction* discouraged him from further NT ventures for some time (1).

is that authorship is not for him a binary alternative of authenticity or pseudonymity. The letter's canonical context invites a sympathetic reading of its strong assertion of authenticity, on historical as well as theological grounds. Some form of 'extending Paul's apostolic witness' accounts more plausibly for the finally received Corpus than the alternative of radical disjunction. An important methodological observation here is that Childs begins with the letter's canonical form and context, and only then addresses other critical concerns, but the interplay moves both ways. This seems to me a good illustration of the creative tension his approach calls for.

The Pastorals raise another aspect of this matter (373–99). Childs notes some attempts (Brox, Trummer, et al.) to read them sympathetically as pseudonymous texts, but these still avoid the major hermeneutical question. Approaching the letters as pseudepigrapha causes a shift in their referentiality so that they can only be read in relation to their postulated historical context: 'The literary genre is actually viewed as something "pseudo", whose true meaning only emerges when the genuine historical setting is reconstructed' (382). So the prehistory of the letters comes to *replace* their canonical context. Again, Childs does not defend direct Pauline authorship, but he rejects the generic category of 'pseudepigrapha' as inapplicable. A different conception of their authorship is required if their canonical presentation is not to be simply discounted.

The Pastorals do indeed show 'temporal and material distance from Paul', but this should be sympathetically interpreted. For Childs, the distance is itself part of the canonical shaping, 'by which a new dimension of the Pauline witness is realized' (384). The genre of the letters is indissolubly bound up with their first-person language. They represent an extension of the personal testimony of the earlier letters, not modifying it but recontextualizing it for a new period:

> [Paul's] relation to the churches in the Pastorals is strikingly different from (say) that with Corinth or Philippi. There is a shift from an active Paul to a passive one, not in a psychological sense, but rather that Paul does not himself break new ground in direct confrontation. Instead, his teachings have become the medium by means of which others are to confront falsehood and error. (390)

By contrast, when the Pastorals are treated as straightforward pseudepigraphy, Paul is displaced from first person to third, from the letters' subject to their object, and the genre is misread.[68] Again, Childs offers no clear-cut resolution of how the 'indirect authorship' of the Pastorals, their extension of the Pauline tradition, came about. Though he does not suggest this, his interpretation would also be compatible with first-hand authorship by Paul, late in life. Childs would perhaps consider that option unlikely, but it is significant that his reading does not stand or fall by this judgement. It shows what happens when such critical questions are allowed to elucidate, rather than subvert, the received canonical form.

---

[68] Childs makes a similar point about Ephesians: 'Regardless of this [authorship] decision, the canonical role of the letter is closely tied to the first-person witness of the Apostle Paul, whose office legitimates his message' (324).

We can now turn to the fuller treatment of the CP in *The Church's Guide for Reading Paul*. Here Childs develops ideas already suggested in his *Introduction* to propose a model for reading the Corpus as a whole. His overarching idea is that Romans and the Pastorals, bookending the Corpus, together govern the interpretation of what comes between. This Childs infers both from the nature of the letters in question and from their position. It is a proposal with several serious flaws and cannot, I believe, be adopted as it stands; but neither should it be dismissed outright. It is a beginning.

In Childs's account of the CP, Romans is not only first but also foremost (65–9). This verdict echoes a swathe of magisterial interpreters, from Augustine to Barth, and from the point of view of *Wirkungsgeschichte* it has obvious purchase. Nevertheless, there are problems with the way Childs privileges the letter. His argument is based on 'its content, position and majestic formulation of the Pauline gospel' (69). The content is uniquely broad, detailed and summative, and whatever Paul's particular intentions may have been, it has in fact been received as a sort of 'historical testament' (Childs follows Bornkamm here). In particular the prescript (1.1–7), by virtue of its scope and the letter's initial position, serves to introduce the whole Corpus.

But is Childs describing here the history of the CP's formation, or its subsequent *Wirkungsgeschichte*? I believe that, in this instance, he identifies the two too confidently. As we have seen, the overwhelming evidence of the earliest sources is that Paul's letters were ordered according to length, with Marcion the only real exception. Romans comes first because it is the longest letter; that it also has a particularly expansive and theologically elevated prescript is, apparently, fortuitous.[69] We also saw evidence, admittedly rough but very striking, that 1 Corinthians was cited much more often than Romans in the first two centuries after Christ (Chapter 1, §2.4.2). Thus it appears less likely that, *at this initial stage of canon formation*, Romans had the theological pre-eminence it would later attain. The question is when the transition occurs from the CP's 'canonical shaping' to its subsequent interpretative history, and I suggest that however natural the primacy of Romans would eventually come to seem, it belongs in the latter category.[70]

The counterexample of Ephesians may illustrate the point. For breadth of address and lack of obvious contingency, it is arguably an even more distinctive letter, and if Romans has an impressive prologue, what of the extended benediction that opens Ephesians? Both letters are steeped in other Pauline texts; both can be taken as epitomes of Pauline theology. Indeed, some may feel that Childs's epithet, a 'majestic formulation of the Pauline gospel', might apply equally to both letters, despite their dissimilarities. Most claims for the uniqueness of Romans are less compelling when considered alongside Ephesians, except that Romans comes first, and it comes first because it is longest. It is true that this primacy would, in time, acquire hermeneutical significance, and I am not questioning the legitimacy of that development, but it did

---

[69] Childs acknowledges that the letters are ordered by length, and that it is only 'conjecture' that Romans subsequently 'took on a special canonical function' (7).

[70] To focus closely on the meaning of a single whole text, like Romans, is now commonplace but arguably less relevant to ancient and medieval interpretation, where (apart from the commentary/homiletic genre) it was normal to quote freely from a range of texts. This may count as another flaw in the historical basis of Childs's model.

not arise from the canonical shaping per se, and should not be unduly weighted in a canonically oriented reading of the Corpus.[71]

Childs's axiom that Romans is less contextually contingent than the other letters, dubious in itself, leads to some questionable exegetical choices. For example, he argues that when the discussion of spiritual gifts in 1 Cor. 12 is reinterpreted in Rom. 12, it is abstracted from its particular context and lifted into 'theological coherence' (147–8), a claim that underplays both the contingency of Romans (which Childs thinks unimportant) and the coherence of 1 Corinthians (where ch. 12 is thoroughly integrated into the letter's theology; see Chapter 4, §3.1). Or again, Martyn's view that Romans should be read through the lens of Galatians is dismissed as 'the reverse of its canonical shaping' (104). Childs argues for a dialectic between universality/coherence and particularity/contingency, but to associate Romans with the former, and the other letters with the latter, is a considerable oversimplification. Moreover, despite the call for dialectic, it tends towards a one-directional hermeneutic in which Romans is normative. (To read one text 'through' another inevitably impacts on how *both* texts are read, but Childs does not consider this.)

At the other end of the Corpus, the Pastorals have a similar, complementary role (69–75). Childs's reading of these letters is essentially unchanged since the 1984 *Introduction*, but their canonical function has been heightened. They belong to the last stage of the CP's formation, and represent an end point in their depiction of a 'passive' and, ultimately, dying Paul (2 Tim. 4.6-8). Paul's ministry has now been passed on to his associates, and he takes on a new, 'personalized' role as the definitive teacher and interpreter of the gospel. In this way, the Pastorals do not rival his earlier letters but, like John the Baptist, point to them with the other scriptures as the source of revelation (166). This 'tritopauline' collection forms a sort of counterpart to Romans in bookending the CP:

> The structure of these books at the beginning and end of the corpus sets the canonical context for its interpretation. They address the crucial hermeneutical issue of the interpretation of Paul, namely, how are his letters in their highly particularized, time-conditioned, historical settings to be used by future generations of Christians? (76)

A small but significant flaw here is the slippage in Childs's references to 'the beginning and end of the corpus'. Historically the Pastorals may represent an 'end', but they do not come last in any known arrangement of the CP, whereas Romans is a 'beginning' in order but not in chronology. Childs's bookend model has to elide these different kinds of directionality. (One could just as well bracket the Corpus between 1 Thessalonians, likely the first to be composed, and either Philemon or Hebrews, variously placed

---

[71] Childs is not unaware that Ephesians has a role somewhat comparable to Romans: 'Ephesians has eliminated most of the highly particularized historical contingencies of Colossians and resorted to a highly universalized theological context addressed to the church at large. ... Canonically speaking, the relation between Colossians and Ephesians has a rough parallel to that between Galatians and Romans' (152–3). Strangely, Childs does not seem to notice that this observation poses a problem for his wider model.

last in the early textual witnesses.) Childs makes a good case that the 'passive' Paul of the Pastorals is significant for the interpretation of the CP as a whole, but when he argues that this complements the purported introductory function of Romans, he is less persuasive. He fails to show that the proposed arrangement arises implicitly from the canonical shaping of the Corpus, either historically or materially; rather, it remains simply his hermeneutical construct.

The limitations of this approach become apparent in Childs's treatment of Ephesians and Colossians. These letters receive relatively little attention, and because he does not accord them the same canonical importance as Romans or the Pastorals, they have less opportunity to speak distinctively. For example, he notes Merklein's suggestion that in Ephesians, Paul is presented as still addressing the church, thus anchoring the letter in the apostolic proclamation (93–4), but does not consider how this might affect its role within the CP. Instead he proceeds directly to his own, similar thesis for the Pastorals. Ephesians and Colossians (here treated together) have become a deuteropauline staging post on the way to the tritopauline goal. The same occurs in the discussion of the church's 'institutionalization' and developing offices, the only point at which Ephesians is discussed at any length (148–53). If the letter does indeed bring 'the fresh ecclesiastical shaping of the faith in the post-Pauline era into conformity with the larger witness of the apostle', the question remains how this development is to be evaluated (151). The answer is again found in the Pastorals, the culmination of the CP's formation, which establish the way in which Paul's teaching is mediated to future generations. The deuteropauline letters appear simply transitional, and so their inherent significance is diminished. Childs's theoretical orientation to the CP could hardly be further from the Baur–Käsemann model, but I would suggest he is still influenced by their familiar linear trajectory.[72]

In his 1984 *Introduction*, Childs made the excellent observation that Ephesians, unlike most Pauline letters, shows in its very composition an awareness of later Christian generations, a deliberate accessibility to a church at some distance from the apostles, and that this intention is itself 'a small step removed from a growing consciousness of the role of the canon'.[73] Like Goodspeed, but without the imaginative improbability of his theory, Childs recognized that the interpretation of Ephesians is closely bound up with the phenomenon of a Pauline collection. It is unfortunate that when, twenty-four years later, he formulated his own guide to the CP, he did not develop this insight further. Perhaps he would acknowledge that his proposals are only partial, that the canonical shaping of the Pauline letters is more multifaceted and admits other kinds of interpretative directionality. In any case, *The Church's Guide for Reading Paul* remains

---

[72] To clarify, Childs does not argue that Colossians and Ephesians are midpoints in the process of institutionalization itself, as does e.g. MacDonald; that inference could easily be drawn, but it is not his substantive claim. Rather, these letters represent successive stages in the reception of Paul in the church's next generation, a process fulfilled in the Pastorals. This still presupposes a single, simple trajectory.

[73] Childs, *New Testament as Canon*, 326. Childs treats ἐν Ἐφέσῳ (1.1) as a late insertion which – since Paul would not have written this kind of letter to those he had personally evangelized – identifies the addressees as second-generation Christians. But this 'canonical commentary' only confirms an intention which is already noticeable throughout the letter, 'in the primary level of the composition'.

a valuable invitation to further reflection. Its discussion of the canonical function of the Pastorals, in particular, is an important contribution. But their elevation as the single *telos* of the one Pauline trajectory, together with the questionable prioritization of Romans, in the end yields an account of the CP which falls disappointingly flat.[74]

Throughout this section, we have seen that the hermeneutic of decadence is by no means as ascendant as it once was, but also that the Baur–Käsemann legacy is still noticeable and sometimes powerful. Among scholars who do not accept it, many still assume a Corpus divided along the lines of authorship. The best alternative model we have found is that of Childs, which lays excellent theoretical groundwork, but does not fully deliver on its promise. Childs's canonical approach will be foundational as I proceed now to outline my own orientation to the CP.

3. The Corpus Paulinum as interpretative dialogue

In her study of hermeneutics within the Corinthian letters, Margaret Mitchell makes this observation:

> The most remarkable thing about the Corinthian correspondence is that, because we have a series of exchanges, we can see Paul interpret his own letters (and glimpse other readings by his addressees, which he disputes). … Even in his own lifetime, Paul's letters – that most dynamic of genres – were disputed, his meaning contested and negotiated in the history of the ongoing relationship within which the letters were situated.[75]

Mitchell traces an ongoing conversation throughout 1–2 Corinthians over the meaning not only of Paul's letters but also of his oral preaching, and even his own body. He adopts a variety of self-hermeneutics, sometimes insisting that he has been literally transparent, sometimes rereading himself more subtly, according to rhetorical exigency. He moves

---

[74] Here we may compare also Christopher R. Seitz, perhaps Childs's most direct academic heir, whose commentary on Colossians foregrounds the letter's place within the CP (*Colossians*, BTCB (Grand Rapids, MI: Brazos, 2014)). As with Childs, I warm to Seitz's theoretical approach, stressing 'the naturalness of a more integrative reading when these [sc. authorship] questions have not in fact been foregrounded, due to the existence of a literary collection that orients them toward one another as a totality' (22–3). And as with Childs, I find the application of the model less successful: in this case, Seitz takes a subgroup of 'prison letters' as the primary context for reading Colossians, another example of unnecessary selectiveness. Part of the problem is Seitz's dependence on Trobisch's unsatisfactory account of the CP's origins (29–31), leading to the improbable suggestion that Ephesians was 'shifted' from before Galatians in order to form the prison group; but as we saw in Chapter 1, the order of the church letters, including the rare inversions Eph.–Gal. and Col.–Phil., is easily explicable by stichometric length. Another interpreter indebted to Childs is Robert W. Wall, who however remains well within the decadence paradigm despite his canonical focus (see n. 10, p. 142 below).

[75] Margaret M. Mitchell, *Paul, the Corinthians, and the Birth of Christian Hermeneutics* (Cambridge: CUP, 2010), 10. See also Mitchell, 'The Corinthian Correspondence and the Birth of Pauline Hermeneutics', in *Paul and the Corinthians: Studies on a Community in Conflict*, FS Margaret Thrall, ed. Trevor J. Burke and J. K. Elliott, NovTSup 109 (Leiden: Brill, 2003), 17–53.

freely between agonistic and apocalyptic paradigms of interpretation, emphasizing the clarity of words or the obscurity of the intention behind them, and in this volatile combination of hermeneutics, a new mode of reading scripture is conceived (63). Thus these letters witness the 'birth of Christian hermeneutics'.

Mitchell's argument is specific to the Corinthian correspondence, because this 'epistolary archive' affords a uniquely longitudinal view of an extended exchange.[76] The process of Paul's self-exegesis is more visible here than anywhere else. Still, she acknowledges that 'the hermeneutical lessons of Corinth would bear fruit in Romans', which reworks some material from earlier letters.[77] In fact, I wish to argue that the implications of this argument extend further than Mitchell takes them, and have tremendous potential significance for reading the CP as a whole. The Corinthian letters are indeed distinctive, but the process of explication they show is just the most developed example of a wider phenomenon. The entire Corpus constitutes a dialogue of continuous self-interpretation.

A few examples will illustrate this suggestion:

1. In 1 Thess. 1-3, a remarkably extended appeal to the Thessalonians' memory, Paul interprets not earlier written texts, but his and his brother apostles' presence, deeds and words. As a simple example, in 3.3-4 Paul reminds the readers that during his founding visit with Silvanus and Timothy, they had spoken of future sufferings. In the light of subsequent events, he now interprets these words as prophetic, confirming that his present afflictions are his appointed lot, and should not unduly disturb the Thessalonians (αὐτοὶ γὰρ οἴδατε ὅτι εἰς τοῦτο κείμεθα· καὶ γὰρ ὅτε πρὸς ὑμᾶς ἦμεν, προελέγομεν ὑμῖν ὅτι μέλλομεν θλίβεσθαι καθὼς καὶ ἐγένετο καὶ οἴδατε). Throughout this earliest instalment of the CP, the memory of the apostolic visits, and especially the apostolic preaching, functions as a kind of 'text' for interpretation. Something similar occurs in many of the letters, occasionally with much greater vigour (Galatians, 2 Corinthians). But it is important that in 1 Thessalonians, where there is no demonstrable reception of other written Pauline texts, we can observe the process of self-interpretation already underway.

2. 2 Thessalonians, as we have seen it interpreted by Childs, works within the CP as a kind of commentary on 1 Thessalonians. It claims to re-present Paul's teaching correctly against a rival account which, uniquely for the CP, has been promulgated in his own name (δι' ἐπιστολῆς ὡς δι' ἡμῶν, 2.2). Paul, or the author representing him, again appeals to his personal preaching in support of the doctrine asserted – 'Don't you remember that I told you these things when I was still with you?' (2.5, cf. 2.15, 3.10) – but this time there is a sharper polemical edge. His message has been wilfully traduced, and is now restated with additional emphasis. This claim resembles the avowal of transparency which Mitchell notes at some points of the Corinthian correspondence. Paul has been consistent; it is the readers who have wavered. In fact, as Childs argues,

---

[76] She argues for the partition of 2 Corinthians into five distinct letters, and so with the entire 1 Corinthians and the non-extant previous letter, for a total of seven attested letters from Paul ('Corinthian Correspondence', 20–2). Her wider thesis does not depend on this analysis, though it works best if 2 Corinthians is somehow partitioned.

[77] Mitchell, *Paul, the Corinthians*, 106.

2 Thessalonians involves considerable 'extension' of the first letter's eschatology, and as in 1–2 Corinthians, the assertion of simple continuity should be recognized as a rhetorical strategy. It buttresses the claim of authority in interpreting Paul's oral and written proclamation (2.15).

The important point here, for my purposes, is that this approach to 2 Thessalonians does not depend on the letter's authorship. It is incompatible with the most extreme option, rightly rejected by Childs, that would place the letter in simple opposition to 1 Thessalonians. But if, in accordance with the canonical shaping, we construe their relationship more sympathetically, we will still have to negotiate the considerable difference between the two letters. Interpretation is not just repetition – though it may sometimes claim to be – and the 'extension' in 2 Thessalonians is quite pronounced, and of a character untypical within the CP. The letter shows one direction in which Pauline eschatology did at some point develop, but which constitutes only a minor branch of the canonically attested tradition. It may be that Paul himself tried it, but found other avenues more rewarding in other contexts; or it may be that he is represented here by a somewhat eccentric disciple. In either case, the eschatology of 2 Thessalonians represents one stream, distinctive but not widely definitive, within the unfolding interpretation of Pauline theology.

3. Paul himself, his life and his apostleship, is an object of interpretation at many points across the CP, for example, Gal. 1–2, 1 Cor. 9, much of 2 Cor., Phil. 3, Eph. 3, 2 Tim. 4. The last example illustrates the late CP's reception of both the figure of the apostle and his earlier texts. The Paul of 2 Tim. 4.6-8 is conscious of his impending death, and looks back on his completed life from a perspective all but outside it. In a startlingly new use of a familiar athletic metaphor, he describes the race as completed (τὸν δρόμον τετέλεκα) and the victor's crown, if not actually attained, as set aside for him (ἀπόκειταί μοι). Part of the background here is 1 Cor. 9.24-27, but the more striking parallel is with Phil. 3.12-14. There, speaking of his conformity with Christ in death and resurrection, Paul insists emphatically that he has not yet achieved his goal, but that his orientation is wholly towards the future (τὰ μὲν ὀπίσω ἐπιλανθανόμενος τοῖς δὲ ἔμπροσθεν ἐπεκτεινόμενος, κατὰ σκοπὸν διώκω εἰς τὸ βραβεῖον). What *is* in the past is Christ's 'winning' of Paul; his own winning of Christ will conform to this pattern (διώκω δὲ εἰ καὶ καταλάβω, ἐφ' ᾧ καὶ κατελήμφθην ὑπὸ Χριστοῦ).

It is hard to imagine the fervidly straining Paul of Phil. 3 ever relaxing into the serene confidence of 2 Tim. 4. The later text is certainly evoking the earlier; a considerable distance has been traversed, but nevertheless, the tension should not be exaggerated. Both letters position writer and readers between an accomplished salvation and an anticipated consummation. The Philippians are exhorted to hold fast to what they have already attained, as they imitate Paul in the continuing journey (3.16-17), while in 2 Tim. 4.8 he still awaits 'that day' to receive his crown. The dialectic of Phil. 3 is not cancelled, but is interpreted from a new perspective, with Paul straddling life and death, speaking as if the end is both at hand and already come. One side or the other is rhetorically assumed by the author: either Paul himself is on the point of death, and writes proleptically, or he has died, and a disciple writes in his name. We cannot be certain which it is, but I do not think the passage's function is greatly altered. Paul has here become an embodied symbol of a dialectic that runs throughout his letters, between knowledge and hope, the certainty of being in Christ and the longing to fully enjoy that identity. As both his life and his Corpus draw to an end, the final resolution of this tension is almost – but not quite – within reach.

One could easily go on. To name a handful of more obvious examples, we could consider the reworking of Gal. 4 on Abraham in Rom. 4, of 1 Cor. 8–10 on table fellowship in Rom. 14–15, of Rom. 6 on baptism in Col. 2, of Colossians generally throughout Ephesians, to say nothing of the many instances Mitchell finds in in 1–2 Corinthians. Equally we could consider theological *topoi* developed across many letters (disputed and undisputed alike), such as the righteousness of faith, the law, participation in Christ, reconciliation, spiritual gifts, the church and Israel and so on. Some of these will be discussed in the following chapters. What I wish to stress here is that the interpretative unfolding of Pauline theology is continuous across the entire CP. At some point in this history, the man himself died, and it is likely that some of the canonical letters in his name bear at least the traces of other hands. We will never know for certain when and how the shift occurred, precisely which letters are affected and in what ways. But my thesis is that the vagaries of authorship are only marginally important for the interpretation of the CP, which is dialogically constituted both during and after the apostle's life.[78]

It might be objected that there is much more going on in the CP than self-interpretation. Undoubtedly; Paul is not his own object. The Corpus is not about him but about Christ, and his primary texts are not his own but the scriptures of Israel. Many parts of the letters are expository, meditative, paranetic and so on, without any immediately reflexive aspect. Nevertheless, they all belong to a conversation, and even the most aphoristic or irenic passages can be read with an eye to their dialogical function, their negotiation of meaning between a writer and readers who have each some existing idea of one another and of the matters discussed, and who draw upon shared texts and traditions. This is by no means the only interpretative approach to the letters, nor will it be useful for every purpose, but it is apposite if one wishes to make sense of the CP as a composite whole. It allows a more constructive construal of difference between texts, in contrast to the oppositional logic of a forensic concern with authorship.

The textual polyphony of the CP, its complex interlacing of similarity and difference, has received much critical attention, but generally under other rubrics: in the case of the homologoumena, as the evolution of Paul's own thought and/or its adaptation to differing contexts; in the case of the antilegomena, as the reception and transformation of Paul's thought by others. I suggest that these processes are more similar than they are different, and that the precise point at which Paul's personal involvement ceased is both unclear and of limited importance. Unburdened by the need to press this distinction, I believe we will gain a clearer view of the composite Pauline text in all its richness and integrity.

The following exegetical chapters will test this proposal. Chapter 3 focuses on a single passage in Ephesians, 2.8-22, with a view to its reception of earlier Pauline

---

[78] This schema of *continuous* self-interpretation, without a caesura at Paul's death, distinguishes my approach from that of Eve-Marie Becker, with which I am otherwise sympathetic (see p. 7 above).

letters. Chapter 4 focuses on a theological theme, the body of Christ, in Ephesians and earlier texts (1 Corinthians, Romans and Colossians). This is of course a highly selective exercise. Ephesians has been chosen as a letter which is generally regarded as pseudonymous, though not quite as universally as the Pastorals; which has suffered from the Baur–Käsemann model, and is still somewhat marginalized in consequence; and which is particularly rich in Pauline intertextuality. It lends itself to my interpretative approach especially well. Nevertheless, I believe the principles illustrated here to be much more widely applicable.

One limitation of the following chapters is that they read Ephesians in relation to earlier CP texts but not later (i.e. the Pastorals and perhaps Hebrews). There are two reasons for this. First, the parallels discussed are simply those which proved most illuminating in these cases. It would be otherwise for different themes or passages: a comparable reading of the portrait of Paul in Eph. 3, for example, would probably consider 2 Tim. 4 among other parallels, as I began to sketch above. And second, my critique is directed principally against the division of the Corpus according to authorship. To respond effectively to this widespread assumption, it is necessary to place most weight on continuity between Ephesians and the undisputed letters.

Finally, it will be apparent that my approach assumes a sympathetic view of the biblical canon. The rationale for pursuing a critical study within such a framework has been ably defended by Childs and others across many publications, and need not be rehearsed here at length. I would simply emphasize once again that Childs's objective, 'to look closely at the text in its received form, and then critically to discern its function for a community of faith', recognizes more accurately than many alternatives the concrete social embeddedness of the canon.[79] The reception of diverse texts into an authoritative collection already reflects, and further defines, a normative reading community. The differences between texts may be considerable, but the canon locates them in a context of shared interpretation, where the coherence of the whole becomes not only a textual but also an ongoing social construction. I have suggested that this process is especially palpable throughout the Pauline letters, and relativizes the importance of their individual authorship; here I would add that when they were gathered into a collection, their original reading community was opened up to include future generations. The theological dialogue whose beginnings are witnessed, and whose boundaries are defined, in the canonical texts, continues to the present day, and to that dialogue the present study seeks to make its contribution.

---

[79] See n. 64, p. 82 above. Childs himself, presenting as primarily a theological interpreter, perhaps undersells his most important conclusion, which is not per se theological: that the canonical form of the biblical texts, though secondary, has its own integrity and solidity because of its communal location.

Part Two

Reading Paul in Ephesians

3

From estrangement to reconciliation

1. Introduction

The task of these two chapters is to put into practice the hermeneutic proposed at the end of Part One. They will attempt integrative exegesis, reading Ephesians alongside other Pauline texts without regard for the authorship question, attentive to the interpretative dialogue that runs between the letters and connects the whole Corpus. I hope to show that, when the canonical context is thus privileged, new and fruitful readings emerge which are otherwise obscured.

No one can doubt that Ephesians is deeply entwined with the other Pauline letters, especially after Goodspeed's bewilderingly vast synoptic table of parallels (even if one accepts only a fraction of them).[1] But the significance of such intertextuality can be variously construed. The interpreter is faced with both similarity and difference, continuity and discontinuity, and must negotiate meaning between them. It is here that the preoccupation with authorship has its most distorting influence on modern readers. Demonstrating a certain thesis of authorship – usually but not always pseudonymity – becomes the *goal* of exegesis, whether intentionally or not. At every point, interpretation is geared towards this underlying question, exaggerating difference and minimizing continuity, or vice versa, as the case may be. Sometimes it is not merely a question of emphasis, but of blindness to what one does not expect to see.

This chapter, the first of our two exegetical studies, offers a reading of the greater part of Eph. 2. A word is needed on the choice of verses. It is always difficult to know where to divide an epistolary text, especially one so seamless as Ephesians. But commentators are almost unanimous in treating 2.11-22 as a unit, and although that has an obvious logic, it can obscure the close connection with the preceding verses. It is easy to overlook how far our exegesis has been shaped by such structural presuppositions. Beginning at 2.8 offers an important corrective to the more usual division, one particularly relevant for this study, as will become clear.

---

[1] Edgar J. Goodspeed, *The Meaning of Ephesians* (Chicago: University of Chicago, 1933), 82–165. Cf. also Mitton's similar synopsis, separately accounting parallels with 1 Peter, in *The Epistle to the Ephesians: Its Authorship, Origin and Purpose* (Oxford: OUP, 1951), 279–315.

Ephesians is so rich in echoes and allusions that, for most verses or units discussed in this chapter, there are a number of possible parallels that could be explored. For most sections I have chosen to focus on one comparison text, with occasional briefer discussion of other parallels along the way, where helpful. First, the treatment of salvation by faith rather than works in Eph. 2.8-10 is considered alongside Rom. 3, showing a greater degree of congruity than is usually recognized. The address to the readers in Eph. 2.11 as 'Gentiles in flesh' is then compared with the unreflective use of 'circumcision' language in Gal. 2, which is similarly called into question by its context. Next, the strong echo of Rom. 9.4–5 in Eph. 2.12, where the advantages of Israel are listed, is reconsidered with reference to the question of non-Christian Jews in Ephesians. The next section (§2.4) is exceptional, tracing a single theme – reconciliation – across a number of Pauline texts, including Eph. 2.13-18, with a more complex pattern of reinterpretation emerging than the prevailing binary construct of 'authentic' versus 'deuteropauline'. Finally, the metaphor of church as building in Eph. 2.19-22 is compared with its earlier occurrence in 1 Cor. 3, showing a creative reworking in Ephesians, focused on a different threat to church unity than concerned Corinth. This method is necessarily selective, and although I have tried to identify the most salient connections, it would undoubtedly be possible to highlight others and so explore different aspects of the text. The aim is to illustrate the possibilities of an integrative interpretation, not to exhaust them.

2. Exegesis

2.1. What kind of works? (Eph. 2.8-10)

Eph. 2.8-10 Τῇ γὰρ χάριτί ἐστε σεσῳσμένοι διὰ πίστεως· καὶ τοῦτο οὐκ ἐξ ὑμῶν, θεοῦ τὸ δῶρον· οὐκ ἐξ ἔργων, ἵνα μή τις καυχήσηται. αὐτοῦ γάρ ἐσμεν ποίημα, κτισθέντες ἐν Χριστῷ Ἰησοῦ ἐπὶ ἔργοις ἀγαθοῖς οἷς προητοίμασεν ὁ θεός, ἵνα ἐν αὐτοῖς περιπατήσωμεν.

Rom. 3.24, 27-30, 4.2 ... δικαιούμενοι δωρεὰν τῇ αὐτοῦ χάριτι διὰ τῆς ἀπολυτρώσεως τῆς ἐν Χριστῷ Ἰησοῦ· ... Ποῦ οὖν ἡ καύχησις; ἐξεκλείσθη. διὰ ποίου νόμου; τῶν ἔργων; οὐχί, ἀλλὰ διὰ νόμου πίστεως. λογιζόμεθα γὰρ δικαιοῦσθαι πίστει ἄνθρωπον χωρὶς ἔργων νόμου. ἢ Ἰουδαίων ὁ θεὸς μόνον; οὐχὶ καὶ ἐθνῶν; ναὶ καὶ ἐθνῶν, εἴπερ εἷς ὁ θεὸς ὃς δικαιώσει περιτομὴν ἐκ πίστεως καὶ ἀκροβυστίαν διὰ τῆς πίστεως. νόμον οὖν καταργοῦμεν διὰ τῆς πίστεως; μὴ γένοιτο· ἀλλὰ νόμον ἱστάνομεν. ... εἰ γὰρ Ἀβραὰμ ἐξ ἔργων ἐδικαιώθη, ἔχει καύχημα, ἀλλ' οὐ πρὸς θεόν.

Although it means careering blithely *in medias res*, it is apt to begin our analysis with Eph. 2.8, a particularly unabashed reappropriation of earlier Pauline language. Here and in what follows, the opposition between faith and works as the means of salvation is concisely invoked, the thesis so thoroughly worked out in Romans and Galatians recalled summarily but with unmistakeable explicitness. An even curter résumé – the three-word parenthesis χάριτί ἐστε σεσῳμένοι – has appeared a few verses earlier (2.5). These phrases do not re-present the argument of the earlier letters, but presuppose it; presumably to the first readers, and certainly to those receiving the canonical CP, they call to mind a familiar theological discourse, foundational to but separate from the present discussion. Much more than mere slogans claiming a Pauline pedigree for a new school of thought, they ground the present passage in a specifically *intertextual* relationship within the CP. There are many texts that might be read alongside Eph. 2.8-10, but the particular collocation of terms – especially the conjunction of 'works' with 'boasting' – alludes most patently to the verses cited from Rom. 3-4.[2] As we will see, however, the connection runs much deeper than shared vocabulary.

Recent interpreters, inclining to magnify the distance between Ephesians and the undisputed letters, have found here a significant departure from the theology of the true Paul. 'Ephesians has refocused the issue from ethnicity to ethics', runs one characteristic summary.[3] The 'works' in question here cannot be 'works of the law', or the author would have said so; whereas for Paul himself, 'works' was shorthand that implied the law, his disciple has broadened this terminology so that it now refers to 'human accomplishment in general'.[4] This may be in order to present Paul's doctrine of salvation in terms more acceptable to Jewish Christians, purged of anti-law polemic;[5] or by de-Judaizing his terminology, to make it more intelligible to the Hellenistic world;[6] or to reapply his symbolic language of grace to the Ephesians' encounter with cosmic powers of evil;[7] or even to distance the author from the contemporary faith-works debate and place the emphasis back on God as the source of both.[8] Despite such differences in the reconstructed context, the view that classic Pauline language has here been 'repurposed' away from its original sense prevails.[9]

---

[2] The continuation of the passage in Ephesians to contrast 'circumcision' and 'uncircumcision' is a further connection (Eph. 2.11; see §2.2 below).
[3] John Muddiman, *The Epistle to the Ephesians*, BNTC (London: Continuum, 2001), 111. Cf. Rudolf Schnackenburg, *Der Brief an die Epheser*, EKKNT 10 (Zürich: Benziger & Neukirchener, 1982), 23: 'Sieht man die Rechtfertigung nicht aus Gesetzeswerken ... als Herzstück paulinischer Theologie an, so findet sich in Eph nur in 2,8f ein Anklang daran. ... Die paulinische Stoßrichtung gegen den jüdischen Heilsweg aufgrund von Gesetzeswerken ist nicht mehr zu spüren.'
[4] Margaret Y. MacDonald, *Colossians and Ephesians*, SP 17 (Collegeville, MN: Liturgical, 2000), 234.
[5] Muddiman, *Ephesians*, 99-100. Cf. also Ulrich Luz: 'Vielleicht war für unseren Verfasser die paulinische Botschaft von der Rechtfertigung ohne die Werke des Gesetzes eher eine antijüdische Kampfeslehre als eine Grundaussage paulinischer Theologie' ('Der Brief an die Epheser', in *Die Briefe an die Galater, Epheser und Kolosser*, by Jürgen Becker and Ulrich Luz, 18th edn, NTD, 8/1 (Göttingen: Vandenhoeck & Ruprecht, 1998), 107-80 (134)).
[6] Ernest Best, *Ephesians*, ICC (London: Clark, 1998), 228.
[7] MacDonald, *Colossians and Ephesians*, 240.
[8] Tet-Lim N. Yee, *Jews, Gentiles and Ethnic Reconciliation: Paul's Jewish Identity and Ephesians*, SNTSMS 130 (Cambridge: CUP, 2005), 68-9. This seems to me an improbable reading which does not identify a 'perceptible development' (68) of Paul's thought at all. In his reluctance to read Ephesians in relation to the CP (65), Yee overlooks the clear theological consonance between the gratuitousness emphasized in e.g. Rom. 3.24 and the present passage; seeing God as the source of all things including faith is in no way a departure from the earlier Paul.
[9] There are some exceptions, including Heinrich Schlier, *Der Brief an die Epheser: Ein Kommentar* (Düsseldorf: Patmos, 1957), 116; and Markus Barth, *Ephesians*, AB 34 (New York: Doubleday, 1974), 244. Both these commentators draw precisely the opposite conclusion from the same intertextual observation: the usual connotations of 'works' within the CP suggest a similar meaning in Ephesians.

However, this approach suffers from isolating vv. 8-10 (or for some, vv. 8-9) from their surrounding context. They are usually treated as a parenthesis, or in the extreme case of Hübner, as a redactional insertion;[10] this in turn is made possible by taking 2.1-10 as a unit distinct from what follows. But the first word of 2.11, Διό, suggests otherwise: the present verses provide the grounds for the claim Paul is about to make about the identity of the readers. I will argue below (§§2.2 and 2.3) that the construction of the readers' self-understanding as Gentiles is crucial to the way this letter presents the gratuity of salvation, and it is just this doctrinal crux that is introduced in 2.8-10. They have received gratuitously as Gentiles what Paul and others received gratuitously as Jews; peace has been made available indiscriminately both to the 'far off' and to the 'near' (2.17) by the same gracious operation.

This is, of course, exactly the point being made in Rom. 3.29-30: God is the God of both Jew and Gentile, circumcision and uncircumcision, and saves both through faith. Reading through Eph. 2 without a partition midway, it is striking how closely it structurally resembles this part of Romans. The parallel is not only in vocabulary but also in line of thought, and once this has been observed, the familiar two-part analysis of the chapter no longer seems adequate:

Rom. 3.9-18, 23	Eph. 2.1-3	All alike have sinned.
Rom. 3.24	Eph. 2.4-5	Nevertheless, God acts in Christ to justify (Rom.)/save (Eph.) those otherwise lost.
Rom. 3.25-26	Eph. 2.4-7	This is to demonstrate (ἐνδείκνυμι) God's nature: his righteousness (Rom.)/the riches of his grace and kindness (Eph.).
Rom. 3.24	Eph. 2.8	It is a gift (δωρεάν, Rom./δῶρον, Eph.).
Rom. 3.27-28, 4.2	Eph. 2.8-9	It is received through faith, not works, to the exclusion of boasting.
Rom. 3.29-30	Eph. 2.11-13	We thus see that God is God of the circumcision and the uncircumcision alike.

There are considerable divergences, of course, and elements and emphases peculiar to each letter, as is to be expected. But their basic trajectories correspond remarkably closely: in fact we may say that the whole of this passage in Ephesians systematically reinterprets the argument of Rom. 3 for a new context. At least in this instance, altogether too much has been made of Ephesians's supposedly post-Pauline novelty.[11]

---

[10] Hans Hübner, 'Glosser in Epheser 2', in *Vom Urchristentum zu Jesus*, ed. Hubert Frankemölle and Karl Kertelge (Freiburg: Herder, 1989), 392–406. Best (*Ephesians*, 229) gives a good summary of reasons to reject this suggestion, not least the lack of any text-critical evidence.

[11] This reading has the added advantage of showing the coherence of Eph. 2 as a whole. Contrast e.g. Peter Tachau's study of the ποτέ-νῦν schema throughout the NT, culminating in a reading of this chapter (*'Einst' und 'Jetzt' im Neuen Testament: Beobachtungen zu einem urchristlichen Predigtschema in der neutestamentlichen Briefliteratur und zu seiner Vorgeschichte*, FRLANT 105

Seen in this light, it is much less plausible that when 'works' are mentioned in Eph. 2.9, all connotations of the law and of division between Jew and Gentile have faded beyond the point of significance. The agency of grace and the impotence of works form the basis for the following discussion of Jew–Gentile reconciliation, suggesting that a Torah-specific sense of 'works' must be at least *included* within the meaning of 2.9. Within a few verses comes further explication, when the obstacle to reconciliation is identified as the law, named for the only time in Ephesians and in decisively negative terms (τὸν νόμον τῶν ἐντολῶν ἐν δόγμασιν, 2.15; see further §2.4 below). So it will not do to say that 2.8-9 merely invokes characteristic Pauline formulae but means something quite different; the consonance with Rom. 3 runs deeper than that. Having established this, we can without prejudice observe that there *is* in fact a certain 'broadening' of works-language here, but in a way that organically expands upon earlier Pauline usage.

First, the salvation introduced in v. 8a is clarified in two parallel clauses describing what it is not (οὐκ ἐξ ...),[12] implying a correspondence between the statements that salvation is not 'from yourselves' and that it is not 'from works'. We have seen that both clauses recall Rom. 3, in the 'giftedness' of grace's operation, and still more in the exclusion of works-boasting (v. 9, cf. Rom. 3.27, 4.2). The more generic claim of v. 8b is somewhat amplified in v. 9: salvation is by no means from yourselves, which is to say, not by means of works. But the law is not mentioned yet, nor is justification or righteousness; that particular overtone of the earlier Paul remains unstated at this point. It is only when we reach v. 11 that the concrete ethnic dimension of the works–grace opposition is made explicit.

However, if vv. 8b and 9 do set up an initially broader sense of 'works', this too follows earlier Pauline usage. The claim of v. 8b, that salvation by grace comes οὐκ ἐξ ὑμῶν, θεοῦ τὸ δῶρον, echoes 2 Cor. 3.5, οὐχ ὅτι ἀφ' ἑαυτῶν ἱκανοί ἐσμεν λογίσασθαί τι ὡς ἐξ ἑαυτῶν, ἀλλ' ἡ ἱκανότης ἡμῶν ἐκ τοῦ θεοῦ, and also 4.7, ἵνα ἡ ὑπερβολὴ τῆς δυνάμεως ᾖ τοῦ θεοῦ καὶ μὴ ἐξ ἡμῶν. In neither verse are 'works of the law' in question, yet both concern the source of the power at work in believers, and exclude any sort of self-reliance. The specification in Eph. 2.9, οὐκ ἐξ ἔργων, draws particularly on Romans, where (in contrast to Galatians) the phrase ἐξ ἔργων frequently occurs without the qualifier νόμου. The strongest parallel is Rom. 9.12, where God's election of Jacob rather than Esau is defined as οὐκ ἐξ ἔργων ἀλλ' ἐκ τοῦ καλοῦντος. The rhetorical thrust is not far from Ephesians: God's people are constituted by God's act alone, apart from *any* human measure of worth. The law remains the definitive case in point, for Ephesians as for Romans, and was doubtless the original source of this

---

(Göttingen: Vandenhoeck & Ruprecht, 1972)). Although Tachau admits some continuity through Eph. 2, with a threefold ποτέ (vv. 1-3, 4-10 and 11-12) answered in v. 13, in his focus on this schema he overlooks the thematic connection of vv. 11-18 with what precedes. Lincoln's response, that a 'then'–'now' contrast is already complete within vv. 1-10 and does not continue beyond that point (*Ephesians*, WBC 42 (Dallas, TX: Word, 1990), 87), is open to the same objection.

[12] Τοῦτο refers to the whole previous clause, rather than to πίστις as has sometimes been suggested (e.g. G. B. Caird, *Paul's Letters from Prison: Ephesians, Philippians, Colossians, Philemon* (Oxford: OUP, 1976), 53), not only because of gender but also because of this parallelism, where both clauses develop v. 8a (Lincoln, *Ephesians*, 112).

familiar Pauline *topos*, but in Rom. 9.12 as in Eph. 2.9 it remains temporarily out of view, inviting a broader reading.[13]

When we continue to Eph. 2.10, the language of 'works' is taken in a somewhat different direction, with practically no ethnic/legal sense discernible. This is effected through the conjunction of the terms ἔργον, ποίημα, κτίζω and προετοιμάζω, which though different belong to the same 'semantic domain',[14] and so recontexualize the readers' works within the wider theological framework of creation. The readers are God's created work (ποίημα, cf. Rom. 1.20) and a new creation in Christ (cf. Eph. 2.15; see §2.4 below). It is in this context only that their own good works are to be understood – or in fact, that they are capable of truly good works. The juxtaposition of vv. 9 and 10 contrasts two different sorts of works: those that proceed 'from yourselves' and lead to boasting, and those that are 'prepared beforehand by God' and characterize the recreated Christian. It is only the latter that are called 'good'.

Ephesians, then, interprets the faith–works dualism of Romans and Galatians so as to exclude the possibility of a quietist reading, one dispensing altogether with the need for tangible acts of faith.[15] That such a reading had currency in NT times is shown by its refutation in Jas 2.14-26, a clear example of a *non*-Pauline text receiving and critically reinterpreting (especially) Rom. 3–4. James's rhetoric is of quite another kind, distancing itself from Paul at least on the surface, yet there is actually considerable agreement between this passage and Eph. 2.10: a faith that does not manifest itself in works is as inconceivable for the Paul of Ephesians as it is for James. But the careful dialectic about the source of works, the counterpoise of vv. 9 and 10, is distinctive to our letter. This is an example where Ephesians may be read as a 'mediating' text, bridging earlier elements of the CP with the wider NT.

In summary, we can conclude that in Eph. 2.8-10 'salvation by works' is excluded through familiar Pauline language; that the context invites some measure of generalization in the sense of 'works' just as surely as it excludes an *absolute* generalization; and that both the narrower and broader senses are in direct continuity with usage in the undisputed letters. This takes us outside the scholarly mainstream and its preoccupation with authorship. As an illustration of the methodological difference, consider how some scholars respond to a distinctively Ephesian turn of phrase in this passage, one I have not so far dwelt upon: that the readers are 'saved' rather than 'justified' by grace through faith (2.5b, 8). Many interpreters exaggerate this point and

---

[13] Contrast the more sweeping judgement of Hoehner: 'It is incorrect to think that "works of the law" is really different from "works". "Works" is a broad term referring to human effort, which is the same as "works of the law" in a Jewish context' (*Ephesians: An Exegetical Commentary* (Grand Rapids, MI: Baker Academic, 2002), 344–5). Hoehner exaggerates real continuity into undifferentiated sameness, an error opposite to that criticized so far in this section. Defending a thesis of Pauline authorship, his tendency is to minimize the distinctiveness of Ephesians.

[14] Yee, *Jews, Gentiles and Ethnic Reconciliation*, 67; however his next claim, that 'ποίημα and ἔργος [sic] are interchangeable' on the basis of some parallelism in the LXX psalms, is implausible. V. 10 does not restate but rather *broadens* the semantic range of v. 9 (a reading which would actually support Yee's argument).

[15] A comparison might also be made here with Phil. 2.12-13, despite the lack of verbal agreement (μετὰ φόβου καὶ τρόμου τὴν ἑαυτῶν σωτηρίαν κατεργάζεσθε· θεὸς γάρ ἐστιν ὁ ἐνεργῶν ἐν ὑμῖν καὶ τὸ θέλειν καὶ τὸ ἐνεργεῖν ὑπὲρ τῆς εὐδοκίας). This account of divine and human agency as complementary rather than competitive is not dissimilar to Eph. 2.10.

construe it as a major realignment, on the basis that nowhere else in the CP is σῴζω used in the perfect. Lindemann, for example, believes that Ephesians fundamentally departs from Paul's thought by dispensing with his 'eschatological reservation', and instead allies itself with gnosticism, treating the believer's real existence as already in heaven.[16] The 'paulinistic' insertions of vv. 5b and 8-9 are attempts by the author to buttress his own thought with the apostle's, but in vain:

> Ihrer theologischen Substanz nach beziehen sich diese Sätze ja gar nicht auf ihren Kontext, d.h. die 'gnostisierenden' Aussagen von V. 5ff, die sich von der paulinischen Theologie vor allem durch die Aufhebung des eschatologischen Vorbehalts unterscheiden, werden gerade in dieser Hinsicht in V. 5b.8f. nicht korrigiert oder auch nur eingeschränkt. Im Gegenteil: dadurch, daß – völlig unpaulinisch! – von der Rettung im Perfekt gesprochen wird, ist das Heilsverständnis von V. 5-7 ausdrücklich bestätigt worden.[17]

For Lindemann, the mere mention of salvation in the perfect tense convicts these verses as gnostic and unpauline. Against this, more measured interpreters have pointed out that, although Paul speaks of salvation in the future more often than not, there is still considerable variation even within the undisputed letters. Particularly relevant comparisons for our passage are 1 Cor. 1.18 and 2 Cor. 2.15, where 'those being saved' and 'those perishing' are designated with present participles (σῳζόμενοι and ἀπολλύμενοι). In view of this usage, together with Paul's blithely inconstant deployment of δικαιόω in the past, present or future as occasion demands,[18] it is absurd to draw an artificial line admitting σῳζόμενοι but excluding σεσῳμένοι as unpauline. Schlier is correct: Paul sees salvation in various aspects, provisionally received as well as awaited in hope, and the present verses fit comfortably on this spectrum.[19]

---

[16] On this point, cf. also Conzelmann: 'Wir sind bereits mit Christus in die Himmel versetzt. Damit befinden wir uns hart am Rande des gnostischen Erlösungsverständnisses' ('Der Brief an die Epheser', in *Die Briefe an die Galater, Epheser, Philipper, Kolosser, Thessalonicher und Philemon*, by Jürgen Becker, Hans Conzelmann and Gerhard Friedrich, 14th edn, NTD 8 (Göttingen: Vandenhoeck & Ruprecht, 1976), 86–124 (97)).

[17] Andreas Lindemann, *Die Aufhebung der Zeit: Geschichtsverständnis und Eschatologie im Epheserbrief*, SNT 12 (Gütersloh: Mohn, 1975), 136–7. Merklein, whose view of Ephesians is on the whole positive, agrees that this perfect tense represents a departure from Paul, such that salvation now consists in believers' relocation to the 'Heilsraum' of the church, and 'Die Soteriologie ist Funktion der Ekklesiologie' ('Paulinische Theologie in der Rezeption des Kolosser- und Epheserbriefes', in *Paulus in den neutestamentlichen Spätschriften: Zur Paulusrezeption im Neuen Testament*, ed. Karl Kertelge, QD 89 (Freiburg: Herder, 1981), 48–9). A more extreme example is Gnilka: he sees a parallel in Rom. 3.24, where grace is emphasized as the principle of salvation, but classifies that verse as pre-Pauline, a liturgical adaptation, just like Eph. 2.5 and 8 (*Der Epheserbrief* (Freiburg: Herder, 1971), 119).

[18] See Barth, *Ephesians*, 221, n. 71, for instances of each.

[19] Schlier, *Epheser*, 110. Another relevant parallel is Rom. 8.24, where σῴζω occurs in the aorist passive (τῇ γὰρ ἐλπίδι ἐσώθημεν), but here the qualification 'in hope' is seized upon as evidence that the meaning is not genuinely past tense (e.g. Muddiman, *Ephesians*, 108). To my mind, this verse shows quite plainly a dialectical view of salvation such as Schlier describes; but there is sufficient evidence of Paul's broad usage without needing to labour this point.

This does not seem to me a particularly radical or surprising conclusion; the oddity is that it should still be so contentious. Lincoln's commentary can serve as an example. After rejecting such excesses as Lindemann's, he discusses the breadth of salvation language in the undisputed letters (citing, as well as the verses already mentioned, 1 Cor. 15.2, 2 Cor. 6.2 and Phil. 2.12), and the close connection in Paul's thought between 'justifying' and 'saving'. And yet he concludes that 'by using the more inclusive term [sc. σῴζω rather than δικαιόω] and indicating its completion, Ephesians constitutes a break with characteristic Pauline usage'.[20] This rather contradicts than sums up his preceding discussion, and illustrates, I would suggest, the distorting influence of a focus on authorship. Difference is construed not as part of a continuous process of reception but as a fundamental 'break' or discontinuity.[21]

Without this distraction, it is possible to read Eph. 2.8-10 as a congruous but innovative development of the Pauline motif of unmerited salvation by faith. It is not only in the pithily compressed formulae of vv. 5b and 8a that Romans and Galatians are recalled, but in the deeper logic of the argument, in which Eph. 2 as a whole is in close concord with Rom. 3: salvation is the gift of God, received through faith not works, alike for circumcision and uncircumcision. We should therefore resist the assumption that the 'works' referred to here cannot be works of the law. Ephesians is also following Pauline precedent, while going further than earlier letters, in pushing beyond this *paradigmatic* sense to a broader claim, that neither salvation nor good works of any kind originate with us. In a context where reprinstinated works of the law apparently represent no threat, the particular basis of the faith–works controversy is still kept in view, as the readers are drawn into a fuller consciousness of their own Gentile identity through the following verses.

2.2. Learning to remember (Eph. 2.11)

Eph. 2.11 Διὸ μνημονεύετε ὅτι ποτὲ ὑμεῖς τὰ ἔθνη ἐν σαρκί, οἱ λεγόμενοι ἀκροβυστία ὑπὸ τῆς λεγομένης περιτομῆς ἐν σαρκὶ χειροποιήτου …

Gal. 2.7-9 ἰδόντες ὅτι πεπίστευμαι τὸ εὐαγγέλιον τῆς ἀκροβυστίας καθὼς Πέτρος τῆς περιτομῆς, ὁ γὰρ ἐνεργήσας Πέτρῳ εἰς ἀποστολὴν τῆς περιτομῆς ἐνήργησεν καὶ ἐμοὶ εἰς τὰ ἔθνη, καὶ γνόντες τὴν χάριν τὴν δοθεῖσάν μοι, Ἰάκωβος καὶ Κηφᾶς καὶ Ἰωάννης, οἱ δοκοῦντες στῦλοι εἶναι, δεξιὰς ἔδωκαν ἐμοὶ καὶ Βαρναβᾷ κοινωνίας, ἵνα ἡμεῖς εἰς τὰ ἔθνη, αὐτοὶ δὲ εἰς τὴν περιτομήν

Perhaps it is surprising that the passage goes on to address the readers as 'Gentiles in flesh', the very distinction that the letter is at such pains to relativize, but this

---

[20] Lincoln, *Ephesians*, 104, restating the argument of Andrew T. Lincoln, 'Ephesians 2.8-10: A Summary of Paul's Gospel?', *CBQ* 45 (1983): 617-30 (620).

[21] The focus on authorship is differently distracting for Mitton, who advocates a version of the Goodspeed theory. Taking these verses and 4.4-6 as examples, he argues that Ephesians borrows so variously from the earlier letters that deliberate, second-hand craftsmanship is the only explanation; this judgement relies upon some very tenuous parallels, however (C. Leslie Mitton, *Ephesians* (London: Oliphants, 1976), 13-15.) Like Goodspeed, Mitton sometimes seems more concerned with the fact of Ephesians's intertextuality than with its meaning.

completes the argument drawn from Rom. 3. The gratuity of salvation is manifested in indiscrimination: Jew and Gentile alike have access to God through Christ. But for this reconciliation to be perceptible, there must first be consciousness of the separation that is overcome, and that is where Paul turns in v. 11. The readers are reminded of who, in the fleshly sense, they *are*. Soon they will recall what they *were* – the object of μνημονεύετε does not appear until v. 12 – but v. 11 remains in the present, and describes a fact of their identity which is somehow enduring.[22] This appeal for a consciously Gentile-Christian self-understanding is a crucial step in the logic of the passage as a whole.

The polarity of circumcision and uncircumcision invoked here is something of a constant throughout the CP. On many occasions, its enduring importance is simply repudiated in favour of a new reality, for example, 'Neither circumcision is anything nor uncircumcision, but new creation' (Gal. 6.15; cf. Gal. 5.6, 1 Cor. 7.19, Col. 3.11). In such instances, Paul repeatedly stresses the soteriological inefficacy of both the rite itself and the resulting social category, and the new unity supersedes the old difference with a sweepingness not evident in Ephesians. Elsewhere, however, the terms are used more neutrally, as for example in the verses quoted above from Gal. 2. In a similar way, Eph. 2.11 refers to two social bodies, but the distinction is admitted only in highly qualified terms. It belongs to the flesh (ἐν σαρκί), a work of human hands (χειροποίητος) whose continuation is merely nominal (λεγόμενος). Although the pejorative force of any of these elements can be separately contested, together they are inescapably dismissive:

1. Σάρξ can have a neutral sense in Paul, denoting the physical body (2 Cor. 7.5, Col. 2.1) or natural kinship (Rom. 4.1, 11.14), but usually it is contrasted with the spiritual or eternal, even when the comparison is relatively benign (Phil. 1.22-24) or not fully explicated (2 Cor. 5.16, Gal. 2.20). In this instance, the negative sense has already been prepared earlier in the chapter, when the readers' past was aligned with the 'desires of our flesh' (Eph. 2.3). Also, the literal sense of the word is inescapable in the case of circumcision, and places the rite squarely on the wrong side of the Pauline dichotomy (cf. e.g. Gal. 6.12-13).

2. Λεγόμενος can also be neutral, as simply 'those called the uncircumcision by those called the circumcision'. But cf. 1 Cor. 8.5-6: 'For even if there are so-called gods [λεγόμενοι θεοί] ... as indeed there are many gods ... yet for us there is one God, the Father.' There is a careful hedging here between the reality or unreality of these 'gods', which altogether implies a contingent or diminished sort of existence. The usage in Eph. 2.11 is similarly distancing: that which is merely λεγόμενος has

---

[22] The words following ὑμεῖς in v. 11 could at first sight be read either appositionally or predicatively, but the former is to be preferred. The recurrence of ὅτι at the beginning of v. 12 introduces the object of μνημονεύετε and shows the syntax to have been interrupted after the first ὅτι in v. 11, ποτέ being picked up again in τῷ καιρῷ ἐκείνῳ. 'Gentiles in flesh', etc., describes not *what* the readers are to remember but *who* is to do the remembering; otherwise we would expect a conjunction before the second ὅτι. (Against Muddiman, *Ephesians*, 116). So I would translate: 'Therefore, remember that once you Gentiles in flesh – the "uncircumcision", so-called by the so-called "circumcision", [itself] handmade in the flesh – that you were at that time without Christ ...'

some sort of reality, but one which pales alongside the spiritual truth discernible in Christ.

3. Χειροποίητος is a familiar term in the LXX, where it refers to idols, but in the NT it is used for dwelling places for God or humankind, usually contrasting the temporal and the eternal.[23] That which is 'handmade' is impermanent; for example, in 2 Cor. 5.1, 'we have a building from God, a house not made by hand [οἰκίαν ἀχειροποίητον], eternal in the heavens'.[24] In the present verse, its significance is to underline the physical concreteness – and so transience – of the symbol of circumcision.[25]

Taken together, then, the address to the readers as Gentiles is so qualified as to strip any enduring detrimental force from this category; and yet the category persists. Paul could simply have omitted to mention it, but it is a curious fact of the CP that the Jew–Gentile distinction keeps surfacing even in those texts which are most concerned with its obsolescence. It appears to be crucial that the Ephesians understand not only that they are now reconciled among God's people in Christ but also that they were formerly estranged, indeed that it is their ethnic nature to be estranged, and that their present inclusion is therefore entirely contingent upon this astonishing divine act of grace. The establishment of Gentile-Christian identity as something fundamentally *incongruous* is central to the function of this passage; it is also a point of deep theological resonance with the wider CP.[26]

In the context of Gal. 2, where the legitimacy of Paul's apostolate is in question, it is part of his defence to distinguish the sphere of his mission from that of the Jerusalem apostles: as Peter is the archetypal apostle to the Jews, so is Paul to the Gentiles. These corporate identities are expressed in the concrete singular nouns περιτομή and ἀκροβυστία, with all the bodily finality they imply, alongside the more neutral ἔθνη. The alternation between the two terminologies is quite free, which shows how

---

[23] This applies to both positive and privative forms of the word. Mk 14.58, Acts 7.48, Heb. 9.11 and 24 all refer to the Jerusalem temple, Acts 17.24 to temples in general. See further Eduard Lohse, 'χειροποίητος, ἀχειροποίητος', in *Theologisches Wörterbuch zum Neuen Testament*, ed. Gerhard Friedrich, vol. 9, 10 vols (Stuttgart: Kohlhammer, 1973), 425–6.

[24] But although we 'have' this dwelling, we also long to put it on (5.2); cf. Col. 2.11, where the 'circumcision not made by hand' has already been received. It is in keeping with Ephesians's general reticence in matters eschatological, relative to Colossians, that this more realized sense should be lacking here.

[25] For this reason, there is something to be said for the literal translation of ἀκροβυστία as 'foreskin', but to apply this English word to a state of being is unacceptably strained. Any distancing force in ἐν σαρκὶ χειροποιήτου is rejected by Yee, who sees this verse as an 'echoic utterance' emphasizing positively a Jewish view of ethnic solidarity, but she downplays far too readily the negative connotations of these terms (*Jews, Gentiles and Ethnic Reconciliation*, 83–6). It should be noted that circumcision language is more benignly reworked elsewhere in the CP. In Rom. 2.25-29, the indissoluble nexus between circumcision and law-observance – a threat in Galatians (e.g. 5.3) – is potentially positive: the keeper of the law (whether Jew or Gentile) has become the true circumcision, in spirit rather than letter. In Phil. 3.2, Paul claims that 'we are the circumcision', and in Col 2.11-13 goes even further by identifying baptism with the 'circumcision of Christ' (the links of this last passage with Eph. 2 are more lexical than substantial). These texts simply represent a different strand of the Pauline reappropriation of circumcision than that discussed here.

[26] The language of 'incongruity' is borrowed from John M. G. Barclay, *Paul and the Gift* (Grand Rapids, MI: Eerdmans, 2015); see the discussion at the end of this section.

entirely unselfconscious Paul's usage is here. 'Circumcision' and 'uncircumcision' are understood as real social groups, the simple equivalent of 'Gentiles' and 'Jews', without explanation; it is only on this basis that the 'pillars' acknowledge the existence of complementary vocations.

The distinction, however, is of no enduring relevance to the baptized, as the letter will go on to argue most forcefully; it refers here to the non-Christian communities who were to be evangelized. The bringing of the gospel will re-evaluate these terms and strip them of their divisiveness. These verses at the beginning of the letter evoke a time and milieu that contrasts with what follows: they recreate an intra-Jewish dialogue, in which the normal Jewish language of ethnic separation can be used unreflectively. We might say, then, that the argument of Galatians as a whole contextualizes this dialogue so as to problematize the language it takes for granted.

It is a very similar sort of hedging that finds expression in Eph. 2.11, and when this is read in conjunction with the neighbouring letter, the overtones become especially significant. Ephesians depends upon and develops Galatians by neither employing uncritically nor dropping altogether the language of circumcision, but problematizing it still further as what we might call a 'retrospective truth' about the readers. Gentileness is a fact about their past, only perceptible from their new present in Christ, where it has ceased to matter. Before becoming Christian, they would never have described themselves in this way; now, it is essential to learn that they *were* Gentile aliens, and in the flesh *are* Gentiles, in order to understand the quality of the grace by which they are now reconciled.[27]

The depreciatory use of σάρξ for circumcision is found most clearly at Gal. 3.3 and 6.12-13, but the negative sense of the term persists throughout the letter (notably in the opposition of Sarah and Hagar (4.22-31) and of flesh and Spirit (5.16-24)), indivisibly from the 'fleshliness' of its main presenting problem. Perhaps the broader Pauline use of 'flesh' as an ontological domain may even have had its origin in the Galatian controversy.[28] Of course, in a literal sense the connection between flesh and circumcision is obvious, but it is principally in Galatians that this is negatively interpreted. This pejorative sense is unavoidably recalled in Eph. 2.11, as is the association of the flesh with immoral conduct (Eph. 2.3; cf. Gal. 5.16). Such a radically negative perspective on circumcision can only be treated so cursorily in Ephesians because the prior argument of Galatians is assumed.

More distinctively, the repeated ἐν σαρκί of Eph. 2.11 also anticipates 2.14, where Christ is said to have broken down the dividing wall ἐν τῇ σαρκὶ αὐτοῦ. This is part of the 'now' complementing the remembered 'then' of 2.11-12, and as such offers a positive

---

[27] As Stephen Fowl puts it, the readers 'need to learn both what being a Gentile meant when they were outside of Christ and what it means now that they are in Christ' (*Ephesians: A Commentary* (Louisville, KY: WJK, 2012), 86). A somewhat different usage is found later in the letter, where the Ephesians are adjured to walk no longer 'as the Gentiles walk', in ignorance and sin that contrasts with 'how you learned Christ' (4.17-20). These foils to the readers' virtue are clearly Gentiles in more than just the flesh. Read side by side, 2.11 and 4.17 locate Ephesians as a transitional text, where the later use of 'Gentiles' to denote non-Christians is emerging, but not yet normal. Cf. 1 Peter, where this is the only sense to be found (2.12 and 4.3).

[28] The word does not occur in the Thessalonian correspondence, the only letters likely to predate Galatians.

'flesh' as a counterpart to the earlier sense. The readers who were once alienated in the flesh have now been reconciled in Christ's flesh. This Christological reinterpretation is not made in Galatians.[29] Crucifixion no less than circumcision is palpably, brazenly a matter of flesh; by locating the problematic part of the Ephesians' past in this domain, Paul aligns it with the victory already achieved by Christ.

So the predicament from which the readers have been delivered becomes perceptible only in retrospect, and the character of grace becomes apparent through the way in which it has been communicated. Before hearing the gospel, the Ephesians would never have considered themselves Gentiles. This status is the contingency of their participation in Christ, fundamental to their Christian identity not as a substantive fact about themselves but as the negative background against which their present reconciliation can be perceived. They need to learn to read their own past anew, not to reinhabit it: hence the highly qualified 'Gentile' language of 2.11.[30]

The Galatians, on the other hand, know only too well that they are the 'uncircumcision'; instead of an instruction to 'remember' their former alienation, they need to be persuaded that their reconciliation has in fact been achieved, that they already participate in it fully through faith in Christ and that submission to the law in the flesh would defeat it, not complete it. The absence of these considerations from the surface of Ephesians obviously suggests a context untroubled by the question of circumcising converts, but the deeper claim at the heart of Galatians – that salvation in Christ comes as an unmerited gift, received through faith – remains just as fundamental to the Pauline gospel in Ephesians as anywhere else. We have seen how it is compactly reformulated in 2.5 and 2.8-9, in language unmistakably evocative of the earlier Paul; in 2.11, I would argue, the social contingency of these statements is similarly recalled. The crucial Pauline logic of Gentile inclusion is reactivated for those removed from the conflict that produced it; in this respect, Ephesians can be seen to mediate Galatians to a wider readership including the modern church.[31]

---

[29] But cf. Rom. 8.3, where Christ is said to 'condemn sin in the flesh'.

[30] Here I am largely in agreement with Benjamin Dunning, who sees two main purposes to this language, that it 'constitutes an implied audience … as a singular and unified group' and 'pulls that audience into the discursive orbit of Pauline theology, wherein the categories of Jew and Gentile have such crucial importance' ('Strangers and Aliens No Longer: Negotiating Identity and Difference in Ephesians 2', HTR 99 (2006): 1–16 (12)). I am less persuaded that the language is discarded after it has 'done its work' in ch. 2, to make way for a 'program of hierarchy and control' in the second half of the letter (13–15).

[31] Various analogies with theological readings of the undisputed letters might be suggested here. As an example, consider Günther Bornkamm on the relation of Rom. 7 and 8. He denies that the past lostness described in ch. 7 is merely a transcended stage of the Christian's development:

> Vielmehr bleibt die Vergangenheit und Verlorenheit des Unerlösten in einem sehr bestimmten Sinne Gegenwart auch für den Christen, nämlich als vergebene und überwundene. Ja, die Vergangenheit wird ihm erst im Glauben durchsichtig. … Die Vergangenheit bleibt darum der abgründige Grund des neuen Seins in Christus. Eben damit wird bezeugt, daß die Gerechtigkeit des Glaubens die *aliena iustitia* Christi und der Mensch im Blick auf sich selbst verloren ist. ('Sünde, Gesetz und Tod', 1950, in *Das Ende des Gesetzes*, BEvT 16 (München: Kaiser, 1961), 51–69 (69))

The 'uncircumcision' evoked in Eph. 2.11-22 could just as aptly be called the 'abgründiger Grund' of the Ephesians' identity in Christ: real only insofar as it is overcome, and perceptible only in retrospect. The familiar Pauline logic of justification, given classic Reformation expression in

In arguing for a higher degree of continuity than is usually admitted between these letters, I have referred to the 'incongruity' of grace presupposed in Ephesians. This draws on John Barclay's recent study of 'the gift' (χάρις) in Paul and other second-temple writers.[32] Barclay argues that, for Paul, God's grace or gift is characterized above all by disregard for conventional criteria of recipients' worth, and that this distinctive understanding arises specifically from the social context of the Gentile mission:

> Paul's notion of the incongruous Christ-gift was originally part of his *missionary theology*, developed for and from the Gentile mission at the pioneering stage of community formation. ... This Gift is experienced and interpreted as an *incongruous gift*. The Gentile mission is formative: non-Jews, wholly unqualified for divine beneficence, are found to be 'called in grace' when they receive the good news of Christ, and are gifted with the Spirit.[33]

Barclay also discusses how this theology was recontextualized in the period after the Gentile mission and in subsequent schools of interpretation. In new social contexts, where the Gentile character of the church is taken for granted, the focus of grace's incongruity is turned inwards upon the church and the individual believer. The process begins within the canon itself:

> The first signs of this contextual shift may be traced in the deutero-Pauline letters, where 'works' are refocused as moral achievements (Eph. 2.8-10; 2 Tim. 1.9; Tit. 3.5) and 'boasting' indicates not the cultural confidence of the Jew in the Torah (or of the Greek in wisdom), but pride in achievement (Eph. 2.9). Grace is a marker of the divine source of worth ('not from you, but the gift of God', Eph. 2.8).[34]

I agree entirely that the Gentile mission is the crucible for Paul's novel theology of incongruous grace, but as discussed in the previous section, I am unpersuaded that οὐκ ἐξ ἔργων (2.9) has nothing to do with the law; I also argued above that such broadening as does occur here is anticipated in the undisputed letters. It seems to me that the Paul of Ephesians remains acutely concerned with the social contingency of his readers' reception of grace. Eph. 2 is indeed a critical passage in the history of the 'contextual shift' that Barclay identifies, but not as an early step towards a subsequently wider departure from the original Paul. Here, rather, the forgetting of the church's increasingly Gentile character – that which above all else defines the incongruity of the grace it has received – is deliberately *resisted*. It is essential for the Ephesians to remember, indeed to learn, that they are Gentiles, precisely in order to appreciate the nature and extent of what God has given them. As the church has become predominantly and

---

Bornkamm's final sentence, is in fact broader than the Romans–Galatians δικαιοσύνη controversy with which it is mainly associated; in our passage, dependence upon grace is made present and vivid for the Ephesians too.

[32] See n. 26 above.
[33] Barclay, *Paul and the Gift*, 566–7; his emphasis.
[34] Ibid., 571.

2.3. No Israel, no Christ (Eph. 2.12)

Eph. 2.12 [μνημονεύετε] ὅτι ἦτε τῷ καιρῷ ἐκείνῳ χωρὶς Χριστοῦ, ἀπηλλοτριωμένοι τῆς πολιτείας τοῦ Ἰσραὴλ καὶ ξένοι τῶν διαθηκῶν τῆς ἐπαγγελίας, ἐλπίδα μὴ ἔχοντες καὶ ἄθεοι ἐν τῷ κόσμῳ.

Rom. 9.3-5 ηὐχόμην γὰρ ἀνάθεμα εἶναι αὐτὸς ἐγὼ ἀπὸ τοῦ Χριστοῦ ὑπὲρ τῶν ἀδελφῶν μου τῶν συγγενῶν μου κατὰ σάρκα, οἵτινές εἰσιν Ἰσραηλῖται, ὧν ἡ υἱοθεσία καὶ ἡ δόξα καὶ αἱ διαθῆκαι καὶ ἡ νομοθεσία καὶ ἡ λατρεία καὶ αἱ ἐπαγγελίαι, ὧν οἱ πατέρες καὶ ἐξ ὧν ὁ Χριστὸς τὸ κατὰ σάρκα, ὁ ὢν ἐπὶ πάντων θεὸς εὐλογητὸς εἰς τοὺς αἰῶνας, ἀμήν.[36]

The Ephesian Christians have been reminded of their fleshly identity in terms that are familiarly Pauline, but especially close to Gal. 2. The past which they are to remember is next described by way of a clear allusion to Rom. 9. Where Romans gives a catalogue of Israel's blessings, Ephesians lists the privations of those separated from her, a mirror image with elements of both closer and more distant correspondence. These include: (1) the partial identification of Christ with Israel; (2) the conjunction of 'covenants' and 'promise'; (3) especially, the plural διαθῆκαι, which is almost unique in the NT;[37] and (4) the complementary conclusions, 'godless in the world' and 'God over all'. The allusion is widely recognized, but Ephesians's reworking of Romans is taken by many critics to show a divergence amounting to irreconcilability, further buttressing the prevailing hypothesis of pseudonymity. The great difference between the two verses, and the wider arguments to which they belong, is the silence of Ephesians about contemporary non-Christian Israel. Martin Rese considers this decisive:

> Something like the unbelieving and hardened Israel, whose existence and fate bothered and moved Paul in Romans 9–11, does not exist for the author of

---

[35] For a contrastive reading of Eph. 2 considerably less sensitive than Barclay's, see James D. G. Dunn, *Beginning from Jerusalem*, Christianity in the Making 2 (Grand Rapids, MI: Eerdmans, 2009), 1110–11. 'One of the most valuable things' the author of Ephesians did was to 'disentangle' two strands of Pauline thought, salvation by faith (2.1-10) and the reconciliation of Jew and Gentile (2.11-22); Paul himself had never quite managed this. According to Dunn, Paul's original monitions against 'works of the law' were only the instantiation in a particular Jewish context of a basic principle, that salvation comes not by any human effort (cf. Hoehner, *Ephesians*, 104, n. 13). Ephesians, anticipating the Reformation, correctly reinterprets this for a Gentile context by rendering it in general terms, helpfully separated from the Jew–Gentile question. This reading contrasts pointedly with my own argument that ethnic particularity is deliberately reinvoked here to teach the readers the true meaning of grace. Dunn takes the supposed division at 2.11 to an extreme; the difference between our readings shows how theologically freighted this analytical decision is.

[36] Textual variants exist with the singulars διαθήκη and ἐπαγγελία, of which the former is very well attested (including by 𝔓⁴⁶ and B), but in each case the plural is undoubtedly the *lectio difficilior* and should be preferred.

[37] Apart from these two verses it occurs only in Gal. 4.24, where the usage is quite different, contrasting the distinct covenants of Sarah and Hagar.

Ephesians. ... In contrast to Paul's point of view in Romans 9–11 the author of Ephesians knows only about a particularity of Israel when looking back to the time before Christ came; after Christ has come the election of Israel has passed over to the Christian church.[38]

For Rese, Eph. 2.12 uses language similar to Rom. 9.4-5 to talk about something fundamentally different; it is not interpretation but repudiation of the earlier Paul. This is not an unusual conclusion. From the New Perspective onwards, much scholarly opinion has rightly been concerned with reemphasizing Paul's concern for Israel κατὰ σάρκα; the silence of Ephesians on this point, even while it picks up some of the threads from Romans, is regarded with suspicion. Rese insists that the NT scholar, who is theologian as well as historian, must take sides on the question of church and Israel, and casts his own vote for Romans.[39] A less sympathetic construal of a silence could hardly be imagined; but it has been to Ephesians's disadvantage that its perspective diverges not only from Romans but also from the priorities of many present-day Pauline scholars.[40]

The opposite position is taken by Markus Barth, who advocates Pauline authorship of Ephesians, and interprets the letter's account of Israel with close reference not only to Rom. 9–11 but also to the parable of the Prodigal Son.[41] It is a creative but unsatisfactory attempt at canonical reading: despite the many points of contact he finds with the parable, in casting non-Christian Israel as the 'older brother' of Luke 15 he accords it a persona, a role in the story, which is simply not there in Ephesians. Barth arrives at the dubious conclusion that 'when Paul speaks of the "one new man" created by God in Christ (Eph. 2.15), he thinks of both Jews and Gentiles just as they are',[42] but given the persistent emphasis on a community fashioned in, through and under Christ, and whose being is constituted by participation in him, this must be regarded as most unlikely.[43]

---

[38] Martin Rese, 'Church and Israel in the Deuteropauline Letters', *SJT* 43 (1990): 19–32 (28–9); see also Rese, 'Die Vorzüge Israels in Rom 9,4f. und Eph 2,12: Exegetische Anmerkungen zum Thema Kirche und Israel', *TZ* 31 (1975): 211–22.

[39] Rese, 'Church and Israel', 22, 32. At the same time Rese concedes that Rom. 9–11 is a minority voice within the NT, and that to give it exclusive priority would require some further hermeneutical justification, a topic deferred to another day. His theological opinion ends up being quite separate from – indeed, arbitrary beside – his historical findings. To me this seems an admission of defeat, a refusal of the invitation to constructive dialogue which is held out by the canonical shaping of the CP.

[40] Another typical example is the censorious conclusion of a survey by Dahl: the author of Ephesians was very interested in the Jewish *roots* of the church, but 'failed to show any concern for the relationship of his audience to contemporary Jews in or outside the church' ('Gentiles, Christians and Israelites in the Epistle to the Ephesians', in *Christians among Jews and Gentiles*, FS Krister Stendahl, ed. George W. Nickelsburg and George W. MacRae (Philadelphia, PA: Fortress, 1986), 31–9 (37)).

[41] Markus Barth, 'Conversion and Conversation: Israel and the Church in Paul's Epistle to the Ephesians', *Interpretation* 17 (1963): 3–24. This question is surprisingly not discussed at length in his commentary, but his view is unchanged: see 269, n. 71 on 'co-citizens with the saints', where he claims that this communion includes non-Christian Jews, both before and after Christ.

[42] Ibid., 9.

[43] There are various other positions that I will not respond to in detail here. For example, MacDonald sees here a community still in tension between 'Jewish' and 'Christian' identities at a time when the

Barth and Rese both show the distorting effects of the preoccupation with authorship. One wants to demonstrate authenticity, the other pseudonymity, and in each case this tacitly becomes the objective of the exegesis. Whereas Rese argues from silence, making much of the absence of non-Christian Israel from Ephesians, Barth must perform considerable interpretative acrobatics to discover that it is there after all. In fact, I believe that Eph. 2 remains deeply consonant with Rom. 9–11, but differs from it in much more than just emphasis, as Barth would have it. It is distinctively focused on Jewish and Gentile identity within the church, not beyond it;[44] but this still involves a certain construal of Israel per se, which may have implications beyond the immediate concern of the text. A comparison of the respective catalogues in Eph. 2.12 and Rom. 9.4-5 will illustrate this.

The past which the Ephesians are to remember is one of alienation from both Christ and Israel. The two belong together: this is the one and only time that Israel is mentioned in Ephesians, and Christ is named in the same breath. Each of the following elements – covenants and promise, hope and God himself – illustrates an aspect of Israel's identity which has now become accessible through Christ, but was formerly out of the readers' reach. They are being reminded of their contingent, incongruous identity as Gentile Christians, and in this context, of how intimately the blessings they now enjoy are identified with God's one chosen nation.

The Gentiles were formerly 'without Christ', but does it follow that Israel was, in those days, somehow 'with Christ'? Most interpreters find here a reference to messianic expectation, no more;[45] but then why would Paul go on to denominate ἐλπίς as just one aspect of what the readers lacked? Schlier goes considerably further: Christ was present for the Jews in the promise, through the law and prophets and even 'quasi-sacramentally' in the wilderness (1 Cor. 10.4).[46] Although this is not altogether inconsistent with Eph. 2, it runs against the grain of the passage, which does not treat Christ as part of Israel's story, but rather views Israel through the lens of Christ. In him, the fullness of the blessings of God's people is disclosed, and so the full extent of the alienation from which the Gentiles have been delivered.

What then should we make of the phrase ἡ πολιτεία τοῦ Ἰσραήλ: why this fuller description, when simply 'alienated from Israel' might have done just as well? There are many possible explanations.[47] To my mind the simplest is that Paul wishes to

---

distinction was not clear-cut, especially in the eyes of the pagan civic authorities ('The Politics of Identity in Ephesians', *JSNT* 26 (2004): 419–44; see also MacDonald, *Colossians and Ephesians*, 252–6). Yee, wishing to bring the New Perspective to bear upon this passage, finds an account of Jewish 'covenantal ethnocentrism' which is not in itself negative (*Jews, Gentiles and Ethnic Reconciliation*, ch. 3). But his attempt to read such language as ἐν σαρκὶ χειροποιήτου sympathetically is unpersuasive; the positive force of the passage is rather in shaping the *readers'* self-understanding.

[44] As is generally recognized. See e.g. Schnackenburg, *Epheser*, 108–9.
[45] E.g. Best, *Ephesians*, 241; Hoehner, *Ephesians*, 355–6.
[46] Schlier, *Epheser*, 120; similarly, Barth, *Ephesians*, 256. There are other possible readings: Yee takes χωρὶς Χριστοῦ to modify τῷ καιρῷ ἐκείνῳ (*Jews, Gentiles and Ethnic Reconciliation*, 99); Muddiman takes it to modify ἀπηλλοτριωμένοι (*Ephesians*, 119), while recognizing that the parallel with Romans 9.4-5 tends against this.
[47] Schnackenburg thinks the author means the equivalent of the OT's קהל, but is unable to use the usual LXX translations, ἐκκλησία or συναγωγή, since they have both acquired more specific meanings. From usage in Josephus and Maccabees, he takes πολιτεία to imply both Israel's God-given constitution and her God-oriented way of life; here it suggests that these things find their fulfilment

underline the concreteness of the people. On a supersessionist reading of Eph. 2, the word πολιτεία may be taken as limiting, distinguishing the merely 'political' Israel of the past from the 'true' Israel now identified with the church; the body politic has been replaced by the body of Christ. But in Eph. 2.12, the πολιτεία is aligned with Christ on the one hand and the covenants, and so on, on the other, so to read it in such a negative sense is contrary. Rather than limiting, then, this expression may in fact emphasize the bodily reality of Israel. The readers have been united not with some transferable ethos but with a concrete, substantial people. In this case, even without explicitly naming the contemporary synagogue, Ephesians in fact *resists* the dehistoricizing of Israel with which it is sometimes credited.

The catalogue of Rom. 9.4-5 begins with a list of six nouns, falling into three pairs: υἱοθεσία–νομοθεσία, δόξα–λατρεία and διαθῆκαι–ἐπαγγελίαι.[48] Paul has named several elements that undisputedly define Israel's character, but tailored the arrangement towards his Christological conclusion. First, the coordination of ἐπαγγελίαι with the distinctive plural διαθῆκαι may imply that, just as the promises of God to Israel are many and yet find their singular fulfilment in Christ (2 Cor. 1.20; cf. Rom. 15.8, Gal. 3.16, Heb. 7.6, etc.), so Christ is the realization of both the old covenant and the new, the covenants of tablet and heart, letter and Spirit (2 Cor. 3.6, Jer. 31.31-34; cf. 1 Cor. 11.25, Heb. 8.8-9). And second, the mention of νομοθεσία (a *hapax legomenon* in the NT) rather than νόμος emphasizes not Israel's law as an artefact but the act of its communication and reception,[49] while the parallel with υἱοθεσία reinforces the verbal element of both compounds. The law, like adoption, arises from God's *action* towards Israel, and this choice of words underlines the giftedness of both.

The doxological conclusion of v. 5 draws all of these benefits together in the person of Christ; he appears as Israel's crowning gift and the consummation of all those just listed.[50] But his place here is qualified in two ways. Unlike the elements listed in v. 4, Christ is not 'theirs' (ὧν) but 'from them' (ἐξ ὧν). This differentiates him also from the patriarchs; they are Israel's foundation, he is her culmination. And unlike them, Christ is from Israel only κατὰ σάρκα; he proceeds from her but does not *belong* to her. This is an ambivalent view of the flesh, since in the same way that Christ is an Israelite, so is Paul (9.3); the people whom he calls simply 'my flesh' (11.14) are also Christ's flesh, and it is just this human family whose salvation Paul both prays for (10.1) and expects (11.26). At the same time, however, Israel's Messiah and the *telos* of her history is one

---

in the church (Rudolf Schnackenburg, 'Die Politeia Israels in Eph 2, 12', in *De la Tôrah au Messie*, FS Henri Cazelles, ed. Maurice Carrez, Joseph Doré and Pierre Greglot (Paris: Desclée, 1981), 467-74). This is a useful analysis of the word, but I will suggest reasons to doubt Schnackenburg's conclusion. Yee draws a rather stretched comparison with the Achaean League to interpret πολιτεία as a 'community of communities'; still he is probably right to see it as a trans-local body politic (*Jews, Gentiles and Ethnic Reconciliation*, 91–6). MacDonald's suggestion, that the readers may have thought themselves excluded from 'any protection offered from Rome's political might' for the Jews, draws a still longer bow (*Colossians and Ephesians*, 242).

[48] As suggested by their ordered placement and rhyming morphology (Brendan Byrne, *Romans*, SP 6 (Collegeville, MN: Liturgical, 1996), 287).

[49] Rese, 'Vorzüge', 216.

[50] This is clearest if v. 5b is taken as appositional to Χριστός, which is my preferred translation ('Christ according to the flesh, *he who is* God over all'). But even if these last words are a self-contained formula of benediction, that itself arises from the catalogue's culmination in Christ.

who relativizes the very flesh that he inhabits: proceeding from this particularity (ἐξ ὧν τὸ κατὰ σάρκα) he is raised to a universality (ὁ ὢν ἐπὶ πάντων) which, as we know by this point of Romans, makes room also for the Gentiles.

These two verses are actually somewhat exceptional in their context. Rom. 9–11 is notoriously complex – which should give pause to any too sweeping claim about its alleged incompatibility with the Paul of later letters – and intertwines many different perspectives on Israel. The highly positive view of Rom. 9.4-5, characterizing the people by a series of blessings which culminate in Christ, remains largely undeveloped in what follows; contrast, for example, 11.28-29, where many similar past blessings are mentioned – election, fathers, gifts, calling – but 'as regards the gospel, they are enemies'. However, removed from its immediate agonistic context, this strand is picked up and developed in a new direction in Ephesians. The catalogue of Eph. 2.12 begins where that of Rom. 9.4-5 concludes, with Christ.[51]

In Eph. 2.11, the value of circumcision, that which excluded the readers, has been sharply relativized; in v. 12, the people of Israel, seen in the light of Christ, are acknowledged positively. An author who believed the πολιτεία τοῦ Ἰσραήλ to have been subsumed into the church, or otherwise to have forfeited its covenant calling, would surely have mentioned it in v. 11 rather than v. 12. Israel in that case would belong in the context of 'law' or 'flesh'. But here, as Schlier comments, 'Die Verheißung und nicht das "Gesetz" ist das Lebensprinzip Israels', consistently with many other Pauline instances.[52] He cites Rom. 4.13 and Gal. 3.16ff., to which we might add the omission of νόμος in favour of νομοθεσία, alongside ἐπαγγελίαι, in Rom. 9.4, and the following statement that τὰ τέκνα τῆς ἐπαγγελίας λογίζεται εἰς σπέρμα (Rom. 9.8). The description of Israel as constituted by promise is crucial to the logic of Rom. 9, but its realization in Christ is only lightly touched upon there. That, however, is the departure point for Eph. 2.12.

For both Romans and Ephesians, Christ is the fulfilment of the promise, but seen from two quite different perspectives. At the beginning of Rom. 9, Paul places himself among his kindred κατὰ σάρκα, and from this Jewish perspective, Christ appears as the *telos* of Israel's blessings. Seen from within covenant history, he represents a broadening, an opening of the door to the Gentiles. In Eph. 2, the perspective is reversed, as Paul directs the readers' attention backwards. From the standpoint of Gentiles lately brought into the covenant, Christ is the lens through whom they view and understand Israel. Romans looks in at the small end of the telescope to see a covenant enlarged through Christ; Ephesians looks in at the large end to see a history particularized through Christ.

I can therefore agree with Rese that Eph. 2.12 considers Israel before Christ, and Rom. 9.4-5 Israel after Christ; but I disagree that this conceals a deeper theological shift in Ephesians, namely that after Christ, Israel has simply *become* the church of Jews and Gentiles.[53] The incongruity of the readers' present salvation arises from a particular history, and it is for that reason, not because of lurking supersessionism, that the glance here is entirely retrospective. In order for the Gentile-Christian Ephesians

---

[51] Pheme Perkins, *Ephesians*, ANTC (Nashville, TN: Abingdon, 1997), 67.
[52] Schlier, *Epheser*, 120-1.
[53] Rese, 'Vorzüge', 219-20.

to learn the *distinctiveness* of the Jewish people, they must look backwards to their own former *dividedness*. The operation of this dialectic within Rom. 9–11 has been helpfully elucidated by Susannah Ticciati, who reads Paul's account of the election of Israel as a 'nondivisive difference', manifesting the absolute difference of God which is non-competitive and non-exclusive:

> The Christ-event, instead of bringing about a binary opposition between old and new Israel, reveals and renews a nondivisive difference between Israel and the nations, Jews and Gentiles. This is the nondivisive difference of election, in which Israel is distinguished from the Gentiles in a way that includes them, and the Gentiles are united with Israel in a way that undergirds Israel's irreducible difference. Israel and the Gentiles share in the same God, but differently.[54]

I would argue that Eph. 2, in its refashioning of the readers' identity in relation to Jewish Christians, corroborates this construal of Israel's difference. Her election is, of course, not thematized here, nor are non-Christian Jews in view, but the readers' attention is directed to Israel in such a way as to accentuate rather than obscure her difference; and this precisely in order to assert that division has given way to unity.

For some interpreters, it will remain problematic that the Paul of Ephesians makes no mention of 'hardened', non-Christian Israel, in contrast with Rom. 9–11. Still, the same can be said of Galatians, leading Lincoln to conclude that with Ephesians, 'the wheel has turned full circle' away from the atypical position of Romans.[55] But I am very suspicious of reading into this silence a change of theological outlook from Romans, rather than just a change of topic. Paul has no need to discuss non-Christian Jews with the Gentile-Christian Ephesians, and so we have simply no data from which to infer a theological shift as significant as that alleged by Rese et al. What we do have, as I read it, is the deliberate reiteration of a 'nondivisive difference' between Jew and Gentile *within* the church – a subtle but insistent reshaping of the readers' self-awareness as dependent upon 'others' whom perhaps they do not know.

On this reading, Eph. 2.12 is much more consonant with its point of reference in Rom. 9.4-5 than has often been supposed, the differences arising from a change of context and perspective rather than a theological *volte-face*. The interpreters who take the latter view make much of a silence that can be more sympathetically construed, a courtesy extended to Galatians but not Ephesians. On the other hand, a harmonizing reading like Barth's, eliding the theological differences, fails to recognize the extent – and so the point – of Ephesians's reworking. Leaving the authorship question aside, however, and reading the

---

[54] Susannah Ticciati, 'The Nondivisive Difference of Election: A Reading of Romans 9–11', *Journal of Theological Interpretation* 6 (2012): 257–78 (276); see also Ticciati, 'Transforming the Grammar of Human Jealousy: Israel's Jealousy in Romans 9–11', in *The Vocation of Theology Today*, FS David Ford, ed. Tom Greggs, Rachel Muers and Simeon Zahl (Eugene, OR: Cascade, 2013), 77–91. (In articulating a sort of divine difference that is visible within the world without dividing it, Ticciati is building upon the work of David Burrell.) More recently, see also Ticciati, 'The Future of Biblical Israel: How Should Christians Read Romans 9–11 Today?', *Biblical Interpretation* 25 (2017): 497–518, for a fascinating critique of interpreters' division between the 'true' and the 'fleshly' Israel.

[55] Andrew T. Lincoln, 'The Church and Israel in Ephesians 2', *CBQ* 49 (1987): 605–24 (620).

text as an integrated part of the whole CP, we can acknowledge its distinctiveness without exaggerating it. It will then appear much more strained to postulate a repudiation of Romans where Ephesians is silent than to infer that *qui tacit consentire videtur*.

2.4. Reconciliation, human and divine (Eph. 2.13-18)

Eph. 2.13-18 νυνὶ δὲ ἐν Χριστῷ Ἰησοῦ ὑμεῖς οἵ ποτε ὄντες μακρὰν ἐγενήθητε ἐγγὺς ἐν τῷ αἵματι τοῦ Χριστοῦ. Αὐτὸς γάρ ἐστιν ἡ εἰρήνη ἡμῶν, ὁ ποιήσας τὰ ἀμφότερα ἓν καὶ τὸ μεσότοιχον τοῦ φραγμοῦ λύσας, τὴν ἔχθραν ἐν τῇ σαρκὶ αὐτοῦ, τὸν νόμον τῶν ἐντολῶν ἐν δόγμασιν καταργήσας, ἵνα τοὺς δύο κτίσῃ ἐν αὐτῷ εἰς ἕνα καινὸν ἄνθρωπον ποιῶν εἰρήνην καὶ **ἀποκαταλλάξῃ** τοὺς ἀμφοτέρους ἐν ἑνὶ σώματι τῷ θεῷ διὰ τοῦ σταυροῦ, ἀποκτείνας τὴν ἔχθραν ἐν αὐτῷ. καὶ ἐλθὼν εὐηγγελίσατο εἰρήνην ὑμῖν τοῖς μακρὰν καὶ εἰρήνην τοῖς ἐγγύς· ὅτι δι' αὐτοῦ ἔχομεν τὴν προσαγωγὴν οἱ ἀμφότεροι ἐν ἑνὶ πνεύματι πρὸς τὸν πατέρα.

Col. 1.19-23 ὅτι ἐν αὐτῷ εὐδόκησεν πᾶν τὸ πλήρωμα κατοικῆσαι
καὶ δι' αὐτοῦ **ἀποκαταλλάξαι** τὰ πάντα εἰς αὐτόν,
εἰρηνοποιήσας διὰ τοῦ αἵματος τοῦ σταυροῦ αὐτοῦ,
δι' αὐτοῦ εἴτε τὰ ἐπὶ τῆς γῆς
εἴτε τὰ ἐν τοῖς οὐρανοῖς.
Καὶ ὑμᾶς ποτε ὄντας ἀπηλλοτριωμένους καὶ ἐχθροὺς τῇ διανοίᾳ ἐν τοῖς ἔργοις τοῖς πονηροῖς, νυνὶ δὲ **ἀποκατήλλαξεν** ἐν τῷ σώματι τῆς σαρκὸς αὐτοῦ διὰ τοῦ θανάτου παραστῆσαι ὑμᾶς ἁγίους καὶ ἀμώμους καὶ ἀνεγκλήτους κατενώπιον αὐτοῦ, εἴ γε ἐπιμένετε τῇ πίστει[56]

Rom. 5.9-11 πολλῷ οὖν μᾶλλον δικαιωθέντες νῦν ἐν τῷ αἵματι αὐτοῦ σωθησόμεθα δι' αὐτοῦ ἀπὸ τῆς ὀργῆς. εἰ γὰρ ἐχθροὶ ὄντες **κατηλλάγημεν** τῷ θεῷ διὰ τοῦ θανάτου τοῦ υἱοῦ αὐτοῦ, πολλῷ μᾶλλον **καταλλαγέντες** σωθησόμεθα ἐν τῇ ζωῇ αὐτοῦ· οὐ μόνον δέ, ἀλλὰ καὶ καυχώμενοι ἐν τῷ θεῷ διὰ τοῦ κυρίου ἡμῶν Ἰησοῦ Χριστοῦ δι' οὗ νῦν τὴν **καταλλαγὴν** ἐλάβομεν.

2 Cor. 5.17-20 ὥστε εἴ τις ἐν Χριστῷ, καινὴ κτίσις· τὰ ἀρχαῖα παρῆλθεν, ἰδοὺ γέγονεν καινά. τὰ δὲ πάντα ἐκ τοῦ θεοῦ τοῦ **καταλλάξαντος** ἡμᾶς ἑαυτῷ διὰ Χριστοῦ καὶ δόντος ἡμῖν τὴν διακονίαν τῆς **καταλλαγῆς**, ὡς ὅτι θεὸς ἦν ἐν Χριστῷ κόσμον **καταλλάσσων** ἑαυτῷ, μὴ λογιζόμενος αὐτοῖς τὰ παραπτώματα αὐτῶν καὶ θέμενος ἐν ἡμῖν τὸν λόγον τῆς **καταλλαγῆς**. Ὑπὲρ Χριστοῦ οὖν πρεσβεύομεν ὡς τοῦ θεοῦ παρακαλοῦντος δι' ἡμῶν· δεόμεθα ὑπὲρ Χριστοῦ, **καταλλάγητε** τῷ θεῷ.

At every point of Eph. 2 we are finding not merely thematic but deep intertextual relationships with earlier Pauline letters. At every point we have also to be selective, since – as Goodspeed so clearly shows – there is a daunting multitude of such

---

[56] A variant attested in 𝔓⁴⁶ and B has ἀποκατηλλάγητε for ἀποκατήλλαξεν. This may well be original (so Bruce M. Metzger, *A Textual Commentary on the Greek New Testament*, 2nd edn (Stuttgart: Deutsche Bibelgesellschaft, 1994), 555, against NA and UBS), but does not substantially change the meaning for our purposes.

connections, ranging from faint echoes to near quotations. In Eph. 2.13-18, to take a few examples, the union of one body in one Spirit recalls 1 Cor. 12.13 (and 6.17); 'peace' as 'access' to God, Rom. 5.1-2; the 'new man', 1 Cor. 15.45 and Col. 3.9; not to mention the many verbal parallels with Col. 1.19-22. Some of these correspondences will be discussed briefly in what follows, but I will focus on 'reconciliation', a word axiomatic to this passage and with wide Pauline resonance. Tracing one thread across various texts, rather than analysing a single parallel, will illustrate how a theological idea can be successively received and reworked across the CP. Before coming to these particulars, however, we will consider Eph. 2.13-18 as a unit, the context which shapes the distinctively Ephesian sense of reconciliation.[57]

With 2.13, Paul turns to the 'now' that corresponds to the 'then' the readers have been learning to remember. The focus here is clearly on the new reconciled reality of the church, but it is still expressed in terms that require recognition of a past difference. There are two images at work in these verses, with at least *prima facie* tension between them: the church is a newly created entity (vv. 14-16) but comprises those formerly 'far off' and 'near' (vv. 13, 17). The Christian community's 'access to the Father' is on the one hand *new*, and on the other, presupposes the existing nearness of Israel, since where the Gentiles have been 'brought near', the Jews already were. An exclusive emphasis on the unique novelty of the church – a supersessionist reading of Eph. 2, as discussed in the last section – disregards the logic of this spatial imagery.

That imagery derives from an allusion in vv. 13-14 and 17 to Is. 57.19:

Is. 57.19 εἰρήνην ἐπ᾽ εἰρήνην τοῖς μακρὰν καὶ τοῖς ἐγγὺς οὖσιν·

Eph. 2.13-14 ὑμεῖς οἵ ποτε ὄντες μακρὰν ἐγενήθητε ἐγγὺς ἐν τῷ αἵματι τοῦ Χριστοῦ.

Αὐτὸς γάρ ἐστιν ἡ εἰρήνη ἡμῶν ...

Eph. 2.17 καὶ ἐλθὼν εὐηγγελίσατο εἰρήνην ὑμῖν τοῖς μακρὰν καὶ εἰρήνην τοῖς ἐγγύς·

The direct allusion, virtually a quotation, comes with v. 17, but this clearly grounds the usage in v. 13 as well.[58] This verse comes from a passage concerned with rebellious Israel, and God's promise is to heal and restore her; by applying it to the reconciliation

---

[57] A good deal has been written about Paul's theology of 'reconciliation': some examples are I. Howard Marshall, 'The Meaning of Reconciliation', 1978, in *Jesus the Saviour: Studies in New Testament Theology* (London: SPCK, 1990), 258-74, surveying the meaning of the word across the CP; Ralph P. Martin, *Reconciliation: A Study of Paul's Theology* (London: Marshall, Morgan & Scott, 1981), somewhat dubiously identifying this theme as the 'centre of Paul's thought and ministry' (3); Seyoon Kim, '2 Cor. 5.11-21 and the Origin of Paul's Concept of "Reconciliation"', *NovT* 39 (1997): 360-84, arguing that the language alludes to the Damascus Road episode; Stanley E. Porter, 'Paul's Concept of Reconciliation, Twice More', in *Paul and His Theology* (Leiden: Brill, 2006), 131-52, chastising Martin and Kim for alleged inattention to recent Greek linguistic theory. These studies look at much the same texts as I do, but with different methods and conclusions; the focus here is limited to how this language is reworked in successive Pauline texts.

[58] Pace Lincoln (*Ephesians*, 138-9). The language of the 'far' being 'brought near' may also reference proselytism, as he argues, but its dependence on Is. 57.19 in v. 17 can hardly fail to shape the interpretation of v. 13 also. The conjunction of 'nearness' with 'peace' is clearly Isaianic in both instances.

of Jews and Gentiles, Paul is accenting a particular strain of Isaiah's theology from the neighbouring context. Is. 56.3-8 is a *locus classicus* for the expansion of the covenant, including the observant eunuch and foreigner among those who will be gathered to God's house of prayer 'for all nations' or 'Gentiles' (πᾶσιν τοῖς ἔθνεσιν). From 56.9 the focus shifts to Israel's own transgressions; so it is a creative move, but by no means an impossible one, to read 57.19 as reaching back beyond this point, and including not only recalcitrant Jews but also the god-fearing Gentiles of 56.3-8 in the ambit of its promised peace. That this is the reading of Ephesians is reaffirmed in the following verses, which vividly recall the universal house of prayer as former 'strangers and sojourners' are built together into a 'new temple' (2.19-22).

This is a characteristically Pauline hermeneutic, whereby an 'inclusive' text, originally about Israel's own restoration, is reread to anticipate the incorporation of the Gentiles through Christ, so becoming a key to the interpretation of the larger scriptural narrative. An example from the undisputed letters is the climactic point of Rom. 9, quoting Hosea: 'I shall call the not-my-people my people, and the not-beloved, beloved' (Rom. 9.25; cf. Hos. 2.25). In Paul's reinterpretation, this describes not only the wayward Israelites of Hosea's time but a consistent pattern through the history of God's saving action, only now fully disclosed. It is 'manifested apart from the law, though borne witness by the law *and the prophets*' (Rom. 3.21). Similarly in Ephesians, at the same time that the readers are joined with Israel into a new people of God, they are also integrated into her scriptural story and become part of its fulfilment, and this is expounded through a prophetic text.

The central verses of our passage, Eph. 2.14-16, explain how the Isaianic peace is actually constituted in Christ. The most pointed accent here is upon the centrality of his own person and work; the leitmotiv of 'peace' is identified precisely and exclusively with him. The initial use of αὐτός rather than ὅς must be translated intensively: it is *he himself*, and no other, who is our peace. This is reinforced through several repetitions of the personal pronoun αὐτός, especially where the reflexive would normally be expected.[59] It is also here, where the prophetic strain of scripture is most prominent, that we find the letter's only explicit reference to the law as such, a wholly negative dismissal.

By way of thematic analysis, we may set these verses out as follows:

F₁	Αὐτὸς γάρ ἐστιν ἡ εἰρήνη ἡμῶν,
P₁	ὁ ποιήσας τὰ ἀμφότερα ἓν
N₁	καὶ τὸ μεσότοιχον τοῦ φραγμοῦ λύσας,

---

[59] Textual variants exist correcting the two instances of ἐν αὐτῷ to ἐν ἑαυτῷ; the second instance is much less well attested, presumably because in that case σταυρός can be taken as the antecedent. This latter reading, although plausible in itself, should be rejected in view of the emphatic fourfold iteration of αὐτός, which strongly implies continuity of referent. Daniel B. Wallace (*Greek Grammar beyond the Basics: An Exegetical Syntax of the New Testament* (Grand Rapids, MI: Zondervan, 1996), 325) lists 2.15 (not 2.16) as a rare example of a reflexive use of αὐτός. I would see the usage in both verses not as 'uncouth' (Barth, *Ephesians*, 295, n. 184) but as marked, underlining the persistent agency of the person of Christ.

N₂	τὴν ἔχθραν ἐν τῇ σαρκὶ αὐτοῦ,
N₃	τὸν νόμον τῶν ἐντολῶν ἐν δόγμασιν καταργήσας,
P₂	ἵνα τοὺς δύο κτίσῃ ἐν αὐτῷ εἰς ἕνα καινὸν ἄνθρωπον
F₂	ποιῶν εἰρήνην
P₃	καὶ ἀποκαταλλάξῃ τοὺς ἀμφοτέρους ἐν ἑνὶ σώματι τῷ θεῷ διὰ τοῦ σταυροῦ,
N₄	ἀποκτείνας τὴν ἔχθραν ἐν αὐτῷ.

The pattern at first looks chiastic, but does not turn out that way. Rather, the foundational note, Christ's constitution of peace (F), is being developed in two tiers at once: his positive work, what he has *made* (P), and his negative work, what he has *destroyed* (N). Interspersed are references to the *place* or *means* of this event (italicized prepositional phrases). These distinctions help to clarify what is going on here; the sense is made somewhat obscure by the intricate syntax and the almost cyclical recurrence of several ideas.[60] I will discuss briefly three points in this passage where Pauline intertextuality is important: one that touches again on the persistent connections with Rom. 3 and two that will be relevant to the reworking of 'reconciliation'.

1. The law. Integral to Christ's act of new creation is the destruction of the existing barrier between Jew and Gentile. Ephesians states with unique directness that the law itself institutes the social division of Jew from Gentile, overcome for Christians. This may be inferred as a corollary of, for example, the instructions on common dining (Rom. 14, 1 Cor. 8-10), but it is made explicit when the law (N₃) is aligned with the 'dividing wall' (N₁) and the 'enmity' (N₂, N₄). Rom. 3 is still very much in the background here: the realignment treated in Romans through the language of 'justifying' is here reframed in terms of 'reconciliation'. Since God is one, and justifies Jew and Gentile in the same way, whatever has previously divided the two peoples is now destroyed, up to and including the law in its negative aspect. Of course, there is ambivalence about the law in Rom. 3 as elsewhere in Paul, and that is evident also in Ephesians, but it is principally the negative side that is developed here.

The letters' agreement on this point is easily overlooked, because the closest verbal parallel to Eph. 2.15 is Rom. 3.31, where similar words are put to a different end: νόμον οὖν καταργοῦμεν διὰ τῆς πίστεως; μὴ γένοιτο. But Rom. 3.27 has already established an opposition between the νόμος πίστεως and νόμος ἔργων, and it is the former, not the latter, that Paul upholds. The triplicate formulation in Eph. 2.15, νόμος τῶν ἐντολῶν ἐν δόγμασιν, belongs with the latter, treating the law as a body of regulation and emphasizing its multiplicity and prescriptiveness. Both Ephesians and Romans are careful to restrict the sense of 'law' to which their most

---

[60] Many commentators have postulated a hymnic source to lie behind this passage, but that theory tends to explain away its difficulties, and should be resisted. As Schnackenburg observes, the prose style here resembles the equally elaborate blessing of ch. 1 (*Epheser*, 107). For a summary of arguments for and against the 'hymn' (concluding against), see Best, *Ephesians*, 247-50.

sweeping indictments are applied.[61] There remains the law as Israel's scripture and symbol; it is in this qualified sense that it is counted among her blessings in Rom. 9.4, a restriction implied by the word νομοθεσία as distinct from νόμος (and as we have seen, the parallel in Eph. 2.12 is charier still and omits it altogether). Later, Ephesians will quote authoritatively from the Pentateuch (Gen. 2.24 at Eph. 5.31, Ex. 20.12 at Eph. 6.2-3), showing the law in its positive, 'scriptural' light, not unlike the quotation of Lev. 19.18 in the generally polemical Galatians (5.14); but that is not the strain developed in Eph. 2. Paul's use of the word νόμος is notoriously elastic, and altogether Ephesians falls well within the spectrum attested in the undisputed letters, inclining to the negative side.

2. The new man. Corresponding to Christ's negative work in destroying the barrier, his positive work is given threefold expression: he has 'made both one', 'created the two into one new man' and 'reconciled both to God'. These three statements should be read in relation to each other, which will be important for understanding what is meant by 'reconciliation', but a word first on the former two. The movement from the neuter in P_1 (ποιήσας τὰ ἀμφότερα ἕν) to the masculine in P_2 (ἵνα τοὺς δύο κτίσῃ ἐν αὐτῷ εἰς ἕνα καινὸν ἄνθρωπον) is probably just a corollary of the shifting imagery, from constructed entities (a dividing wall) to persons. The former anticipates the building metaphor of vv. 19-22, where one new temple is being made out of diverse materials; the latter restates the same idea in terms closer to the Christological heart of the present verses. The change of verb from ποιέω to κτίζω, from craftsmanship to creation, can be similarly understood, but the effect is to move into much more pointed connection with the parallel texts, particularly 2 Cor. 5 (the καινὴ κτίσις) and Col. 1 (reconciliation in the person of Christ).

V. 15 has been badly served by translators. The ESV is typical of modern versions: 'that he might create in himself one new man in place of the two'. The problem is already embryonically present in the AV, 'for to make in himself of twain one new man', or Luther, 'auf daß er aus zweien einen neuen Menschen in ihm selber schüfe'. These versions have in common a syntactical transposition, by which the 'one new man' rather than 'the two' becomes the object of the verb, and the preposition εἰς is suppressed. More strictly: 'that in himself he might create the two into one new man'. The paraphrase may seem harmless enough, but it loses the connection with Col. 1.20 (ἀποκαταλλάξαι τὰ πάντα εἰς αὐτόν). Moreover, the ESV's intruding 'in place of' shows where it can lead: the misconstrual that the new has displaced the old, that former identities have been simply superseded, rather than reshaped through the removal of division.[62] This passage continues the dialectic we have already observed between the newness of the Gentile Christians' identity and its dependence on Jewish particularity; similarly here, Isaiah's peace is reinterpreted both as the overcoming of hostility

---

[61] In this 'qualifying' reading of the phrase τῶν ἐντολῶν ἐν δόγμασιν, I am in agreement with Muddiman (*Ephesians*, 133).

[62] The Vulgate's reading is interesting for a different reason: 'ut duos condat in semet ipsum in unum novum hominem'. This is obviously much closer to the original, with one exception: the choice of 'ipsum' rather than 'ipso' implies the identification of the new man with Christ himself. I agree that the text prompts this inference, but the Latin flags it much more baldly than does the Greek.

between existing parties and as a new creation. To collapse the tension in favour of either novelty or continuity is a tempting but erroneous simplification.[63]

3. In one body. The various prepositional phrases italicized in the analysis above (p. 116–17), taken together, are exceptionally emphatic. Christ has wrought his reconciliation 'in his flesh ... in him[self] ... in one body ... through the cross ... in him[self]'. In the space of just three short verses, the Christ-event, his person and death, could hardly be more decisively underlined; the similarly rich sequence of prepositional phrases in Col. 1.19-22 lies behind this. V. 16a is of chief interest here, where the Ephesians have been reconciled *in* one body, *to* God, *through* the cross. Note that the word ἀποκαταλλάσσω is not used directly of the union between Jew and Gentile: they are said to be reconciled to God, not to one another. Their interior concord, the 'horizontal' dimension, is expressed here in the oneness of the body, and as one body, they are 'vertically' reconciled with God.[64]

The syntax here is intricate and there is some ambiguity in the order of ideas. Ἵνα governs both κτίσῃ and ἀποκαταλλάξῃ, so the new creation and the reconciliation together state the result or (more likely) purpose of the destruction of the wall, and so on: 'that in himself he might create the two into one new man – making peace – and reconcile both in one body to God through the cross'. This seems to be conceptually (though not chronologically) a two-stage process: the two parties joined into one, and then in that new, single body, reconciled to God. In fact τοὺς δύο κτίσῃ ... εἰς ἕνα seems to amplify, rather than to ground, ποιήσας τὰ ἀμφότερα ἕν, and in that sense may be more consecutive than final, but the real purpose is the completion of reconciliation in the 'vertical' relationship.[65]

On this reading, ἀποκαταλλάξῃ identifies the ultimate purpose of Christ's work, and ἐν ἑνὶ σώματι summarizes the way in which it is achieved, the one new man who has been newly created of Jew and Gentile, the one body in which they are together brought near to God. Taking P_1, P_2 and P_3 together, Christ is said to have 'made both one', 'created the two in himself into one new man' and 'reconciled both in one body to God'. Ultimate, vertical reconciliation to God, the summative point of the passage, depends upon and takes place within horizontal reconciliation into one new body. Even without any further development of the σῶμα theme, its relation to 1 Cor. 12 and Rom. 12 is unmistakeable, an area to be greatly amplified in Eph. 4 and 5. This will be the subject of our next chapter, and here I simply note the importance of the

---

[63] Lincoln's comment tends in this direction: 'The "new man" created in Christ (2.15) is a third entity, distinct from and superseding the former categories of Jew and Gentile; to suppose that the readers have been integrated into Israel underestimates the newness of this community' (*Ephesians*, xcii-xciii). But integration into Israel on the one hand, and the supersession of former categories on the other, are not the only alternatives.

[64] R. Martin argues that reconciliation with God is the intention of the underlying 'hymn', and that the author has extended this to include also human reconciliation (*Reconciliation*, 174). But without the scaffolding of the speculative hymn thesis, Martin's conclusion that the 'dividing wall' refers in the first instance to divine–human alienation looks very improbable. The relation between the horizontal and vertical dimensions of reconciliation seems to me just as central irrespective of the source history.

[65] The syntax becomes tortuous if the four aorist participles are taken to be strictly parallel, which makes the double-barrelled ἵνα clause parenthetical, and yields the following:

connection: the church is 'one body' precisely and only as the body *of Christ*. That is to say, the 'one body' here can stand for the community of believers only because it first stands for Christ's own personal body. The same, I would argue, can also be said of the antecedent phrase that defines the 'one body' here. The 'one new man' is, in the first instance, Christ himself, and by participation in his corporate identity, the church of Jew and Gentile.

So much for the distinctive Ephesian context of reconciliation. How does this build upon the earlier texts quoted above? We will follow them in reverse chronological order, beginning with Col. 1.19-23a, which is of course the closest parallel. It gives the only other NT attestation of the word ἀποκαταλλάσσω, a double compound of the kind so dear to Ephesians and Colossians.[66] It shares the emphasis on making peace (εἰρηνοποιήσας), the agency of the cross (διὰ τοῦ αἵματος τοῦ σταυροῦ αὐτοῦ), the location in one body (ἐν τῷ σώματι) and the final directedness towards God (παραστῆσαι ὑμᾶς … κατενώπιον αὐτοῦ). As is often the case with these two letters, however, the close correspondence can mask the distinctiveness of Ephesians's new interpretation.

These verses of Col. 1 see a transition from the Christ-hymn, ending in v. 20, to the readers in v. 21 (and eventually to Paul at the end of v. 23), reflected in the two occurrences of the word ἀποκαταλλάσσω. The first (v. 20) is a Christological statement, a summation of what has preceded: the image of God, all things created through him, the head of the body, and so on. Christ's relationship with God and his role in creation are expressed in brief as cosmic reconciliation (τὰ πάντα εἰς αὐτόν).[67] The transition from hymn to personal address is from the universal to the particular, and when the readers are told that they too have been reconciled (v. 22), this is grounded in what has just been said of all creation: it is not first and foremost *their* story, but they are participants in a prior and grander reconciliation. In their case it means being brought from a state of alienation and hostility into the presence of God; interpersonal reconciliation is not at all in focus.

The measure of Ephesians's reworking is evident from the quite different usage of the words ἀπηλλοτριωμένοι and ἐχθροί. In Col. 1.21-22, they describe the former

> For it is he who is our peace: he who made both one, and broke down the dividing wall, the enmity, in his flesh, made void the law of the commandments in [all its] ordinances – so as to create the two in himself into one new man, making peace, and to reconcile both to God in one body through the cross – [he who] killed the enmity in himself.

That analysis prioritizes syntactical pedantry over sense; it is better to treat the ἀποκτείνας phrase simply as an afterthought.

[66] Is there any real difference in meaning between καταλλάσσω and ἀποκαταλλάσσω? Best, *Ephesians*, 264, cites the view of Chrysostom, among others, that the double compound suggests the 'restoration of a once-lost unity', only to rule this out because Christ is the subject of the verb (in Ephesians, that is), whereas prelapsarian union was with God. But apart from the fact that this rather begs the theological question – why could Paul not suggest that Christ was in Paradise? – the reconciliation in Eph. 2.16 is in any case *to God*. I see no reason to reject Chrysostom's reading.

[67] The subject here is πᾶν τὸ πλήρωμα, and Christ is referred to with the personal pronoun (ἐν αὐτῷ … δι᾽ αὐτοῦ … εἰς αὐτόν). I suspect that this diction is carried over into Eph. 2 even though the subject is there changed to Christ, and that this lies behind the marked use of the personal rather than reflexive pronoun (see n. 59 above). That explanation does not make it any less emphatic, of course.

divine–human relationship: they were alienated and hostile 'in mind, by evil deeds' (τῇ διανοίᾳ ἐν τοῖς ἔργοις τοῖς πονηροῖς) but are now brought before God (ἁγίους καὶ ἀμώμους καὶ ἀνεγκλήτους κατενώπιον αὐτοῦ). The Ephesians, on the other hand, were alienated (ἀπηλλοτριωμένοι) from the people of Israel (2.12), and the hostility (ἔχθρα) destroyed by Christ refers at least in the first instance to the Jew–Gentile division (2.14; cf. more ambiguously 2.16). On the other hand, the word ἀποκαταλλάσσω is reserved in Ephesians as in Colossians for the 'Godward' relationship. So from this cluster of related vocabulary, all used 'vertically' in Colossians, Ephesians reworks some but not all into a 'horizontal' sense so that the Jew–Gentile relationship is expressed with powerful echoes of divine–human concord. It may be strictly correct to say that Eph. 2 does not treat 'the reconciliation of Jew and Gentile', since ἀποκαταλλάσσω is not used in that way, but that is a trifle pedantic. Eph. 2 reworks Col. 1 to show horizontal reconciliation as the corollary, even the condition of the vertical.

The cosmic scope of Col. 1 is less immediately evident in Eph. 2: the whole human race is certainly embraced in this reconciliation to God, but it begins from and ends with the readers in particular, and there is no mention of non-human creation.[68] Still one can hear lingering overtones of the universal in the language reworked from Colossians. In Col. 1.20, the whole creation (τὰ πάντα) is reconciled εἰς αὐτόν; this builds upon the earlier statement that τὰ πάντα δι' αὐτοῦ καὶ εἰς αὐτὸν ἔκτισται (1.16). When, in Eph. 2.15, we are told that Jew and Gentile are created (κτίζω) in him into (εἰς) one new man, the resonance is unmistakeable. A Christological reading of the καινὸς ἄνθρωπος then suggests itself much more vividly, and immediately makes sense both of the creation language and of the especially persistent emphasis on the person of Christ. The drama of the universe is encapsulated in the reconciliation of Jew and Gentile. All things and both peoples are reconciled into him – the new man – and through him, to God.[69]

A similar observation may be made about Eph. 2.16, where the readers are said to be reconciled 'in one body, to God, through the cross'. If the 'body' here means a social group, that can hardly escape the theological weighting given to the term in later chapters; on the other hand, given the proximity to 'the cross', it may mean Christ's physical body. In fact Col. 1 distinguishes between the two senses, referring both to Christ's body the church (1.18) and to the 'body of his flesh' which died (1.22). Eph. 2 does not make this distinction and, by omitting Colossians's reference to 'his flesh', resists an exclusively 'physical' interpretation of the body. Ephesians here brings together what Colossians separates, and so anticipates the fuller discussion in Eph. 4

---

[68] This is taken by one commentator as 'a case where it may be felt that Col. is secondary to Eph.' (R. McL. Wilson, *A Critical and Exegetical Commentary on Colossians and Philemon*, ICC (London: Clark, 2005), 155). Wilson is following C. F. D. Moule's suggestion (*The Epistles of Paul the Apostle to the Colossians and to Philemon*, CGTC (Cambridge: CUP, 1957), 71) that Ephesians's idea of reconciliation is 'more intelligible' because this is an interpersonal rather than a cosmic term. In fact, Colossians's usage seems to me a perfectly normal example of metaphorical religious language, quite consonant with the letter's generally personalized and hostile view of the cosmos.

[69] The creation of two into one new man clearly complements the division of Adam in Gen. 2, and so recalls the Adamic Christology of 1 Cor. 15 and Rom. 5. It is only suggested here, but will become clearer in Eph. 5; see Chapter 4, §3.4 below.

and 5: the church is a body only insofar as it is Christ's body. The body which died and the body which lives are closely identified in this letter, and that is already suggested in 2.14-16.

Finally, the conditionality introduced with Col. 1.23 – 'if indeed you persist in the faith …' – is absent from Ephesians. Probably we should take this εἴ γε clause to modify παραστῆσαι rather than the finite and complete ἀποκατήλλαξεν: Christ has achieved the reconciliation of all things, including you, with the *object* of presenting you blameless before God, but that end depends upon your persistence. We may say that the ethical concern of Colossians has been reworked into a social-religious focus in Ephesians. Ephesians will, of course, offer exhortation enough in due course, but at this point the appeal is not to right behaviour but to right self-understanding, and the paranetic note is not to the purpose.[70]

'People do not go to documents to pillage words and ignore their thought', runs one sceptical comment on this intertextual relationship.[71] Best thinks that the similarities between Col. 1.19-22 and Eph. 2.14-16 should be attributed to a common source, or a common 'school', rather than a literary relationship.[72] To my mind, the opposite conclusion is more probable. Where familiar diction is turned to new purposes, or ideas arranged in a new constellation, we have evidence of reception and interpretation, whether by the same author or some other. Ephesians categorically does not 'ignore the thought' of Colossians, any more than it slavishly reproduces it, but does exactly what a later, interpretative text would be expected to do: reworks its material critically and creatively for its own rhetorical purpose.[73]

Following the trail back one step further, we come to Romans. Rom. 5.10 is particularly pertinent to the treatment of reconciliation in both Eph. 2 and Col. 1; if 2 Cor. 5 is the earliest source of Paul's reconciliation language, it is in Rom. 5 that he first relates it specifically to the death of Christ, and names the enmity which is overcome in him. This passage, Rom. 5.1-11, is of course much debated and can be approached from many angles. For our purposes, the interplay between present and future – justification received and salvation awaited – is a helpful point of departure. The distinction is teased out in Rom. 5.9-10 through a double couplet:

---

[70] R. Martin makes a great deal of the ethical side of Col. 1.19-22, in fact arguing that in this letter, 'reconciliation is primarily concerned with the *restoration of personal relationships*' (*Reconciliation*, 121; his emphasis), partly because of the implied reference to 2 Cor. 5. Actually I think that Col. 1 can be read in this way *only* if both 2 Corinthians and Ephesians are kept in mind; Colossians alone does not place the same weight on the interpersonal. It is all concerned with the 'Godward' relationship, cosmically in v. 20, personally in vv. 21-22.

[71] Best, *Ephesians*, 265.

[72] For fuller discussion see Ernest Best, 'Who Used Whom? The Relationship of Ephesians and Colossians', NTS 43 (1997): 72–96.

[73] E. P. Sanders reads Colossians itself in a similar, unnecessarily contrastive way: for him, the letter's pseudonymity is practically proven by the differences between this passage and 2 Cor. 5 and Rom. 5 ('Literary Dependence in Colossians', JBL 85 (1966): 28–45 (37–9)). He claims that when familiar language is applied to new and different purposes, we should recognize the hand of an imitator. Sigurd Grindheim rightly responds, 'It is characteristic of Paul that he reapplies his core ideas to the practical issues at hand' ('A Deutero-Pauline Mystery? Ecclesiology in Colossians and Ephesians', in *Paul and Pseudepigraphy*, ed. Stanley E. Porter and Gregory P. Fewster, PaSt 8 (Leiden: Brill, 2013), 173–95 (179, n. 11)).

A₁ πολλῷ οὖν μᾶλλον δικαιωθέντες νῦν ἐν τῷ αἵματι αὐτοῦ
B₁ σωθησόμεθα δι' αὐτοῦ ἀπὸ τῆς ὀργῆς.
A₂ εἰ γὰρ ἐχθροὶ ὄντες κατηλλάγημεν τῷ θεῷ διὰ τοῦ θανάτου τοῦ υἱοῦ αὐτοῦ,
B₂ πολλῷ μᾶλλον καταλλαγέντες σωθησόμεθα ἐν τῇ ζωῇ αὐτοῦ.

The precise parallel in syntax is between A–B₁ and B₂, but in each case the present condition is amplified first (A), and then the corresponding future salvation (B). In the latter case, the verb is identical (σωθησόμεθα), with the result that a strong correspondence is established between the two former verbs, δικαιόω and καταλλάσσω. Accordingly, when Ephesians adopts much of the logic of Rom. 3, but develops it in terms of 'reconciliation' rather than 'justification', it is following a precedent already set in Rom. 5.[74]

In fact, according to these verses, reconciliation sums up and even incorporates justification. The two couplets stand in a sort of implicit nested structure. Each follows Paul's familiar πολλῷ μᾶλλον reasoning, stepping from the lesser to the greater, but less obviously, the second couplet stands in a similar, consecutive relation to the first: 'If (justified in blood) → (saved from wrath), *how much more* (reconciled through death) → (saved in life)'. A₂ may look like an intrusion into an otherwise neat syntactic parallel, but its function is to reformulate the conclusion of A–B₁ into a new premise for B₂. To paraphrase: '... we shall be saved from wrath; that is to say, although we were by rights his enemies, we have been reconciled to God through his son's death. How much more then, being so reconciled through his death, shall we be saved in his life!' We are saved both *from* something and *for* something, and the latter, being the object of the whole operation, is the greater. So Paul will even go so far as to boast in it (5.11).[75] Justification is swallowed up in reconciliation, which in turn draws beyond itself to its object, God; these ideas are suggested only in embryo here, but developed more fully in Ephesians.

If this reading is correct, it sheds light upon a curiosity of Eph. 2: despite being so deeply grounded in the logic of Rom. 3, it contains no language of 'justifying' or 'righteousness' at all, with δικ- terminology appearing only in the paranetic material of Eph. 4–6. This is because Ephesians reads Rom. 3 through the lens of Rom. 5, not Rom. 4. The Paul of Romans has to demonstrate the gratuity of salvation, but the Paul of Ephesians need only invoke it. The doctrine itself is apparently not in dispute, though perhaps less familiar to the readers, but its implications for enduring Christian life and identity are very much in focus. This is the stuff of Rom. 5–8 rather than 1–4, so it is entirely logical that Eph. 2 follows the trend set by the transitional Rom. 5.1-11, and adopts the language of reconciliation as apter to the task than justification.

---

[74] R. Martin resists too 'facile' an identification of the two verbs (*Reconciliation*, 138), which is quite right, but I am suggesting analogy rather than identity.

[75] Thus closing the circle with 5.1-2. The passage as a whole defends a 'good' sort of boasting, as against the boast in the law and its works (2.17, 23, 3.27, 4.2). To translate καυχάομαι here as 'rejoice' (AV, etc.) misses this point entirely.

The one other mention of reconciliation in Romans has a similar structure to the couplets of 5.9-10, but the context is very different:

Rom. 11.15 εἰ γὰρ ἡ ἀποβολὴ αὐτῶν καταλλαγὴ κόσμου, τίς ἡ πρόσλημψις εἰ μὴ ζωὴ ἐκ νεκρῶν;

Although this passage is, like Eph. 2, directly about the relationship of Jews and Gentiles, the primary meaning of καταλλαγή evidently remains reconciliation of the world to God, rather than between the peoples. But in view of what follows – the olive tree allegory begins in the next verse – it is possible to detect a hint of the horizontal dimension too. At the least, Paul is here introducing the motif of cosmic reconciliation into a controversy explicitly about Jew–Gentile relations, which is a step further than he goes in Rom. 5, and may well have prompted the further amplification that occurs in Eph. 2.

In 11.15 as in 5.10-11, reconciliation has already been achieved, and is interpreted as the pledge of something greater yet to come: there being 'saved by his life', here 'life from the dead'. In ch. 11 we learn that this consummation will coincide with the final inclusion of all Israel, for which Paul so urgently longs, further sharpening the already acute tension between present and future. Such temporal tension is less pronounced in Ephesians.[76] As we have seen, the letter views the Israel–church question from a standpoint of fulfilment, which goes some way to elucidating its distinctive sense of 'reconciliation'. In Eph. 2, unlike Romans, 'life' is not mentioned at all; the keynote is 'peace', of which accomplished reconciliation is an effective instrument. As in Romans, it points beyond itself, but to a condition already present, not a resurrection awaited. In Ephesians Paul invites his readers to look not forward but back: they will fully appropriate their present peace and reconciliation only by understanding their former alienation.

We should also note a particularly close parallel between Rom. 5 and Col. 1 which is not altogether followed in Ephesians:

Rom. 5.10a	εἰ γὰρ ἐχθροὶ ὄντες κατηλλάγημεν τῷ θεῷ
	διὰ τοῦ θανάτου τοῦ υἱοῦ αὐτοῦ
Col. 1.21-22	Καὶ ὑμᾶς ποτε ὄντας ... ἐχθροὺς ...
	νυνὶ δὲ ἀποκατήλλαξεν ... διὰ τοῦ θανάτου

The identification of reconciliation with Christ's death, in particular, is traceable to Romans, and relates to the close analogy between justification and reconciliation. It is amplified in Colossians through the mention of 'the blood of the cross' (1.20; cf. Rom. 5.9, δικαιωθέντες νῦν ἐν τῷ αἵματι αὐτοῦ) and 'the body of his flesh' (1.22). In Eph. 2,

---

[76] This commonplace observation is often overstated, but that does not mean it is without truth. An example of the exaggeration is Lindemann's study of Ephesians, its thesis indicated in the title, *Die Aufhebung der Zeit*. This is another instance where the relentless need to make Ephesians different has skewed interpretation, magnifying its distinctiveness to the point of caricature.

most of these words appear (not θάνατος), but scattered throughout the passage such that the tight nexus of 'death' and 'reconciliation' is loosened. When it comes to the explicit mention of the cross, Ephesians is markedly less graphic:

Eph. 2.16 ἀποκαταλλάξῃ τοὺς ἀμφοτέρους ἐν ἑνὶ σώματι τῷ θεῷ διὰ τοῦ σταυροῦ, ἀποκτείνας τὴν ἔχθραν ἐν αὐτῷ.

The verb ἀποκτείνω is not an obvious way to express the neutralization of enmity, and receives some of the weight of the preceding word, σταυρός, the violence of literal crucifixion being at least partly sublimated into the metaphorical. What is killed on the cross? The enmity between Jew and Gentile.[77] Eph. 2 does not retreat from the sacrificial language of Rom. 5 and Col. 1, but does shift the emphasis away from the physical death of Jesus to its ecclesial significance. One reason for this may be closer identification between the 'one body' on the cross (2.16) and the 'one body' of the church (4.4): the body in which we are reconciled is the living body of Christ. (More on this in Chapter 4, §3.4.)

Finally, then, to 2 Corinthians, the fountainhead of this stream of Pauline thought.[78] It is a letter that concerns reconciliation at multiple levels, but only in 5.18-20 do the words καταλλάσσω and καταλλαγή occur, and consistently with later CP usage, God is the goal. Elsewhere, the reconciliation between Paul and the Corinthians, or within the Corinthian church, is discussed in other terms (e.g. the ubiquitous παρακαλέω). The analogy has often been recognized;[79] one scholar, whose own concern is only with Paul's appeal for interpersonal reconciliation, argues that this aspect is given 'greater weight and significance' by the way it frames the specifically theological claim of ch. 5.[80] Such breadth in the concept of reconciliation, while the word itself is limited to the divine–human relationship, foreshadows the later letters and especially Ephesians. Three other aspects that will recur consistently are also present here, though not quite as we have seen them elsewhere: reconciliation is received through participation in Christ, is cosmic in scope and is a fact already achieved. The following discussion will amplify each of these.

The verses leading up to 5.18 place particular emphasis on participation in Christ. 'One has died for all, therefore all have died', and live for him (5.14-15); and those who are 'in him', if seen truly (not according to the flesh), are a 'new creation' (5.16-17). At

---

[77] Cf. Col. 2.14, where the 'record against us in prescriptions' (τὸ καθ' ἡμῶν χειρόγραφον τοῖς δόγμασιν) is 'nailed to the cross'.

[78] The 'secular' use of καταλλάσσω in 1 Cor. 7.11 (the reconciliation of a wife to her estranged husband) is not relevant. It has been proposed that in 2 Cor. 5, pre-Pauline material is being reworked (Martin, *Reconciliation*, 93–7, referring also to the earlier work of Käsemann), but that is not generally accepted and seems to me quite unnecessary. Of course, if Campbell's chronology is correct, Ephesians would be the point of origin and 2 Corinthians among the receiving texts. This is an exemplary case where Campbell would need to show that his proposal could make better *exegetical* sense than the conventional chronology followed here.

[79] Some of the relevant scholarship is cited in Ivar Vegge, *2 Corinthians – a Letter about Reconciliation: A Psychagogical, Epistolographical and Rhetorical Analysis*, WUNT 2 239 (Tübingen: Mohr Siebeck, 2008), 51, n. 212.

[80] Ibid., 52.

5.18, there is an abrupt change of grammatical subject to God; the subject of discourse apparently changes, too, and we find ourselves talking about reconciliation without any clearly defined transition. The segue simply runs τὰ δὲ πάντα ἐκ τοῦ θεοῦ, which apparently means that it is these things just discussed – participation in Christ – which are now approached under the rubric of reconciliation.[81] The question of agency is of particular interest here: καταλλάσσω is treated as a quasi-reflexive verb, in fact, with God both subject and (indirect) object. God reconciles – to himself. This he does through Christ, and finally he devolves the corresponding ministry to 'us' (whether Paul, the apostles or the church as a whole). The elements are set out in v. 18 and closely repeated, with amplification, in the following verse:[82]

5.18		τὰ δὲ πάντα ἐκ τοῦ θεοῦ
	(1)	τοῦ καταλλάξαντος ἡμᾶς ἑαυτῷ
	(2)	διὰ Χριστοῦ
	(3)	καὶ δόντος ἡμῖν τὴν διακονίαν τῆς καταλλαγῆς,
5.19		ὡς ὅτι θεὸς
	(2)	ἦν ἐν Χριστῷ
	(1)	κόσμον καταλλάσσων ἑαυτῷ,
		(μὴ λογιζόμενος αὐτοῖς τὰ παραπτώματα αὐτῶν)
	(3)	καὶ θέμενος ἐν ἡμῖν τὸν λόγον τῆς καταλλαγῆς.

There is, then, an outward trajectory in the agency of reconciliation, God → Christ → us → you, and in its horizon from us to the whole world; at the same time, there is a gravitational attraction back to the God who originates this process, and is also its final object. For this reason I think it is more than stylistic variation when God's work 'through Christ' (v. 18) is rearticulated as God's 'being in Christ' (v. 19), just as believers too are 'in Christ' (v. 17).[83] Christ is not merely the means by which reconciliation is wrought, but himself the place in which it is effected, the meeting point of God and humanity. God acts in Christ to make himself and humanity one, and not only humanity but the whole κόσμος (v. 19). So although the shift from 'new creation' in v. 17 to 'reconciliation' in vv. 18-20 initially seems abrupt, it is a logical connection. The

---

[81] Most exegetes read τὰ δὲ πάντα in this way, i.e. 'all this', since the more literal 'all things' makes little sense; see e.g. Margaret E. Thrall, *A Critical and Exegetical Commentary on the Second Epistle to the Corinthians*, ICC (Edinburgh: Clark, 1994), 429, and references there. The theme of participation is taken still further in the concluding v. 21: ἵνα ἡμεῖς γενώμεθα δικαιοσύνη θεοῦ ἐν αὐτῷ.

[82] The ambiguous connection ὡς ὅτι is best understood epexegetically, 'that is to say' (so e.g. Thomas Schmeller, *Der zweite Brief an die Korinther*, vol. 1, EKKNT 8 (Neukirchen: Neukirchner & Patmos, 2010), 331).

[83] I read ἦν and καταλλάσσων as distinct in sense, not a single periphrastic verb, and therefore ἐν Χριστῷ as the complement of θεός rather than an adverbial phrase. This is probably a minority view (see references in ibid.). The fact that Paul normally attributes 'being in Christ' to believers does not make it any less likely that he would here say the same of God; on the contrary, it lends that claim additional theological depth (against Thrall, *2 Corinthians*, 433).

new creation extends to the bounds of the universe, but only insofar as it participates in Christ, who brings all things together by reconciling them to God.

Participation in Christ is central to reconciliation also for Col. 1 and Eph. 2, but each develops it in a somewhat different direction.[84] The relentless Christological prepositional phrases that both letters attach to reconciliation – ἐν αὐτῷ, δι' αὐτοῦ and so on – are ultimately traceable to the 2 Cor. 5 emphasis on God's action *in Christ*. For Colossians, the greater weight falls upon Christ as both the origin and goal of creation; since all things were created 'for him' (1.16), it is only natural that all things should be reconciled to God 'through him' (1.20). The correspondence is in some ways extremely close: Col. 1.19-20 (ὅτι ἐν αὐτῷ εὐδόκησεν πᾶν τὸ πλήρωμα κατοικῆσαι καὶ δι' αὐτοῦ ἀποκαταλλάξαι τὰ πάντα εἰς αὐτόν) is really no less than an interpretative riff on 2 Cor. 5.19a (θεὸς ἦν ἐν Χριστῷ κόσμον καταλλάσσων ἑαυτῷ).[85] 2 Cor. 5.19 states explicitly that the whole created order (κόσμος) is the object of reconciliation, an accent echoed briefly in Rom. 11.15 and developed more extensively in Col 1, but more muted in Rom. 5 and Eph. 2.[86]

With its increased emphasis on Christ's role at the beginning of all things, Colossians loses the distinctiveness of the *new* creation. For Ephesians, though, it is newness in particular that is brought to the fore. The constructive work of Christ is to 'create the two in himself into one new person' (ἵνα τοὺς δύο κτίσῃ ἐν αὐτῷ εἰς ἕνα καινὸν ἄνθρωπον). This is no mere echo, but an exegetical gloss on the καινὴ κτίσις of 2 Cor. 5.17. In the earlier letter, the phrase could be taken severally – everyone who participates in Christ is personally 'recreated' – or epiphenomenonally – when anyone is in Christ, new creation 'occurs'.[87] As interpreted in Ephesians, however, the new creation is a single 'new person', not only an individual but a corporate identity in whom the readers are able to participate. This sounds suspiciously like a variation on the 'body of Christ' motif, as sure enough the following verse makes plain ('to reconcile both *in one body* to God …'). Ephesians here is grounded in the deeply incarnational logic of 2 Cor. 5 but, characteristically, tends towards an ecclesiological interpretation in its reworking of the earlier letter.[88]

---

[84] Rom. 5 is the odd one out in this respect. On the other hand, the words μὴ λογιζόμενος αὐτοῖς τὰ παραπτώματα αὐτῶν (2 Cor. 5.19) have a similar function to ἐχθροὶ ὄντες (Rom. 5.10). In this instance it is the Romans, not the 2 Corinthians vocabulary, that is taken up in Colossians and Ephesians.

[85] Which incidentally means that Colossians supports the non-periphrastic reading of ἦν … καταλλάσσων.

[86] The word κόσμος does not occur in this part of Colossians, but the whole hymnic passage paraphrases it emphatically. We have already noted that, although the cosmic scope of reconciliation is not explicit in Eph. 2, it is still a significant overtone. It is also arguably suggested in Rom. 5 when the discussion proceeds immediately to the cosmic scope of sin (5.12–13) and, by implication, Christ's remedy.

[87] The phrase in 2 Cor. 5.17 has many other possible interpretations. I agree with Thrall's summary (*2 Corinthians*, 426): 'This Christ "in whom" the believer lives is the last Adam, the inaugurator of the new eschatological humanity. Hence, believers themselves become newly-created: the most obvious explanation of καινὴ κτίσις is that it means "newly created being", in whom the lost divine likeness is regained.' If this is right, then Eph. 2.15 is an *accurate* gloss.

[88] Later in Ephesians, the invitation to participate in the 'new man' becomes more explicit: ἐνδύσασθαι τὸν καινὸν ἄνθρωπον τὸν κατὰ θεὸν κτισθέντα (4.24). Cf. the similar use of ἐνδύω in Col. 3.10 and

The other familiar aspect of reconciliation in 2 Cor. 5 is its alignment with the completed work of Christ rather than the awaited future, but there is a certain ambiguity here which is unlike the later letters. It corresponds to the differing agencies associated with the verb. Where God is the subject, the work is complete;[89] but the 'ministry' and 'message' of reconciliation are not so delimited, and logically must be ongoing. So the following v. 20 sees Paul actually carrying out the ministry he has just claimed as his own, urging the Corinthians to be reconciled to God. The passive imperative καταλλάγητε implies a mixed agency: the readers are to do something, but its substance is to allow something to be done to them.[90] Reconciliation, then, is a fact already established and achieved by God, but it can still be transmitted by God's ministers and, especially, appropriated or reappropriated by God's people.[91]

The eschatological dialectic is especially marked if the first-person pronouns in vv. 18-19 are taken inclusively, as seems best.[92] 'God has reconciled us *all* to himself – now you lot, be reconciled to God.' Paul appeals to the readers to become what they are – to accept and embrace anew what they have already been given. In this respect, 2 Cor. 5 is quite unlike Rom. 5, where reconciliation belongs on the past side of a clear temporal divide, and Col. 1, where the final object of reconciliation (παραστῆσαι ὑμᾶς ...) is conditional upon the readers' persistence. It does, however, closely resemble the larger shape of Eph. 2, where the readers are invited to relearn their identity as Gentile Christians. In this case, it is not so much that Ephesians develops a different strand from the other letters, as that its rhetorical context more nearly approaches 2 Corinthians, and to that extent the resonance between the two letters is richer.

If Paul's theology of reconciliation finds its earliest and most extended expression in 2 Corinthians, it is reworked in Romans, Colossians and Ephesians in three quite distinct ways. Each retains some elements of the first source, but often not the same ones. The participatory Christology is more enthusiastically taken up in Colossians and Ephesians than in Romans; the cosmic scope is developed in Colossians but more muted in Romans and Ephesians; Colossians develops the sacrificial element introduced in Romans, which is still present but softened in Ephesians; the ambiguity in agency and eschatology is treated differently in each letter, with Ephesians approaching

---

1 Cor. 15.53-54, but more especially Gal. 3.27 and Rom. 13.14, where the reference is explicitly to 'putting on Christ'.

[89] However one interprets ἦν ... καταλλάσσων (see n. 83 above), the imperfective participle is dependent on the finite verb for its time reference. 5.18 lacks a finite verb, but from the explication in 5.19 it must be taken as implicitly past tense.

[90] Or perhaps it should be read with a middle or reflexive sense, a possibility advocated by Reimund Bieringer, '"Reconcile Yourselves to God": An Unusual Interpretation of 2 Corinthians 5.20 in Its Context', in *Jesus, Paul and Early Christianity*, FS Henk Jan de Jong, ed. Rieuwerd Buitenwerf, Harm W. Hollander and Johannes Tromp (Leiden: Brill, 2008), 11-38. Bieringer rightly points out that reconciliation is inherently reciprocal, and that stressing the human side should not imply any competition with divine agency (36).

[91] The mixed agency is more pointed in 5.20 than is sometimes realized. If the genitive absolute τοῦ θεοῦ παρακαλοῦντος δι' ἡμῶν is treated as a true parenthesis, it runs, 'So we are ambassadors on Christ's behalf, as we urge you on Christ's behalf – God appealing through us – be reconciled to God.' The continuation in 6.1, Συνεργοῦντες δὲ καὶ παρακαλοῦμεν μὴ εἰς κενὸν τὴν χάριν τοῦ θεοῦ δέξασθαι ὑμᾶς, further underlines both Paul's participation in the agency of God in Christ and the need for the Corinthians' cooperation in realizing the gift they have already received.

[92] So e.g. Thrall, *2 Corinthians*, 430, but it is another disputed point.

2 Corinthians most nearly. And so on. The hermeneutical point, which I hope has become clear, is that the pattern of reception and interpretation does not divide neatly down the middle, with 2 Corinthians and Romans on one side, Colossians and Ephesians on the other – unless, that is, one has decided beforehand to impose this schema on other grounds. To do so is to obscure the complexity of the picture and miss many of the most interesting inflections.

2.5. Foundation and capstone (Eph. 2.19-22)

Eph. 2.19-22 Ἄρα οὖν οὐκέτι ἐστὲ ξένοι καὶ πάροικοι ἀλλ᾽ ἐστὲ συμπολῖται τῶν ἁγίων καὶ οἰκεῖοι τοῦ θεοῦ, ἐποικοδομηθέντες ἐπὶ τῷ θεμελίῳ τῶν ἀποστόλων καὶ προφητῶν, ὄντος ἀκρογωνιαίου αὐτοῦ Χριστοῦ Ἰησοῦ, ἐν ᾧ πᾶσα οἰκοδομὴ συναρμολογουμένη αὔξει εἰς ναὸν ἅγιον ἐν κυρίῳ, ἐν ᾧ καὶ ὑμεῖς συνοικοδομεῖσθε εἰς κατοικητήριον τοῦ θεοῦ ἐν πνεύματι.

1 Cor. 3.9-17 θεοῦ γάρ ἐσμεν συνεργοί, θεοῦ γεώργιον, θεοῦ οἰκοδομή ἐστε. Κατὰ τὴν χάριν τοῦ θεοῦ τὴν δοθεῖσάν μοι ὡς σοφὸς ἀρχιτέκτων θεμέλιον ἔθηκα, ἄλλος δὲ ἐποικοδομεῖ. ἕκαστος δὲ βλεπέτω πῶς ἐποικοδομεῖ. θεμέλιον γὰρ ἄλλον οὐδεὶς δύναται θεῖναι παρὰ τὸν κείμενον, ὅς ἐστιν Ἰησοῦς Χριστός. εἰ δέ τις ἐποικοδομεῖ ἐπὶ τὸν θεμέλιον χρυσόν, ἄργυρον, λίθους τιμίους, ξύλα, χόρτον, καλάμην, ἑκάστου τὸ ἔργον φανερὸν γενήσεται, ἡ γὰρ ἡμέρα δηλώσει, ὅτι ἐν πυρὶ ἀποκαλύπτεται· καὶ ἑκάστου τὸ ἔργον ὁποῖόν ἐστιν τὸ πῦρ [αὐτὸ] δοκιμάσει. εἴ τινος τὸ ἔργον μενεῖ ὃ ἐποικοδόμησεν, μισθὸν λήμψεται· εἴ τινος τὸ ἔργον κατακαήσεται, ζημιωθήσεται, αὐτὸς δὲ σωθήσεται, οὕτως δὲ ὡς διὰ πυρός.

Οὐκ οἴδατε ὅτι ναὸς θεοῦ ἐστε καὶ τὸ πνεῦμα τοῦ θεοῦ οἰκεῖ ἐν ὑμῖν; εἴ τις τὸν ναὸν τοῦ θεοῦ φθείρει, φθερεῖ τοῦτον ὁ θεός· ὁ γὰρ ναὸς τοῦ θεοῦ ἅγιός ἐστιν, οἵτινές ἐστε ὑμεῖς.

By now it is clear that Eph. 2 is intimately integrated with the earlier Pauline letters. Its theological core adheres particularly closely to Rom. 3, but it also depends crucially on allusions to Galatians, 2 Corinthians and elsewhere in Romans, to say nothing of the intricate relationship with Colossians. Now we turn to 1 Corinthians. Like the theme of reconciliation just discussed, the material drawn from this letter enlarges upon the consequences of the readers' incorporation into God's people, and the coherence of the new whole. We have come a long way from the curt reformulation of Rom. 3 in Eph. 2.8, but the many different strands are so skilfully integrated that the transition is hardly noticeable.

Building and dwelling as a metaphor for the church is common throughout the NT, and in the epistles particularly through various cognates and compounds of οἰκέω; 1 Cor. 3 is the earliest and most extended example, and it reappears at length in two later texts, this passage from Eph. 2 and also 1 Pet. 2.4-8 (which I will discuss only incidentally).[93] In Eph. 2 as in 1 Cor. 3, the context concerns the unity of the church;

---

[93] 1 Peter is, quite rightly, no longer regarded as a Pauline text (see e.g. John H. Elliott, *1 Peter*, AB 37B (New York: Doubleday, 2000), 37–40). But the reaction against this old school of thought may perhaps prejudice interpreters in a similar way to the authorship question within the CP, so that

in both cases, the same subject will later be treated more thoroughly under the rubric of the body of Christ; in both cases, the building metaphor serves to illustrate the necessary cohesion of the church, her structural unity resting in Christ, and the indwelling presence of God in the whole. The two letters address different kinds of potential disunity: conflicted parties in 1 Corinthians, Jew and Gentile in Ephesians. The Ephesian Paul, having addressed the Jew–Gentile question head-on in the language of Romans and Galatians, turns now to 1 Corinthians to expand upon the church's growth as a harmonious communion between members and God.

There are really not one but two building metaphors in 1 Cor. 3. In vv. 10-15, the focus is on the builders: whether they are building on the correct foundation, and the relative fireworthiness of their different materials. With v. 16 there is an abrupt transition, and the readers are themselves identified with the building, now called a 'temple'. Eph. 2 follows a similar pattern, beginning with the process of building and ending with the 'temple', the 'spirit' and God's indwelling presence, but in this case, the readers are identified with the building from the outset (ἐστὲ ... ἐποικοδομηθέντες ἐπὶ τῷ θεμελίῳ). The two distinct images from 1 Corinthians have been amalgamated. 1 Peter takes this a step further still, explicitly combining the concrete and the spiritual in the initial address: ὡς λίθοι ζῶντες οἰκοδομεῖσθε οἶκος πνευματικός (2.5). Peter is concerned less with internal unity than with the distinctive holiness of the church, hardly alien to Ephesians (see 4.17-24), but no more the point of Eph. 2 than of 1 Cor. 3. So Ephesians, once again, occupies a mediating position between the earlier Pauline and the non-Pauline text.

There can be no doubt that Eph. 2 is consciously both drawing upon and modifying 1 Cor. 3. A comparison of vocabulary is telling: in the nine verses quoted from 1 Cor. 3, we have one instance each of οἰκοδομή and οἰκέω and four of ἐποικοδομέω. In the space of just four verses of Eph. 2, by contrast, we find no less than six different cognate lexemes: οἰκεῖος, πάροικος, ἐποικοδομέω, οἰκοδομή, συνοικοδομέω and κατοικητήριον; none are repeated, and three are *hapax legomena* for the NT. This undoubtedly reflects the preference in Ephesians for compound words, but should not be written off as merely stylistic; rather, Ephesians here broadens the semantic range of a metaphor that was, in 1 Corinthians, relatively clear-cut. It is not only God's dwelling within a structure of people but also the readers' own belonging, their 'residency' that is in question now. This can be seen clearly in the way that Eph. 2.19 functions as a transitional verse. It harks back to 2.12, summarizing the intervening discussion ('Ἄρα οὖν): 'Remember that you were strangers, but now ... So then, you are no longer strangers.' But at the same time, it conjoins to the vocabulary of the earlier verse new terms that lead into what follows:

ἀπηλλοτριωμένοι τῆς *πολιτείας* τοῦ Ἰσραὴλ (2.12)
→ *συμπολῖται* τῶν ἁγίων *καὶ οἰκεῖοι* τοῦ θεοῦ (2.19)

> Pauline–Petrine continuity is underplayed. The present study makes no assumptions about literary dependencies outside the CP, but intertextual connections between Pauline and non-Pauline texts clearly exist, irrespective of how they got there. This is part of the broader story of the NT's reception as a canonical whole, but cannot be properly investigated here. (See Mitton, *Authorship, Origin and Purpose*, 176-97, for the case for 1 Peter's dependence on Ephesians.)

ξένοι τῶν διαθηκῶν τῆς ἐπαγγελίας (2.12)
→ οὐκέτι ... ξένοι καὶ πάροικοι (2.19)

Via this intermediate sense of 'residency', οἰκέω terminology is introduced as a foil to the readers' former alienation, and then from 2.20 takes over in a plainer building metaphor. The transition is effected very smoothly, and may in fact conceal the breadth this language is now being made to cover. 1 Cor. 3.9, by comparison, is a less subtle hinge-verse, making the move from horticulture to architecture rather abruptly: θεοῦ γεώργιον, θεοῦ οἰκοδομή ἐστε.

Eph. 2.20 introduces two further technical building terms, θεμέλιος and ἀκρογωνιαῖος. Only the former is found in 1 Cor. 3, but the two occur together in Isaiah:

Is. 28.16 Ἰδοὺ ἐγὼ ἐμβαλῶ εἰς τὰ θεμέλια Σιων λίθον πολυτελῆ ἐκλεκτὸν ἀκρογωνιαῖον ἔντιμον εἰς τὰ θεμέλια αὐτῆς, καὶ ὁ πιστεύων ἐπ᾽αὐτῷ οὐ μὴ καταισχυνθῇ.

There is a view that this verse 'was combined with Ps. 117.22 (LXX) to create an early Christian proof-text for the crucifixion and resurrection of Jesus',[94] but in fact 1 Pet. 2.6 is the only NT text to quote them both. A number refer only to the psalm;[95] Rom. 9.33 quotes Is. 28.16, but modifies it considerably to segue into Is. 8.14.[96] I agree that these three verses were, quite probably, associated together in early Christianity, but their distinctive treatments in different NT texts should not be smoothed over. In both Romans and 1 Peter, the two references to the θεμέλια are omitted from the quotation of Is. 28; in the latter case, this harmonizes Isaiah with the psalm (which mentions only the κεφαλὴ γωνίας). Eph. 2.20 is the only NT text to bring together the two words θεμέλιος and ἀκρογωνιαῖος, as per Is. 28. We may say that this echo of the prophet in 1 Cor. 3 is strengthened to a definite allusion in Eph. 2, and becomes an actual quotation in 1 Pet. 2, though there in a way that also reflects Rom. 9. Here again, Ephesians occupies a mediating position.

However, the 'stone' motif is put to unique use in Ephesians. The proper translation of ἀκρογωνιαῖος has long been debated; it is clear at least that for Isaiah it is a foundation stone, whereas for the *Testament of Solomon* (chs 22–23) it is a capstone.[97] If we suppose that both 1 Peter and Ephesians follow the latter sense, then the identification of this stone with the θεμέλια in Is. 28.16 would suggest a disorientingly topsy-turvy architecture, and require amendment. 1 Peter solves the problem by omitting θεμέλια, Ephesians by making a distinction between the two stones: unlike 1 Cor. 3.10-12, the θεμέλιος is the apostles and prophets, and Christ is reassigned to the role of

---

[94] Muddiman, *Ephesians*, 142.
[95] Mt. 21.42, Mk 12.10 and Acts 4.11.
[96] *Pace* Fowl (*Ephesians*, 98), there is no reason to see an allusion to the psalm in Rom. 9.33; nor, *pace* Lincoln (*Ephesians*, 155), to Is. 28.16 in Lk 20.17-18, despite the combination there of the psalm with Is. 8.14-15.
[97] See esp. R. J. McKelvey, 'Christ the Cornerstone', NTS 8 (1962): 352–9, with references to the discussion in the preceding decades.

ἀκρογωνιαῖος. It is mainly because of this distinction that I side with the minority of interpreters who read the latter as 'keystone' or 'capstone' rather than (ground-level) 'cornerstone'.[98]

The precise architectural location, however, is less important than Christ's role in *joining* distinct elements and holding them together, which on any reading the ἀκρογωνιαῖος must do. The transition into building imagery at this point of Eph. 2 is no arbitrary rhetorical sidestep, but further develops the theological thrust of the preceding verses: that God has made a new people not *ex nihilo*, but by uniting in Christ those who were previously divided. As in 1 Corinthians, Paul uses this language to emphasize the unity of the church, but as the particular threat to unity differs, so does the role of Christ in the metaphor. In Corinth, the problem is fissiparous factions who need to learn that there can be no new, separate church: Christ is their one and irreplaceable foundation. The Ephesian Christians, on the other hand, have been graciously integrated into God's people, and are not to forget it: Christ is the crux-stone joining them and others into one building. Hence the emphasis in vv. 21-22 on growing together: συναρμολογουμένη αὔξει … συνοικοδομεῖσθε.

The 'foundation' in Ephesians thus becomes the 'apostles and prophets'. The similar coupling of these two words in 3.5 and 4.11, where the context is unambiguously ecclesial, makes it clear that the primary sense of 'prophets' is Christian. That need not exclude a suggestion of the prophets of Israel, however, an inference singularly appropriate to the theme of Jew–Gentile union; such at least was Origen's view,[99] but it has fallen out of favour in our more literally minded age. At any rate, the church's foundation is identified with the personal testimony to Christ rather than with Christ in his own person. This is not so far from another Pauline example:

Rom. 15.20 οὕτως δὲ φιλοτιμούμενον εὐαγγελίζεσθαι οὐχ ὅπου ὠνομάσθη Χριστός, ἵνα μὴ ἐπ' ἀλλότριον θεμέλιον οἰκοδομῶ

1 Cor. 3.11 forbids the laying of a θεμέλιος ἄλλος, not ἀλλότριος, which makes all the difference. The substance of the foundation does not vary, but the one who lays it may;[100] from there it is a short step to Eph. 2.20. The foundation is *of* the apostles and prophets in a subjective sense, but objectively, its content remains Christ. That at least is the implication when the Pauline texts are read together.

---

[98] So Lincoln, *Ephesians*, 155–6; and Barth, *Ephesians*, 317–19. The reappearance of much of the same vocabulary in Eph. 4.16, where Christ is the 'head', also supports this view. McKelvey denies that any distinction is made, on the insufficient grounds that the two words 'stand in too close proximity for the writer not to be thinking of the lower part of the building [in both cases]' (356) – the proximity in no way implies identity – and is too literalistic in judging the growth of the bodily οἰκοδομή in 4.16 incompatible with the image of a capstone (359).

[99] Origen and Jerome, *The Commentaries of Origen and Jerome on St. Paul's Epistle to the Ephesians*, ed. and trans. Ronald E. Heine (Oxford: OUP, 2002), 138–9.

[100] 'Während θεμέλιος in V 10 die grundlegende Tätigkeit des Apostels meinte, ist hier also die gekreuzigte Jesus Christus selbst als Inhalt der apostolischen Verkündigung Grund und Maß allen Gemeindeaufbaus' (Wolfgang Schrage, *Der erste Brief an die Korinther*, vol. 1, EKKNT 7 (Zürich: Benziger & Neukirchener, 1991), 298).

So I agree entirely with Barth:

> The notion that Christ supports and rules the church primarily from the past, as it were by things historical and laid beneath the ground, has to be complemented by an equally strong eschatological element.¹⁰¹

Christ is the first and the last, the foundation and the capstone. This presents no great difficulty for a conceptuality as theologically dextrous as that of Ephesians. Looking backward, Christ is perceived objectively through the testimony of apostles and prophets, including that of Israel, if we are willing to take 'prophets' in the broader sense. Looking forward, he is perceived eschatologically as the consummation of all, the head crowning and ruling the body.¹⁰² The heavenward perspective is especially characteristic of Ephesians, but in the present passage, where the readers are being adjured to remember their origins, it must be integrated also with the historical.

Eph. 2.21-22 brings the address back to the readers with a closing couplet:

v. 21	v. 22
ἐν ᾧ	ἐν ᾧ
πᾶσα οἰκοδομὴ	καὶ ὑμεῖς
συναρμολογουμένη αὔξει	συνοικοδομεῖσθε
εἰς ναὸν ἅγιον	εἰς κατοικητήριον τοῦ θεοῦ
ἐν κυρίῳ,	ἐν πνεύματι.

The position of καί in v. 22 requires the translation 'also', and if the clear parallelism were insufficient, shows that a comparison is intended between the church as a universal whole (πᾶσα οἰκοδομή) and the readers in particular. You too are built together in him, in just the same way as the whole. The Ephesians' internal unity is of a piece with the unity of the universal church; in fact, it is just this vision of their integration into a bigger story that Paul has been driving at these several verses. If the readers are in danger of forgetting their secondary Gentile status, that amounts to a sort of parochialism, temporal and geographical; part of the letter's strategy is to bring them back into conscious dependence upon the broader communion of saints, both the foundation on which they rest and the greater structure of which they are a part. The Jerusalem collection comes to mind: Paul had to remind the Corinthians of their interdependence with saints far away (2 Cor. 8.13-14), and the predominantly Gentile Romans of their spiritual debt to the Jews (Rom. 15.27).

---

¹⁰¹ Barth, *Ephesians*, 319.
¹⁰² The close interrelation of 'body' and 'building' language is shown both by the easy segue from 2.16 into the present passage, and by the three recurrences of the word οἰκοδομή in ch. 4. Eph. 4.16 is especially pertinent: τὸ σῶμα συναρμονολούμενον ... ποιεῖται εἰς οἰκοδομὴν ἑαυτοῦ ἐν ἀγάπῃ. This is the only NT occurrence of συναρμολογέω apart from Eph. 2.21. MacDonald is right that 'the body metaphor ... has merged with architectural imagery in order to create a vision of a human spiritual dwelling' (*Colossians and Ephesians*, 250).

In the language of reconciliation and, more decidedly, in the metaphor of God's building, Eph. 2 has moved from the world of Romans and Galatians to that of the Corinthian correspondence. For the fundamental question, the unity of Jew and Gentile in Christ, the former letters were the more pertinent, and Rom. 3 in particular shapes the theological spine of the passage. But into this Paul has grafted material from his more Gentile-oriented letters, turning it to a new and previously unimagined purpose. What could the Romans learn from Corinthian controversies, or vice versa? A good deal, in fact. What we have observed here, in other words, is Ephesians playing an integrating role within the CP, drawing together diverse strands of Pauline theology and allowing them to combine in a new and mutually enriching pattern.

3. Conclusions

In Chapter 1, we saw that as far back as can be traced, the CP included Ephesians at its heart. The letter was read and received as part of a whole, embedded in it *physically* through the very manuscripts by which it was transmitted. In this chapter, taking that canonical context as the normative frame for exegesis, we have seen that Ephesians is also embedded *textually* in the CP, and not just at the level of thematic overlap or occasional verbal echoes. The connection runs much deeper than a general milieu shared by a postapostolic 'Pauline school', a construct sufficiently vague to offer no real exegetical advantage: Ephesians may or may not have been steeped in a Pauline 'school', but it is unmistakeably steeped in Pauline *texts*.

We have observed an author, whether Paul or someone else, engaged in a deliberate, sophisticated conversation with earlier letters. As a shorthand we can say that Ephesians is reinterpreting other Pauline texts, but that should not be taken to imply a single, one-dimensional mode of engagement. Sometimes Ephesians expands upon what went before; sometimes it shifts focus or perspective; sometimes it reshapes earlier language for new purposes; sometimes it is prompted to quite new reflection; and so on. The earlier letters play a variety of roles in this dialogue; Ephesians does not silence or replace them, but it does enable them to speak into new contexts. Each letter continues to address the community in its own voice, with its own distinctive emphases, and indeed is heard the more distinctly for its interaction with the others.

The exegesis in this chapter does not depend on any particular view about Ephesians's authorship. Instead, as I argued in Chapter 2, this letter participates in a continuous process of receiving and interpreting Paul, extending throughout his whole Corpus, whatever the identity of the person or persons historically responsible. The prevailing scholarly trend, by contrast, is for the interpretation of this and other antilegomena to be primarily oriented to the question of authorship. It is an ever-present though often invisible undercurrent in exegesis, with the text constantly interrogated as evidence buttressing the interpreter's preferred thesis. This is true for advocates of authenticity and of pseudonymity – though the latter is the more widespread position now and has accordingly received more attention here – and even sometimes for those who take an agnostic position. My contention is that this preoccupation fundamentally distorts the interpretation of the text, concealing the complexity and variety of its intertextuality, and oversimplifying its theological character. The case study of Eph. 2.8-22 has borne this out in a number of ways:

1. A higher degree of continuity has been observed between Ephesians and the earlier letters than is usually admitted. The most striking example is the close parallel, not only in vocabulary but also in line of thought, between this passage and Rom. 3. The prevailing view, that Ephesians makes reference to the old faith–works controversy but fundamentally alters the sense of the terms, fails to see the depth of shared logic.

2. On a number of occasions when Ephesians diverges significantly from some earlier Pauline sources, it draws closer to others. A few examples among many: the partial broadening of 'works' in 2.5 and 8, the enduring, fleshly sense of 'circumcision' in 2.11 and the wholly dismissive treatment of the law in 2.15. These have all been shown to correspond closely to some passages in the undisputed letters, while differing from others. Ephesians takes its place *among* a diverse Pauline collection, not *against* a univocal 'historical Paul'.

3. Our wider survey of the theme of reconciliation has also shown the division of the CP into 'authentic' and 'deuteropauline' corpora to be misleading. The pattern of reinterpretation is much more variegated and complex. The texts converge and diverge in a number of different ways, as various aspects of the common theme are refined or emphasized for new contexts; they resist marshalling into the two traditional camps.

4. Ephesians has emerged as an *integrating* text in two ways. First, in a number of instances Ephesians appears to serve a wider mediating role, bridging the gap between the CP and other NT texts; this has been merely observed here, but it could be further investigated. Second, as has been more conclusively shown, Ephesians seamlessly works together strands from many different Pauline letters; in particular, a basic argument drawn from the Jew–Gentile controversies of Galatians and Romans is engrafted with quite 'foreign' material from the Corinthian letters, where this issue is less prominent.

What have we learnt about the actual meaning of Ephesians? One crucial emphasis is the acute incongruousness of God's grace, an aspect of Paul's gospel apparently less familiar to the community addressed. The readers emerge as Gentile Christians removed from the context of Jew–Gentile church conflict, perhaps of a somewhat later generation than those troubled by circumcision in Galatia or table fellowship in Corinth or Rome. The paradigmatic demonstration of salvation's incongruity – that the God of Israel should reach out indiscriminately to the constitutionally wicked Gentiles – was less vividly present to them. The recovery of the logic of Rom. 3 for this new context, the construction of the readers' identity as Gentiles in flesh and the reorientation of their memory towards the irreducible particularity of Israel, teaches them that their place in the economy of salvation is contingent. Only in this way can a full appreciation of Christ's unifying work come about. They must know their former estrangement before they can understand their present reconciliation, but it can only be learnt retrospectively.

In this way, Ephesians mediates certain central aspects of the earlier Pauline letters to a new generation. It may serve a similar purpose for modern readers, so much further removed from the simmering social crucible where the gospel of grace was first refined. That is not to suggest that Ephesians should be privileged as the only or the principal lens through which to read the rest of the CP. It is one perspective among several. One can read Galatians through Ephesians, or Ephesians through Galatians – the interpreter's choice will vary according to occasion and context, critical and hermeneutical creativity – and either way, it will affect the meaning found in *both* letters. Meanwhile, internal tension remains a permanent fact about the Corpus, inviting exploration, and defying every attempt to synthesize it under a single totalizing interpretation. What must above all be resisted is the narrowing of vision such that only the allegedly 'authentic' is granted hermeneutical priority.

4

The body and the Corpus

1. Introduction

The previous chapter illustrated a canonically integrated approach to Ephesians through a reading of one particular passage. The present chapter takes a somewhat different tack, and focuses not on a single text but on a single theological theme: the body of Christ. We will investigate how this subject is treated throughout Ephesians and across other relevant Pauline letters. The body of Christ is a suitable subject for several reasons: it is a classically Pauline theologoumenon, attested broadly across the CP and theologically pivotal both to Ephesians and to one undisputed letter, 1 Corinthians; it is foundational to the hotly contested arena of ecclesiology, and so has generated much lively commentary; it is for some interpreters the paradigmatic instance of Ephesians's divergence from the authentic Paul; and, as such, it exemplifies how theological and confessional predispositions can weight the interpretation of the CP.

So my concern here is not only with how Ephesians develops earlier Pauline discussions of the body of Christ but also with how the variation across the Corpus is evaluated by modern interpreters. For some, Ephesians reaffirms and perhaps elaborates what Paul had already set out in 1 Corinthians; for others, it categorically misconstrues the apostle; for others again, it hardly rates a mention. Such wide divergence among readers is remarkable, and this chapter sets out from that point. We will begin by comparing some modern accounts of the Pauline body of Christ motif, focusing on the work of Ernst Käsemann, Gregory Dawes, Dale Martin and Robert Jenson, and drawing on several others along the way. Some of these interpreters are explicitly concerned with Ephesians, while others touch on it sparingly or not at all, but all are relevant to this study, because the question is how the Pauline body of Christ is construed *as a whole*, and whether and how Ephesians has a distinctive voice in that construal. The range of interpreters to be consulted is broad, bringing together systematic and biblical scholars, a procedure warranted by the subject matter. As will become apparent, widely divergent figures like Käsemann and Jenson address the Pauline letters with similar theological questions, however they may differ in method. This is hardly accidental; it is the nature of the biblical text's *Wirkungsgeschichte* that it shapes the parameters of theological discussion, and sets its agenda, to a considerable extent. After reviewing these various interpretations, we will proceed to exegesis of relevant Pauline texts.

Two particular questions will be important throughout:

1. How widely do earlier and later letters differ on this subject, and how is that difference evaluated? In particular, does Ephesians 'catholicize' Paul's view of the body of Christ? This goes to the heart of the suspicion towards the letter among much biblical scholarship of the last two centuries. We have seen in Chapter 2 how the Baur–Käsemann model, where the CP gradually declines into *Frühkatholizismus*, has widely skewed interpretation of Paul's letters (and continues to be influential even when no longer openly espoused). Ecclesiology is the primary locus of this debate, both as regards ministerial office – less relevant for Ephesians, more so for the Pastorals – and the body of Christ. The exegetical engagement with Käsemann in this chapter will flesh out the more general critique of his model in Chapter 2. But the decadence hermeneutic is hardly peculiar to him. Consider for example Schweitzer:

> Indem der Verfasser des Epheserbriefes die Vorstellung des Leibes Christi und Spekulationen über Christus und die Kirche nebeneinander bringt, zeigt er an, daß ihm die ursprüngliche Natur der Vorstellung des mystischen Leibes Christi nicht mehr gegenwärtig ist. Er hat kein Bewußtsein mehr davon, daß in ihr alles, was über die Kirche sowie über Christus und die Kirche ausgesagt werden kann, in erschöpfender Weise ausgedrückt ist.[1]

Authentic Pauline somatic ecclesiology is 'exhaustively expressed' in the undisputed letters, and misunderstood in Ephesians: this view of the subject, closely anticipating Käsemann's, can stand as a summary hypothesis to be tested in what follows.

2. What is the ontological reference of Paul's body language? More plainly, is the body of Christ a metaphor? Many biblical scholars give an affirmative answer to this question; still more simply assume one. The assumption may seem natural where the tools of analysis are principally linguistic and literary – interestingly, it seems to be less common among systematic theologians – but in any case, it should be questioned. Does the Paul of Ephesians, or indeed the Paul of 1 Corinthians, intend this language only as a figure of speech, or is it to be taken as somehow really, substantively *true*? Undoubtedly, it sometimes *functions* metaphorically, as for instance in Eph. 4.16 where the body's articulation is described in medical terms, or 1 Cor. 12.14-26 with its dialogue between eye and hand, head and foot. But is that all?

Certainly 'metaphor' is a broad term in literary and linguistic studies, and perhaps it would be possible to apply it here in an extremely strong sense, as conveying a truth no less real than the literal. However, I would suggest that 'you are God's field, God's building' (1 Cor. 3.9) and 'you are the body of Christ' (1 Cor. 12.27) are two quite different modes of predication for Paul. If we call the former metaphorical, as we surely must, the same label cannot be applied to the latter without obscuring this distinction. Nor can such language properly be called 'literal', since it takes the words well beyond their ordinary referential meaning. In fact, the conventional polarity of

---

[1] Albert Schweitzer, *Die Mystik des Apostels Paulus* (Tübingen: Mohr, 1930), 121–2. Schweitzer is referring to not only the head of Eph. 1.22-23 and the spouse of Eph. 5 but also the doxological formula ἐν τῇ ἐκκλησίᾳ καὶ ἐν Χριστῷ Ἰησοῦ (3.21).

literal–metaphorical is too blunt an analytical tool to be useful here. Words are malleable and polysemous: they can be adapted to new and surprising contexts, and existing meanings can be stretched, according to an author's purpose. This phenomenon can include metaphor, along with various other tropes, but is not limited to them. So I will occasionally refer to the 'extended' use of language, meaning polysemy which goes beyond the literal without being a trope, in attempting a more precise interpretation of Paul's σῶμα Χριστοῦ.

2. Interpretations of the body of Christ

2.1. Decadence: Ernst Käsemann

The body of Christ had been the subject of Käsemann's doctoral dissertation, and it continued to exercise him throughout his life. His interpretation did evolve somewhat over time, and I will focus on his later views, set out most thoroughly in his 1969 essay on the subject.[2] Paul's body of Christ is, for Käsemann, emphatically not a metaphor, one image for the church among others; equally, though, it is not the mystical body of Catholic dogma, a union between the crucified body of the man Jesus and the institution of the church. 'Der erhöhte Christus hat wirklich einen irdischen Leib, und die Glaubenden werden mit ihrem ganzen Sein realiter darin eingegliedert' (182); yet, Paul's account of this body presupposes a particular mythological background, and to treat it as a distinct metaphysical doctrine is to disregard this history. Käsemann positions himself between what he considers the opposite misreadings of Catholics and Protestants, and so must occupy a precariously narrow space.

Käsemann proceeds by way of *religionsgeschichtlich* analysis of the antecedent traditions lying behind Paul's language. In the first place, he argues that the connection between the eucharistic and ecclesial body of Christ (1 Cor. 10.16-17) is a comparison newly introduced by Paul. The eucharistic formulation originally had nothing to do with ecclesiology; it referred to Christ's body only by analogy with his blood, and not to believers' union with his ecclesial body, but rather their 'mystery-like' (*mysterienhaft*) sacramental participation in his death. From this Paul 'leaps' to Christians' incorporation in the body of the *exalted* Christ through the Spirit, maintaining however a clear distinction between the two bodies (193–4). Käsemann may be right that sacramental participation, on the one hand, and incorporation into the community, on the other, were originally distinct ideas in earliest Christianity, separately associated with the 'body of Christ'. But his insistence that Paul *keeps* them distinct, having brought them together in 1 Cor. 10, is more tendentious. He is concerned that the church not become an extension of the incarnation, of the earthly,

---

[2] Ernst Käsemann, 'Das theologische Problem des Motivs vom Leib Christi', in *Paulinische Perspektiven* (Tübingen: Mohr Siebeck, 1969), 178–210. A helpful review of Käsemann's thought in this area is given by David Way, *The Lordship of Christ: Ernst Käsemann's Interpretation of Paul's Theology* (Oxford: Clarendon, 1991), 237–49.

crucified Jesus, but only the manifestation of the risen Lord's reign on earth; we will see, however, that there is no need to impose these alternatives upon the Pauline texts.

Although he does not develop the point here, Käsemann's use of the term 'mystery-like' suggests that the early theology of eucharistic participation drew upon religious traditions antecedent to Christianity. A similar, more significant interpretative move is foundational to his argument in this essay, and indeed all his writings on the subject. Like his brother Bultmannian Schlier, Käsemann inherited the assumption that a pre-Christian gnostic 'Anthropos myth' – of a heavenly redeemer who would incorporate the cosmos into his body – was the formative background to Paul's body of Christ language. This reconstruction was highly speculative, and became much less plausible as acquaintance with actual 'gnostic' texts increased; yet still in 1969, Käsemann's account of the body of Christ depended upon it.[3] He distinguishes between the 'organizational' view of the body, the unity of diverse members (which he associates with stoic antecedents),[4] and the 'individual' view, the exalted Christ filling the world (which he traces to the 'Anthropos myth') (201-2). The latter is, for Käsemann, historically and theologically primary: the body of Christ means first the presence of the risen Lord, and only derivatively the solidarity of many Christians.

As David Way observes, although Käsemann is ostensibly moving away from the 'gnostic model' by this stage, he in fact still depends upon its conceptuality.[5] This must be counted a major weakness in his interpretation. His identification of the genuine Pauline gospel relies upon the isolation of distinct antecedent traditions, and the reconstruction of how Paul appropriated and transformed them. But, by the time of the Romans commentary, he was beginning to acknowledge the instability of the *religionsgeschichtlich* edifice.[6] Can his theological conclusions stand without it?

Similar historical assumptions govern his treatment of the 'deuteropauline' letters.[7] Paul's own interest is not in the church per se, but only in how it manifests Christ's presence; for this reason, the body of Christ appears in paranetic contexts, but is never thematized. That changes in Colossians and Ephesians, however, where it is spoken of 'doxologically'. The difference emerges most clearly when Christ is called the head: he is then somehow separated from the body, and the church is ascribed a sort of independence over and against her Lord, in contrast with what the authentic letters call the rule of the Spirit. In the deuteropauline letters, we find the church not simply as the earthly body of the ascended Lord, extending through time and space, but herself a distinct subject, ascending into the heavenly regions. The discussion of the church, which for Paul was always secondary, became in the next generation a question of dogma, as the need for stronger unity and structure came to the fore. With Ephesians,

---

[3] It is abandoned in the Romans commentary, however, where Käsemann instead speaks of a generic 'cosmic body' motif across pre-Platonic, stoic and oriental thought (*An die Römer*, 3rd edn, HNT 8A (Tübingen: Mohr Siebeck, 1974), 323-4).
[4] The best-known example is Livy's fable of Menenius Agrippa, where the state is described as an uneasy union of the stomach with other bodily members. As Dale Martin discusses, though, the 'society-as-body topos' had much broader currency than just among the stoics (see §2.3 below).
[5] Way, *Lordship of Christ*, 246.
[6] He comments on the enduring obscurity around the body motif, represented by the various, overlapping theories of its origins (Käsemann, *Römer*, 325).
[7] For the following, see Käsemann, 'Das theologische Problem', 204-10.

the rot has set in: its departure from genuine Pauline ecclesiology is '[das] erste Indiz einer bis heute anhaltenden Fehlinterpretation'.[8]

Nevertheless, however regrettable the deuteropauline compromise may be, Käsemann finds himself unable to reject it unequivocally. Throughout the various lectures and articles in which he addressed this topic over his career, he maintained a consistent dialectic between regret at the domestication of Paul by the church and resignation that some such process was not only historically necessary but even somehow legitimate in light of fading eschatological expectation. In the 1949 lecture on 'Amt und Gemeinde im Neuen Testament', for instance, he laments that the Protestant church has never succeeded in ordering itself according to a truly Pauline doctrine of charismata, while admitting that such a step would simply open the door to *Schwärmertum*, as it did in Corinth. If Paul himself could not prevent this, what is the later church to do? Some sort of staid compromise appears inevitable, with the church at best remaining conscious of her provisionality, permanently dependent upon the creative action of grace.[9] This dialectic remains largely unchanged in the 1969 essay's claim for a centre ground between Protestant and Catholic errors.

It will be evident that Käsemann's position depends entirely on a thesis of deuteropauline pseudonymity, no less than on his equally tendentious reconstruction of pre-Pauline traditions. It is only by setting Ephesians over against 1 Corinthians that he can justify his anti-metaphysical reading of the body. We noted in Chapter 2 Käsemann's conceptual disjunction between gospel and church, which he sees played out within the NT as a disjunction between different texts (see p. 66 above); the present case exemplifies this hermeneutic. His convictions about the acceptable contours of a plausibly Pauline theology determine the shape of his canon, limiting not only which letters can be regarded as authoritative but also what can legitimately be found in the undisputed letters. As we will see in what follows, this leads him to misread the extent

---

[8] Ibid., 191. Cf. Ernst Käsemann, 'Paulus und der Frühkatholizismus', 1963, in *Exegetische Versuche und Besinnungen* (Göttingen: Vandenhoeck & Ruprecht, 1964), 245: '[Der Epheserbrief] begründet ... die Verbindung von Ekklesiologie und Christologie sakramental, so daß nun die Nachfolge Jesu die Konsequenz, nicht aber die Basis des Christenstandes abgibt.'

[9] Ernst Käsemann, 'Amt und Gemeinde im Neuen Testament', 1949, in *Exegetische Versuche und Besinnungen*, vol. 1, 2 vols (Göttingen: Vandenhoeck & Ruprecht, 1960), 109-34 (133-4). The image of a 'two-front war' – the true gospel under attack from both nomism and enthusiasm (*Schwärmertum*) – of course reflects a Lutheran perspective on sixteenth-century hostilities, and was read back into Paul's context originally by Wilhelm Lütgert in the early twentieth century. Käsemann was exceptional in continuing to espouse this view after it had been generally forgotten. On this, see Klaus Haacker, 'Rezeptionsgeschichte und Literarkritik: Anfragen an die Communis Opinio zum Corpus Paulinum', TZ 65 (2009): 219-22. The idea of a 'libertine' party alongside the Judaizers, at least in Galatia, predated Lütgert (see John M. G. Barclay, *Obeying the Truth: A Study of Paul's Ethics in Galatians* (Edinburgh: Clark, 1988), 16-18), but the military metaphor was his. An example: 'Die christliche Gemeinde hat von Anfang an zwischen zwei Fronten gestanden. ... Auf der einer Seite standen die Vertreter des Gesetzes, aber auf der anderen Seite stand von Anfang an ein Feind, der diesem ersten diametral gegenüberstand: die Verdreher der Freiheitspredigt. Die Gemeinde stand zwischen Nomisten und Antinomisten, so wie die Reformatoren zwischen der alten Kirche und den Schwärmern.' (D. W. Lütgert, *Freiheitspredigt und Schwarmgeister in Korinth: Ein Beitrag zur Charakteristik der Christuspartei*, Beiträge zur Förderung christlicher Theologie, 12.3 (Gütersloh: Bertelsmann, 1908), 7-8.)

to which the body of Christ is already a matter of 'dogmatic' importance especially in 1 Corinthians.[10]

Käsemann's great antagonist in this debate was Schlier; we have already noted his highly critical (though not unappreciative) review of Schlier's Ephesians commentary.[11] The antecedent 'Anthropos myth' was an assumption shared by both scholars, and their disagreement hinged to some extent on how it was reworked in the Pauline letters. Käsemann considers Schlier guilty of a category error: he takes the language too literally, failing to realize how completely Paul has transformed his source. The body of Christ language certainly *looks* like its reference is ontological, but that is the legacy of its pre-Pauline history, not the apostle's actual intention.[12] Schlier stands in the same tradition as the author of Ephesians in misunderstanding Paul's ecclesiology, and by misreading Ephesians *as* Pauline, compounds the mistake.

In his commentary, Schlier like Käsemann sees a clear distinction between the earlier and later letters, where the former have a more organizational, the latter a more cosmic view of the body of Christ, reflecting respectively stoic and gnostic influence. Notably, though, for Schlier this is compatible with consistent Pauline authorship: the different perspectives are complementary rather than contradictory, and Paul's original thought is developed and even completed in the later letters.[13] Still more telling is his quite different response to the loss of the Bultmannian mythological framework. His last work, a Pauline theology published in the year of his death, is intended as a quasi-systematic rather than historical study. It makes no reference to the prehistory of the body of Christ motif, but reads it in if anything a still more integrated way across the CP.[14] The crucified body of Christ is made present as a space or dimension of salvation (*Heilsraum, Heilsdimension*) through the Spirit, who incorporates believers as its members through the sacraments.[15] In setting this out, Schlier draws equally on the language of Ephesians and 1 Corinthians. Perhaps it shows the strength of his

---

[10] Käsemann's view that the multiplicity of NT texts validates, even mandates ongoing ecumenical diversity is shared by Robert W. Wall ('Ecumenicity and Ecclesiology: The Promise of the Multiple Letter Canon of the New Testament', in *The New Testament as Canon: A Reader in Canonical Criticism*, ed. Eugene E. Lemcio and Robert W. Wall (Sheffield: JSOT, 1992), 184–207). This essay's reading of ecclesiology across the NT epistles, despite its 'canonical' orientation, follows a straightforward decadence schema of the CP: Ephesians and Colossians take Paul's σῶμα Χριστοῦ 'from metaphor to myth' in a 'potentially dangerous' exaltation of the church (200), and already betray an 'institutional mentality' which will gain corrupting hegemony by the time of the Pastorals (205–6).

[11] See n. 30, p. 66 above.

[12] 'Ich kann jedenfalls die, religionsgeschichtlich betrachtet, zweifellos ontologisch formulierte Aussagenreihe, auf welche Schlier sich beruft, schlechterdings nicht ontologisch interpretieren und meine, daß hier der tiefste Unterschied zwischen uns aufbricht' (Ernst Käsemann, 'Das Interpretationsproblem des Epheserbriefes,' 1961, in *Exegetische Versuche und Besinnungen* (Göttingen: Vandenhoeck & Ruprecht, 1964), 257).

[13] Heinrich Schlier, *Der Brief an die Epheser: Ein Kommentar* (Düsseldorf: Patmos, 1957), 90–6.

[14] Heinrich Schlier, *Grundzüge einer paulinischen Theologie* (Freiburg: Herder, 1978), 194–200.

[15] 'Wird die Kirche also "Leib Christi" von Paulus genannt, so ist das für ihn nicht eigentlich bildhaft gemeint, sondern bezeichnet eine reale Identität mit dem Kreuzesleib als der Heilsdimension. Sie heißt "Leib Christi", weil sie der durch den heiligen Geist entschränkte Heilsraum des Kreuzesleibes Christi ist, dessen, der von den Toten erweckt ist' (ibid., 197). Schlier and Käsemann are equally emphatic in rejecting a merely metaphorical interpretation of the body of Christ.

canonically holistic reading that it can withstand the loss of its dubious mythological scaffolding in a way that Käsemann's divisive reading cannot.

Before moving on, we should note another oft-repeated claim which indirectly echoes Käsemann. Lincoln is representative of many commentators when he writes that in Ephesians, like Colossians, the body of Christ 'has become a depiction of the universal church as distinct from the more local application of the image in 1 Cor. 12 or Rom. 12'.[16] But Best correctly points to examples in 1 Corinthians where the body means the universal church – at the eucharist (10.16-17), through baptism (12.13) and knowing multiple apostles (12.27-28) – and concludes that if this difference exists, it is not absolute.[17] It is true that Ephesians as a whole is less obviously particular than most Pauline letters, and certainly less identifiable with a particular congregation than 1 Corinthians. But to exaggerate the movement from local to universal recalls the decadence paradigm, and resembles Käsemann's hypothesized trajectory from stoic (intra-communal) to gnostic (cosmically ontological) models of the body, with equally questionable foundation in the text.[18]

2.2. Metaphor: Gregory Dawes

Gregory Dawes's monograph on Eph. 5.21-33 aims for a new interpretation that resists the passage's unapologetically patriarchal ethic without dismissing it as a morally or theologically irrelevant text.[19] His approach is to analyse the function of 'head' and 'body' language throughout the letter in the light of metaphor theory, or at least some selected examples of it.[20] Within this framework, he distinguishes between the conclusions explicitly drawn in the *Haustafel* text and a more egalitarian ethic which he argues is the real implication of its logic. It is undoubtedly true that there are tensions within Eph. 5 which undermine its unilateral subordination of the wife to the husband, and I agree that this should be exploited exegetically, but here I am only concerned with Dawes's reading of the letter's somatic language. In my view, he underestimates its realism, and his metaphorical framework is ultimately inadequate to interpret it. This is important because, although the other main interpreters discussed here do not read σῶμα Χριστοῦ metaphorically, Dawes is representative of the modern exegetical mainstream in doing so.

Dawes considers 'head' and 'body' to be two distinct but not separate metaphors throughout Ephesians, arguing that they both draw upon a common underlying

---

[16] Andrew T. Lincoln, *Ephesians*, WBC 42 (Dallas, TX: Word, 1990), xciv.
[17] Ernest Best, *Ephesians*, ICC (London: Clark, 1998), 191.
[18] A similar observation applies to the word ἐκκλησία, which is already acquiring a universal application within the undisputed letters. See Sigurd Grindheim, 'A Deutero-Pauline Mystery? Ecclesiology in Colossians and Ephesians,' in *Paul and Pseudepigraphy*, ed. Stanley E. Porter and Gregory P. Fewster, PaSt 8 (Leiden: Brill, 2013), 175–7.
[19] Gregory W. Dawes, *The Body in Question: Metaphor and Meaning in the Interpretation of Ephesians 5.21-33*, Biblical Interpretation 30 (Leiden: Brill, 1998).
[20] Yorke objects that Dawes's selectivity gives a somewhat naive impression of this complex field (Gosnell L. O. R. Yorke, 'Review of Gregory Dawes, *The Body in Question*', JBL 121 (2002): 378–80). This is borne out in the subsequent exegesis, which benefits little from the initial chapters on theory. (Yorke's own approach, however, has still graver shortcomings; see below.)

imaginative construct or 'model' of the body. This may seem obvious but is in fact a necessary rebuttal of Yorke's thesis that 'head' and 'body' are entirely independent metaphors.[21] For Yorke, 'head' is a Christological title, in no way related to the 'body of Christ', which refers to a generic human body as a metaphor for the church, and not at all to the physical body of Jesus. Dawes rightly responds that, since in Ephesians the words κεφαλή and σῶμα regularly occur together, and in the context of other body language, they most certainly interpret one another.[22]

Dawes does not consider the possibility of a non-metaphorical body of Christ, although he is aware that the language is sometimes used realistically. He identifies just one occasion where the word σῶμα is to be taken literally, the injunction to husbands to love their wives 'as their own bodies' (5.28), but it is not clear why this verse in particular is so singled out. He rightly accepts that the 'deictic' (predicative) sense of ὡς is strongest here – 'love your wives *as being* your own bodies' (97–9) – and concludes that the 'most basic lexical sense, namely that of the physical body', must be meant (153); but that the wife is her husband's body is plainly *not* the 'basic lexical sense' of the word. As we have discussed, the schema of literal versus metaphorical meaning is a blunt description of linguistic polysemy, and this verse is a case in point. Like any other word, σῶμα has a range of applications even within normal usage, and here it is being further extended. The marital union of bodies is indeed an ontological fact for this text, and therefore not to be called 'metaphorical', but no more is it 'literal'; that polarity is simply not applicable, yet the 'exceptional' case of 5.28 shows how Dawes's analysis is bound by it. Each instance of somatic language is made to fall within one of these two categories.

Moreover, the union of Christ and the church is, for Paul, every bit as real as the marital union, and it is here that the limits of a metaphorical interpretation tell most keenly. According to Dawes, while in Eph. 5 both the church and marriage are related to the body metaphorically, their relationship to one another is by way of analogy (Chapter 3 and pp. 195–8). But he finds that the analogy does not really work, because of the text's 'slippage' from the literal bodily union of husband and wife to the metaphorical union of Christ and church: 'The author merely creates the impression that the two are comparable by a sort of linguistic sleight of hand, using (in different senses) the same language of both unions' (224). But this approach should be turned on its head. The fact that, for this text, marriage and church *are* comparable bodily unions should delineate how we interpret the somatic language, not vice versa. Dawes simply does not consider the possibility that, in both cases, the language is realistic in an 'extended', metaphysical or sacramental sense.

We may also question whether 'analogy' is the appropriate category here. When Paul places marital and ecclesial relationships either side of a ὡς or καθώς, there is clearly a comparison taking place, but of what kind? I would suggest that, in ordinary

---

[21] Gosnell L. O. R. Yorke, *The Church as the Body of Christ in the Pauline Corpus: A Re-Examination* (Lanham, MD: University of America, 1991). Other exponents of this position opposed by Dawes are Herman Ridderbos and J. K. McVay (Dawes, *Body in Question*, 119).

[22] Yorke's improbable position enables him to conclude that the ecclesial use of σῶμα does not change at all across the CP, which supports his preferred thesis of authentic authorship. This is another example of the preoccupation with Ephesians's provenance skewing its interpretation.

usage at least, 'analogy' denotes a relation that is purely *contingent*, as when Jesus compares the kingdom of God to a mustard seed. Its purpose is illustrative, and the meaning does not extend beyond the scope of the illustration. The comparison of Eph. 5, however, describes a relation that is *intrinsic*: marriage and the church are connected at a metaphysical level, and the full significance of that connection is not exhausted by the textual account of it. It would be better to call this 'allegory', in the Alexandrian sense where a deeper meaning is concealed within the text; indeed, Origen cites Eph. 5.32, alongside Gal. 4.24, as an apostolic warrant for the allegorical interpretation of the Torah.[23]

Although he insists that the metaphors of head and body are related, Dawes does distinguish between two discrete senses of σῶμα in Ephesians: a 'partitive' sense where head and body are differentiated (e.g. 1.22-23) and a 'unitive' sense where they are not (e.g. 2.16). The usage is not entirely consistent, and the two senses may even clash, as in 4.15-16 where the head is differentiated from the 'whole body'. In the *Haustafel*, the disjunction becomes more pronounced: the partitive sense applies in vv. 22-24, where women/the church are to submit to their husbands/Christ as a distinct 'head', but the unitive sense applies in vv. 25-32, where women and men together are Christ's body. The implication, overlooked by the letter's author, is that the latter verses at least are 'reversible': the woman should also love her husband 'as her own body' (200–6).

Dawes argues that the 'unitive' sense must have priority over the 'partitive' in the same way that Aristotle insists on the primacy of the whole over the parts, the body over the members, within the πόλις. Yet he considers the very similar somatic language of 1 Cor. 12 and Rom. 12 an example of the 'unitive' sense (204). This inconsistency arises from treating the head/body distinction as 'partitive' in the first place. Where head and body are mentioned together, Dawes sees a contrast between discrete 'parts' and their corresponding roles, which becomes problematic when mapped onto familial relationships. But in Eph. 1.22-23 and 4.15-16, the distinction is not between one part of the body and another, but between the body as a whole, and the one *whose* body it is. To name Christ 'head' identifies him certainly as both ruler and source of the church, but more fundamentally, as the subject in relation to whom the church is, objectively, his body.

This seems to me a critically important point for interpreting Paul's somatic theology. It is intrinsic to the idea of a body that it is identified with a particular subject, but is not, at least conceptually, coextensive with that subject. I both *am* my body and *have* my body; it is intelligible both to identify fully with my body and also to speak of it as an object over against myself. Paul refers frequently to ordinary human bodies, sometimes stressing the identification between self and body ('Do you not know that your bodies are members of Christ?', 1 Cor. 6.15), more often the distance between them ('I chastise my body and keep it in subjection', 1 Cor. 9.27). But to speak of 'my body' at all – rather than simply 'I' – already implies some degree of distance between

---

[23] Origen, *Homilies on Numbers*, ed. Christopher P. Hall, trans. Thomas P. Scheck (Downers Grove, IL: IVP Academic, 2009) 11.1.10-11 (p. 51); noted by Rudolf Schnackenburg, *Der Brief an die Epheser*, EKKNT 10 (Zürich: Benziger & Neukirchener, 1982), 344, n. 912. These are important examples for Origen where Paul finds an allegorical meaning that does not cancel the literal.

the speaking subject and the embodied self. Here we may draw on Bultmann, who memorably comments that that for Paul, 'der Mensch *hat* nicht ein σῶμα, sondern er *ist* σῶμα'.[24] But this statement does not apply to every instance of the word, which he goes on to argue sometimes means 'body' (*Leib*), sometimes simply the whole person. The constant is that σῶμα denotes the person as an object distinguishable from the self, '[der Mensch] ... *sofern er ein Verhältnis zu sich selbst hat, sich in gewisser Weise von sich selbst distanzieren kann*'.[25] Taken to an extreme, this definition can obscure that σῶμα always has an inherent, primarily *physical* sense;[26] but the basic observation makes good sense of the variety of Pauline usage.

What applies to the ordinary human σῶμα is also relevant to its extended use for the church. If the church can be called σῶμα Χριστοῦ, that implies both identification between the people and their Lord, and also distinction between Christ as a subject and his body as an object. When Paul addresses this topic in 1 Corinthians, the emphasis falls often (not always) on identification, but when it is further developed in Ephesians, the situation becomes more complex. At some points, the subject–object distinction is not emphasized, and the church is simply Christ's body as his whole presence or fullness. At others, where the personal identity of Christ is emphasized in relation to the church, he is generally called the 'head'. Eph. 5.22-24 is an example of the latter, but when the passage continues in 5.25-32, although the word κεφαλή disappears, the subject–object distinction remains, differently expressed. Returning to Dawes, then, I can find no contradiction here between 'unitive' and 'partitive' senses of the body, any more than between literal and metaphorical. There are simply shades of meaning, related variations on a Pauline idea which is inherently complex.

If Paul's somatic language is interpreted as consistently realistic, the 'slippage' that Dawes detects in 5.21-32 disappears. That is not to say that there is no friction within the passage; it is just of another kind. The stark asymmetry of the Ephesians *Haustafel* – undoubtedly intrinsic to its intended meaning, as Dawes recognizes – is clearly in tension with its more egalitarian claims.[27] The appeal for mutual subordination of v. 21 conflicts with the unilaterally gendered character of the following instructions, while participation in Christ's body in v. 30 makes no distinction between the sexes. Dawes's treatment of these points is the stronger part of his argument; his reading of the body of Christ as a metaphor, however, can in the end only account for the text by rejecting the coherence of its conceptual framework.

The two principal interpreters discussed so far devote considerable attention to the body of Christ in Ephesians. The next two focus much more on the earliest and fullest example of Paul's somatic theology, 1 Corinthians, and Ephesians arises incidentally if at all. How the choice of texts affects the interpretation of 'Paul's' theology is one of the concerns of this study. Ephesians recedes from the foreground for a time now, but with the object of an ultimately more holistic view of the Pauline σῶμα Χριστοῦ.

[24] Rudolf Bultmann, *Theologie des Neuen Testaments* (Tübingen: Mohr Siebeck, 1953), 191; his emphasis.
[25] Ibid., 192; his emphasis.
[26] See n. 34 below.
[27] This matter has been thoroughly discussed elsewhere, and I will not develop it further here. See esp. Francis Watson, *Agape, Eros, Gender: Towards a Pauline Sexual Ethic* (Cambridge: CUP, 2000), ch. 6.

2.3. Ideology: Dale Martin

Dale Martin's influential study of 1 Corinthians critiques how the ideology of the body was constructed in Paul's cultural milieu, examining philosophical and medical as well as biblical texts. Martin explains the usage of his key term:

> *Ideology* ... refers to the relation between language and social structures of power. It is the linguistic, symbolic matrix that makes sense of and supports a particular exercise of power and the power structures that exist. ... Ideology, in my usage, is a more serviceable concept than 'ideas', 'theology', or 'beliefs', because it avoids reference to authorial intention: the person who uses ideology or is influenced by it need not be aware that this is the case.[28]

I question whether the latter distinction really holds; one may be unconsciously influenced by ideas, theology and beliefs. Moreover, the 'linguistic, symbolic matrix' of a culture shapes the whole complex of its social relations, including the normal human faculty for mutuality and cooperation, and so to consider it exclusively in terms of 'power' seems to me reductive. But *The Corinthian Body* remains instructive within an understanding of ideology qualified along these lines. I will not engage with Martin's analysis of power dynamics, where we differ in ways not relevant to this study, but with his discussion of how Paul stretches σῶμα and related terms beyond their ordinary sense, and especially how alien that 'ordinary' sense is for a modern reader. The ancient conceptual framework for the body, and therefore the body of Christ, may be less perspicuous than we suppose.

Martin's first chapter sketches the history of the ancient Mediterranean idea of the body, arguing that it is far removed from a familiar Cartesian separation between the natural/physical and the supernatural/nonphysical, and so between the body and the mind or soul.[29] For Aristotle, incorporeal things such as fire, air and water are still made of 'stuff', and simply lack order; for the Epicureans, everything in the cosmos is a body unless it is 'void, place or room'; for the Stoics, the only truly incorporeal things are those which do not exist but can be imagined, such as centaurs or giants. In each of these systems of thought, the soul is part of nature, and not properly called 'incorporeal'. Plato, who most closely anticipates modern dualism, still envisages a soul which is variously located in the body, constituted of στοιχεία, affected by the humours, and so on, and in this sense is still 'bodily' or 'physical'. Rather than the stark separation of Descartes, in Plato we find 'something more like a spectrum of essences than a dichotomy of realms' (12).

Drawing mainly on medical treatises, Martin discusses how the ancient body was less sharply distinguished than the modern from the surrounding world, participating in it (quite nonmetaphorically) as a microcosm, 'a small version of the universe at large' (16). The stuff of the cosmos constituted the body, passing in and out through different

---

[28] Dale B. Martin, *The Corinthian Body* (New Haven, CT: Yale University Press, 1995), xiv.
[29] For the following, see ibid., 4–14. It should be noted that Martin's account of the various philosophical positions is quite cursory; in particular, his opposition between Platonic and Cartesian views of *pneuma* is too simple. See n. 33 below.

poroi corresponding to the senses, and affecting the soul as well as physiological phenomena; the boundary between personal and cosmic bodies was fluid, and the distinction between the 'physical' and the 'psychological' simply did not exist (17–19). In summary:

> The self was a precarious, temporary state of affairs, constituted by forces surrounding and pervading the body, like radio waves that bounce around and through the bodies of modern urbanites. In such a maelstrom of cosmological forces, the individualism of modern conceptions disappears, and the body is perceived as a location in a continuum of cosmic movement. The body – or the 'self' – is an unstable point of transition, not a discrete, permanent, solid entity. (25)

Is the intellectual context, so described, incompatible with the distinct subjective and objective senses I have associated with somatic language, the body one *has* and the body one *is*? I do not think so; but Martin's observations help to clarify that this is a relative rather than an absolute distinction, which indeed reflects the range of usage in Pauline texts. There are more subjective and more objective instances, but they shade into one another and cannot be sharply delineated. We should certainly not map this distinction onto a stark metaphysical dualism (e.g. by understanding the subject who *has* a physical body simply as its nonphysical mind or soul). On the other hand, Martin's equation of 'body' and 'self' in the passage just quoted is hard to square with a text like 1 Cor. 9.27, 'I chastise my body and keep it in subjection'.

Martin devotes much discussion to the body politic, arguing that the widespread 'society-as-body topos' functioned ideologically to uphold a conservative regime of 'benevolent patriarchalism'; Paul, however, deployed it contrariwise, inverting the prevailing hierarchies and subordinating stronger members to weaker.[30] The *topos* functions analogically – the members of a microcosmic human body correspond to the members of the macrocosmic social body – but this does not make it metaphorical. The body *is*, not is *like*, a microcosm (16). If the 'self' is indeed so unstable and precarious, then a simple opposition between individual and collective bodies is not possible; rather, bodies of all kinds have their being by participating in the elements of the universe, fluidly and permeably. On this understanding, the relation between the body of Christ and the bodies of Christians must be concrete and realistic, not just imaginative, and a reading like Dawes's is excluded.

The question of this relation arises again in the second half of the study, dealing with rival aetiologies of disease: is disease caused by the imbalance of humours within the body, or by the invasion of polluting elements from without? Martin argues that the 'strong' party in Corinth took the former, more educated view, but Paul sided with the lower-class 'weak' in favouring the latter. The resulting conflict plays out in a number of issues to do with the body: the man consorting with his stepmother (1 Cor. 5), those visiting prostitutes (1 Cor. 6), idol food (1 Cor. 8–10), the veiling of virgins and the mis-eating of the eucharist (1 Cor. 11). In all of these cases, Paul's concern is that the

---

[30] Ibid., esp. 39–47 and 92–6, and throughout ch. 3.

pollution of the bodies of particular Christians pollutes the whole body of Christ and renders it liable to corruption. The Christian person is identified with Christ not at an immaterial level, 'spiritually' in a modern sense, but by sharing in the substantial element of Christ's *pneuma*: taking the example of 1 Cor. 6, 'the man's body is therefore an appendage of Christ's body, totally dependent on the pneumatic life-force of the larger body for its existence' (176). By consorting with a prostitute, the man brings Christ into substantial encounter with the corrupt body of the wider cosmos, and brings the corruption into the ecclesial body.

Martin's study is helpful in reframing how Paul is able to conceive the body of Christ realistically. The fluidity and permeability of bodies in his cultural milieu, their common participation in the constitutive elements of the cosmos, in contrast with the modern separation between material and immaterial realms, makes more lucid Paul's identification between the Christian and the ecclesial body. The thrust of Martin's rhetoric, however, can take him perilously near to dissolving the intelligibility of somatic language altogether:

> Although I have sometimes spoken of the individual body of the offender and the social body of the church, the terms should be taken not as references to 'real things' but simply as heuristic and momentary tropes. ... One may argue that the modern concept of the individual is simply unavailable to Paul. (173)

The 'modern concept of the individual', however, is a very inexact formulation, and I doubt whether modern and ancient thought on this subject are so wholly incommensurable as this statement would suggest. We moderns have various ways of talking about distinct and particular persons, many of which are compatible with Paul and other ancient authors simply because then as now, life is lived *by* distinct and particular persons, which is to say distinct and particular bodies. Martin's argument that bodily boundaries were more fluid in ancient thought is persuasive; his suggestion that the personal body was just a linguistic construction is not.

A related question is the distinction between the body as a subject and as an object. Martin would possibly exclude this as anachronistic, but though the terminology can be disputed, there remains in Paul a range of levels and kinds of identification between the self and the body, as we have seen. Sometimes he simply is his body; sometimes it is an object to him. Analogously, Christ is both identified with the church and encountered by it as an other; he is both the body's ruler and its subject. The question to Martin might be put thus: What difference does it make that Paul's community is the body *of Christ* and not simply the body of the church? A polis may be conventionally understood as a body, but it is not understood as the body *of* its governor. Paul speaks of the body of Christ as a *personal* body, which is not generally true of the society-as-body *topos*.[31]

The beginning of an answer lies in the substantive union between Christ and people through a shared *pneuma*, identified but not greatly developed by Martin; for a fuller

---

[31] As we will see presently, Jenson's work on the eucharistic and ecclesial body in 1 Corinthians is helpful here.

treatment of this subject, we turn to Troels Engberg-Pedersen on the 'material Spirit' in Paul.[32] Engberg-Pedersen finds a close correspondence between the Stoic conception of *pneuma* and that of (the undisputed) Paul. For example, it would be obvious to a Stoic reader that the σώματα ἐπουράνια and σώματα ἐπίγεια of 1 Cor. 15.40 are to be identified, respectively, with the σῶμα πνευματικόν and σῶμα ψυχικόν of 15.44: of course heavenly bodies, those at the top of the *scala naturae*, are made up of *pneuma* (28). This element constitutes Christ's resurrection body, and will equally constitute the bodies of Christians at the resurrection, but at the same time is already present in them; thus can Paul speak of being 'in Christ' or Christ 'in him'. (One can only imagine what Käsemann would make of this, with his horror of any *corpus Christi mysticum* eliding the absolute difference between Christ and the church.)

Importantly, though, there is no conflict between a material conception of *pneuma* and its operation on human *understanding*. Engberg-Pedersen distinguishes between the 'purely instrumental' role of the *pneuma* – as when it raises Jesus from the dead (Rom. 8.11) – and a 'cognitive' role – as when it reveals God to the Corinthians (1 Cor. 2.10). But in both cases, it is the same element at work. Accordingly, 'there is absolutely no inconsistency in understanding [*pneuma*] as a physical entity and as a cognitive power that generates understanding' (65). Within such a holistic view, the strikingly 'physicalist' readings proposed by Engberg-Pedersen do not necessarily contradict prevailing cognitive and even metaphorical readings, which may be valid as far as they go, but complement and deepen them. He argues for 'a radical extension of the traditional way of reading [Paul] so as to include a whole dimension (the physical and bodily one) that has hitherto not been given its due'.[33]

Although it is not a major focus of his study, Engberg-Pedersen's account of the material *pneuma* has important implications for our interpretation of the spirit-filled body of Christ. Of the body described in 1 Cor. 12, he writes,

> Since the pneuma is itself a physical entity, the body that is Christ is in fact a real, physical body – it is coextensive with (if not just identical with) the pneumatic body that Paul will go on to talk about in chapter 15 of the letter. … Paul's talk of the 'single body' in verse 13 is not just a case of metaphorical speech. He intends it literally as referring to an entity that is a (tri-dimensional) body just as much as a

---

[32] Troels Engberg-Pedersen, *Cosmology and Self in the Apostle Paul: The Material Spirit* (Oxford: OUP, 2010). Engberg-Pedersen is indebted to Martin, in fact dedicating this book to him, but not uncritical of his account. He demurs from some of the more provocatively sweeping analysis in *The Corinthian Body*, e.g. the 'Marxist-inspired', class-based opposition between 'religious' and 'philosophical' thought (18).

[33] Ibid., 181. Engberg-Pedersen is more nuanced than Martin on Platonic views of the *pneuma*, especially Middle Platonism as received by patristic authors. For Martin, the immaterial spirit is a product of the Cartesian era, but as Engberg-Pedersen notes, the same view can be found in the Wisdom of Solomon and then Philo, 'from whom it migrated into the church fathers and later tradition' (16). One example of this might be Origen, who in *Princip.* is at pains to prove that *pneuma* – and therefore God – is *not* bodily: e.g. 'sed et his, qui per hoc quod dictum est quoniam deus spiritus est corpus esse arbitrantur deum, hoc modo respondendum est. consuetudo est scripturae sanctae, cum aliquid contrarium corpori huic crassiori et solidiori designare uult, spiritum nominare, sicut dicit: *littera occidit, spiritus autem uiuificat*' (*Traité des principes*, ed. Henri Crouzel and Manlio Simonetti, vol. 1, SC 252 (Paris: Cerf, 1978), 1.1.42–6).

normal, physical body, only it is made up of a different kind of 'stuff' from a body of flesh and blood. (174)

Such literalism does not exclude the cognitive function of Paul's 'body of Christ', any more than that of his purely pneumatological language. Just as the *pneuma* both is physical and generates understanding, so the pneumatically constituted body is both a concrete phenomenon and a conceptual framework. There should therefore be no difficulty in recognizing the metaphorical *aspects* of Paul's somatic language without rendering the whole discourse as exclusively, or indeed primarily, metaphor.[34]

Throughout *The Corinthian Body*, Martin introduces various comparisons to other undisputed Pauline letters, but hardly touches on the 'deuteropaulines' or Pastorals, letters which are also wholly absent from Engberg-Pedersen's *Cosmology and Self*. Yet the later development of the σῶμα Χριστοῦ motif raises questions where their approaches might be highly relevant. In particular, the relation between Christ as head and the church as his body takes on thematic importance, and the place of believing humanity in the cosmological 'maelstrom' receives heightened attention. It would perhaps be an interesting exercise to extend the analysis of these interpreters to the Ephesian body, particularly in the areas of ascension, headship and marriage. But at any rate, they show that a relentlessly realistic view of the body of Christ is not an invention of the 'Pauline school', but is thoroughly grounded in the undisputed writing of the apostle.

2.4. Ontology: Robert Jenson

In his *Systematic Theology*, Robert Jenson asks where the body of the risen Christ is to be located.[35] He follows Calvin in presupposing that anything called a body must, axiomatically, have its *place*,[36] but this poses a theological problem for post-Ptolemaic cosmology: there is no longer a fitting place within creation for the risen body of Christ. Where did Jesus ascend *to*? Formerly, he could be located in the outermost stratum of created space, the rarefied sphere of heaven, but this is impossible in a

---

[34] It is interesting to compare the realism of Martin and Engberg-Pedersen with that of Albert Schweitzer, who in some respects anticipates them. Schweitzer places great stress on the common corporeality (*Leiblichkeit*) shared by Christ and believers: this is no less than 'Die ursprüngliche und zentrale Gedanke der Mystik Pauli' (*Die Mystik*, 116). Paul's σῶμα Χριστοῦ is for Schweitzer a real physical entity, shared by Christ and Christians alike, in which participation goes both ways, Christ suffering for us and we for Christ: 'Die Vertauschbarkeit der Beziehungen geht darauf zurück, daß die betreffenden Existenzen in derselben Leiblichkeit naturhaft untereinander zusammenhängen und eine in die andere übergehen' (127). Yet for Schweitzer, this remains in the end a question of 'mysticism' rather than, as Engberg-Pedersen maintains, 'elemental pneumatic cosmology' (*Cosmology and Self*, 69). Contrast also Bultmann, for whom the conception of πνεῦμα as material (*Stoff*) is a 'mythology' to be distinguished from Paul's real intention (*Theologie*, 195). In view of the σῶμα πνευματικόν of 1 Cor. 15, Bultmann can only sustain this view by defining σῶμα as an *entirely* relational category – the person as an object to the self – divested of any inherently physical sense.
[35] For the following, see Robert W. Jenson, *Systematic Theology*, vol. 1 (Oxford: OUP, 1997), 201–6.
[36] If this seems to conflict with Martin's account of the fluid ancient body, recall that he discerns a dispute between Paul and the 'strong' about the relative firmness of the body's boundaries. That there are boundaries – however permeable – is a given.

Copernican universe, where in principle no one place is nearer God than any other. In their consequent bafflement, swathes of modern Christians have – effectively if not formally – simply relinquished belief in a bodily resurrection, and interpreted this language in a non-material, 'spiritualized' way. Jenson responds by way of Paul's somatic theology in 1 Corinthians (the whole letter, not just ch. 12).[37] From this one undisputed letter, Jenson develops a particularly rich Pauline account of church, sacraments and body; his reading challenges the view that Ephesians elevates Paul's ecclesiology and reifies his view of the body to the point of distortion.

First, Jenson excludes the possibility that the body of Christ is a metaphor.[38] Paul exploits its metaphorical possibilities, but across the various relevant passages in 1 Corinthians, 'there is no way to construe "body" as a simile or other trope that does not make mush of Paul's arguments' (1.205). Rather, he speaks about the body of Christ in the same way he speaks about ordinary human bodies: a person's 'body' means their availability as an object to self and others. (The echo of Bultmann is clear.) This is true not only in the fleshly body of everyday experience but also after the resurrection into a 'spiritual body' (1 Cor. 15.44). Similarly, when Paul speaks of Christ's eucharistic or ecclesial body, he means his availability as an object to us, in the sacrament and in the assembly. It is crucial for Jenson that Paul's ecclesial use of the term is grounded in the eucharistic. 'We many are one body, for we all partake of the one bread' (1 Cor. 10.17), while the Corinthians' divided eucharist fails to 'discern the body' (11.29).

> [In 1 Cor. 11.29,] we want to ask which body Paul has in mind, the bread about which he has just reported the dominical words 'This is my body', or the congregation that is in fact the offended entity and which he has just earlier called Christ's body. Paul's text makes sense only when we grasp that he means both at once, and would reject our question as meaningless. ... We must learn to say: the entity rightly called the body of Christ is whatever object it is that is Christ's availability to us as subjects; by the promise of Christ, this object is the bread and cup and the gathering of the church around them. There is where creatures can locate him, to respond to his word to them. (1.205)

---

[37] It is a common mistake to read the σῶμα Χριστοῦ of Ephesians and Colossians in relation only to ch. 12 of 1 Corinthians, when in fact this passage belongs within the broader and more complex somatic theology of the whole letter. For example, although Gregory Fewster's study is refreshingly integrative (see n. 16, p. 7 above), his conclusion – that the headship of Christ in Ephesians is a charism analogous with prophecy, teaching, etc. – reflects this selective focus.

[38] He invokes Käsemann here, noting however that, 'faithfully to the prejudices of his school', the German excludes a metaphysical reading lest conclusions like Jenson's own should follow (Robert Jenson, *Systematic Theology*, vol. 2 (Oxford: OUP, 1999), 212, n. 9.). Cf. also John A. T. Robinson, *The Body: A Study in Pauline Theology* (London: SCM, 1952), 51:

> To say that the Church is the body of Christ is no more of a metaphor than to say that the flesh of the incarnate Jesus or the bread of the Eucharist is the body of Christ. None of them is 'like' His body (Paul never says this): each of them *is* the body of Christ, in that each is the physical complement and extension of the one and same Person and Life.

Jenson acknowledges the influence of Robinson's study.

For Jenson, this is the only possible response to the Copernican conundrum. The risen body of Christ is not to be located in a separate sphere, but in that space within creation where Christ has chosen to make himself available. This is not so far from Käsemann, who spoke of the 'Herrschaftsbereich des Auferstandenen',[39] or indeed from Schlier's 'Heilsraum' and 'Heilsdimension'; for Käsemann, though, it was necessary to bracket such expressions off from any possible identification with the incarnate Jesus. Jenson, Schlier, Robinson and many others (from both sides of the Reformation divide) are not so delicate.

In his second volume, elaborating the ecclesiological implications of this reading, Jenson responds to the objection that close identification of the church with Christ tends to obliterate the distinction between them. It is precisely because of the eucharistic centre of the Corinthian somatic language that this concern is misplaced:

> The object that is the church-assembly is the body of Christ, that is, Christ available to the world and to her members, just in that the church gathers around objects distinct from herself, the bread and cup, which are the availability *to her* of the same Christ. (2.213)

Here again we encounter this increasingly familiar dialectic, that a subject is both identified with and distinct from its outwardly available presence. *Ad extra*, the church simply represents the presence of Christ, but within her own communion, she encounters him as an other. This distinction, on Jenson's account already implicit in 1 Corinthians, is further developed in Colossians and Ephesians, most obviously through the description of Christ as head – which Jenson does not discuss – but also through the spousal language of Eph. 5. The one citation he does introduce from Ephesians is to invoke the church as Christ's 'bride' and therefore other than him (5.31-32).[40] Where Dawes sees confusion between literal and metaphorical – and 'partitive' and 'unitive' – senses of σῶμα, Jenson sees a consistent dialectic between oneness and otherness. The consequent continuity between earlier and later Pauline letters should not pass unnoticed by biblical scholars, although he does not develop the point here.[41]

---

[39] 'Der Christusleib ... ist für den Apostel gerade in seiner Leiblichkeit die Wirklichkeit der Gemeinde, sofern sie als Herrschaftsbereich des Auferstandenen die neue Welt darstellt' (Käsemann, 'Amt und Gemeinde', 113).

[40] Jenson, *Systematic Theology*, 2.213 (of course, the text of Ephesians does not exactly say this). Cf. Anthony J. Kelly, '"The Body of Christ: Amen!": The Expanding Incarnation', TS 71 (2010): 792–816, who distinguishes between the 'body-subject' and 'body-object'. Although the human body can be reduced to an object for sexual, labour or scientific exploitation, 'the consideration of *somebody* only in this way, detached from personal consciousness, is obscene' (804). Theology goes astray when it considers the body of Christ in a purely objective way. Like Jenson, Kelly grounds his reading of Paul's σῶμα Χριστοῦ in 1 Corinthians, before turning to Eph. 5 for the expression of Christ's relation to his ecclesial body (808).

[41] Jenson does develop a similar point elsewhere in relation to ministerial office in the Pastoral letters. Their presentation of a self-perpetuating office looks beyond the apparently shorter horizon of the early Paul, a fact treated as unproblematic by Catholics and ignored by Protestants. Against both tendencies, Jenson urges theologians 'both to acknowledge that the development shown in the Pastorals is a kind of retreat and to say that God called it' (Robert W. Jenson, *Unbaptized God: The Basic Flaw in Ecumenical Theology* (Minneapolis, MN: Fortress, 1992), 116). Cf. Jenson, *Systematic Theology*, 2.228–30. Not unlike Childs or Aageson, Jenson sees a 'catholicizing' trajectory in the

Jenson's rather radical interpretation unsurprisingly provokes controversy, not only among those constitutionally unsympathetic but also among natural allies. One example of the latter is Susan Wood, whose explicitly Catholic response to Jenson's ecclesiology is at once appreciative and critical. According to Wood, Jenson is not merely consonant with Catholic ecclesiology but exceeds it, elevating the church 'beyond creaturely status'.[42] He identifies Christ and the church too readily, and his subject–object distinction is not sufficient to avoid confusion between them; Wood suggests that the relationship is better described as subject–subject (182). I am dubious about this criticism: in Jenson's account, bodily presence is precisely the availability of one subject to another, and Christ's embodiment ensures that the subject–subject relation between him and the church is truly reciprocal.[43]

Wood is right, though, that Jenson could make more use of the category of 'sacramentality' in speaking about the church itself.[44] Drawing on *Lumen Gentium* and its description of the church as 'sacrament-like' (*veluti sacramentum*), she discusses how this mode of presence differs from the simply historical, being less bound to the temporal and spatial limitations of normal bodily existence. There is only one body, but there are many loaves and cups; or again, eating the bread of the eucharist does not cause pain to the body of the man Jesus. The category of sacramental presence avoids too ready an identification between Christ and the church, while having a 'heavier ontological density than the "merely symbolic" or "sign"' (184, n. 8). This all seems to me quite consonant with Jenson's position, and the use of more explicitly sacramental language perhaps anticipates a possible misunderstanding rather than correcting an actual flaw.

Writing at the same time as Jenson, another theologian to explore the relation between Jesus's eucharistic and ecclesial body is Graham Ward.[45] Acknowledging Martin's account of fluidity and permeability in the ancient Mediterranean body, Ward maintains that such blurring of boundaries does not sufficiently account for the eucharistic 'this is my body', and its direct identification of Jesus's person with the bread:

> That ontological scandal is the epicentre for the shock-waves which follow. For it is actually the translocationality that is surprising – as if place and space itself are

---

later Pauline letters without evaluating it negatively. The same approach apparently informs his reading of Ephesians, though he does not say so.

[42] Susan K. Wood, 'Robert Jenson's Ecclesiology from a Roman Catholic Perspective', in *Trinity, Time and Church: A Response to the Theology of Robert W. Jenson*, ed. Colin E. Gunton (Grand Rapids, MI: Eerdmans, 2000), 178–87 (180).

[43] Here Jenson is following Hegel, arguing that when one subject is available as an object to the other, but not vice versa, this can only mean the enslavement of one party (*Systematic Theology*, 2.214; cf. also 1.155–6).

[44] For the following, see Wood, 'Jenson's Ecclesiology', 182–4.

[45] Graham Ward, 'Transcorporeality: The Ontological Scandal', BJRL 80 (1998): 235–52; and Ward, 'The Displaced Body of Jesus Christ', in *Radical Orthodoxy: A New Theology*, ed. John Milbank, Catherine Pickstock and Graham Ward (London: Routledge, 1999), 163–81. Interestingly, Ward like Jenson is influenced by Robinson's 'still seminal' study of Paul's body language ('Transcorporeality', 238, n. 7).

being redefined such that one can be a body here and also there, one can be this kind of body here and that kind of body there.[46]

Ward coins the term 'transcorporeality' for this phenomenon. Note that the nexus between body and place is not broken here, but expanded: the body of Jesus is encountered in particular places, in concrete and apprehensible ways, but is also continually *dis*placed, unable to be held onto and explained.

After the ascension, Jesus's earthly body – 'the body of the gendered Jew' – is withdrawn to make way for his body the church, 'the fullness of him who fills all in all', as Ward quotes from 'Colossians' [sic].[47] In his earlier article on this subject, the same verse is translated differently (but attributed correctly): 'The Church is Christ's body, the completion of him who himself completes all things everywhere.'[48] Ward is not concerned with the letter's authorship, but neither, it seems, with any substantive difference from the earlier Paul, nor indeed from the gospels, which are his main point of reference for the institution of the eucharist. The importance of Ephesians in his argument is that it uniquely attests to the expansiveness of the ascended Christ's bodily presence, of his 'transcorporeal' immanence through all creation, in the church. So emphatic is Ward on this point that he ends up considerably beyond Jenson:

> God in Christ dies and the church is born. One gives way to the other, without remainder. The relationship between Jesus and the church is processional, as the relationship between the trinitarian persons is processional.[49]

I will not attempt a proper response to Ward's fascinating and complex analysis.[50] At this point I would only observe that the danger detected by Käsemann in Schlier and indeed in Ephesians itself, and which troubled Wood in Jenson, seems a more legitimate concern here: that the difference between the person of Christ and the church as his body is elided. Perhaps this does not do justice to the nuance of Ward's position. But it does seem to me that attention to the full spectrum of somatic language across the CP, and in Ephesians in particular, averts this danger, requiring instead a constant dialectic between Christ's total presence in his ecclesial body and his distinction as a subject over against that body. In his attentive reading of 1 Corinthians, Jenson is alive to this dialectic; in my view, it emerges still more strongly in the Ephesian account of the body of Christ.

---

[46] Ward, 'Displaced Body', 168.
[47] Ibid., 175–6 (and a couple of paragraphs later, Gal. 3.28 is miscited as Phil. 2.12!).
[48] Ward, 'Transcorporeality', 247.
[49] Ward, 'Displaced Body', 177.
[50] Ward also discusses the textual mediation of the body of Christ, in fact of all bodies. Although he insists that the words of institution are 'not a simile … not a metaphor … not an analogy … not a symbol' ('Transcorporeality', 237; similarly, 'Displaced Body', 168), he concludes that, in his account of 'transcorporeality', 'the body accepts its own metaphorical nature insofar as it is received and understood only in and through language. Only God sees and understands creation literally' ('Transcorporeality', 251). This is an example of an understanding of metaphor so 'thick' that it can be theologically apposite in this context, but it is quite different from the reductively literary reading of Paul's σῶμα Χριστοῦ that I am opposing.

Table 3 Aspects of Σῶμα Χριστοῦ in 1 Corinthians and Romans

many in one/ unity and diversity	union with Christ	sharing in the death of Christ	body is named as Christ's	baptism into a person/ body	constituted by food and drink	the Spirit/ spiritual
—	1 Cor. 10.4 (proleptically)	—	—	1 Cor. 10.2 (into Moses)	1 Cor. 10.3-4	1 Cor. 10.3-4
1 Cor. 10.17	1 Cor. 10.16	1 Cor. 10.16 (blood)	1 Cor. 10.16	—	1 Cor. 10.16-17	—
1 Cor. 11.17-22 (negatively)	1 Cor. 11.23-29	1 Cor. 11.26 (proclaiming)	1 Cor. 11.24-25, 27	—	1 Cor. 11.23-29	—
1 Cor. 12.12-27	1 Cor. 12.27	—	1 Cor. 12.27	1 Cor. 12.13	—	1 Cor. 12.1-13
—	Rom. 6.3-11	Rom. 6.3-11	—	Rom. 6.3-4	—	—
—	Rom. 7.4	Rom. 7.4	Rom. 7.4	—	—	(Rom. 7.6)
Rom. 12.4-8	Rom. 12.5	—	(Rom. 12.5, one body *in* Christ)	—	—	—

3. Exegesis

The σῶμα Χριστοῦ in the CP is not so much a distinct doctrine as the central nexus in a cluster of related ideas. It is associated with Paul's general participatory understanding of Christian life, with baptism and the eucharist, with the bodily lives of believers, with the unity of diverse gifts and groups and with the Spirit. Clearly, it would be impossible to address every tangentially relevant text. Table 3 sets out how some of these related ideas occur together at a number of important *loci* in 1 Corinthians and Romans, and shows why I do choose to include some texts like 1 Cor. 10.1-4 and Rom. 6.3-11 that do not mention the actual phrase σῶμα Χριστοῦ. The choice of texts from Colossians and Ephesians is more self-evident.

3.1. 1 Corinthians

The first text of major relevance is 1 Cor. 10.16-17, but the earlier verses of the same chapter provide important context for Paul's first mention of the eucharistic body. The rhetorical thrust here is a warning against idolatry, and particularly the danger of bodily mingling with hostile spiritual powers.[51] The catastrophic experience of Israel in the desert is introduced as a paradigmatic counterexample. By bringing together

---

[51] The argument of 1 Cor. 8–10 is notoriously difficult, especially the apparent contradiction between 10.1-22 and 8.4-13/10.23-30. There are many interpretations of this difference, but without going into that question, I consider it unmistakeable from 10.1-22 that Paul considers idolatry a real, present and bodily threat to the Corinthians. That is all that matters for our purposes.

several different scriptural episodes, Paul presents the whole trajectory of wilderness apostasy as anticipating the Corinthians' peril: their ancestors are not just cautionary tales for them, but their τύποι (10.6).

In view of what will follow, it is striking how 1 Cor. 10.1-4 describes the wilderness generation in the language of physical participation: their solidarity comes through 'baptism into Moses' (10.2) and the consumption of spiritual food and drink (10.3-4). Moreover, in a gnomic parenthesis, the rock from which they drank is identified as Christ himself (10.4). Although Martin hardly touches on these verses, perhaps because they do not mention the body as such, they are a good example of the fluid interpersonal boundaries he emphasizes. The elements which envelop the Israelites – cloud and sea – and which they ingest – manna and water – constitute a real physical union between them, with their leader Moses, and especially with the divine source of their sustenance.[52] The chief significance of Christ's petrific peregrination in 10.4 is that the Israelites are ultimately united with the same person that the Corinthians are. To paraphrase: 'You, like your fathers, are participants in Christ; and you, like them, can nevertheless be destroyed through idolatry.'[53]

The following verses refer to incidents from Ex. 32 (10.7), Num. 25 (10.8), Num. 21 (10.9) and Num. 16–17 (10.10); the whole comes under the general head of 'desiring evil things' (10.6), recalling the 'tombs of desire' incident in Num. 11. As Watson argues, these various episodes may be taken as different expressions of the root problem, desire, in each case leading to death.[54] It is noteworthy, though, how the kinds of desire recounted here relate to the immediate problem of 1 Cor. 10. The affair of the quails in Num. 11 and the 'testing' of Num. 21 arise from the Israelites' dissatisfaction with the 'spiritual food and drink' provided in the desert (we might even say they failed to 'discern the body' in what they were consuming). The crisis of Num. 25 involves not only πορνεία but also idolatry and the eating of food offered to idols (25.2). Although Paul singles out πορνεία – itself a major Corinthian issue, we know, and equally concerned with bodily boundaries – the other transgressions are if anything more pertinent. And the golden calf of Ex. 32 is, of course, the archetypal idolatry. It is invoked here via an otherwise tangential verse, a reference to the people's eating

---

[52] The alternative reading, prevalent in the modern age, is to consign the 'spiritual' to the realm of supernatural immateriality. E.g. Weiss takes the spiritual food and drink, like the spiritual body of 15.44, to denote 'etwas Übernatürliches, Himmlisches' (*1. Korintherbrief*, 251); similarly, Lietzmann translates πνευματικόν in 10.3-4 as 'überirdisch' and further glosses it as 'übernatürlich, göttlich' (*An die Korinther I, II*, 2nd edn, HNT 9 (Tübingen: Mohr Siebeck, 1923), 46). Studies like Martin's and Engberg-Pedersen's have shown this approach to be unsatisfactory.

[53] This is another place where Paul's straightforwardly realistic language tends now to be read metaphorically, e.g. the desert prefigurations of baptism and the eucharist are 'fanciful analogies' (Richard B. Hays, *Echoes of Scripture in the Letters of Paul* (New Haven, CT: Yale University, 1989), 91; similarly in his commentary). For a survey of views on the relation between Christ and the rock, see Anthony C. Thiselton, *The First Epistle to the Corinthians: A Commentary on the Greek Text*, NIGTC (Grand Rapids, MI: Eerdmans & Paternoster, 2000), 727–30. I agree that 'it is better to allow the exegesis to determine how we understand τύπος' than the reverse (730), but I am not sure that Thiselton actually does so. In the direct predicate of 10.4, by far the simplest reading indicates the presence of the pre-existent Christ; all the alternatives are more or less laboured.

[54] Francis Watson, *Paul and the Hermeneutics of Faith*, 2nd edn (London: Bloomsbury, 2016), 334–8.

and drinking the offerings sacrificed before the idol (32.6); again, the significance can hardly have been lost on the Corinthians.[55]

The danger to the wilderness generation was not merely disobedience or even desire in a general sense, but the desire for other gods. By first setting out their shared corporeality with Moses and ultimately with Christ, through baptism and spiritual food and drink, Paul heightens the bodily character of the people's subsequent apostasy. Through partaking of idol food, through rejecting the Lord's food and drink and through πορνεία, they exchange their union with Christ for union with idols. That is not just a parallel to the Corinthians' present predicament; it is the same thing. Such is the context when Paul turns to the eucharistic communion in the body of Christ. This is his crowning argument against idolatry, one which he implies should self-evidently convince sensible people (10.14-15):

1 Cor. 10.16-17 Τὸ ποτήριον τῆς εὐλογίας ὃ εὐλογοῦμεν, οὐχὶ κοινωνία ἐστὶν τοῦ αἵματος τοῦ Χριστοῦ; τὸν ἄρτον ὃν κλῶμεν, οὐχὶ κοινωνία τοῦ σώματος τοῦ Χριστοῦ ἐστιν; ὅτι εἷς ἄρτος, ἓν σῶμα οἱ πολλοί ἐσμεν, οἱ γὰρ πάντες ἐκ τοῦ ἑνὸς ἄρτου μετέχομεν.

The former of these verses makes a natural climax to the surrounding argument. The spiritual food and drink of the church, the eucharist, constitutes a real participation (κοινωνία) in the body and blood of Christ. Comparable ontological communion occurs through the manna and rock water of the wilderness generation, through the idol food that they ate, through the sacrifices offered and eaten by contemporary Israel (10.18) and through the cup and table of demons for which the Corinthian 'strong' feel themselves free (10.20) (κοινωνοί in both these latter cases). If 10.16 quotes a liturgical formula, that would cohere with its function here, since Paul treats the words as axiomatic: in view of the corporeal communion established between readers and Christ through the eucharist, all rival communions are necessarily excluded, especially communion with demons.

The identification between the people and Christ's body is not complete in 10.16. They are not here told that they *are* the body of Christ, only that they are participants in his blood and his body. This verse still maintains an 'otherness' between Christ and people, which becomes especially important in relation to chs 11 and 12, as Jenson shows. The body is also secondary to the blood in this verse, which may perhaps reflect, as Käsemann argues, an original emphasis of the eucharistic formula on sharing in Jesus's *death*. That makes the transition to 10.17 all the more significant, for there the focus moves to the unity of diverse members rather than solidarity in Jesus's sacrifice.

---

[55] The 'grumbling' episode (1 Cor. 10.10) does not so easily fit this pattern. The incident in question (the Korah rebellion of Num. 16–17, rather than Num. 14; see ibid., 336–7) involves a more than usually absolute rejection of Moses's and Aaron's leadership, and so may relate more to the people's repudiation of their 'baptism into Moses' than to their communion in spiritual food and drink. The final warning against provoking the Lord to jealousy (10.22) is a further reference to Israel's idolatry, the verb παραζηλόω echoing Deut. 32.21 and Ps. 77.58.

The shift is obvious if the passage is read omitting v. 17; the argument flows much more naturally. Paul must have good reason for adding what is effectively an aside.[56]

The verse is a pleonastic chiasm, doubly underlining the oneness of the bread and its causal connection (ὅτι ... γάρ) with the oneness of the ecclesial body. The point could hardly be more emphatic. Communion in the body of Christ via the eucharistic bread means corresponding communion between the partakers; to be severally incorporated with one Lord entails equal incorporation with one another. Moreover, the noun σῶμα is here predicated directly of believers, so that they are more than just participants in the body, they *are* the body. The eucharistic and ecclesial bodies are related not contingently, but intrinsically, in two ways: partaking in Christ's eucharistic body means (1) being *identified with* that body and, consequently, (ii) being *united* to one another. The distinction between Christ and his body recedes here.[57]

Again, Käsemann may be right in suggesting that the conjunction between the eucharistic and the ecclesial bodies is a Pauline innovation.[58] But his insistence that Paul in fact keeps the two bodies separate, despite making a 'comparison' between them, is far from convincing, and betrays discomfort (one cannot help feeling Käsemann would rather Paul had *not* made the comparison). He sees the mystery-like incorporation into the historical Jesus's death (10.16) and the unity of the Christian community (10.17) as two different things, but this is only possible by taking σῶμα to have opposite meaning in the two verses; that is, by exactly reversing the force of Paul's emphatic causal connection. By sifting the text for hypothetical sources, he obscures the consistency of the actual Pauline argument. The dynamic of the one and the many will be further teased out in 1 Cor. 11 and (especially) 12; 10.17 anticipates this later discussion, and shows it to be integral to the very idea of the σῶμα Χριστοῦ. But it is also relevant to the immediate context.

Although the presenting problem in 1 Cor. 8–10 is idol food, Paul couches it in terms of the love and upbuilding owed by the strong to the weak. The indulgence of their 'knowledge' comes at the cost of their weaker brethren. When it comes to the divided eucharist of ch. 11, once again a privileged party is feasting to the exclusion of the poor. The spiritual gifts discussed in chs 12–14 are also the occasion of division, with the 'inspired' excluding those who do not understand their glossolalia. In each case, Paul refers to the body of Christ as the foundation and mandate of the congregation's unity, obliging the strong to modify their behaviour. The oneness of the body is no less relevant in ch. 10 than in the later iterations; although it is not thematized at 10.16-17 as it later will be, it is wholly apposite in a part of the letter deeply concerned with mutual responsibility.

---

[56] Characteristically, Weiss suggests, albeit tentatively, excluding this 'mystically' oriented verse as an insertion (*1. Korintherbrief*, 259).

[57] For the many commentators who treat σῶμα as a metaphor, it is easy to reduce this intrinsic relation to an analogy, since the predicate in v. 17 is then understood only descriptively. E.g. Gordon D. Fee, *The First Epistle to the Corinthians*, NIGTC (Grand Rapids, MI: Eerdmans, 1987), 469–70; Richard B. Hays, *First Corinthians*, Interpretation (Louisville, KY: Knox, 1997), 167–8; or Thiselton, *1 Corinthians*, 769–70. We have already seen good reason to reject this approach. Thiselton's use of Ricoeur's 'split reference' gives a fuller, but still ultimately unsatisfactory, account of the 'metaphor'.

[58] Käsemann, 'Das theologische Problem', 193–4.

Participation in the eucharist, unity among Christians and their identity with the body of Christ are in 10.16-17 three aspects of a single phenomenon. The first two are further developed in ch. 11, with subtler reference also to the last, which will return explicitly in ch. 12. At 11.2, Paul turns from the question of idolatry to two issues of 'tradition', the covering of women's but not men's heads at prayer (vv. 2-16) and divisions at the eucharist (vv. 17-34). Paul is able to commend (ἐπαινέω) the Corinthians for faithfully handing on tradition (παραδίδωμι, παράδοσις) in the former case but not the latter (vv. 2, 17, 22-23); indeed, the former trouble may be only with certain dissidents (Εἰ δέ τις δοκεῖ φιλόνεικος εἶναι, v. 16). For our purposes, the relevant point here is tradition itself, and relation to the wider church. Paul's clincher argument in v. 16 is that to depart from established practice is to contradict the practice of the other 'churches of God'. This touches on the Corinthians' besetting sin of factionalism, but on a broader scale: the danger is that one local church becomes a schismatic party separated from the others. It is not only a question of synchronic oneness – the common communion of different local churches – but also of diachronic oneness – the faithfulness of the church in a single, persisting identity. Continuity of tradition is essential to both.

Unsurprisingly, then, when Paul turns to the internal divisions at the Corinthian eucharist, he is warm in rebuke. In fact the simultaneous feasting of some and fasting of others so deeply contradicts the received practice that it can no longer be called the Lord's supper at all (v. 20). His response is to rehearse the tradition itself, the liturgical words (vv. 23-26)[59] which make the strongest possible argument for diachronic unity. The eucharist is an iterative action (ὁσάκις, vv. 25, 26), situated between past and future events (τὸν θάνατον τοῦ κυρίου ... ἄχρι οὗ ἔλθῃ, v. 26), in which the remembered and anticipated Lord is brought into the present (ἀνάμνησις, vv. 24-25). Here more than anywhere else, the gathered community receives its identity as a single fellowship, persisting through time, just as they receive elements named as the Lord's own body and blood.

Those partaking of the one eucharistic body, in common with Christians past and present and with Jesus himself, *must* be one body in their internal communion. That is the point of the syllogism introduced by Paul at 10.16-17, and it is the whole logic of 11.17-34. The gorging rich are censured now not merely because they are causing internal unrest, but because by failing to realize that one bread entails one body, they are denying the nature of the eucharist itself. If they appreciated the force of the words of institution, they would understand that it is Christ himself they encounter in this meal, and that to abuse it is to abuse him (ἔνοχος [εἶναι] τοῦ σώματος καὶ τοῦ αἵματος τοῦ κυρίου, v. 27). That is the significance of 'discerning the body', and the reason the following verses are so gravely admonitory.

---

[59] Most commentators take the traditional material to end with v. 25, and v. 26 to be Paul's reflection on it, e.g. Thiselton, *1 Corinthians*, 886; Wolfgang Schrage, *Der erste Brief an die Korinther*, vol. 3, EKKNT 7 (Zürich: Benziger & Neukirchener, 1999), 44. Schrage notes the move from the first to the third person, but to my mind that does not imply breaking off the traditional or liturgical words. To single out only Christ's *death* would be a curious rhetorical choice in the context if this is indeed Paul's comment.

The example of Israel in the desert has already shown that bodily participation in Christ is no infallible prophylactic. One can share in the common baptism and the common meal and yet still be cut off, like 'most of them' (10.5). So it is no surprise in 11.19 to find Paul interpreting the Corinthian factions in a similar, probative light: they will reveal who is 'genuine' (δόκιμος). This is spelt out in 11.27-34. At the eucharist, one is to 'test' oneself (δοκιμάζω, v. 28) and only thus partake, that is if on examination, one will not do so 'unworthily' (ἀναξίως, v. 27). It is instructive to compare the group of cognate words that amplify this in what follows:

29	One eats and drinks judgement (κρίμα) on oneself if not discerning (διακρίνω) *the body*
30	(Deleterious consequences manifest at Corinth)
31	But if we discerned (διακρίνω) *ourselves*, we would not be judged (κρίνω)
32	Judged (κρίνω) by the Lord, we are disciplined so as not to be condemned (κατακρίνω)
33-34	So wait for one another, lest your gathering be for judgement (κρίμα)

Judgement (κρίνω/κρίμα) is salutary and not ultimately fatal, as distinct from condemnation (κατακρίνω). Even the sickness and death experienced in Corinth comes under the head of judgement or discipline (παιδεύω, v. 30); it does not (yet) amount to condemnation. Conversely, the alternative to negative judgement is positive discernment (διακρίνω). And it is here that the critical point becomes clear. The parallel between vv. 29 and 31 is exact and deliberate. To discern *the body* means to discern *ourselves*: correctly recognizing Christ in the eucharist means recognizing him in the community. Both aspects equally characterize the true perception which is the alternative to judgement.[60]

So Paul identifies the people with the body, and the meal with the body and blood of Christ, at just the same time, and thus confirms that 10.16-17 was no aberration. Those who correctly discern Christ's body and blood in the bread and cup know that partaking, they are themselves integrated into that body (cf. 10.16); and those who correctly discern themselves as Christ's body cannot be divided as the Corinthians are (cf. 10.17).[61] As before, the connection between the eucharistic and ecclesial bodies is intrinsic and causative, not merely contingent, and we cannot with Käsemann reduce it to a 'comparison'. We must agree with Jenson: to force an alternative between these

---

[60] Against Lietzmann, for whom ἑαυτὸν διακρίνειν (v. 31) and ἑαυτὸν δοκιμάζειν (v. 28) are synonymous ('sich selbst prüfen'), but contrast with τὸ σῶμα διακρίνειν (v. 29) ('den Leib unterscheiden') (*Korinther*, 60–1). But this runs quite contrary to Paul's careful choice of words.

[61] Similarly Mitchell: the argument that eucharistic and ecclesial bodies are discerned together 'works rhetorically because in 10.16-17 Paul laid down the premises which also function in this later argument' (Margaret M. Mitchell, *Paul and the Rhetoric of Reconciliation: An Exegetical Investigation of the Language and Composition of 1 Corinthians*, HUT 28 (Tübingen: Mohr Siebeck, 1991), 265, n. 442, citing in support Bornkamm and Conzelmann, among others).

senses of σῶμα is simply to resist the close correlation which is the point of Paul's argument.

Finally we come to ch. 12, the passage which is perhaps most readily associated with the Pauline teaching about Christ's body. Our discussion will in fact be quite brief, since as we have seen, the deeper theological foundations have already been laid in chs 10 and 11. What follows in ch. 12 is a consistent development of these ideas, applied to the contentious question of spiritual gifts. The particular grounds for the controversy will not become clear until ch. 14, but Paul begins with a more general discussion of the ordering of gifts; one reason may be that his governing image, the body of Christ, arises so naturally from the preceding discussion of the eucharist. While it is usual, and correct, to read ch. 12 as part of the larger unit of chs 12-14, that should not obscure the close connections with the previous chapters. This is especially important because if those connections are overlooked, it is easier to read ch. 12 as an unremarkably metaphorical example of the 'society-as-body topos'.

The introductory verses 12.1-3 anticipate the eventual concern with glossolalia: the criterion for what is truly of the Spirit is not 'inspired utterance' per se, but the 'intelligible content' of that utterance conforming with the Christian confession.[62] The rest of the chapter falls into two main parts, discussing first gifts of the Spirit, then unity and diversity in the body. The body is not mentioned in vv. 1-11, nor the Spirit in vv. 14-31, and these two distinct sections stand in a straightforward analogical relation. God appoints many and various members to the body, and dissension between them would be absurd (vv. 14-20); God arranges that lesser members receive greater honour, which entails the solidarity of the whole, rather than the apportioning of suffering and joy to different parts (vv. 21-26). So it is with you, Christ's body, among whom God appoints various roles (vv. 27-31), corresponding to the various gifts distributed by God's Spirit for the common good (vv. 4-11). The analogy is so clear, the use of the body so plainly illustrative (with the talking foot, ear and eye), that it is unsurprising many interpreters have concluded Paul's somatic language is just a grand simile or metaphor. That interpretation, however, founders on the pivotal verses 12.12-13, the crux of the chapter and the one point where the two key terms of σῶμα and πνεῦμα are brought together.

1 Cor. 12.12-13 Καθάπερ γὰρ τὸ σῶμα ἕν ἐστιν καὶ μέλη πολλὰ ἔχει, πάντα δὲ τὰ μέλη τοῦ σώματος πολλὰ ὄντα ἕν ἐστιν σῶμα, οὕτως καὶ ὁ Χριστός· καὶ γὰρ ἐν ἑνὶ πνεύματι ἡμεῖς πάντες εἰς ἓν σῶμα ἐβαπτίσθημεν, εἴτε Ἰουδαῖοι εἴτε Ἕλληνες εἴτε δοῦλοι εἴτε ἐλεύθεροι, καὶ πάντες ἓν πνεῦμα ἐποτίσθημεν.

'Just as the body ... so also Christ.' At first glance, 12.12 looks like a straightforward comparison that will not particularly stretch the ordinary sense of σῶμα, in keeping with the analogy that dominates the chapter. But crucially, Paul does not write οὕτως καὶ ἡ ἐκκλησία, but ὁ Χριστός. Unlike the usual 'society-as-body topos', the comparison here is not with an organization but with a person.[63] We have already

---

[62] Fee, *1 Corinthians*, 575.
[63] So Lietzmann identifies in this verse a leap (*Gedankensprung*) from the conventional comparative topos to Pauline mysticism (*Korinther*, 63). For him as for Schweitzer, the category of 'mysticism'

observed in relation to Martin's work that this aspect of personal identity is distinctive to Paul's adaptation of the conventional idea. Whereas Menenius Agrippa compares body with polis, Paul compares body with body: human with divine, personal with transpersonal. The identity of Christ's body with the Christian community is by now presumed, in light of the previous chapters; otherwise, this comparison with *Christ* would be unintelligible. The analogical development in ch. 12 does not depart from the earlier somatic theology, but building on that foundation, expands its social or organizational dimension.

In 12.13 the relationship between σῶμα and πνεῦμα is finally made explicit, in terms which hark back to 10.1-4 and complete the sacramental typology begun there. The baptism foreshadowed in the wilderness has now been received, and the spiritual drink that mysteriously united the Israelites with Christ now nourishes those in his body. Far from being 'fanciful analogies', the τύποι introduced in ch. 10 are genuine anticipations of exactly what is now realized in the church, namely bodily participation in the one God of Israel and Jesus Christ. That at least is so in the case of 'spiritual drink', which Paul made clear united the Israelites with Christ (10.4). Baptism 'into Moses' is more obviously a partial foreshadowing of the Christian rite, but still clearly means for Paul a real kind of bodily participation in the same God.

Christian baptism is described here as ἐν ἑνὶ πνεύματι and εἰς ἓν σῶμα. The identity of this particular σῶμα is unambiguous after the previous verse: Christ has a body that may be compared to a human body (v. 12), and by receiving his Spirit you have been made part of it (v. 13).[64] The oneness of the body evidently corresponds to the oneness of the Spirit, which has been so repeatedly stressed in vv. 4-11; 'oneness' is in fact the common element that relates the chapter's two halves. That all share in a single Spirit necessarily means that the body will be one. So natural has this association come to seem with long familiarity that it requires an effort to notice its logic. The Spirit in v. 13 is the means by which the Christian many have been brought into one body; it is no less than the physical substance of their union. Here more than anywhere else in Paul's somatic theology, it is essential to remember the materiality of the Spirit in his worldview, or else the concreteness of the union will be overlooked. Baptism represents real contact with Christ's Spirit; 'drinking' represents the real reception of the same Spirit into a person's body (whether through baptismal water, or the eucharist, or both), and therefore a substantive bodily link with Christ himself and all others who have similarly partaken. In neither ch. 10 nor 11 nor 12 is bodily communion with Christ a figure of speech or an idealization. It is the expression, as plain as Paul can make it in the terms available to him, of what it means for Jesus Christ's πνεῦμα to be actually in the bodies of believers.[65]

---

allows the cognitive sincerity of Paul's participatory theology to be acknowledged without conceding its concrete realism.

[64] Cf. Engberg-Pedersen: 'Paul begins with a straightforward comparison: "just as ... so it is ...". By verse 13, however, the entity ("Christ") which was compared with a normal, physical body has itself *become* a body, one that is constituted by the pneuma' (*Cosmology and Self*, 174).

[65] The modern failure to comprehend the material dimension of Paul's pneumatology can dramatically constrain the sympathetic appreciation of his theology as a whole, not least his somatic ecclesiology. This is illustrated by Weiss's extraordinarily plaintive comment on 12.13. Rightly recognizing that the Spirit constituting Christians as one body is to be identified with Christ himself, he muses,

3.2. Romans

1 Corinthians offers the most thorough treatment of the body of Christ among the undisputed letters, but in Romans, though the subject is less extensively discussed, there is some important development. It is treated thematically for only a few verses (12.4-8), recapitulating one element of 1 Cor. 12, the cooperation of different gifts in the church analogously to different bodily members. But the familiarity of the image should not mask the distance from the earlier letter: there is no mention here of baptism, the rule of God over the body, or the shared suffering and rejoicing of members, let alone the eucharistic constitution of the body in 1 Cor. 10 and 11. Above all, the role of the Spirit (or the spiritual) does not arise. It is only the cooperative element that is recalled; in fact we find here simply the familiar 'society-as-body topos', expressed in Christian terms to be sure, but not particularly distinctive because the body in question is Christ's own. This, I think, reflects the immediate context of very general paranesis, with Paul making a brief point about the interdependence of gifts alongside other quite broad ethical instructions. That is probably the reason that the readers are called not the body *of* Christ, but one body *in* Christ: the focus is kept on the unity of members, not the theological ontology of the body.

If that were all, Romans might seem to offer only a partial and perfunctory rehearsal of 1 Cor. 12, and we could pass over it quickly. But in fact one earlier verse touches our subject more closely:

Rom. 7.4 ὥστε, ἀδελφοί μου, καὶ ὑμεῖς ἐθανατώθητε τῷ νόμῳ διὰ τοῦ σώματος τοῦ Χριστοῦ, εἰς τὸ γενέσθαι ὑμᾶς ἑτέρῳ, τῷ ἐκ νεκρῶν ἐγερθέντι

At a glance, this verse may seem of dubious relevance. Surely the phrase διὰ τοῦ σώματος τοῦ Χριστοῦ refers to the fleshly body of Christ on the cross, meaning that only through the event of Calvary can the Romans be said to have died to the law? No doubt; still if Paul wished to say no more than that, it would be surprising to introduce the *body* here, rather than say simply 'through the death of Christ' or 'the cross of Christ'. The point of interest is that the readers' participation in Christ's death should be expressed in the words σῶμα Χριστοῦ.

This passage continues the argument of Rom. 6, where baptism into and participation in Christ's death is expressed in strongly concrete, bodily terms (vv. 1-11), and the readers are accordingly enjoined to devote their mortal body (σῶμα θνητόν) and members (μέλη) to new life (12-19). Although the phrase σῶμα Χριστοῦ does not occur in ch. 6, the conceptuality is closely related: to be 'in Christ' is described as an embodied union of the believer's personal suffering, death and resurrection with

> Wie dies gedacht werden kann, daß die scharfumrissene Persönlichkeit des erhöhten Christus zugleich die gestaltlos durch viele Wesen hindurch flutende göttliche Kraft des Pneuma sei, ist für uns ein fast unlösbares Problem …; es ist die unvermeidliche Begleiterscheinung der mystischen Frömmigkeit. Wenn nicht nur in einem, sondern in allen Gläubigen Christus sein soll und zugleich alle Gläubigen in Christo, so muß die Vorstellung von Christus erweicht, aufgelöst, in pantheisierender Weise entpersönlicht werden, und dafür ist diese Gleichsetzung mit dem πνεῦμα der Ausdruck. (*1. Korintherbrief*, 303)

his. In 7.1-6, Paul elaborates the implications of this union with respect to the law: the death of the 'body of Christ' is efficacious to set the readers free only because they have just been shown to be united with precisely that body. To take διὰ τοῦ σώματος τοῦ Χριστοῦ at 7.4 as a reference *exclusively* to the historical person of Jesus exactly reverses the argument of ch. 6, that his own death and resurrection is not a single past phenomenon, but incorporates the readers, presently and bodily. Robinson, who sees so clearly the coherence of Pauline thought on this subject, reads it rightly:

> Here the words [διὰ τοῦ σώματος τοῦ Χριστοῦ] mean *both* 'through the fact that Christ in His flesh-body died to the law' *and* 'through the fact that you are now joined to and part of that body'.[66]

I would observe also that the address here is in the plural: embodiment with Christ is not an individual affair but equally entails union with other Christians. In other words, this is an ecclesial as well as a personal statement, at least by implication. Although this 'organizational', corporate dimension of the σῶμα Χριστοῦ is not developed here, it is precisely that aspect which is later introduced in Rom. 12.4-8. Personal and ecclesial participation in the body of Christ are conceptual corollaries, whether they are explicitly discussed together, as in 1 Corinthians, or not, as in Romans.

An interesting twist then arises. In the notoriously asymmetrical analogy of the widow in Rom. 7.1-6, Christ occupies two places: he is the one who has died, and so by sharing in his death, believers are freed from the law. But he is also the one who has been raised, the one to whom they can now belong. In his body, they die, and are set free – for him. This is, I think, the one place in the undisputed letters where the body of Christ, and Christ himself, are named as being in a distinct relation to one another. He is both identified with his body and stands apart from it as an other. Inasmuch as they are in Christ's body, believers are simply identified with him, die and are set free with him. But still there remains the uncontainable Christ to encounter this body anew, from without.

This is an important observation. If correct, the distinction stands in continuity with 1 Cor. 10–11 as read by Jenson, where at once the church is Christ's body to the world, and the bread of the eucharist is Christ's body to the church. The relationship is formulated more directly here than it ever is in 1 Corinthians, however. This verse then also anticipates the much more developed account of Christ's 'otherness' from his body in Colossians and, especially, Ephesians. Interpreters like Käsemann, suspicious on theological grounds, insist that in the undisputed letters, Christ is never described in distinct relation to his own body, but although that thesis holds for 1 Corinthians, in my opinion it falters at Rom. 7.4. If there is indeed the kernel of such a distinction in this verse, of course it need not necessarily have grown into

---

[66] Robinson, *The Body*, 47. Only a small minority of modern interpreters take a similar view (another example is C. H. Dodd, *The Epistle of Paul to the Romans* (London: Hodder & Stoughton, 1932), 101–2). The consensus is to exclude any ecclesial or indeed eucharistic reference from σῶμα Χριστοῦ here. Käsemann's view is that, like 1 Cor. 10.16, it draws on pre-Pauline eucharistic usage referring only to the crucified body (*Römer*, 181).

the fuller expression of Christ as head or spouse. That is one possible interpretative option, one which in fact was taken up in the later letters, but it was not an inevitable development, and it is still possible to play down its importance if Romans is read apart from the wider CP. A canonically integrative reading will not take this line, however. There is a continuity here which should correct an exaggerated opposition between the 'authentic' and 'deuteropauline' σῶμα Χριστοῦ.

3.3. Colossians

Colossians and Ephesians have much in common in their treatment of Christ's body, but as we have seen elsewhere, they turn out to differ more extensively below the surface. I will give an overview here of the motif's development in Colossians, but reserve more detailed discussion and comparison for the following section on Ephesians.

Nowhere in the undisputed letters is the church actually called a 'body' in so many words. 'You' or 'we' are the body of Christ; this is discernible in the church (1 Cor. 12.27-28), and derives from κοινωνία in the eucharistic body (10.16-17, 11.24); but σῶμα and ἐκκλησία are not joined in a literal copula. It is in Col. 1 that this first occurs, at the same time that Christ is first called the head of the body: αὐτός ἐστιν ἡ κεφαλὴ τοῦ σώματος τῆς ἐκκλησίας (1.18). The relationship between the two genitives is epexegetical apposition, not subordination; the body *is* the church.[67] This will be confirmed in a direct copula a few verses later: ὑπὲρ τοῦ σώματος αὐτοῦ [sc. Χριστοῦ], ὅ ἐστιν ἡ ἐκκλησία (1.24). The reference to the church is a slight departure in the hymn, which has so far been focusing on Christ's relationship with 'all things', and for that reason it is sometimes regarded as an authorial insertion into traditional material.[68] That is unnecessary, though, as the transition makes perfect sense: the preceding verses have been concerned with Christ's role in creation, those following with redemption.

An eschatological perspective has already been suggested at the end of v. 16, where we are told that all things were created not only through him but also *for* him. Christ defines the end of the cosmos as well as its origin. Now we learn that he who was firstborn of creation (v. 15) is also 'firstborn of the dead, that *in all things* he might be preeminent' (v. 18) – that is, in the new creation as well as the old. It is just at this juncture that he is called, in close correspondence, both the head of the body, the church, and the beginning (ἀρχή, v. 18) of the resurrection. The church is introduced here as the sphere in which Christ's eschatological priority is manifest: poised between his patent presence at the beginning and at the end, this 'body' is the particular space, and indeed the particular time, where he is to be found in the middle of history.[69]

---

[67] As is generally agreed; see e.g. R. McL. Wilson, *A Critical and Exegetical Commentary on Colossians and Philemon*, ICC (London: Clark, 2005), 145.

[68] By Lohse among others; see Jerry L. Sumney, *Colossians: A Commentary*, NTL (London: WJK, 2008), 71.

[69] Contrast Paul Foster: unlike 1 Cor. 12, where it is about relationships between Christians, in Col. 1.18 'the body metaphor has only one function, to emphasize Christ's preeminence in the church' (*Colossians*, BNTC (London: Clark, 2016), 192). The assumption that the somatic language must be metaphorical considerably narrows the range of its possible reference, in both letters.

This limitation marks an important difference from Ephesians. Christ is not, in the Colossians account, in or through the whole of creation. When the hymn speaks about 'all things', they are subsequent to him, created through him, reconciled through him, but not filled by him. In this letter, the word πλήρωμα (1.19, 2.9) refers only to the fullness of *God* (or 'deity', θεότης), which dwells bodily (σωματικῶς) in Christ, and in 2.10, extends through him to the faithful (ἐστὲ ἐν αὐτῷ πεπληρωμένοι). This is a fairly straightforward conceptualization of the church as body, with perceptible boundaries: God's particular embodiment in the incarnation continues to be available in the corporate community whose head is the risen Christ. The head is described metaphorically in 2.19 as the source of growth, but the relationship between Christ as the head and the church as his body is not explored in detail here as it will be in Ephesians.

In fact, although the somatic ecclesiology of Colossians is more explicit than that of 1 Corinthians or Romans, it is also in one sense less complex. The ambiguity between Christ's identification with his body, and his encountering it as an other, does not surface in this letter. A good illustration of the difference is Col. 1.22, where we learn that Christ effected reconciliation through his earthly body, called specifically τὸ σῶμα τῆς σαρκὸς αὐτοῦ (1.22). This language distinguishes it from the neighbouring references to his body the church (1.18, 24).[70] The conceptuality is quite circumscribed: Christ's mortal and ecclesial bodies are presumably related, but in each particular utterance, we know what the immediate reference is. I argued above that in Rom. 7.4, σῶμα Χριστοῦ refers both to the mortal body on the cross and to the church which is joined to the risen Lord, an ambiguity which arises naturally out of the participatory language of Rom. 6. Colossians straightens things out by specifying which body is which; Ephesians, in turn, will restore the ambiguity and develop it further. Once again, a simple chronological trajectory proves inadequate to plot the theological development of the CP.

The body is thematically important also in the central part of Col. 2, where Paul warns the readers against rival teaching. Without going into the hoary question of what exactly constituted the 'Colossian heresy', it is worth observing that the threat is presented as an alternative to living as the body of Christ. In 2.8-10, the *emptiness* of the rival philosophy (κενὴ ἀπάτη) is contrasted with the divine *fullness* dwelling bodily in Christ and believers, while the authority of the στοιχεῖα τοῦ κόσμου is subordinated to Christ as head (κεφαλὴ πάσης ἀρχῆς καὶ ἐξουσίας). In 2.11-14, the readers are united with their risen Lord after putting off the 'body of the flesh', their new life defying the erstwhile 'uncircumcision of the flesh'. In 2.16-17, the contested religious observances are only a 'shadow' (σκία) of what is to come, whereas the σῶμα is Christ's, a resonance with the broader theological theme often lost in translation (where σῶμα becomes e.g. 'substance' (RSV) or 'reality' (NIV)). And in 2.18-19, the hypothetical opponent suffers from a distended νοῦς τῆς σαρκός, and is separated from the organically growing union of head and body.

---

[70] So e.g. ibid., 205.

So life in the σῶμα Χριστοῦ is contrasted both with the flesh and with insubstantial emptiness, which together characterize the apparent threat to the Colossian Christians. There is consequently a certain earthy concreteness to the somatic ecclesiology of this letter. The vastness of the cosmos described should not obscure this fact: Paul is teaching his readers to understand their place in the world, where their own physical life fits into their context. They are part of the embodiment, in the middle of history, of the one who rules and encompasses the whole creation. Universal scope and grounded particularity belong equally to this self-understanding.

3.4. Ephesians

In Ephesians, the body of Christ returns to centre stage, taking on a thematic centrality previously seen only in 1 Corinthians. The climax of its treatment, and the point of greatest originality, comes with the combined discussion of church and marriage in ch. 5, but by that stage the idea has already been developed in ways distinctive to this letter. In what follows, I will comment on each of the relevant passages.

> **Eph. 1.22-23** …καὶ πάντα ὑπέταξεν ὑπὸ τοὺς πόδας αὐτοῦ καὶ αὐτὸν ἔδωκεν κεφαλὴν ὑπὲρ πάντα τῇ ἐκκλησίᾳ, ἥτις ἐστὶν τὸ σῶμα αὐτοῦ, τὸ πλήρωμα τοῦ τὰ πάντα ἐν πᾶσιν πληρουμένου.

This is the first mention of the body in Ephesians, and sets the tone for its treatment throughout the letter. It forms a bridge from the doxological and intercessory material of the opening chapter, along with the 'vertical' Christological reflection that has immediately preceded, to the more concrete, 'horizontal' discussion of the church as a reconciled community in ch. 2. The intersection of these two dimensions is the characteristic location of the body of Christ in the letter.

This part of Ephesians corresponds to the Colossians Christ-hymn, and from there is taken the explicit identification of the church as Christ's body, and of him as head. The somatic language no longer needs to be introduced but can be taken for granted, and increasingly becomes itself the object of theological reflection. Colossians and Ephesians do not create this new material *ex nihilo* or impose it arbitrarily upon Pauline thought, but to some extent crystallize what was before implied, and develop it further. The 'reification' of somatic ecclesiology, if we may call it that, does seem to represent a more settled conceptualization of the church, and there should be no problem agreeing with Käsemann and others that this reflects growing institutionalization with the passage of time, but the development need not be understood negatively. It is natural that as the church became better established, ecclesiological reflection should come increasingly to the fore. Ephesians in particular conceives of a church extended not only spatially (as in the undisputed letters) but also diachronically, for example by being 'built on the foundation of the apostles and prophets' (2.20).

In 1 Cor. 12.21, the head is simply one representative member of the body, alongside eye, hand and feet. In Eph. 1.22, head and feet are again mentioned together, but here they are sharply distinguished. The corporeal language begins when the catalogue of things subordinated to Christ is summed up in the quotation of Ps. 8.7, πάντα ὑπέταξεν ὑπὸ τοὺς πόδας αὐτοῦ, which is seamlessly continued, καὶ αὐτὸν ἔδωκεν κεφαλὴν ὑπὲρ πάντα. Just as all things are beneath Christ's feet, so he is head above all: a natural extension of the Psalmist's imagery, and a unit of sense apparently complete in itself.[71] Ἔδωκεν would then be translated 'appointed', exactly as in 4.11 where it is applied to different roles 'appointed' within the body. But the following words, τῇ ἐκκλησίᾳ, express an indirect object and so shift the sense of ἔδωκεν: God 'gave him *as* head above all things *to* the church'. What seemed at first to name Christ's role within the whole cosmos ends up defining that role in relation to the church.

It has often been noted that this is an asymmetrical relationship: Christ is head over all things, but it is the church, not 'all things', that is called his body.[72] His 'headship' seems then to have a dual force. In relation to the cosmos, Christ is supreme and universal authority, head *over*; in relation to the church, he is organic source and apex, head *of*. The first aspect expresses separation between an exalted Christ and a subordinated creation; the second, his presence in creation through an immanent body. But the two aspects are not unconnected. In the undisputed letters, the horizontal dimension of somatic language is generally associated with unity, whether of diverse members and gifts or of Jew and Gentile; we will see both of these later in Ephesians too. But in these early verses, we find a much more radical interpretation. The body is glossed by a second noun phrase in apposition: the church is Christ's σῶμα as his πλήρωμα, 'the fullness of him who fills all in all'.[73] The body is *interpreted as* fullness. Christ's exaltation as head above all things does not diminish his presence in creation; on the contrary, it enables his presence to permeate the whole universe, in contrast, presumably, with the limited physical space occupied by the body of his flesh. We may say that in this verse, Christ's body is presented as the mode of his immanence in creation, and his immanence is as cosmic in scope as is his headship.

Throughout Ephesians, the church is consistently described as the body in connection with Christ's exaltation, even when he is not named as 'head'. The Colossians hymn, by contrast, quite lacks this vertical dimension.[74] There, although Christ is named as head of the church, the relationship between the two is not really

---

[71] George Howard exaggerates the importance of this point, claiming that 'the primary thrust of the author lies in the correlative relationship between the metaphors "head" and "feet" ... the "body" metaphor is subordinate to the other two' ('The Head/Body Metaphors of Ephesians', NTS 20 (1974): 350–6 (356)). But 'body' persists throughout Ephesians in a way that 'feet' does not.

[72] E.g. Dawes, *Body in Question*, 141. Dawes has an interesting suggestion for locating the difference: the Jew–Gentile union shows that the 'summing up of all things in Christ' (1.10; ἀνακεφαλαιώσασθαι, echoing κεφαλή) is already accomplished in the church, while the world's struggle with hostile powers continues (cf. 6.10-20) (148–9).

[73] Of the many linguistic ambiguities in 1.22-23, the most important is the voice of πληρουμένου. The view that it has passive force – that Christ *is filled* (viz. by God) – depends upon taking the phrase τὰ πάντα ἐν πᾶσιν adverbially, as equivalent to παντάπασιν (so ibid., 241–2, following de la Potterie and Moule; similarly, Best, *Ephesians*, 184–5). But this would be a roundabout and obscure choice of words, when the phrase looks so decidedly like an accusative object. I side with most modern interpreters in preferring an active sense (e.g. Schnackenburg, *Epheser*, 81–2; Margaret Y. MacDonald, *Colossians and Ephesians*, SP 17 (Collegeville, MN: Liturgical, 2000), 221; Lincoln, *Ephesians*, 76: 'It would seem particularly strange for the writer to depict the Church as already "the fullness" but Christ as still being filled').

[74] The pairing of heaven and earth (Col. 1.16, 20) is simply an emphatic periphrasis for the whole of creation; the distance between them is not considered.

explored. As we have seen, this question is already implicit when the undisputed letters speak of Christ's body, and it receives some attention there without being thematized in its own right. Ephesians adopts the more reified somatic language of Colossians, and in these terms develops the Christ–church relationship more extensively, both in these early verses and still more dramatically in ch. 5.

One result of this deepening ecclesiological reflection is an increasing strain on the conceptualization of the body. A body – even an unstable, fluid body as in Martin's account – occupies space and has limits, however permeable. A church which is the space occupied by Christ in the world, and yet does not itself occupy the whole world, is readily comprehensible as a 'body', and that is what we find in Colossians. But how can it also be the mode of Christ's immanence 'filling all in all' (Eph. 1.23)? There is a sort of dual identification going on here, in which Christ is both identified with his body the church and at the same time is beyond its bounds. At several points, I have noted the inherent ambiguity that a body cannot be exhaustively, coextensively identified with its subject. In Ephesians, I believe, this is exploited and stretched further than in any other Pauline letter. But it is not without precedent: with Jenson, we saw Paul distinguish in 1 Corinthians between the church embodying Christ in the world and the eucharistic elements embodying Christ in the church. Looking inwards, the church meets Christ as an other in his body for the meal; to this we may add that looking outwards, the church meets Christ as an other in his filling of the whole cosmos, even beyond the discernible boundaries of his embodied presence. The church is his fullness, but yet encounters him as one filling creation still further, drawing her beyond her own containment to the ends of the earth.

These two verses not only introduce the language of Christ's body to Ephesians, they also stretch it to the brink. They represent a concentrated, complex dialectic between the universal and the particular, the transcendent and the immanent, the vertical and the horizontal, held together in Christ as head of the body. Little wonder they have long been a *crux interpretum*. They introduce the 'extended' sense of the body to Ephesians, and cannot be reduced to simple metaphorical or literal terms without distortion. In particular, the dual sense of the 'head' as both above and integrated within the body must be maintained to avoid misinterpretations throughout the letter.[75]

Eph. 2.14-16 Αὐτὸς γάρ ἐστιν ἡ εἰρήνη ἡμῶν, ὁ ποιήσας τὰ ἀμφότερα ἓν καὶ τὸ μεσότοιχον τοῦ φραγμοῦ λύσας, τὴν ἔχθραν ἐν τῇ σαρκὶ αὐτοῦ, τὸν νόμον τῶν ἐντολῶν ἐν δόγμασιν καταργήσας, ἵνα τοὺς δύο κτίσῃ ἐν αὐτῷ εἰς ἕνα καινὸν ἄνθρωπον ποιῶν εἰρήνην καὶ ἀποκαταλλάξῃ τοὺς ἀμφοτέρους ἐν ἑνὶ σώματι τῷ θεῷ διὰ τοῦ σταυροῦ, ἀποκτείνας τὴν ἔχθραν ἐν αὐτῷ.

---

[75] An extreme example is Yorke's improbable view that in Ephesians, body and head are two independent, unconnected metaphors:

> The passing metaphorical reference to Christ's feet ... strongly suggests that for Paul, κεφαλή and σῶμα do not constitute anatomical components at all ... If they did, then σῶμα here would have to be defined not only as an acephalous entity (with Christ as head), but also as an acephalous, footless amputee (since Christ now has the feet as well). (Yorke, *Church as the Body of Christ*, 106, apropos 1.22-3)

I have already discussed this passage in relation to reconciliation (Chapter 3, §2.4), and will not re-tread that ground, but it raises new questions when considering the body. In the earlier discussion, we saw that the interpersonal dimension which is more muted in the Colossians parallel becomes central to – even a prerequisite of – these verses' account of reconciliation with God. The goal of the passage is peace (εἰρήνη occurs four times, vv. 14, 15, 17 twice), and Christ's body is its means and location, the place where believers are joined to one another and so to God. Like 1.22-23, the horizontal and the vertical are here brought together, but the balance of emphasis has now shifted towards the horizontal. Unlike the earlier verses, the concern is not cosmic but intra-ecclesial; Christ's headship, and the relation of the body to the universe, are not at issue here.

But the knotty question arises whether this 'body' means the church, the earthly body of the man Jesus or both. Nowadays the preference is for an exclusively ecclesiological reading.[76] Against this is the parallelism between ἐν ἑνὶ σώματι and several neighbouring references to Christ (ἐν τῇ σαρκὶ αὐτοῦ (v. 14) and ἐν αὐτῷ (vv. 15 and 16); see n. 59, p. 116 above, against the possibility that the last of these means the cross). This identifies the body closely with Christ himself. The structure of the double ἵνα-clause illustrates the point:

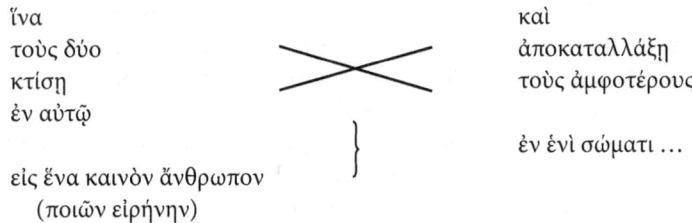

In the first half of the clause, the place or means of the new creation is simply Christ himself (ἐν αὐτῷ), and the goal is the one new person; in the second, the new, single body so created then becomes the place or means of reconciliation, whose goal is God. In substance the one body corresponds to the one person; in role, to Christ. This makes perfect sense if both 'one new person' and 'one body' are understood as primarily *Christological* designations of the church.

The opposite view, that the reference here is exclusively to Jesus's earthly body, is now largely discounted.[77] The chief obstacle is the modifier '*one* body', which would in this case be redundant. Εἷς is persistently coupled with δύο/ἀμφότεροι in this passage so that the one body corresponds to the 'one' remade out of two (v. 14), the one new person (v. 15) and the one Spirit (v. 18), all of which contrast with the divided humanity before Christ.[78] The clear implication is that ἓν σῶμα means a united community. This

---

[76] E.g. Best, *Ephesians*, 265; Lincoln, *Ephesians*, 144–5; MacDonald, *Colossians and Ephesians*, 246–7.
[77] A handful of modern interpreters espouse this view, e.g. Barth, albeit somewhat half-heartedly; he notes that its pedigree includes Chrysostom and Theodoret (*Ephesians*, 2 vols, AB 34 (New York: Doubleday, 1974), 297–8).
[78] V. 18 also anticipates the conjunction of 'one body' and 'one Spirit' in 4.4 (Stephen E. Fowl, *Ephesians: A Commentary* (Louisville, KY: WJK, 2012), 96).

parallelism links 'in one body' to other expressions for the church, just as the syntactic parallelism links it to other expressions for Christ himself. A deliberately ambiguous, dual reference is the best solution.[79]

Personal representations of the community are common throughout Ephesians: in addition to the present passage, cf. the ἀνὴρ τέλειος of 4.13 and the γυνή of 5.28-32 – both passages that develop the theologoumenon of Christ's body – and the παλαιὸς and καινὸς ἄνθρωπος of 4.22-24. Taken together, these represent not so much different iterations of the same idea as a constellation of related imagery, showing a strong partiality in this letter for a theology of corporate personality.[80] All of the images are Christologically grounded – even the wife, albeit less directly. Corporate personality is a thoroughly Pauline mode of thought – as witness Rom. 5.12-21, 7.7-25, 1 Cor. 15.21-23, Gal. 3.27-28, to name but a few examples – and is ultimately grounded in Paul's Adamic Christology.[81] While the figure of Adam is not immediately relevant here, in Ephesians the idea of participation in the person of Christ reaches its most sustained development.

The 'one body' of 2.15 undoubtedly refers to the church, but only as the church is represented by, and participates in, the person of Christ. There remains the question of *how* Christ is envisaged. Is his 'body' here simply a more vivid name for his 'presence' post-ascension? The next words, διὰ τοῦ σταυροῦ, bring us emphatically back down to earth, and to Jesus's own embodied history. The way in which the new person, the one new body, is reconciled to God is precisely through the death of Jesus's fleshly body on the cross. And in case this were not enough, it goes on, ἀποκτείνας τὴν ἔχθραν ἐν αὐτῷ. Why ἀποκτείνας? There are plenty of other verbs that would fit more literally with ἔχρθα. But the reference is to the crucifixion: the enmity between God and humanity was not merely overcome or destroyed but *killed* in Christ. His ecclesial body is indeed something radically new, but it remains inescapably grounded in his mortal body.[82]

The language of Christ's body has both ecclesial and fleshly reference: the double usage itself implies some sort of relation between the two.[83] This is another case where Ephesians has complicated the relatively straightforward sense of Colossians. The earlier letter, we have seen, distinguishes between Christ's earthly body (τὸ σῶμα τῆς

---

[79] So Muddiman, who comments that 'a certain porosity between the doctrines of Christ and the Church is one of the distinguishing features of the thought of Ephesians' (*The Epistle to the Ephesians*, BNTC (London: Continuum, 2001), 135).

[80] The attempts of some commentators to read the καινὸς ἄνθρωπος of 2.15 in an individual sense disregard this wider tendency in the letter, as well as the constant reiteration of participation in Christ (ἐν αὐτῷ) in the immediate context. Best, for example, says that in 4.24 'the new being is not a corporate being but a transformed individual', which supports his preferred individual reading of 2.15 (*Ephesians*, 262). But this is simply to beg the question. The address in 4.20-24 is consistently to the second-person *plural*, and a corporate reading of ἄνθρωπος in that context is not merely possible but preferable. We have also noted that the parallel with Col. 1, where all things are created εἰς αὐτόν (1.16), clarifies that the reference here is to Christ in the first instance (see p. 121 above). Barth identifies the καινὸς ἄνθρωπος with the wife rather than Christ himself (*Ephesians*, 309), an intriguing but improbable suggestion.

[81] As noted by e.g. Schlier, *Epheser*, 92; and Lincoln, *Ephesians*, 143.

[82] The neighbouring parallel ἐν τῇ σαρκὶ αὐτοῦ (v. 14) further confirms this. See Barth, *Ephesians*, 300, n. 205, for various other collocations of the terms 'body', 'flesh' and/or 'blood' with comparable force.

[83] Many interpreters agree that both senses are indicated here, e.g. Schlier, *Epheser*, 135; Dawes, *Body in Question*, 158-60.

σαρκὸς αὐτοῦ, 1.22) and his body the church (1.18, 24). In Ephesians, by contrast, no such clear distinction is made, leading potentially to a more radical identification between the church and her Lord. It was this letter rather than Colossians that so perturbed Käsemann. But of course we need not share his negative evaluation. As we have already seen in Eph. 1.22-23 and will see again in 4.9-16, the church is identified with the body of the *ascended* Christ, but it is a body both crucified and resurrected that ascends into heaven. Christ dying on the cross, Christ risen in the garden and Christ at the right hand of the Father remains one person, one body, eternally bearing the wounds of the passion. Accordingly, when we read that the church is reconciled to God ἐν ἑνὶ σώματι … διὰ τοῦ σταυροῦ, we should understand that the community constituted by the ascended Christ's Spirit continues to share in the identity of his flesh. The ambiguity inherent when speaking of his *bodily* presence – reaching from Mary's womb to the corners of the cosmos – is just what gives this language its power.

Eph. 3.6 …εἶναι τὰ ἔθνη συγκληρονόμα καὶ σύσσωμα καὶ συμμέτοχα τῆς ἐπαγγελίας ἐν Χριστῷ Ἰησοῦ διὰ τοῦ εὐαγγελίου

Here again the body functions primarily to depict the unity of Jews and Gentiles in the church. But on this occasion it is mentioned only in passing, sandwiched among other similar terms in a subordinate couple of verses. It is Paul's own identity that is at issue in 3.1-13, and he is cast axiomatically as apostle to the Gentiles, just as in the undisputed letters: the definition of the μυστήριον in 3.6 is a summary statement of the distinctive gospel that characterizes his ministry and so auspices the present letter. Along with most interpreters, I take the clause καθὼς προέγραψα ἐν ὀλίγῳ (3.3) to refer to the preceding chapters of Ephesians, rather than earlier letters.[84] The implication is that this brief account of the μυστήριον recapitulates the essence of what has already been said on the topic, rather than introducing new material. We would naturally expect the body to be mentioned in any such summary: if anything, the surprise is that it is not more prominent.

The explanation, if any be needed, is that the distinctiveness of Paul's apostolic identity, his mission to the Gentiles, is most apparent in the horizontal dimension of reconciliation. So the emphasis here falls on what is now held in common by both human parties, summarized in three parallel σύν-compounds: the Gentiles are co-heirs (cf. 1.11, 18), co-sharers in the promise (cf. 2.12) and, inconspicuously in the middle, 'co-body', effectively another way of saying 'one body'.[85] This is not inconsistent with chs 1 and 2 as a whole, where body language occurs amidst various other ecclesial images,

---

[84] It would be congenial to my thesis to find here a reference to the nascent CP, but as discussed in Chapter 1, we cannot postulate anything more than occasional and relatively local letter exchanges at the time of Ephesians's composition. In any case, Paul's previous correspondence on this subject can hardly be described as ἐν ὀλίγῳ. So Schnackenburg, *Epheser*, 133; Lincoln, *Ephesians*, 175; Best, *Ephesians*, 302–3; MacDonald, *Colossians and Ephesians*, 262–3; against Edgar J. Goodspeed, *The Meaning of Ephesians* (Chicago: University of Chicago Press), 41–3.

[85] Structurally, the parallelism is phonetic rather than syntactic: συγκληρονόμα and συμμέτοχα function adjectivally, agreeing with the neuter plural ἔθνη, whereas σύσσωμα is obviously a singular noun. This must be simply for assonance.

such as spatial distance (2.13-14, 17) and God's building (2.20-22). When it comes to the fore in chs 4 and 5, it will serve a slightly different function. At this point of ch. 3, its particular symbolic potencies – the organic cooperation of different members, the distinctive relation to Christ as head, the 'filling' of the cosmos – are not especially important, and so it is not dwelt upon.[86]

Eph. 4.4-6 Ἕν σῶμα καὶ ἕν πνεῦμα, καθὼς καὶ ἐκλήθητε ἐν μιᾷ ἐλπίδι τῆς κλήσεως ὑμῶν· εἷς κύριος, μία πίστις, ἕν βάπτισμα, εἷς θεὸς καὶ πατὴρ πάντων, ὁ ἐπὶ πάντων καὶ διὰ πάντων καὶ ἐν πᾶσιν.

The body of Christ is pervasive in Eph. 4.1-16. The word σῶμα occurs three times (vv. 4, 12 and 16) and κεφαλή once (v. 15), but this vision of the church provides the framework and background for the whole passage. Here as in chs 1–3, its most immediate function is to emphasize unity among believers. The theme is initially transparent (4.1-6), but as the passage unfolds, unity turns out once again to be a function of Christology – one church reflects the image of one Lord and one Father (vv. 5-6) – and human reconciliation to be a corollary of Christ's exaltation and filling of all things (vv. 7-10). The link between ascension and spiritual gifts, made via the citation of Ps. 67.19 (v. 8), leads into discussion of complementary offices (vv. 11-12) and finally of maturity and growth into Christ (vv. 13-16). At v. 12 and vv. 15b-16, these successive stages of the appeal are grounded back into the governing language of the body, which has however remained present in the background, partly through echoes of earlier Pauline letters.

Paul has urged the Ephesians as one bound in the Lord (δέσμιος, 4.1) to maintain the unity of the Spirit in the shared bond of peace (συνδέσμῳ, 4.3); it is the subtlest of verbal echoes, but enough to suggest the common participation of author and readers in a single unifying 'bond'. The apostle's captivity can be reinterpreted positively as a closer, tighter adhesion to Christ (he is a prisoner not ὑπὲρ κυρίου but ἐν κυρίῳ (4.1)), and so can the Ephesians' union with one another. The particular virtues singled out for their cultivation are conspicuously oriented towards social concord: ταπεινοφροσύνη, πραΰτης, μακροθυμία, ἀλλήλων ἀνέχειν (4.2). 'Oneness' is the centre of this paranetic material from its first words, and so when vv. 4-6 begin to ring their variations on this theme, it is simply a change of key, the elevation of Paul's appeal into a higher, more poetic register.[87]

Unlike in 2.14-18, 'one' is no longer contrasted with 'two' or 'both'. The unity of Jew and Gentile, so critical to the theological appeal of the earlier chapters, has receded here: the attention to the readers' cohesion and stability, for the peaceful cooperation of diverse gifts and offices, betrays no concern about ethnic or partisan tension. To read the first three chapters of Ephesians alone, one would think that the Jew–Gentile

---

[86] No problem arises here for a nonmetaphorical reading, since clearly neither συγκληρονόμα nor συμμέτοχα is meant metaphorically.

[87] It is perfectly possible that pre-Pauline hymnic or credal material is reflected in vv. 4-6, as per the critical consensus, but like Fowl (*Ephesians*, 133), I doubt whether it makes much material difference to the interpretation.

question was the author's main preoccupation; it is remarkable that it then disappears so completely in the letter's second half.[88] The implication, I believe, is that for the Ephesian Paul this remains a matter of theologically foundational importance even where it is not a pressing pastoral concern. In our discussion of 2.8-22, we saw how carefully the readers' identity as Gentile Christians was educed and expounded: the contingency of their own salvation, their dependence on incongruous grace and their incorporation into a story both cosmic and eternal could not be grasped apart from this self-understanding. The church's internal cohesion and peace, as set out in ch. 4, builds on the basis that the earlier chapters have established, the oneness of Jew and Gentile in Christ.

The interdependence of 'one body' and 'one Spirit', implicit in 2.14-18 and made axiomatic here (4.4), obviously recalls 1 Cor. 12, though the Spirit remains a more muted subject in Ephesians, often mentioned but rarely thematized. In fact, relatively few of the successive 'ones' in vv. 4-6 are of thematic importance for the letter as a whole: we hear no more about baptism, and little about faith in an objective sense. The point seems rather to be their cumulative force, culminating in the one God who is above, through and in all things. This clearly harks back to Christ 'over all things' and 'filling all in all' (1.22-23), and becomes the substantive theme of the following verses.

Eph. 4.7-10 Ἑνὶ δὲ ἑκάστῳ ἡμῶν ἐδόθη ἡ χάρις κατὰ τὸ μέτρον τῆς δωρεᾶς τοῦ Χριστοῦ. διὸ λέγει· *ἀναβὰς εἰς ὕψος ᾐχμαλώτευσεν αἰχμαλωσίαν, ἔδωκεν δόματα τοῖς ἀνθρώποις*. τὸ δὲ ἀνέβη τί ἐστιν, εἰ μὴ ὅτι καὶ κατέβη εἰς τὰ κατώτερα [μέρη] τῆς γῆς; ὁ καταβὰς αὐτός ἐστιν καὶ ὁ *ἀναβὰς* ὑπεράνω πάντων τῶν οὐρανῶν, ἵνα πληρώσῃ τὰ πάντα.

The repetition of ἕν at the beginning of v. 7 sounds initially like a continuation of the hymnic catalogue of the preceding verses, but the sense shifts from corporate wholeness to individual distinctiveness, from *one* body to *each one* of us. The interdependence of diverse gifts – a 1 Cor. 12 or Rom. 12 sort of view – remains prominent in the Ephesian account of the body. But it is secondary to that other aspect we have seen especially in 1.22-23, associated with Christ's ascension and consequent filling of all things. The present verses are critical in making the connection between these two ideas. V. 8 quotes Ps. 67.19, where the ascended one is identified as the giver of gifts. The parenthetical exegesis of vv. 9-10 clarifies that when the psalm refers to Christ's ascension, this also entails his filling of the whole cosmos.[89] So the psalm plays a crucial

---

[88] The corresponding contrast between 'you' and an exclusive 'we' also vanishes here. In fact the former contrast has been reversed: in 4.17 it is between 'you' and the ἔθνη, now meaning 'non-Christians'. This is an early example of a usage that would in time become widespread (e.g. Mt. 6.32, 1 Pet. 4.3 or throughout Hermas, e.g. 4.2, 6.5).

[89] It does not make much difference for our purposes whether κατέβη εἰς τὰ κατώτερα μέρη τῆς γῆς (v. 9) is taken as a reference to the incarnation or the descent into hell. In my view, the parallel with ὑπεράνω πάντων τῶν οὐρανῶν in the following verse suggests the latter, a reading widely favoured in the patristic period. Caird makes the lovely suggestion that the 'descent' refers to Pentecost (*Paul's Letters from Prison: Ephesians, Philippians, Colossians, Philemon* (Oxford: OUP, 1976, 71), but it is hard to get around Best's objection that these verses make no reference to the Spirit (*Ephesians*, 385). Muddiman suggests that the two verbs should be taken simultaneously: 'The crucified Christ "raised up on high" at that very moment plumbed the depths; his humiliation was his exaltation,

role in defining the parameters of Ephesians's somatic language, although it does not itself mention the body at all.

Eph. 4.11-16 Καὶ αὐτὸς ἔδωκεν τοὺς μὲν ἀποστόλους, τοὺς δὲ προφήτας, τοὺς δὲ εὐαγγελιστάς, τοὺς δὲ ποιμένας καὶ διδασκάλους, πρὸς τὸν καταρτισμὸν τῶν ἁγίων εἰς ἔργον διακονίας, εἰς οἰκοδομὴν τοῦ σώματος τοῦ Χριστοῦ, μέχρι καταντήσωμεν οἱ πάντες εἰς τὴν ἑνότητα τῆς πίστεως καὶ τῆς ἐπιγνώσεως τοῦ υἱοῦ τοῦ θεοῦ, εἰς ἄνδρα τέλειον, εἰς μέτρον ἡλικίας τοῦ πληρώματος τοῦ Χριστοῦ, ἵνα μηκέτι ὦμεν νήπιοι, κλυδωνιζόμενοι καὶ περιφερόμενοι παντὶ ἀνέμῳ τῆς διδασκαλίας ἐν τῇ κυβείᾳ τῶν ἀνθρώπων, ἐν πανουργίᾳ πρὸς τὴν μεθοδείαν τῆς πλάνης, ἀληθεύοντες δὲ ἐν ἀγάπῃ αὐξήσωμεν εἰς αὐτὸν τὰ πάντα, ὅς ἐστιν ἡ κεφαλή, Χριστός, ἐξ οὗ πᾶν τὸ σῶμα συναρμολογούμενον καὶ συμβιβαζόμενον διὰ πάσης ἁφῆς τῆς ἐπιχορηγίας κατ' ἐνέργειαν ἐν μέτρῳ ἑνὸς ἑκάστου μέρους τὴν αὔξησιν τοῦ σώματος ποιεῖται εἰς οἰκοδομὴν ἑαυτοῦ ἐν ἀγάπῃ.

It becomes plainer in the following verses that the diversity of gifts is a part of the broader somatic theology. The serpentine syntax leads the reader through several variations on this theme, but at three points returns to the interdependence of gifts. The recurrence of related vocabulary is highlighted here:

4.7-8	Ἑνὶ δὲ **ἑκάστῳ** ἡμῶν *ἐδόθη* ἡ χάρις κατὰ τὸ **μέτρον** τῆς δωρεᾶς τοῦ Χριστοῦ ... *ἔδωκεν δόματα τοῖς ἀνθρώποις*.
4.11-12	Καὶ αὐτὸς ἔδωκεν τοὺς μὲν ἀποστόλους (κτλ.) ... εἰς <u>οἰκοδομὴν τοῦ σώματος</u> τοῦ Χριστοῦ ...
4.16	κατ' ἐνέργειαν ἐν **μέτρῳ ἑνὸς ἑκάστου** μέρους τὴν αὔχησιν τοῦ <u>σώματος</u> ποιεῖται εἰς <u>οἰκοδομὴν</u> ἑαυτοῦ ἐν ἀγάπῃ.

The passage moves from gifts (vv. 7-8) to offices (vv. 11-12) to members (v. 16).[90] The difference in measure (vv. 7, 16) and kind (v. 11) of gifts is interpreted as both an expression of the ascended Christ's lordship, following Ps. 67, and a pragmatic ordering for the body's edification. The debt to 1 Cor. 12 is obvious, though the analogy between complementary offices and body parts is presumed rather than stated here, and Ephesians is characteristically more irenic, betraying no anxiety about competitiveness or pride: the dignity of 'lesser' members seems now to be taken for granted.

The one anxiety that does surface is for the readers' stability in teaching and resistance to deceit (v. 14). The background is Col. 2.16-23, from which the motif of organic growth is taken, but whereas those verses raise quite specific concerns about the Colossians' faith and practice, the Ephesians receive only the most general admonition.

---

as Paul (1 Cor. 2.8) and John (Jn 12.28) would have agreed' (*Ephesians*, 195). Yes indeed; but *pace* Muddiman, this is not incompatible with an infernal reading.

[90] Μέλη does not occur until 4.25, except in a textual variant (μέλους for μέρους in 4.16, attested in ACΨ *inter alia*). But the two words are effectively synonymous in the context of the body (see BADG s.v. μέλος §2 and μέρος §1.b.β).

Conversely, there is increased emphasis on unity (the body is συναρμολογούμενον, Eph. 4.16, rather than ἐπιχορηγούμενον, Col. 2.19). And once again, in reworking material from Colossians, Ephesians complicates things considerably. In the earlier letter, Christ as head was simply the source of the body's growth (ἐξ οὗ πᾶν τὸ σῶμα ... αὔξει τὴν αὔξησιν τοῦ θεοῦ, Col. 2.19). But now that the body is understood as the manifestation of the *ascended* Christ, the head becomes the goal as well as the source of growth, and the body ends up working its own increase (αὐξήσωμεν εἰς αὐτὸν τὰ πάντα, ὅς ἐστιν ἡ κεφαλή, Χριστός, ἐξ οὗ πᾶν τὸ σῶμα ... τὴν αὔξησιν τοῦ σώματος ποιεῖται, Eph. 4.15-16).

It is not the letter's most syntactically felicitous moment, but it makes its point, which is quite different from Colossians. The readers need, in both senses of the expression, to *grow up*: to reach a maturity in faith that can withstand the buffeting of stray doctrine, and to keep drawing closer to the complete image of Christ. In this way, the language of the body acquires a new and distinctively Ephesian accent, foregrounding teleology. The unity enunciated in vv. 1-6 is still in view here, as a counterpart of maturity: the readers will attain the 'unity of faith' as they graduate from the plural νήπιοι (v. 14) into the singular, shared identity of Christ, the ἀνὴρ τέλειος (v. 13). They grow together as they grow up into him; his body already bears his image *in nuce*, and ripens in integration as it does in stature.

This is a point where the metaphorical aspect of the body of Christ is certainly in play, and also under some strain: in the ordinary course of things, one does not 'grow into' one's head. For Yorke, the strain is too much, and 'head' and 'body' must be treated as separate metaphors.[91] For Dawes, the 'imaginative conflict' persisting throughout the whole letter – between the 'unitive' and 'partitive' senses of σῶμα – comes to a crunch here in 4.15-16, and the two senses clash.[92] My own view is that the strain is not between different metaphors or aspects of the one metaphor but between the metaphorical and nonmetaphorical use of body language. Christ has been the ἀνὴρ τέλειος, into whose full stature his body is growing; then he is named as head, recalling the two senses of 1.22-23, head *over* the cosmos as its ruler and head *of* his body as its source; finally in v. 16 his headship is related organically to the body's physiology. Only at the end of the passage is the usage unmistakably metaphorical.

There is a subtle allusion here also to 1 Cor. 13.9-12, where Paul contrasts the νήπιος with the ἀνήρ, the partial (τὸ ἐκ μέρους) with the complete (τὸ τέλειον), and anticipates a future, perfect knowledge (ἐπιγνώσομαι καθὼς καὶ ἐπεγνώσθην). This eschatology crowns the surrounding discussion of spiritual gifts and life in the body of Christ: love relativizes every other gift and discloses it as temporary. Knowledge, tongues, prophecy and so on in 1 Corinthians are partial (ἐκ μέρους) primarily in a temporal sense. When Eph. 4 recalls the whole discussion in brief, this diachronic element is still present: unity, knowledge (ἐπίγνωσις), the ἀνὴρ τέλειος are yet to be attained, the goal of growth (4.13-15). But this moves seamlessly into a present-tense synchronic perspective, in which the partialness of the different members is inherent to the ordering of the body, described as a harmonious organic whole, growing under

---

[91] E.g. Yorke, *Church as the Body of Christ*, 108–9.
[92] Dawes, *Body in Question*, 120, 165.

the government of the crowning gift, love (v. 16). The eschatology of 1 Cor. 13 and the somatic theology of 1 Cor. 12 are integrated here into a single account of the body.

There follow particular directions for how the Ephesians are to be unlike the benighted 'Gentiles' (now meaning non-Christians). Some familiar motifs recur here, in particular the καινὸς and παλαιὸς ἄνθρωπος of 2.15, and we have seen that, on the basis of 4.22-24, some commentators prefer to take this in an individual sense (see n. 80, p. 172 above). As I have argued, though, the contrasting ἄνθρωποι recall more explicit Adamic Christology from earlier Pauline letters, and so should be interpreted as corporate personalities. The readers, having 'learnt Christ' (v. 20), must discard the old man for the new, one whose cosmically expansive presence will draw the individual beyond personal participation into membership of the body. This is made clear in v. 25: ὅτι ἐσμὲν ἀλλήλων μέλη. The ethical transformation to which the readers are invited, which as in 4.1-3 emphasizes virtues of mutual responsibility and concord, is theologically grounded in their corporate sharing in the body of Christ, one ἄνθρωπος with many μέλη.

Eph. 5.21-33 Ὑποτασσόμενοι ἀλλήλοις ἐν φόβῳ Χριστοῦ, αἱ γυναῖκες τοῖς ἰδίοις ἀνδράσιν ὡς τῷ κυρίῳ, ὅτι ἀνήρ ἐστιν κεφαλὴ τῆς γυναικὸς ὡς καὶ ὁ Χριστὸς κεφαλὴ τῆς ἐκκλησίας, αὐτὸς σωτὴρ τοῦ σώματος· ἀλλ' ὡς ἡ ἐκκλησία ὑποτάσσεται τῷ Χριστῷ, οὕτως καὶ αἱ γυναῖκες τοῖς ἀνδράσιν ἐν παντί. Οἱ ἄνδρες, ἀγαπᾶτε τὰς γυναῖκας, καθὼς καὶ ὁ Χριστὸς ἠγάπησεν τὴν ἐκκλησίαν καὶ ἑαυτὸν παρέδωκεν ὑπὲρ αὐτῆς, ἵνα αὐτὴν ἁγιάσῃ καθαρίσας τῷ λουτρῷ τοῦ ὕδατος ἐν ῥήματι, ἵνα παραστήσῃ αὐτὸς ἑαυτῷ ἔνδοξον τὴν ἐκκλησίαν, μὴ ἔχουσαν σπίλον ἢ ῥυτίδα ἤ τι τῶν τοιούτων, ἀλλ' ἵνα ᾖ ἁγία καὶ ἄμωμος. οὕτως ὀφείλουσιν [καὶ] οἱ ἄνδρες ἀγαπᾶν τὰς ἑαυτῶν γυναῖκας ὡς τὰ ἑαυτῶν σώματα. ὁ ἀγαπῶν τὴν ἑαυτοῦ γυναῖκα ἑαυτὸν ἀγαπᾷ. Οὐδεὶς γάρ ποτε τὴν ἑαυτοῦ σάρκα ἐμίσησεν ἀλλ' ἐκτρέφει καὶ θάλπει αὐτήν, καθὼς καὶ ὁ Χριστὸς τὴν ἐκκλησίαν, ὅτι μέλη ἐσμὲν τοῦ σώματος αὐτοῦ. ἀντὶ τούτου καταλείψει ἄνθρωπος [τὸν] πατέρα καὶ [τὴν] μητέρα καὶ προσκολληθήσεται πρὸς τὴν γυναῖκα αὐτοῦ, καὶ ἔσονται οἱ δύο εἰς σάρκα μίαν. τὸ μυστήριον τοῦτο μέγα ἐστίν· ἐγὼ δὲ λέγω εἰς Χριστὸν καὶ εἰς τὴν ἐκκλησίαν. πλὴν καὶ ὑμεῖς οἱ καθ' ἕνα, ἕκαστος τὴν ἑαυτοῦ γυναῖκα οὕτως ἀγαπάτω ὡς ἑαυτόν, ἡ δὲ γυνὴ ἵνα φοβῆται τὸν ἄνδρα.

Nowhere is the seamlessness of Ephesians more apparent than at the beginning of this passage. 5.21 is usually treated as the opening of a new paragraph, which is probably necessary, the direction to 'submit to one another' standing like a title over the household code that follows. But at the same time, we have not had a main verb since 5.18 (πληροῦσθε ἐν πνεύματι), and ὑποτασσόμενοι is the last in a string of dependent participles: this verse is an ending before it is a beginning, a summary of the preceding paranesis that also launches a new theme. Αἱ γυναῖκες τοῖς ἰδίοις ἀνδράσιν is in turn dependent on v. 21, lacking even a non-finite verb, and can still less stand as a separate beginning.[93] So although these verses can be read as a unit, their appeal for mutual

---

[93] Several textual witnesses supply a verb in v. 22, but this is a predictable correction, and the shorter text of 𝔓46B is to be preferred (so NA28).

subjection is also the culmination of the long sequence of paranetic material beginning at 4.1. Both personal and social conduct have been discussed, the whole has been repeatedly grounded back into the corporate language of Christ's body, and now in the household code this theologoumenon is given its most extensive and distinctively Ephesian interpretation. It is undoubtedly a difficult passage, but on close reading a particularly rich one.[94]

Eph. 5.21–6.9 is a reworking of Col. 3.18–4.1, so extensive that interpreters have long recognized this comparison as one of cardinal importance for our letter. The Colossians *Haustafel* is relatively bare, but the first pair of injunctions, to husbands and wives, becomes in Ephesians the locus of substantial and innovative theological reflection.[95] At three points in this passage, Paul justifies a particular appeal to wives or husbands by a corresponding observation about Christ and the church. Wives are to submit to husbands *because* the husband's headship is analogous to Christ's (vv. 22-24); husbands are to love their wives *in the same way* that Christ loved the church, giving himself up for her in order to present her spotless to himself (vv. 25-27); to love their wives as their own bodies, *in the same way* that Christ loves his own body, the church (vv. 28-30). Then, quoting Gen. 2.24 in proof of this last claim, Paul applies it explicitly to the church, before finally clarifying that the household instructions also remain relevant in their literal sense (vv. 31-33). What is going on? Ecclesiology is an odd avenue by which to approach domestic paranesis, and especially in comparison with Colossians, the weight placed upon this first article of the *Haustafel* is overwhelming. Why such prominence for the discussion of marriage, and why is it so interwoven with the church?

Many interpreters do not actually address this question. It seems to be a common assumption that the two subjects are simply analogous in a way that the Ephesian Paul finds convenient for catechetical purposes. Ecclesiology is a preoccupation of the letter as a whole, so when attention turns to the relationship of husband and wife, he chooses to explicate it by analogy with Christ and the church. Dawes, for example, considers the church–body and marriage–body relationships metaphorical, but the church–marriage relationship analogical (see §2.2 above). We have seen the problems: he neglects the realism of Paul's language in describing both kinds of somatic union, and introduces two artificial distinctions, literal/metaphorical and partitive/unitive, which make the text appear contradictory. Moreover, Dawes's account does not sufficiently explain the integration of the two subjects. It does not do justice to the theological weight of what is said about both; it is not accidental that these verses have been highly influential in the history of Christian thought about both marriage *and* the church.

---

[94] Against e.g. Mitton, who finds this passage 'lacking in systematic construction and in strong internal connexions. If it is read in public with oratorical skill, it can sound most impressive. If it is studied item by item and analysed in detail, it is less satisfactory' (C. Leslie Mitton, *Ephesians* (London: Oliphants, 1976), 210).

[95] The following injunctions to children/fathers and slaves/masters differ much less dramatically from Colossians. The most significant expansion is the citation of the fifth commandment in relation to children's obedience (Eph. 6.2-3), which is characteristic of Ephesians's deepened engagement with scripture.

The connection between these two different sorts of transpersonal 'body' is itself the passage's most striking novelty, and goes to the heart of its meaning.

Another possibility is that the Ephesian Paul is considerably more interested in ecclesiology than domestic matters, and so while dutifully producing a *Haustafel* along the lines of Colossians, he uses one part of it as a pretext to talk about something quite different. Muddiman, for example, distinguishes sharply between the mundane directions given about marriage itself and the author's real preoccupation with the union of Christ and the church, 'into which human marriages may provide some kind of earthly insight'; for this reason, it is a grave mistake to see here the germ of a sacramental view of marriage.[96] One problem with this reading is that the text insists on real domestic as well as ecclesial relevance: 'I am applying this to Christ and to the church; *nevertheless, you also* [πλὴν καὶ ὑμεῖς], every one, [must act accordingly]' (vv. 32-33). Another, greater obstacle is vv. 28-30, where husbands are to love their wives as their own bodies, 'just as' (καθώς) Christ loves his body, the church. This comparison represents the bodily unions of marriage and church in terms equally solemn and realistic: to take one but not both as metaphorical goes against the grain of the argument. The parallel works both ways, because the relation described is allegorical rather than analogical, intrinsic rather than contingent.

The Ephesian injunctions to husbands and wives have their foundation in the ontological condition of the marriage relationship, which can *only* be adequately articulated with reference to Christ and the church. One clue lies in the way in which the scriptural quotation of v. 31 fits into its context: 'For nobody [ever] hated his own flesh, but nourishes and cherishes it, just as Christ the church, because we are members of his body. *For this reason* [ἀντὶ τούτου], a man shall leave father and mother ...' The quotation of Gen. 2.24 could easily have been more smoothly introduced, e.g. καθὼς γέγραπται, καταλείψει ἄνθρωπος ..., but instead Paul chooses to integrate it into the surrounding syntax by including the consecutive phrase.[97] This creates at least the appearance of a causal connection between the church's participation in the body of Christ and the ontological participation of marriage.

A significant textual variant in v. 30 shows that, at least for some early readers, the text was taken this way. In Gen. 2.23, Adam identifies Eve as 'bone of my bones and flesh of my flesh' (ὀστοῦν ἐκ τῶν ὀστέων μου καὶ σὰρξ ἐκ τῆς σαρκός μου), and as 'taken out of her husband' (ἐκ τοῦ ἀνδρὸς αὐτῆς ἐλήμφθη αὕτη). These statements form the antecedent for ἕνεκεν τούτου in v. 24: it is because of their origin in a common flesh that man and woman become again one flesh. The majority textual tradition of Eph. 5.30, represented in several uncials and known by Irenaeus, works Gen. 2.23 into the

---

[96] Muddiman, *Ephesians*, 271. This passage, especially 5.32 (which in Latin reads *sacramentum hoc magnum est*), certainly contributed to the inclusion of marriage among the sacraments of the church, though the precise significance of the rite has been variously interpreted, and remains a confessional fault line. On this see Schnackenburg, *Epheser*, 346-9. Muddiman is not alone in seeing marriage per se as less significant here: cf. among others Goodspeed, *Meaning*, 61-2; and A. J. Kostenberger, 'The Mystery of Christ and the Church: Head and Body, "One Flesh"', *Trinity Journal* 12 (1991): 79-94.

[97] The LXX has ἕνεκεν τούτου, but the difference is insignificant; no attempted correction appears in the textual history.

quotation that follows: ὅτι μέλη ἐσμὲν τοῦ σώματος αὐτοῦ ἐκ τῆς σαρκὸς αὐτοῦ καὶ ἐκ τῶν ὀστέων αὐτοῦ. ἀντὶ τούτου ... The italicized words are absent from 𝔓⁴⁶ℵ*AB and are therefore unlikely to be original, but their effect is to make plain what I suggest is already implicit: a rereading of Gen. 2 in which the union of man and woman into 'one flesh' is grounded in the union of many people in the one body of Christ. It is our sharing in his 'flesh and bone' that lies behind marriage.[98]

The following statement that 'this μυστήριον is great' (5.32) supports this reading. Consistently with the other uses of the term in Ephesians (1.9, 3.1-10 and, more generically, 6.19), μυστήριον denotes a formerly hidden purpose of God. In 1.10, it is defined as the recapitulation (ἀνακεφαλαιώσασθαι) of all things in Christ; in 3.6, as the union of Gentiles and Jews into a common body (σύσσωμα). (It is noticeable that the language of 'head' and 'body', even in these places where it is not thematized, is still associated with the μυστήριον.) To what precisely does the word refer in 5.32, the institution of marriage or the quotation of Gen. 2.24? These alternatives, which date back to von Soden,[99] are not particularly helpful. The scriptural verse can be presumed by author and readers to give a *true* aetiology of the institution, whose deepest meaning has only now become visible in the light of Christ. Marriage as attested in scripture is a great μυστήριον: both an allegory of, and a participation in, the reunion of divided humanity in the corporate personhood of its saviour, consistently with God's eternal purpose.[100]

The second half of 5.32 also has its linguistic challenges. The identical phrase ἐγὼ δὲ λέγω occurs repeatedly in the antitheses of Mt. 5, where it is emphatically authoritative and adversative. Paul, however, gives no indication of opposing another interpretation of Gen. 2.24. The δέ should indeed be read adversatively here, but the contrast is between past hiddenness and present disclosure: 'This text and the matter it refers to are deeply mysterious; *nevertheless I, Paul*, am able to explain it to you.' More perplexing is the expression λέγω εἰς. The only comparable NT occurrence is Acts 2.25, Δαυὶδ γὰρ λέγει εἰς αὐτόν, introducing a quotation from Ps. 15. This is close to Eph. 5.32 in that the psalm text is 'applied' to Jesus, identifying him as its true referent; nevertheless, the subject of λέγω is not Peter, who is preaching, but David. In that case, the author of scripture *speaks* (intransitive) about Jesus, but in Eph. 5, Paul *applies* scripture (transitive) to Christ and the church. This would be a unique use of λέγω, but should not be ruled out on that account. Alternatively, we could infer that λέγω introduces indirect speech: τὸ μυστήριον τοῦτο μέγα ἐστίν· [ὃ] ἐγὼ δὲ λέγω [εἶναι] εἰς Χριστὸν καὶ εἰς τὴν ἐκκλησίαν. 'I declare that this mystery *is for* – has its fulfilment in – Christ and the church.' This has the advantage of bringing out the teleological character

---

[98] Although it would strengthen this argument, I cannot bring myself to agree with Muddiman (*Ephesians*, 268) that the longer text is likely to be original.

[99] See the discussion in J. Paul Sampley, *'And the Two Shall Become One Flesh': A Study of Traditions in Ephesians 5.21-33*, SNTSMS 16 (Cambridge: CUP, 1971), 90–1.

[100] The meaning of μυστήριον has been much discussed. For a valuable recent study see T. J. Lang, *Mystery and the Making of a Christian Historical Consciousness: From Paul to the Second Century*, BZNW 219 (Berlin: de Gruyter, 2015). Lang finds in the use of the term, beginning with Paul and continuing into such figures as Justin, Irenaeus and Tertullian, a consistent schema of hiddenness–disclosure which characterizes a novel early-Christian conception of history.

of the repeated εἰς.¹⁰¹ Either of these readings is possible, but common to both is that λέγω has a hermeneutical force here, explaining the correct interpretation of scripture, a fact that is especially clear in view of the Acts parallel. It is a mistake to smooth this over, as happens for example in the AV, 'This is a great mystery: but I speak concerning Christ and the church.'¹⁰²

For Ephesians, the union of the faithful in the church and the union of husband and wife are related intrinsically, and not just analogically, because in each case the final goal of the union is the person of Christ. That is not to suggest that the marital union has no integrity of its own, distinct from the wider ecclesial union, but rather that the church is the *telos* of marriage, the eschatological union that Eden foreshadows and begins to anticipate. That, I think, is the point of the emphatic pronouncement in 5.32: the μυστήριον disclosed in primeval marriage Paul now declares to apply to Christ and the church. Because Adam is not actually named, it is easily missed that this is the one place in Ephesians where Adamic Christology is made explicit, but that is certainly the effect of the Genesis quotation. It is Christ as the *eschatos Adam*, the authentically representative human person, into whom all things and all people are finally gathered, an integration which from the first has been tangibly anticipated in marriage, and is now decisively enacted in the church.¹⁰³

This reading, I suggest, satisfactorily answers the questions of why ecclesiology is interwoven into the Ephesians *Haustafel*, and of the relationship between these two apparently discrete subjects. To paraphrase: 'From marriage, we learn something of the mystery of the bodily union brought about in Christ, and see that it was anticipated from the beginning of creation. From this mystery, in turn, we learn the true extent of marriage's significance. Go and live accordingly!' Seen in this light, it is both apt and cogent, though also highly creative, as an elaboration of the comparatively straightforward parallel in Colossians.

One final observation. There is a close relationship between the command to husbands to love their wives and to the readers generally to 'walk in love':

---

[101] The second εἰς is omitted in B but well attested elsewhere.

[102] BADG cites Eph. 5.32 twice under λέγω, once alongside Acts 2.25 and parallels from Euripides and Xenophon, meaning 'speak about' (§1.b.α) – this does not do justice to the hermeneutical function of either NT verse – and again on its own, meaning 'interpret with reference to' (§2.e).

[103] There is clear resonance here with the Adamic Christology latent at various points throughout the letter, including the *creation* of Jew and Gentile into a καινὸς ἄνθρωπος in 2.15. Best is dubious about Adamic Christology at 5.32: 'Paul knowing Hebrew and Greek would probably see the shadow of Adam when he came on the word ἄνθρωπος, but [the author of Ephesians] was probably not Paul and even if he was a Jew we cannot assume he had a detailed knowledge of Hebrew' (*Ephesians*, 556). This is another example of the hypothesis of pseudonymity skewing interpretation in the direction of discontinuity and difference. Stephen Francis Miletic, on the other hand, goes too far when he finds Adamic overtones in Christ's role as σωτήρ and κεφαλή in 5.23 ('*One Flesh*': *Eph. 5.22-24, 5.31, Marriage and the New Creation*, AnBib 115 (Rome: Pontificio Istituto Biblico, 1988)). This in turn builds upon Sampley's argument that Gen. 2.24 is foundational to the wife's subordination in Eph. 5.22-24 (*One Flesh*, esp. 112–14), through reasoning which has been rightly criticized by Lincoln ('The Use of the OT in Ephesians', *JSNT* 4 (1982): 16–57 (35–6)). The fact that later texts such as the Gospel of Philip make quite different use of Eden in reading this passage (see Pheme Perkins, *Ephesians*, ANTC (Nashville, TN: Abingdon, 1997), 133–6) does not affect the Adamic reading proposed here.

5.2	περιπατεῖτε ἐν ἀγάπῃ
	καθὼς καὶ ὁ Χριστὸς ἠγάπησεν *ἡμᾶς*
	καὶ παρέδωκεν ἑαυτὸν ὑπὲρ *ἡμῶν* …
5.25	Οἱ ἄνδρες, ἀγαπᾶτε τὰς γυναῖκας
	καθὼς καὶ ὁ Χριστὸς ἠγάπησεν *τὴν ἐκκλησίαν*
	καὶ ἑαυτὸν παρέδωκεν ὑπερ *αὐτῆς* …

For our purposes, the interesting point is not the verbal correspondence itself, but the continuation of the parallel in the following statements of purpose. In 5.2, Christ gives himself up for us as an 'offering and sacrifice *to God* as a sweet-smelling odour'; in 5.26, he gives himself up for the church 'that he might sanctify her, having purified [her] with the washing of water in the word, that he might present the church *to himself*. In the former case, he is himself the pure offering presented to God; in the latter, he purifies the church and presents her to himself. He is identified both with the offering itself and the God receiving it. It is the ambiguity of the body that makes this possible: because the church is his own body, it can be presented with him to God, a very close identification; because he is the head of the body, or the husband of the bride, he can be distinguished from the church.

At first, the submission of wives is linked to that of the church (vv. 22-24), and then the love of husbands is linked to Christ's self-sacrifice (vv. 25-27); here the distinctness of the parties is in focus, and the body is an 'other' to its head. Then marital love is linked to the close identification between self and body, Christ and church (vv. 28-30), and from this follows the scriptural μυστήριον of bodily union in one flesh (vv. 31-32). Oneness and otherness are stressed equally, in both the marital and ecclesial relationships. The ease with which Ephesians can move across this dialectic means that neither side can be privileged without distorting the argument. The dialectic itself we have already met in the earlier letters, especially in the relation of the eucharistic and ecclesial bodies in 1 Corinthians, but the equipoise and fluidity of its exposition is unique to Ephesians. This is the fullest and most intricate expression of somatic theology in the CP, and represents a kind of end point for the development of this Pauline idea.

4. Conclusions

This chapter has found the theology of Christ's body to be consistently and coherently developed throughout the CP. Against metaphorical interpretations, represented here by Dawes, we found the usage to be thoroughly realistic, beginning with 1 Corinthians, which, as the most extensive treatment in the undisputed letters, is the critical test case. This conclusion draws partly on Martin's discussion of how the body was understood in the ancient Mediterranean, and Engberg-Pedersen's account of *pneuma* as a material element; the enervated, immaterial 'spirit' that emerges from a purely metaphorical reading of 1 Cor. 12 does not belong in Paul's world. But the same conclusion arises also from a straightforwardly ontological reading of the sacramental language in 1 Cor. 10 and 11, in which we have found Jenson a reliable companion. It is evident in his work, as in Robinson's and Ward's, that a consistently realistic interpretation of the σῶμα Χριστοῦ tends towards a more integrated reading of the CP, even where that is not always fully explored. If we are right to read 1 Corinthians as we do, then what we find in Romans, Colossians and especially Ephesians looks less like misconstrual or betrayal, and more like variation and reinterpretation.

That is not to suggest, however, that no significant differences remain. Even if he were to concede that a substantive, sacrament-like view of the church as the body of Christ persists through the whole CP, Käsemann would still object to the fundamental Ephesian 'misinterpretation': that the distinction between Christ as head and the church as body opens up a conceptual fissure between the two, obscuring the church's total dependence on Christ and ultimately allowing it not merely to represent him, but to replace him. Although I dissent from Käsemann's theological evaluation, there remains an element of truth in the exegetical observations he draws upon. Nowhere in the undisputed letters is the relationship between Christ and the church discussed *as such*; he is not called her source or ruler, her head or spouse. But as we have seen, there is already in these letters the beginnings of a distinction between Christ and his body. I have argued that this is not just an extension but an inevitable corollary of Paul's somatic ecclesiology. If the church can really be called Christ's 'body', it follows from the nature of bodily existence that he will both identify with it as a subject and encounter it as an object. That is exactly what we find in the different dimensions of his bodily presence in 1 Corinthians. Similar thought lies behind Rom. 6–7, coming to the surface at 7.4, and in Colossians it becomes explicit when Christ is first named as the 'head of the body'.

Ephesians moves with particular ease between these 'subjective' and 'objective' conceptualizations of the body. We have seen that both senses are present through the letter, that Christ as 'head' is associated with the latter and that for interpreters like Dawes this constitutes a conceptual fault line. I have argued instead that this ambiguity inherent in somatic language makes it uniquely applicable to the interrelation of Christ and the church. Nowhere in Ephesians, or elsewhere in the NT for that matter, is it claimed that the church simply *is* Christ; there is always a reservation of identity. Christ's agency is never absorbed into the church. And yet, the participation is so profound that the only identity that *can* be attributed to the church is Christ's. This mystery is indeed great. It should not surprise us to find in 1 Corinthians – the earliest forays exploring it – many pregnant suggestions whose full potential will be explored only in later Pauline letters. Having now given some attention to this process, I must demur from Schweitzer's assessment that the undisputed letters 'exhaustively express' all that can be said about the church as Christ's body (p. 138 above). Rather, what there begins to bud blossoms copiously in the latter letters, a growth integral and organic.

Conclusion: *Corpus conpactum et conexum*

Let us in every respect grow up into him who is the head, Christ, from whom the whole body, united and knit together by every supporting ligament, by the proper working of each single member, brings about the body's growth for its edification in love. (Eph. 4.15-16)

The Corpus Paulinum, like the church that formed it, is a differentiated but cohesive body. No two members are the same; no one member is dispensable. Although each letter has its own background, they share a common reception, and it is only as this complex whole that they come down to us. And although each letter casts its distinctive light on the man Paul and his milieu, it is the interaction of the Corpus that communicates his legacy. When Origen described Ephesians as the heart, he exemplified the character not only of the one letter but of 'the whole body, united and knit together'.

The last two centuries have seen our perspective completely transformed. We now have a sharper focus on the particularities of each individual text, but at the cost of an atomism that divides what earlier readers had joined together. There has been not merely a reweighting of interpretative dialectic, a shift of emphasis from the whole to the part, but a radical redefinition of what both whole and part actually are. The deepest kind of intertextual coherence is found no longer in the context of reception and transmission, but only at the level of composition. The critical corpus of seven 'authentic' letters has come to displace the canonical CP as the larger unit of interpretation. Correspondingly, the nature of the individual letters is also changed, most dramatically for the antilegomena, whose historical reference is understood no longer as Paul himself, but as later church traditions.

In the first part of this study, we reviewed the construction of these two rival canons, the formation and dissolution of the church's CP. In Chapter 1, we saw that from the beginning, Paul's letters circulated beyond their immediate recipients, and that apparently quite quickly, they came to be transmitted and read exclusively as a collection, in due course as a Corpus like our own. The early sources for this nascent CP are more consistent than we might have expected; the MSS, in particular, show surprisingly little variation in scope. We were open to the possibility that different levels in the Corpus's formation might be discernible, and might have enduring hermeneutical significance, but in fact found little grounds for such distinctions, even in the case of the Pastorals, where modern scholarship has tended to overstate the evidence. It is significant that Hebrews, the only letter whose place was certainly marginal, is also the only one whose authorship was seriously disputed. There can be little doubt that those early readers who shaped the Corpus believed the letters to be Paul's own, and excluded what was known to be pseudonymous (witness Tertullian on the *Acta Pauli* or the Muratorian Fragment on 'Laodiceans' and 'Alexandrians').

So when Pauline authorship began to be subjected to historical criticism, it shook an exegetical foundation which had been in place some seventeen centuries. Little wonder the reaction to Schleiermacher's *Sendschreiben* on 1 Timothy was so dramatic. As we saw in Chapter 2, alongside many hostile responses, more sympathetic figures like Eichhorn and de Wette took up his philological critique and developed it further. In due course, however, it was radicalized by Baur, who deepened the distinction of authorship into a division between the genuine Pauline gospel and its regrettable Catholic domestication. Although Baur's position was extreme and controversial, it has had considerable influence in the subsequent history of Pauline exegesis, most notably in a wide-ranging, confessionally inflected hermeneutic of decadence. We saw several examples of the enduring legacy of this model, most markedly but by no means uniquely in Käsemann.

I have suggested that contemporary exegesis has yet to come fully to terms with the implications of the authorship question. A tension is perceived between the phenomenon of pseudepigraphy and the CP's canonical formation, and although there are now a variety of interpretative approaches available, none that we considered addresses this tension quite satisfactorily. In Childs, however, we found a recovered canonical perspective with the potential to circumvent it, engaging not only with the biblical texts' composition but also with the form in which they are received and used by particular communities of faith. While agreeing with Childs's theoretical approach, I argued that in adapting it to the CP he was not entirely successful, and so attempted to develop an alternative.

Taking a cue from Mitchell's work on the Corinthian letters, I proposed that the CP be understood as a self-interpretative dialogue, reading each letter in the light of the others, and not filtering their interplay by authorship. This hermeneutic acknowledges the tensions between texts, which may reflect not only different local contexts but also different authors and generations, but it does not make such questions of provenance a major focus. I argued that the rich polyphony of the Corpus can be heard more distinctly when the letters are not artificially separated into the camps of 'authentic' and 'spurious'. By viewing the CP as an integrated whole, this approach is consistent not only with its formation but also with the letters' intrinsic intertextual, self-referential nature. The canonical shaping of these texts is secondary but not arbitrary; it corresponds closely to their character also at the level of composition.

The second part of the study put this hermeneutic into practice, taking Ephesians as the focal text. Our reading in Chapter 3 of Eph. 2.8-22 affirmed the integrative character of this letter. We found an unexpected level of agreement with Rom. 3, not only in superficial verbal echoes but in the whole line of thought; we saw also how seamlessly the familiar Jew–Gentile logic of Romans and Galatians is interwoven with threads from the more Gentile-oriented Corinthian letters. We noted that when Ephesians draws away from one undisputed letter, it often draws closer to another, and particularly in the survey of reconciliation across four letters, saw that the complex and varied patterns of reinterpretation do not align well with the traditional authorship division. In Chapter 4, we took this thematic approach further with a reading of the body of Christ across the CP. We found a substantial but consistent development of this subject through the four relevant letters. This conclusion contrasts with the decadence view, represented by Käsemann, which sees the somatic ecclesiology of Colossians and especially Ephesians as a catholicizing misconstrual of Paul, and also with the widespread metaphorical interpretation, represented by Dawes. My reading was grounded in a reconsideration of the body of Christ in 1 Corinthians, where I argued the treatment is deeply realistic and indeed sacramental throughout. The later development of this subject breaks new ground, especially on the relationship between Christ and the church, but it does so by exploiting suggestions already latent in the earlier, undisputedly Pauline discussion.

I hope that the results of these exegetical chapters vindicate the hermeneutical model set out in the first part. If so, they indicate a direction that could be explored much further. The focus on Ephesians has naturally shaped this study in certain ways that would not apply equally to every text or question, but *mutatis mutandis*, other letters can be read within the same framework, and other theological topics addressed. As another intertextual approach was once described, this is 'less a matter of method than of sensibility'.[1] My purpose has not been to provide a blueprint for a particular exegetical procedure, so much as to illustrate the possibilities of renewed attentiveness to the dynamic integrity of the CP, unconstrained by a preoccupation with authorship. If persuasive, this approach could be further developed in any number of ways, including moving beyond the CP to the wider Christian canon.

No special priority is being claimed for Ephesians: like Romans, it is an especially integrative text and obscure in its immediate contingency; like the Pastorals, it shows a concern for the future transmission of the faith. But whereas Childs accorded those two 'bookends' a privileged position governing the interpretation of other Pauline letters, I would resist elevating any particular letter in that way. Ephesians is not being substituted here for the 'authentic' corpus as the norm for reading Paul. No subset of the CP should have such a normative function; as far as possible, we should avoid reducing its polyphonic intricacy to a simple melody with accompaniment. Certainly, any particular reflection must begin with a particular text, but whether we set out from Ephesians or Galatians, 2 Thessalonians or 1 Timothy, can vary with the context and the question; and wherever we begin, such intertextual readings will change the meaning we find in all the texts concerned.

Still, for some readers there will remain a problem. What of the Paul of history? Are not the earlier, undisputed letters vividly imprinted with his particular personality, in a way less palpable in Ephesians or the Pastorals? Without necessarily conceding the premise, I do think this objection raises an important issue that I have not yet directly addressed: the role of the canon in connecting the church with her origins. Before the rise of modern critical scholarship, no conflict was perceived between the authorship

---

[1] Richard B. Hays, *Echoes of Scripture in the Letters of Paul* (New Haven, CT: Yale University Press, 1989), 21.

of the Pauline letters and their reception into the Corpus. The canonical texts formed a tangible link between the apostles who had personally composed them and the church of the present, mediated through generations of ecclesial interpretation. The critique of authorship fractured this link, distinguishing between composition and canonization, and in doing so posed a significant religious problem. Christianity is a historical faith, grounded in the events of a particular time and place, with which it must somehow remain connected. The continuity of the present church with the apostles was jeopardized when those founding figures were no longer reliably accessible in their texts.

This anxiety, I believe, helps to explain the kind of response typified by Baur. He locates the church's historical foundation no longer in the NT writings but behind them, in the shrouded, indistinct moments of Christian origins. The faith's true kernel was distorted by its canonical transmission, and must be recovered through a process of archaeological winnowing. We have seen how Baur and Käsemann characterize Paul's gospel as the enemy of tradition, periodically re-emerging to shatter ecclesial convention. Although theirs is an extreme position, I suggest the underlying assumptions are more widespread: that earlier sources provide more reliable access to Christian truth, and that subsequent reception and transmission represents a deterioration. This is the historiographical foundation for the hermeneutics of decadence, but it is also reflected in more moderate approaches than Baur's or Käsemann's, in the narration of a simple trajectory from Paul to the early church, from the authentic to the deutero- and tritopauline, so often with subtle preference for the former. The same assumptions lie behind the conservative defence of traditional authorship, a constant from Schleiermacher's earliest reviewers to the present, as well as the enthusiastic detection of pseudepigraphy among antagonists of the church like Ehrman.

Yet the phenomenon of canonical pseudepigraphy need not provoke such a divisive response. It threatens only the most superficial conceptualization of the church's continuity. The Christian faith is indeed grounded in a particular history, but that history is not confined before any one point, whether Easter, Pentecost, the death of the apostles, the formation of the canon or any other watershed. From the very beginning, from the first reception of the risen Christ among his disciples, the church has existed as an interpreting community, struggling to make sense of her faith and to pass it on to others. There is no uninterpreted, pre-ecclesial gospel. Nor, to return to our more immediate concern, is there any uninterpreted Paul. As we have seen, even his earliest writings do not stand alone, but contribute to an ongoing conversation, which is developed throughout the canonical letters and continues in postbiblical texts and traditions. In all probability, Paul himself was not the only contributor to the Corpus received in his name, but the involvement of other authors only deepens a dialogical character present from the beginning. The church of today, the continuation of the community that received and reshaped these letters, participates in this dialogue still.

The various layers of textual interpretation that make up the CP may well be critically differentiated – though this will always involve a certain amount of speculation – and a portrait of the apostle refined accordingly. But such reconstruction of the historical Paul remains an auxiliary task to the interpretation of his Corpus; the congruity of the different texts does not depend on it. As he himself had occasion to observe, Paul is not the object of his own gospel. The tangle and the mystery of his letters and of his person find their coherence in the one to whom they testify, in Christ who is the head of Paul and Paul's Corpus as he is the head of his whole body, the church, the source of her unity and the goal of her growth.

Bibliography

Biblical text

The OT is cited from the LXX throughout, and follows its chapter and verse divisions.
Aland, Barbara, Kurt Aland, Johannes Karavidopoulos, Carlo M. Martini and Bruce M. Metzger, eds. *Nestle–Aland Novum Testamentum Graece*. 28th edn. Stuttgart: Deutsche Bibelgesellschaft, 2012.
Rahlfs, Alfred, and Robert Hanhart, eds. *Septuaginta*. Editio altera. Stuttgart: Deutsche Bibelgesellschaft, 2006.
Weber, Robert, and Roger Gryson, eds. *Biblia Sacra Vulgata*. 5th edn. Stuttgart: Deutsche Bibelgesellschaft, 2007.

New Testament manuscripts

Bastianini, Guido, Gabriella Messeri, Franco Montanari, Rosario Pintaudi and Vittorio Bartoletti, eds. *Papiri Greci e Latini*. Vol. 15: ni. 1453–1574. Firenze: Istituto Papirologico, G. Vitelli, 2008.
Gallazzi, Claudio. 'Frammenti di un codice con le epistole di Paolo'. *Zeitschrift für Papyrologie und Epigraphik* 46 (1982): 117–22.
Grenfell, Bernard P., and Arthur S. Hunt, eds. *The Oxyrhynchus Papyri*. Vol. 4. London: Egypt Exploration Fund, 1904.
Grenfell, Bernard P., and Arthur S. Hunt, eds. *The Oxyrhynchus Papyri*. Vol. 13. London: Egypt Exploration Fund, 1919.
Hunt, Arthur S., ed. *Catalogue of the Greek Papyri in the John Rylands Library Manchester*. Vol. 1: Literary Texts (Nos. 1–61). Manchester: Quaritch, Sherratt & Hughes, 1911.
Kenyon, Frederic G. *The Chester Beatty Biblical Papyri*. Vol. 3 Supp.: Pauline Epistles (Text). London: Walker, 1936.
Wessely, Karl, ed. *Studien zur Palaeographie und Papyruskunde*. Vol. 12: Griechische und koptische Texte theologischen Inhalts III. Leipzig: Haessel, 1912.
Wouters, Alfons, ed. *The Chester Beatty Codex Ac 1499: A Graeco-Latin Lexicon on the Pauline Epistles and a Greek Grammar*. Chester Beatty Monographs 12. Leuven: Peeters, 1988.

Patristic works

Translations are my own except where otherwise cited.
Cyprian. 'Ad Fortunatum'. In *Opera*, edited by R. Weber, 1.181–216. CCSL 3. Turnhout: Brepols, 1972.
Cyprian. 'Ad Quirinum'. In *Opera*, edited by R. Weber, 1.1–179. CCSL 3. Turnhout: Brepols, 1972.

Ehrman, Bart D., ed. and trans. *The Apostolic Fathers*. 2 vols. Loeb 24. Cambridge, MA: Harvard University, 2003.
Epiphanius. *Panarion haer. 34–64*. Edited by Karl Holl. 2nd edn. 1922. GCS Epiphanius II. Berlin: Akademie, 1980.
Epiphanius. *The Panarion of Epiphanius of Salamis: Book I (Sects 1–46)*. Translated by Frank Williams. NHS 63. Leiden: Brill, 2009.
Epiphanius. *The Panarion of Epiphanius of Salamis: Books II and III, De Fide*. Translated by Frank Williams. 2nd edn. NHS 79. Leiden: Brill, 2013.
Eusebius. *Ecclesiastical History*. Edited and translated by Kirsopp Lake. Vol. 1. 2 vols. Loeb 153. Cambridge, MA: Harvard University, 1926.
Lake, Kirsopp, ed. and trans. *The Apostolic Fathers*. 2 vols. Loeb 24–25. London: Heinemann, 1912–13.
Origen. 'Against Celsus'. Translated by Frederick Crombie. ANF 4.395–669. 1885. Peabody, MA: Hendrickson, 1994.
Origen. *Contre Celse*. Edited and translated by Marcel Borret. Vol. 2. 3 vols. SC 136. Paris: Cerf, 1968.
Origen. *Homilies on Numbers*. Edited by Christopher P. Hall. Translated by Thomas P. Scheck. Downers Grove, IL: IVP Academic, 2009.
Origen. *Traité des principes*. Edited by Henri Crouzel and Manlio Simonetti. Vol. 1. SC 252. Paris: Cerf, 1978.
Origen and Jerome. *The Commentaries of Origen and Jerome on St. Paul's Epistle to the Ephesians*. Edited and translated by Ronald E. Heine. Oxford: OUP, 2002.
Tertullian. *Adversus Marcionem*. Edited and translated by Ernest Evans. 2 vols. Oxford: Clarendon, 1972.
Tertullian. 'De Praescriptione Haereticorum'. In *Opera*, edited by R. F. Refoulé, 1.185–224. CCSL 1–2. Turnhout: Brepols, 1954.
Tertullian. 'The Five Books against Marcion'. Translated by Peter Holmes. ANF 3.269–475. 1885. Peabody, MA: Hendrickson, 1994.
Tertullian. 'The Prescription against Heretics'. Translated by Peter Holmes. ANF 3.243–65. 1885. Peabody, MA: Hendrickson, 1994.
Tertullian. *Traité de la prescription contre les hérétiques*. Edited by R. F. Refoulé. Translated by P. de Labriolle. SC 46. Paris: Cerf, 1957.
Tertullian. *Traité du baptême*. Edited by R. F. Refoulé. Translated by M. Drouzy. SC 35. Paris: Cerf, 1952.
Victorinus. 'Commentary on the Apocalypse'. In *Latin Commentaries on Revelation*, edited and translated by William C. Weinrich, 1–22. ACT. Downers Grove, IL: IVP Academic, 2011.
Victorinus. *Sur l'apocalypse suivi du fragment chronologique et de la construction du monde*. Edited and translated by M. Dulaey. SC 423. Paris: Cerf, 1997.

General

Aageson, James W. *Paul, the Pastorals and the Early Church*. Peabody, MA: Hendrickson, 2008.
Aland, Kurt. 'Die Entstehung des Corpus Paulinum'. In *Neutestamentliche Entwürfe*, 302–50. München: Kaiser, 1979.

Aland, Kurt, ed. *Kurzgefasste Liste der griechischen Handschriften des Neuen Testaments*. 2nd edn. ANTF 1. Berlin: de Gruyter, 1994.
Aland, Kurt, ed. *Repertorium der griechischen christlichen Papyri*. Vol. 1: Biblische Papyri. PTS 18. Berlin: de Gruyter, 1976.
Aland, Kurt, and Barbara Aland. *The Text of the New Testament: An Introduction to the Critical Editions and to the Theory and Practice of Modern Textual Criticism*. Translated by Erroll F. Rhodes. German 1981. Grand Rapids, MI: Eerdmans, 1987.
Allenbach, J., A. Benoît, D. A. Bertrand, A. Hanriot-Coustet, P. Maraval, A. Pautler and P. Prigent, eds. *Biblia Patristica: Index des citations et allusions bibliques dans la littérature Patristique*. Vol. 1: Des origines à Clément d'Alexandrie et Tertullien. Paris: Centre National de la Recherche Scientifique, 1975.
Anderson, Charles P. 'The Epistle to the Hebrews and the Pauline Letter Collection'. HTR 59 (1966): 429–38.
Armstrong, Jonathan. 'Victorinus of Pettau as the Author of the Canon Muratori'. VC 62 (2008): 1–34.
Aune, David E. 'Reconceptualizing the Phenomenon of Ancient Pseudepigraphy: An Epilogue'. In *Pseudepigraphie und Verfasserfiktion in frühchristlichen Briefen*, edited by Jörg Frey, Jens Herzer, Martina Janssen and Clare K. Rothschild, 789–824. WUNT 246. Tübingen: Mohr Siebeck, 2009.
Barclay, John M. G. *Obeying the Truth: A Study of Paul's Ethics in Galatians*. Edinburgh: Clark, 1988.
Barclay, John M. G. *Paul and the Gift*. Grand Rapids, MI: Eerdmans, 2015.
Barker, Don. 'The Dating of New Testament Papyri'. NTS 57 (2011): 571–82.
Barnett, Albert E. *Paul Becomes a Literary Influence*. Chicago: University of Chicago Press, 1941.
Barth, Markus. 'Conversion and Conversation: Israel and the Church in Paul's Epistle to the Ephesians'. *Interpretation* 17 (1963): 3–24.
Barth, Markus. *Ephesians*. 2 vols. AB 34. New York: Doubleday, 1974.
Baur, F. C. *Kirchengeschichte der drei ersten Jahrhunderte*. 3rd edn. Geschichte der christlichen Kirche 1. Tübingen: Fues, 1863.
Baur, F. C. *Paulus, der Apostel Jesu Christi: Sein Leben und Wirken, seine Briefe und seine Lehre*. 2nd edn. 2 vols. Leipzig: Fues, 1866–7.
Becker, Eve-Marie. 'Text und Hermeneutik am Beispiel einer textinternen Hermeneutik'. In *Die Bibel als Text: Beiträge zu einer textbezogenen Bibelhermeneutik*, edited by Oda Wischmeyer and Stefan Scholz, 193–215. NET 14. Tübingen: Francke, 2008.
Becker, Eve-Marie. 'Von Paulus zu "Paulus": Paulinische Pseudepigraphie-Forschung als literaturgeschichtliche Aufgabe'. In *Pseudepigraphie und Verfasserfiktion in frühchristlichen Briefen*, edited by Jörg Frey, Jens Herzer, Martina Janssen and Clare K. Rothschild, 363–86. WUNT 246. Tübingen: Mohr Siebeck, 2009.
BeDuhn, Jason David. *The First New Testament: Marcion's Scriptural Canon*. Salem, OR: Polebridge, 2013.
Best, Ernest. *Ephesians*. ICC. London: Clark, 1998.
Best, Ernest. 'Who Used Whom? The Relationship of Ephesians and Colossians'. NTS 43 (1997): 72–96.
Bieringer, Reimund. '"Reconcile Yourselves to God": An Unusual Interpretation of 2 Corinthians 5.20 in Its Context'. In *Jesus, Paul and Early Christianity*, FS Henk Jan de Jong, edited by Rieuwerd Buitenwerf, Harm W. Hollander and Johannes Tromp, 11–38. Leiden: Brill, 2008.

Black, C. Clifton. 'The Johannine Epistles and the Question of Early Catholicism'. *NovT* 28 (1986): 131–58.
Bornkamm, Günther. 'Sünde, Gesetz und Tod'. 1950. In *Das Ende des Gesetzes*, 51–69. BEvT 16. München: Kaiser, 1961.
Brakke, David. 'Early Christian Lies and the Lying Liars Who Wrote Them'. *JR* 96 (2016): 378–90.
Brakke, David. 'A New Fragment of Athanasius's Thirty-Ninth Festal Letter: Heresy, Apocrypha, and the Canon'. *HTR* 103 (2010): 47–66.
Brown, Raymond E. 'The Unity and Diversity in New Testament Ecclesiology'. *NovT* 6 (1963): 298–308.
Bultmann, Rudolf. *Theologie des Neuen Testaments*. Tübingen: Mohr Siebeck, 1953.
Burkett, Delbert. *An Introduction to the New Testament and the Origins of Christianity*. Cambridge: CUP, 2002.
Byrne, Brendan. *Romans*. SP 6. Collegeville, MN: Liturgical, 1996.
Caird, G. B. *Paul's Letters from Prison: Ephesians, Philippians, Colossians, Philemon*. Oxford: OUP, 1976.
Campbell, Douglas A. *Framing Paul: An Epistolary Biography*. Grand Rapids, MI: Eerdmans, 2014.
Carroll, Kenneth L. 'The Expansion of the Pauline Corpus'. *JBL* 72 (1953): 230–7.
Childs, Brevard S. 'The Canonical Shape of the Prophetic Literature'. *Union Seminary Review* 32 (1978): 46–55.
Childs, Brevard S. *The Church's Guide for Reading Paul: The Canonical Shaping of the Pauline Corpus*. Grand Rapids, MI: Eerdmans, 2008.
Childs, Brevard S. *The New Testament as Canon: An Introduction*. London: SCM, 1984.
Clabeaux, John J. *A Lost Edition of the Letters of Paul: A Reassessment of the Text of the Pauline Corpus Attested by Marcion*. CBQMS 21. Washington, DC: Catholic Biblical Association of America, 1989.
Clivaz, Claire. 'A New NT Papyrus: $\mathfrak{P}^{126}$ (PSI 1497)'. *Early Christianity* 1 (2010): 158–62.
Conzelmann, Hans. 'Der Brief an die Epheser'. In *Die Briefe an die Galater, Epheser, Philipper, Kolosser, Thessalonicher und Philemon*, by Jürgen Becker, Hans Conzelmann and Gerhard Friedrich, 86–124, 14th edn. NTD 8. Göttingen: Vandenhoeck & Ruprecht, 1976.
Conzelmann, Hans. 'Paulus und die Weisheit'. *NTS* 12 (1966): 231–44.
Corssen, Peter. 'Zur Überlieferungsgeschichte des Römerbriefs'. *ZNTW* 10 (1909): 1–45, 97–102.
Dahl, Nils A. 'Gentiles, Christians and Israelites in the Epistle to the Ephesians'. In *Christians among Jews and Gentiles*, FS Krister Stendahl, edited by George W. Nickelsburg and George W. MacRae, 31–9. Philadelphia, PA: Fortress, 1986.
Dahl, Nils A. 'Interpreting Ephesians: Then and Now'. In *Studies in Ephesians*, 461–73. WUNT 131. Tübingen: Mohr Siebeck, 2000.
Dahl, Nils A. 'The Origin of the Earliest Prologues to the Pauline Letters'. *Semeia* 12 (1978): 233–77.
Dahl, Nils A. 'The Particularity of the Pauline Epistles as a Problem in the Ancient Church'. In *Neotestamentica et Patristica*, edited by Oscar Cullmann, 261–71. NovTSup 6. Leiden: Brill, 1962.
Dahl, Nils A. 'Welche Ordnung der Paulusbriefe wird vom Muratorischen Kanon vorausgesetzt?' *ZNTW* 52 (1961): 39–53.
Dawes, Gregory W. *The Body in Question: Metaphor and Meaning in the Interpretation of Ephesians 5.21-33*. Biblical Interpretation 30. Leiden: Brill, 1998.

de Bruyne, Donatien. 'Prologues bibliques d'origine Marcionite'. *Revue Bénédictine* 24 (1907): 1–16.
de Wette, W. M. L. *Kurze Erklärung der Briefe an die Colosser, an Philemon, an die Ephesier und Philipper*. Kurzgefasstes exegetisches Handbuch zum Neuen Testament, 2.4. Leipzig: Weidmann'sche Buchhandlung, 1843.
de Wette, W. M. L. *Kurze Erklärung des Briefes an die Galater und der Briefe an die Thessalonicher*. Kurzgefasstes exegetisches Handbuch zum Neuen Testament, 2.3. Leipzig: Weidmann'sche Buchhandlung, 1841.
de Wette, W. M. L. *Lehrbuch der historisch kritischen Einleitung in die kanonischen Bücher des Neuen Testaments*. Berlin: Reimer, 1826.
Dennison, Charles D. 'Ernst Käsemann's Theory of Early Catholicism: An Inquiry into the Success of the "Lutheran Gospel"'. MA, Duquesne University, 1984.
Dodd, C. H. *The Epistle of Paul to the Romans*. London: Hodder & Stoughton, 1932.
Downs, David J. '"Early Catholicism" and Apocalypticism in the Pastoral Epistles'. *CBQ* 67 (2005): 641–61.
Duff, Jeremy. '𝔓⁴⁶ and the Pastorals: A Misleading Consensus?' *NTS* 44 (1998): 578–90.
Duncan, George S. *St. Paul's Ephesian Ministry: A Reconstruction with Special Reference to the Ephesian Origin of the Imprisonment Epistles*. London: Hodder & Stoughton, 1929.
Dunn, James D. G. *Beginning from Jerusalem*. Christianity in the Making 2. Grand Rapids, MI: Eerdmans, 2009.
Dunn, James D. G. *Neither Jew nor Greek*. Christianity in the Making 3. Grand Rapids, MI: Eerdmans, 2015.
Dunn, James D. G. *Unity and Diversity in the New Testament: An Inquiry into the Character of Earliest Christianity*. 3rd edn. London: SCM, 2006.
Dunning, Benjamin H. 'Strangers and Aliens No Longer: Negotiating Identity and Difference in Ephesians 2'. *HTR* 99 (2006): 1–16.
Ehrman, Bart D. *Forgery and Counterforgery: The Use of Literary Deceit in Early Christian Polemics*. New York: OUP, 2013.
Elliott, J. K. *The Apocryphal New Testament: A Collection of Apocryphal Christian Literature in an English Translation*. Oxford: OUP, 1993.
Elliott, John H. *1 Peter*. AB 37B. New York: Doubleday, 2000.
Engberg-Pedersen, Troels. *Cosmology and Self in the Apostle Paul: The Material Spirit*. Oxford: OUP, 2010.
Epp, Eldon Jay. 'Issues in the Interrelation of New Testament Textual Criticism and Canon'. In *The Canon Debate*, edited by Lee Martin McDonald and James A. Sanders, 485–515. Peabody, MA: Hendrickson, 2002.
Evanson, Edward. *The Dissonance of the Four Generally Received Evangelists, and the Evidence of Their Respective Authenticity, Examined; with That of Some Other Scriptures, Deemed Canonical*. 2nd edn. Gloucester: Walker, 1805.
Fee, Gordon D. *The First Epistle to the Corinthians*. NICNT. Grand Rapids, MI: Eerdmans, 1987.
Ferguson, Everett. 'Review of Geoffrey Mark Hahneman, *The Muratorian Fragment and the Development of the Canon*'. *JTS* 44 (1993): 691–7.
Fewster, Gregory P. 'Hermeneutical Issues in Canonical Pseudepigrapha: The Head/Body Motif in the Pauline Corpus as a Test Case'. In *Paul and Pseudepigraphy*, edited by Stanley E. Porter and Gregory P. Fewster, 89–111. PaSt 8. Leiden: Brill, 2013.
Finegan, Jack. 'The Original Form of the Pauline Collection'. *HTR* 49 (1956): 85–104.
Foster, Paul. *Colossians*. BNTC. London: Clark, 2016.
Fowl, Stephen E. *Ephesians: A Commentary*. Louisville, KY: WJK, 2012.

Frede, Hermann Josef. *Altlateinische Paulus-Handschriften*. Vol. 4. Vetus Latina. Freiburg: Herder, 1964.
Frede, Hermann Josef. 'Die Ordnung der Paulusbriefe und der Platz des Kolosserbriefs im Corpus Paulinum'. In *Epistulae ad Philippenses et ad Colossenses*, 290–303. Vetus Latina 24. Freiburg: Herder, 1969.
Furnish, Victor Paul. *1 Thessalonians, 2 Thessalonians*. ANTC. Nashville, TN: Abingdon, 2007.
Gamble, Harry Y. *Books and Readers in the Early Church: A History of Early Christian Texts*. New Haven, CT: Yale University Press, 1995.
Gamble, Harry Y. *The New Testament Canon: Its Making and Meaning*. Philadelphia, PA: Fortress, 1985.
Gamble, Harry Y. 'The New Testament Canon: Recent Research and the Status Quaestionis'. In *The Canon Debate*, edited by Lee Martin McDonald and James A. Sanders, 267–94. Peabody, MA: Hendrickson, 2002.
Gamble, Harry Y. 'The Pauline Corpus and the Early Christian Book'. In *Paul and the Legacies of Paul*, edited by William S. Babcock, 265–80. Dallas, TX: Southern Methodist University, 1990.
Gamble, Harry Y. 'Pseudonymity and the New Testament Canon'. In *Pseudepigraphie und Verfasserfiktion in frühchristlichen Briefen*, edited by Jörg Frey, Jens Herzer, Martina Janssen and Clare K. Rothschild, 333–62. WUNT 246. Tübingen: Mohr Siebeck, 2009.
Gamble, Harry Y. 'The Redaction of the Pauline Letters and the Formation of the Pauline Corpus'. JBL 94 (1975): 403–18.
Gamble, Harry Y. *The Textual History of the Letter to the Romans: A Study in Textual and Literary Criticism*. SD 42. Grand Rapids, MI: Eerdmans, 1977.
Gnilka, Joachim. *Der Epheserbrief*. Freiburg: Herder, 1971.
Goodspeed, Edgar J. *The Key to Ephesians*. Chicago: University of Chicago Press, 1956.
Goodspeed, Edgar J. *The Meaning of Ephesians*. Chicago: University of Chicago Press, 1933.
Goodspeed, Edgar J. *New Solutions of New Testament Problems*. Chicago: University of Chicago Press, 1927.
Grindheim, Sigurd. 'A Deutero-Pauline Mystery? Ecclesiology in Colossians and Ephesians'. In *Paul and Pseudepigraphy*, edited by Stanley E. Porter and Gregory P. Fewster, 173–95. PaSt 8. Leiden: Brill, 2013.
Haacker, Klaus. 'Rezeptionsgeschichte und Literarkritik: Anfragen an die Communis Opinio zum Corpus Paulinum'. TZ 65 (2009): 209–28.
Hagen, Kenneth. *Hebrews Commenting from Erasmus to Bèze, 1516–1598*. BGBE 23. Tübingen: Mohr Siebeck, 1981.
Hahneman, Geoffrey Mark. *The Muratorian Fragment and the Development of the Canon*. Oxford: Clarendon, 1992.
Harnack, Adolf von. *Die Briefsammlung des Apostels Paulus und die anderen vorkonstantinischen christlichen Briefsammlungen*. Leipzig: Hinrichs, 1926.
Harnack, Adolf von. 'Excerpte aus dem Muratorischen Fragment (saec. XI. et XII.)'. TLZ 23 (1898): 131–4.
Harnack, Adolf von. *Marcion: Das Evangelium vom fremden Gott. Eine Monographie zur Geschichte der Grundlegung der katholischen Kirche*. TUGAL 45. Leipzig: Hinrichs, 1921.
Hatch, William H. P. 'The Position of Hebrews in the Canon of the New Testament'. HTR 29 (1936): 133–51.

Hays, Richard B. *Echoes of Scripture in the Letters of Paul*. New Haven, CT: Yale University Press, 1989.
Hays, Richard B. *First Corinthians*. Interpretation. Louisville, KY: Knox, 1997.
Herzer, Jens. 'Zwischen Mythos und Wahrheit: Neue Perspektiven auf die sogenannten Pastoralbriefe'. *NTS* 63 (2017): 428–50.
Hill, C. E. 'The Debate over the Muratorian Fragment and the Development of the Canon'. *WTJ* 57 (1995): 437–52.
Hoehner, Harold E. *Ephesians: An Exegetical Commentary*. Grand Rapids, MI: Baker Academic, 2002.
Howard, George. 'The Head/Body Metaphors of Ephesians'. *NTS* 20 (1974): 350–6.
Hübner, Hans. 'Glosser in Epheser 2'. In *Vom Urchristentum zu Jesus*, edited by Hubert Frankemölle and Karl Kertelge, 392–406. Freiburg: Herder, 1989.
Hurtado, Larry W. *The Earliest Christian Artifacts: Manuscripts and Christian Origins*. Grand Rapids, MI: Eerdmans, 2006.
Jenson, Robert W. *Systematic Theology*. 2 vols. Oxford: OUP, 1997–9.
Jenson, Robert W. *Unbaptized God: The Basic Flaw in Ecumenical Theology*. Minneapolis, MN: Fortress, 1992.
Käsemann, Ernst. 'Amt und Gemeinde im Neuen Testament'. 1949. In *Exegetische Versuche und Besinnungen*, 1.109–34. Göttingen: Vandenhoeck & Ruprecht, 1960.
Käsemann, Ernst. *An die Römer*. 3rd edn. HNT 8A. Tübingen: Mohr Siebeck, 1974.
Käsemann, Ernst. 'Begründet der neutestamentliche Kanon die Einheit der Kirche?' 1951. In *Exegetische Versuche und Besinnungen*, 1.214–23. Göttingen: Vandenhoeck & Ruprecht, 1960.
Käsemann, Ernst. 'Das Interpretationsproblem des Epheserbriefes'. 1961. In *Exegetische Versuche und Besinnungen*, 2.253–61. Göttingen: Vandenhoeck & Ruprecht, 1964.
Käsemann, Ernst. *Das Neue Testament als Kanon*. Göttingen: Vandenhoeck & Ruprecht, 1970.
Käsemann, Ernst. 'Paulus und der Frühkatholizismus'. 1963. In *Exegetische Versuche und Besinnungen*, 2.239–52. Göttingen: Vandenhoeck & Ruprecht, 1964.
Käsemann, Ernst. 'Das theologische Problem des Motivs vom Leib Christi'. In *Paulinische Perspektiven*, 178–210. Tübingen: Mohr Siebeck, 1969.
Käsemann, Ernst. 'Unity and Diversity in New Testament Ecclesiology'. *NovT* 6 (1963): 290–7.
Keck, Leander E. 'Faith Seeking Canonical Understanding: Childs's Guide to the Pauline Letters'. In *The Bible as Christian Scripture: The Work of Brevard S. Childs*, edited by Christopher R. Seitz and Kent Harold Richards, 103–17. SBLBSNA 25. Atlanta, GA: SBL, 2013.
Kelly, Anthony J. '"The Body of Christ: Amen!": The Expanding Incarnation'. *TS* 71 (2010): 792–816.
Kim, Seyoon. '2 Cor. 5.11-21 and the Origin of Paul's Concept of "Reconciliation"'. *NovT* 39 (1997): 360–84.
Knox, John. *Marcion and the New Testament: An Essay in the Early History of the Canon*. Chicago: University of Chicago Press, 1942.
Knox, John. *Philemon among the Letters of Paul*. 2nd edn. 1935. London: Collins, 1960.
Kostenberger, A. J. 'The Mystery of Christ and the Church: Head and Body, "One Flesh"'. *Trinity Journal* 12 (1991): 79–94.
Kreinecker, Christina M. 'The Imitation Hypothesis: Pseudepigraphic Remarks on 2 Thessalonians with Help from Documentary Papyri'. In *Paul and Pseudepigraphy*, edited by Stanley E. Porter and Gregory P. Fewster, 197–219. PaSt 8. Leiden: Brill, 2013.

Küng, Hans. 'Der Frühkatholizismus im Neuen Testament als kontroverstheologisches Problem'. In *Das Neue Testament als Kanon*, edited by Ernst Käsemann, 175–204. Göttingen: Vandenhoeck & Ruprecht, 1970.

Lang, T. J. 'Did Tertullian Read Marcion in Latin? Grammatical Evidence from the Greek of Ephesians 3.9 in Marcion's Apostolikon as Presented in the Latin of Tertullian's Adversus Marcionem'. ZAC 21 (2017): 63–72.

Lang, T. J. *Mystery and the Making of a Christian Historical Consciousness: From Paul to the Second Century*. BZNW 219. Berlin: de Gruyter, 2015.

Leppä, Outi. *The Making of Colossians: A Study on the Formation and Purpose of a Deutero-Pauline Letter*. Publications of the Finnish Exegetical Society 86. Göttingen: Vandenhoeck & Ruprecht, 2003.

Lietzmann, Hans. *An die Korinther I, II*. 2nd edn. HNT 9. Tübingen: Mohr Siebeck, 1923.

Lieu, Judith M. *Marcion and the Making of a Heretic: God and Scripture in the Second Century*. New York: CUP, 2015.

Lieu, Judith M. 'Marcion and the New Testament'. In *Method and Meaning*, FS Harold W. Attridge, edited by Andrew B. McGowan and Kent Harold Richards, 399–416. Atlanta, GA: SBL, 2011.

Lincoln, Andrew T. 'The Church and Israel in Ephesians 2'. CBQ 49 (1987): 605–24.

Lincoln, Andrew T. *Ephesians*. WBC 42. Dallas, TX: Word, 1990.

Lincoln, Andrew T. 'Ephesians 2.8-10: A Summary of Paul's Gospel?' CBQ 45 (1983): 617–30.

Lincoln, Andrew T. 'The Letter to the Colossians'. *New Interpreter's Bible* 11.551–669. Nashville, TN: Abingdon, 2000.

Lincoln, Andrew T. 'The Use of the OT in Ephesians'. JSNT 4 (1982): 16–57.

Lindemann, Andreas. *Die Aufhebung der Zeit: Geschichtsverständnis und Eschatologie im Epheserbrief*. SNT 12. Gütersloh: Mohn, 1975.

Lindemann, Andreas. 'Die Sammlung der Paulusbriefe im 1. und 2. Jahrhundert'. In *The Biblical Canons*, edited by Jean-Marie Auwers and H. J. de Jonge, 321–51. BETL 163. Leuven: Leuven University & Peeters, 2003.

Lohse, Eduard. 'χειροποίητος, ἀχειροποίητος'. In *Theologisches Wörterbuch zum Neuen Testament*, edited by Gerhard Friedrich, 9.425–6. Stuttgart: Kohlhammer, 1973.

Lovering, Eugene H. 'The Collection, Redaction and Early Circulation of the Corpus Paulinum'. PhD, Southern Methodist University, 1988.

Lovering, Eugene H. 'Review of David Trobisch, *Die Entstehung der Paulusbriefsammlung*'. JBL 110 (1991): 736–8.

Lütgert, D. W. *Freiheitspredigt und Schwarmgeister in Korinth: Ein Beitrag zur Charakteristik der Christuspartei*. Beiträge zur Förderung christlicher Theologie, 12.3. Gütersloh: Bertelsmann, 1908.

Luz, Ulrich. 'Der Brief an die Epheser'. In *Die Briefe an die Galater, Epheser und Kolosser*, by Jürgen Becker and Ulrich Luz, 107–80, 18th edn. NTD 8/1. Göttingen: Vandenhoeck & Ruprecht, 1998.

Luz, Ulrich. 'Erwägungen zur Entstehung des "Frühkatholizismus": Eine Skizze'. ZNTW 65 (1974): 88–111.

MacDonald, Margaret Y. *Colossians and Ephesians*. SP 17. Collegeville, MN: Liturgical, 2000.

MacDonald, Margaret Y. 'Early Catholicism'. In *The SCM Dictionary of Biblical Interpretation*. London: SCM, 1990.

MacDonald, Margaret Y. *The Pauline Churches: A Socio-Historical Study of Institutionalization in the Pauline and Deutero-Pauline Writings*. SNTSMS 60. Cambridge: CUP, 1988.

MacDonald, Margaret Y. 'The Politics of Identity in Ephesians'. *JSNT* 26 (2004): 419–44.
McKelvey, R. J. 'Christ the Cornerstone'. *NTS* 8 (1962): 352–9.
Markschies, Christoph Johannes. *Christian Theology and Its Institutions in the Early Roman Empire*. Translated by Wayne Coppins. German 2009. Waco, TX: Baylor University, 2015.
Marshall, I. Howard. 'The Meaning of Reconciliation'. 1978. In *Jesus the Saviour: Studies in New Testament Theology*, 258–74. London: SPCK, 1990.
Martin, Dale B. *Biblical Truths: The Meaning of Scripture in the Twenty-First Century*. New Haven, CT: Yale University, 2017.
Martin, Dale B. *The Corinthian Body*. New Haven, CT: Yale University Press, 1995.
Martin, Ralph P. *Reconciliation: A Study of Paul's Theology*. London: Marshall, Morgan & Scott, 1981.
Meade, David G. *Pseudonymity and Canon: An Investigation into the Relationship of Authorship and Authority in Jewish and Earliest Christian Tradition*. WUNT 39. Tübingen: Mohr, 1986.
Merklein, Helmut. 'Paulinische Theologie in der Rezeption des Kolosser- und Epheserbriefes'. In *Paulus in den neutestamentlichen Spätschriften: Zur Paulusrezeption im Neuen Testament*, edited by Karl Kertelge, 25–69. QD 89. Freiburg: Herder, 1981.
Merz, Annette. 'The Fictitious Self-Exposition of Paul: How Might Intertextual Theory Suggest a Reformulation of the Hermeneutics of Pseudepigraphy?' In *The Intertextuality of the Epistles*, edited by Thomas L. Brodie, Dennis R. MacDonald and Stanley E. Porter, 113–32. NTM 16. Sheffield: Sheffield Phoenix, 2006.
Metzger, Bruce M. *The Canon of the New Testament: Its Origin, Development and Significance*. Oxford: Clarendon, 1987.
Metzger, Bruce M. *A Textual Commentary on the Greek New Testament*. 2nd edn. Stuttgart: Deutsche Bibelgesellschaft, 1994.
Miletic, Stephen Francis. *'One Flesh': Eph. 5.22-24, 5.31, Marriage and the New Creation*. AnBib 115. Rome: Pontificio Istituto Biblico, 1988.
Mitchell, Margaret M. 'The Corinthian Correspondence and the Birth of Pauline Hermeneutics'. In *Paul and the Corinthians: Studies on a Community in Conflict*, FS Margaret Thrall, edited by Trevor J. Burke and J. K. Elliott, 17–53. NovTSup 109. Leiden: Brill, 2003.
Mitchell, Margaret M. *Paul and the Rhetoric of Reconciliation: An Exegetical Investigation of the Language and Composition of 1 Corinthians*. HUT 28. Tübingen: Mohr Siebeck, 1991.
Mitchell, Margaret M. *Paul, the Corinthians, and the Birth of Christian Hermeneutics*. Cambridge: CUP, 2010.
Mitton, C. Leslie. *Ephesians*. London: Oliphants, 1976.
Mitton, C. Leslie. *The Epistle to the Ephesians: Its Authorship, Origin and Purpose*. Oxford: OUP, 1951.
Mitton, C. Leslie. *The Formation of the Pauline Corpus of Letters*. London: Epworth, 1955.
Morgan, Robert. 'Paul's Enduring Legacy'. In *The Cambridge Companion to St. Paul*, edited by James D. G. Dunn, 242–55. Cambridge: CUP, 2003.
Moule, C. F. D. *The Epistles of Paul the Apostle to the Colossians and to Philemon*. CGTC. Cambridge: CUP, 1957.
Mowry, Lucetta. 'The Early Circulation of Paul's Letters'. *JBL* 63 (1944): 73–86.
Muddiman, John. *The Epistle to the Ephesians*. BNTC. London: Continuum, 2001.
Muratori, Lodovico Antonio. 'De literarum statu, neglectu et cultura in Italia'. In *Antiquitates Italicae medii aevi*, 3.809–80. Milan: Societas Palatina, 1740.

Murphy-O'Connor, Jerome. *Paul the Letter-Writer: His World, His Options, His Skills*. GNS 41. Collegeville, MN: Liturgical, 1995.

Nienhuis, David R. *Not by Paul Alone: The Formation of the Catholic Epistle Collection and the Christian Canon*. Waco, TX: Baylor University, 2007.

Novenson, Matthew V. 'Review of Douglas A. Campbell, *Framing Paul: An Epistolary Biography*'. RBL, October 2016.

O'Brien, Peter T. *The Letter to the Ephesians*. PNTC. Grand Rapids, MI: Eerdmans, 1999.

Parker, D. C. *An Introduction to the New Testament Manuscripts and Their Texts*. Cambridge: CUP, 2008.

Patsch, Hermann. 'Die Angst vor dem Deuteropaulinismus: Die Rezeption des "kritischen Sendschreibens" Friedrich Schleiermachers über den 1. Timotheusbrief im ersten Jahrfünft'. ZTK 88 (1991): 451–77.

Perkins, Pheme. *Ephesians*. ANTC. Nashville, TN: Abingdon, 1997.

Pokorný, Petr. *Der Brief des Paulus an die Kolosser*. THKNT, 10/I. Berlin: Evangelische Verlagsanstalt, 1987.

Porter, Stanley E. *The Apostle Paul: His Life, Thought, and Letters*. Grand Rapids, MI: Eerdmans, 2016.

Porter, Stanley E. 'Paul and the Pauline Letter Collection'. In *Paul and the Second Century*, edited by Michael F. Bird and Joseph R. Dodson, 19–36. LNTS 412. London: Clark, 2011.

Porter, Stanley E. 'Paul and the Process of Canonization'. In *Exploring the Origins of the Bible: Canon Formation in Historical, Literary, and Theological Perspective*, edited by Craig A. Evans and Emanuel Tov, 173–202. Grand Rapids, MI: Baker, 2008.

Porter, Stanley E. 'Pauline Authorship and the Pastoral Epistles: A Response to R. W. Wall's Response'. BBR 6 (1996): 133–8.

Porter, Stanley E. 'Pauline Authorship and the Pastoral Epistles: Implications for Canon'. BBR 5 (1995): 105–23.

Porter, Stanley E. 'Paul's Concept of Reconciliation, Twice More'. In *Paul and His Theology*, edited by Stanley E. Porter, 131–52. PaSt 3. Leiden: Brill, 2006.

Porter, Stanley E. 'When and How Was the Pauline Canon Complied? An Assessment of Theories'. In *The Pauline Canon*, edited by Stanley E. Porter, 95–127. PaSt 1. Leiden: Brill, 2004.

Porter, Stanley E., and Kent D. Clarke. 'Canonical-Critical Perspective and the Relationship of Colossians and Ephesians'. *Biblica* 78 (1997): 57–86.

Price, Robert M. 'The Evolution of the Pauline Canon'. *Hervormde Teologiese Studies* 53 (1997): 36–67.

Quinn, Jerome D. 'P46 – The Pauline Canon?' CBQ 36 (1974): 379–85.

Rese, Martin. 'Church and Israel in the Deuteropauline Letters'. SJT 43 (1990): 19–32.

Rese, Martin. 'Die Vorzüge Israels in Rom 9,4f. und Eph 2,12: Exegetische Anmerkungen zum Thema Kirche und Israel'. TZ 31 (1975): 211–22.

Richards, E. Randolph. 'The Codex and the Early Collection of Paul's Letters'. BBR 8 (1998): 151–66.

Richards, E. Randolph. *Paul and First-Century Letter Writing: Secretaries, Composition and Collection*. Downers Grove, IL: InterVarsity, 2004.

Robinson, John A. T. *The Body: A Study in Pauline Theology*. London: SCM, 1952.

Robinson, Theodore H. 'The Authorship of the Muratorian Canon'. *Expositor* VII (1906): 481–95.

Rogge, Joachim, and Gottfried Schille, eds. *Frühkatholizismus im ökumenischen Gespräch*. Berlin: Evangelische Verlagsanstalt, 1983.

Rollmann, Hans. 'From Baur to Wrede: The Quest for a Historical Method'. SR 17 (1988): 443–54.
Rothschild, Clare K. *Hebrews as Pseudepigraphon: The History and Significance of the Pauline Attribution of Hebrews*. WUNT 235. Tübingen: Mohr Siebeck, 2009.
Sampley, J. Paul. *'And the Two Shall Become One Flesh': A Study of Traditions in Ephesians 5.21-33*. SNTSMS 16. Cambridge: CUP, 1971.
Sand, Alexander. 'Überlieferung und Sammlung der Paulusbriefe'. In *Paulus in den neutestamentlichen Spätschriften: Zur Paulusrezeption im Neuen Testament*, edited by Karl Kertelge, 11–24. QD 89. Freiburg: Herder, 1981.
Sanders, E. P. 'Literary Dependence in Colossians'. JBL 85 (1966): 28–45.
Schäfer, Karl Theodor. 'Marcion und die ältesten Prologe zu den Paulusbriefen'. In *Kyriakon*, edited by Patrick Granfield and Johnannes Jungmann, 1.135–50. Münster: Aschendorff, 1970.
Schenke, Hans-Martin. 'Das Weiterwirken des Paulus und die Pflege seines Erbes durch die Paulus-Schule'. NTS 21 (1975): 505–18.
Scherbenske, Eric W. *Canonizing Paul: Ancient Editorial Practice and the Corpus Paulinum*. New York: OUP, 2013.
Schleiermacher, Friedrich. *Hermeneutics and Criticism and Other Writings*. Edited and translated by Andrew Bowie. Cambridge Texts in the History of Philosophy. Cambridge: CUP, 1998.
Schleiermacher, Friedrich. *Ueber den sogenannten ersten Brief des Paulos an den Timotheos: Ein kritisches Sendschreiben an J. C. Gass*. Berlin: Realschulbuchhandlung, 1807.
Schlier, Heinrich. *Der Brief an die Epheser: Ein Kommentar*. Düsseldorf: Patmos, 1957.
Schlier, Heinrich. *Grundzüge einer paulinischen Theologie*. Freiburg: Herder, 1978.
Schmeller, Thomas. *Der Zweite Brief an die Korinther*. 2 vols. EKKNT 8. Neukirchen: Neukirchner & Patmos, 2010–15.
Schmid, Ulrich. *Marcion und sein Apostolos: Rekonstruktion und historische Einordnung der marcionitischen Paulusbriefausgabe*. ANTF 25. Berlin: de Gruyter, 1995.
Schmidt, J. E. C. 'Vermuthungen über die beyden Briefe an die Thessalonicher'. In *Bibliothek für Kritik und Exegese des neuen Testaments und älteste Christengeschichte*, 2.3.380–6. Habamer: Gelehrtenbuchhandlung, 1801.
Schmithals, Walter. 'Zur Abfassung und ältesten Sammlung der paulinischen Hauptbriefe'. In *Paulus und die Gnostiker*, 175–200. TF 35. Hamburg–Bergstedt: Reich, 1965.
Schmitz, Hans-Josef. *Frühkatholizismus bei Adolf von Harnack, Rudolph Sohm und Ernst Käsemann*. Düsseldorf: Patmos, 1977.
Schnackenburg, Rudolf. *Der Brief an die Epheser*. EKKNT 10. Zürich: Benziger & Neukirchener, 1982.
Schnackenburg, Rudolf. 'Die Politeia Israels in Eph 2, 12'. In *De la Tôrah au Messie*, FS Henri Cazelles, edited by Maurice Carrez, Joseph Doré and Pierre Greglot, 467–74. Paris: Desclée, 1981.
Schnelle, Udo. *Theologie des Neuen Testaments*. Stuttgart: Vandenhoeck & Ruprecht, 2007.
Schofield, Ellwood Mearle. 'The Papyrus Fragments of the Greek New Testament'. PhD, Southern Baptist Theological Seminary, 1936.
Schrage, Wolfgang. *Der erste Brief an die Korinther*. 4 vols. EKKNT 7. Zürich: Benziger & Neukirchener, 1991–2001.
Schreiner, Thomas R. *Paul: Apostle of God's Glory in Christ*. Downers Grove, IL: InterVarsity & Apollos, 2001.

Schürmann, Heinz. 'Frühkatholizismus im Neuen Testament: Neun fragende Thesen'. *Catholica* 51 (1997): 163-8.
Schweitzer, Albert. *Die Mystik des Apostels Paulus*. Tübingen: Mohr, 1930.
Seitz, Christopher R. *Colossians*. BTCB. Grand Rapids, MI: Brazos, 2014.
Skeat, T. C. 'The Origin of the Christian Codex'. *Zeitschrift für Papyrologie und Epigraphik* 102 (1994): 263-8.
Staats, Reinhart. 'Ignatius und der Frühkatholizismus: Neues zu einem alten Thema'. VF 48 (2003): 80-92.
Standhartinger, Angela. 'Colossians and the Pauline School'. NTS 50 (2004): 572-93.
Stanton, Graham N. 'The Fourfold Gospel'. NTS 43 (1997): 317-46.
Stendahl, Krister. 'The Apocalypse of John and the Epistles of Paul in the Muratorian Fragment'. In *Current Issues in New Testament Interpretation*, edited by William Klassen and Graydon F. Snyder, 239-45. London: SCM, 1962.
Strawbridge, Jennifer R. *The Pauline Effect: The Use of the Pauline Epistles by Early Christian Writers*. SBR 5. Berlin: De Gruyter, 2015.
Sumney, Jerry L. *Colossians: A Commentary*. NTL. London: WJK, 2008.
Sundberg, Albert C. 'Canon Muratori: A Fourth-Century List'. HTR 66 (1973): 1-41.
Sundberg, Albert C. 'Towards a Revised History of the New Testament Canon'. In *Studia Evangelica*, edited by F. L. Cross, IV/1.452-61. TUGAL 102. Berlin: Akademie, 1968.
Tachau, Peter. *'Einst' und 'Jetzt' im Neuen Testament: Beobachtungen zu einem urchristlichen Predigtschema in der neutestamentlichen Briefliteratur und zu seiner Vorgeschichte*. FRLANT 105. Göttingen: Vandenhoeck & Ruprecht, 1972.
Thielman, Frank. *Ephesians*. BECNT. Grand Rapids, MI: Baker, 2010.
Thiselton, Anthony C. *The First Epistle to the Corinthians: A Commentary on the Greek Text*. NIGTC. Grand Rapids, MI: Eerdmans & Paternoster, 2000.
Thrall, Margaret E. *A Critical and Exegetical Commentary on the Second Epistle to the Corinthians*. 2 vols. ICC. Edinburgh: Clark, 1994.
Ticciati, Susannah. 'The Future of Biblical Israel: How Should Christians Read Romans 9-11 Today?' *Biblical Interpretation* 25 (2017): 497-518.
Ticciati, Susannah. 'The Nondivisive Difference of Election: A Reading of Romans 9-11'. *Journal of Theological Interpretation* 6 (2012): 257-78.
Ticciati, Susannah. 'Transforming the Grammar of Human Jealousy: Israel's Jealousy in Romans 9-11'. In *The Vocation of Theology Today*, FS David Ford, edited by Tom Greggs, Rachel Muers and Simeon Zahl, 77-91. Eugene, OR: Cascade, 2013.
Towner, P. H. 'The Present Age in the Eschatology of the Pastoral Epistles'. NTS 32 (1986): 427-48.
Trobisch, David. *Die Entstehung der Paulusbriefsammlung: Studien zu den Anfängen christlicher Publizistik*. NTOA 10. Freiburg (Schweiz): Universitätsverlag, 1989.
Trobisch, David. *The First Edition of the New Testament*. Oxford: OUP, 2000.
Trobisch, David. *Paul's Letter Collection: Tracing the Origins*. Minneapolis, MN: Fortress, 1994.
Twelftree, Graham H. *People of the Spirit: Exploring Luke's View of the Church*. Grand Rapids, MI: SPCK & Baker, 2009.
Vegge, Ivar. *2 Corinthians - a Letter about Reconciliation: A Psychagogical, Epistolographical and Rhetorical Analysis*. WUNT 2 239. Tübingen: Mohr Siebeck, 2008.
Verheyden, Joseph. 'The Canon Muratori: A Matter of Dispute'. In *The Biblical Canons*, edited by Jean-Marie Auwers and H. J. de Jonge, 487-556. BETL 163. Leuven: Leuven University & Peeters, 2003.

Vinzent, Markus. *Marcion and the Dating of the Synoptic Gospels*. Studia Patristica, Sup. 2. Leuven: Peeters, 2014.
Walker, William O. 'Acts and the Pauline Corpus Reconsidered'. JSNT 24 (1985): 3–23.
Wall, Robert W. 'Ecumenicity and Ecclesiology: The Promise of the Multiple Letter Canon of the New Testament'. In *The New Testament as Canon: A Reader in Canonical Criticism*, edited by Eugene E. Lemcio and Robert W. Wall, 184–207. Sheffield: JSOT, 1992.
Wall, Robert W. 'Pauline Authorship and the Pastoral Epistles: A Response to S. E. Porter'. BBR 5 (1995): 125–8.
Wallace, Daniel B. *Greek Grammar beyond the Basics: An Exegetical Syntax of the New Testament*. Grand Rapids, MI: Zondervan, 1996.
Ward, Graham. 'The Displaced Body of Jesus Christ'. In *Radical Orthodoxy: A New Theology*, edited by John Milbank, Catherine Pickstock and Graham Ward, 163–81. London: Routledge, 1999.
Ward, Graham. 'Transcorporeality: The Ontological Scandal'. BJRL 80 (1998): 235–52.
Watson, Francis. *Agape, Eros, Gender: Towards a Pauline Sexual Ethic*. Cambridge: CUP, 2000.
Watson, Francis. '"Every Perfect Gift": James, Paul and the Created Order'. In *Muted Voices of the New Testament: Readings in the Catholic Epistles and Hebrews*, edited by Katherine M. Hockey, Madison N. Pierce and Francis Watson, 121–37. LNTS 565. London: Clark, 2017.
Watson, Francis. *Gospel Writing: A Canonical Perspective*. Grand Rapids, MI: Eerdmans, 2013.
Watson, Francis. *Paul and the Hermeneutics of Faith*. 2nd edn. London: Bloomsbury, 2016.
Watson, Francis. *Paul, Judaism, and the Gentiles: Beyond the New Perspective*. Grand Rapids, MI: Eerdmans, 2007.
Way, David. *The Lordship of Christ: Ernst Käsemann's Interpretation of Paul's Theology*. Oxford: Clarendon, 1991.
Weiss, Johannes. 'Der Eingang des ersten Korintherbriefs'. *Theologische Studien und Kritiken* 73 (1900): 126–30.
Weiss, Johannes. *Der erste Korintherbrief*. KEK. Göttingen: Vandenhoeck & Ruprecht, 1910.
White, Benjamin L. *Remembering Paul: Ancient and Modern Contests over the Image of the Apostle*. Oxford: OUP, 2014.
Wilson, R. McL. *A Critical and Exegetical Commentary on Colossians and Philemon*. ICC. London: Clark, 2005.
Wood, Susan K. 'Robert Jenson's Ecclesiology from a Roman Catholic Perspective'. In *Trinity, Time and Church: A Response to the Theology of Robert W. Jenson*, edited by Colin E. Gunton, 178–87. Grand Rapids, MI: Eerdmans, 2000.
Wright, N. T. *Paul and the Faithfulness of God*. 2 vols. London: SPCK, 2013.
Yee, Tet-Lim N. *Jews, Gentiles and Ethnic Reconciliation: Paul's Jewish Identity and Ephesians*. SNTSMS 130. Cambridge: CUP, 2005.
Yorke, Gosnell L. O. R. *The Church as the Body of Christ in the Pauline Corpus: A Re-Examination*. Lanham, MD: University Press of America, 1991.
Yorke, Gosnell L. O. R. 'Review of Gregory Dawes, *The Body in Question*'. JBL 121 (2002): 378–80.

Zahn, Theodor. *Geschichte des neutestamentlichen Kanons*. 2 vols. Erlangen: Deichert, 1888–92.
Zahn, Theodor. *Grundriß der Geschichte des neutestamentlichen Kanons: Eine Ergänzung zu der Einleitung in das Neue Testament*. 2nd edn. Leipzig: Deichert, 1904.
Zuntz, Günther. *The Text of the Epistles: A Disquisition upon the* Corpus Paulinum. London: OUP, 1953.

Index of Authors

Patristic

Cyprian 21, 52, 54
Epiphanius 42–7, 49
Eusebius 1–2, 15, 50
Origen 1–2, 10, 36–7, 39, 53, 78, 132, 145, 150, 185
Tertullian 1, 16, 34–6, 38–40, 42–8, 51, 53, 57, 62, 77, 186
Victorinus 47, 52

Modern

Aageson, James W. 75, 153
Aland, Barbara 23, 26–8
Aland, Kurt 17–18, 22–3, 26–8, 30–4, 38, 53
Anderson, Charles P. 28
Armstrong, Jonathan 52
Aune, David E. 3

Barclay, John M. G. 104, 107–8, 141
Barker, Don 23
Barnett, Albert E. 19
Barth, Markus 97, 101, 109–10, 113, 116, 133, 171–2
Baur, F. C. 2, 4, 9, 21, 46–7, 57–68, 71–4, 78, 81, 87–8, 92, 138, 186, 188
Becker, Eve-Marie 7–8, 91
BeDuhn, Jason David 42–3, 47
Best, Ernest 97–8, 110, 117, 120, 122, 143, 169, 171–3, 175, 182
Bieringer, Reimund 128
Black, C. Clifton 67–9
Bornkamm, Günther 40, 85, 106–7, 161
Brakke, David 3, 15
Brown, Raymond E. 66–7
Bultmann, Rudolf 62, 146, 151–2
Burkett, Delbert 69
Byrne, Brendan 111

Caird, G. B. 99, 175
Campbell, Douglas A. 76–9, 81–2, 125
Carroll, Kenneth L. 19
Childs, Brevard S. 9, 58, 72, 75, 81–90, 92, 153, 186–7
Clabeaux, John J. 43
Clarke, Kent D. 5
Clivaz, Claire 25
Conzelmann, Hans 19, 68, 101, 161
Corssen, Peter 47

Dahl, Nils A. 21, 37–8, 46–8, 51–2, 74–5, 109
Dawes, Gregory W. 143–6, 148, 153, 169, 172, 177, 179, 183–4, 187
de Bruyne, Donatien 47
de Wette, W. M. L. 58–61, 78, 186
Dennison, Charles D. 65
Dodd, C. H. 165
Downs, David J. 68, 71
Duff, Jeremy 24, 47
Duncan, George S. 77
Dunn, James D. G. 6, 69–73, 108
Dunning, Benjamin H. 106

Ehrman, Bart D. 3–5, 7, 19, 42, 76, 188
Elliott, J. K. 44
Elliott, John H. 129
Engberg-Pedersen, Troels 150–1, 157, 163, 183
Epp, Eldon Jay 24
Evanson, Edward 59

Fee, Gordon D. 159, 162
Ferguson, Everett 49–50
Fewster, Gregory P. 7–8, 152
Finegan, Jack 24, 31, 45–6
Fowl, Stephen E. 105, 131, 171, 174
Frede, Hermann Josef 20–1, 30–4, 39–40, 46, 51, 53–4
Furnish, Victor Paul 76

Gamble, Harry Y. 15–16, 19–20, 22, 28, 35–6, 38, 42, 45, 52–3
Gnilka, Joachim 101
Goodspeed, Edgar J. 18–19, 22, 28, 34–6, 46, 55, 79, 87, 95, 102, 114–15, 173, 180
Grindheim, Sigurd 122, 143

Haacker, Klaus 64, 68–9, 141
Hagen, Kenneth 59
Hahneman, Geoffrey Mark 49–52
Harnack, Adolf von 16–17, 34, 43, 45–6, 49, 52
Hatch, William H. P. 25
Hays, Richard B. 157, 159, 187
Herzer, Jens 59, 75
Hill, C. E. 50
Hoehner, Harold E. 73, 100, 108, 110
Howard, George 169
Hübner, Hans 98
Hurtado, Larry W. 26, 28

Jenson, Robert W. 137, 149, 151–5, 158, 161–2, 165, 170, 184

Käsemann, Ernst 9, 58, 65–9, 71–5, 81, 87–8, 92, 125, 137–43, 150, 152–3, 155, 158–9, 161, 165, 168, 173, 184, 186–8
Keck, Leander E. 82
Kelly, Anthony J. 153
Kim, Seyoon 115
Knox, John 18–20, 45–7, 55, 79
Kostenberger, A. J. 180
Kreinecker, Christina M. 76
Küng, Hans 66–7

Lang, T. J. 42, 181
Leppä, Outi 76
Lietzmann, Hans 17, 35, 157, 161–3
Lieu, Judith M. 36, 42–3
Lincoln, Andrew T. 6, 76, 99, 102, 113, 115, 119, 131–2, 143, 169, 171–3, 182
Lindemann, Andreas 16, 101–2, 124
Lohse, Eduard 104, 166
Lovering, Eugene H. 15, 17, 19, 21, 32–3, 35–6, 40, 53–4
Lütgert, D. W. 141
Luz, Ulrich 67, 97

MacDonald, Margaret Y. 73–4, 87, 97, 109–11, 133, 169, 171, 173
Markschies, Christoph Johannes 49–50
Marshall, I. Howard 115
Martin, Dale B. 80–1
Martin, Ralph P. 115, 119, 122–3, 125, 140, 147–51, 154, 157, 163, 170, 183
McKelvey, R. J. 131–2
Meade, David G. 3–4
Merklein, Helmut 75, 101
Merz, Annette 6–7
Metzger, Bruce M. 51, 114
Miletic, Stephen Francis 182
Mitchell, Margaret M. 9, 88–9, 91, 161, 186
Mitton, C. Leslie 19, 71–2, 96, 102, 130, 179
Morgan, Robert 72
Moule, C. F. D. 121, 169
Mowry, Lucetta 19
Muratori, Lodovico Antonio 49–50
Murphy-O'Connor, Jerome 16, 21

Nienhuis, David R. 51
Novenson, Matthew V. 79

O'Brien, Peter T. 73

Parker, D. C. 22
Patsch, Hermann 59
Perkins, Pheme 112, 182
Pokorný, Petr 74–5
Porter, Stanley E. 5–7, 16, 19–20, 22, 54–5, 73, 115
Price, Robert M. 16

Quinn, Jerome D. 21

Rese, Martin 108–13
Richards, E. Randolph 20
Robinson, John A. T. 152–4, 165, 184
Robinson, Theodore H. 181
Rogge, Joachim 67
Rollmann, Hans 64
Rothschild, Clare K. 28

Sampley, J. Paul 181–2
Sand, Alexander 19
Sanders, E. P. 122
Schäfer, Karl Theodor 47–8
Schenke, Hans-Martin 19–20

Scherbenske, Eric W. 48
Schille, Gottfried 67
Schleiermacher, Friedrich 9, 57–60, 64, 186, 188
Schlier, Heinrich 66–7, 75, 97, 101, 110, 112, 140, 142–3, 153, 155, 172
Schmeller, Thomas 126
Schmid, Ulrich 43, 46
Schmidt, J. E. C. 59
Schmithals, Walter 19, 35
Schmitz, Hans-Josef 67
Schnackenburg, Rudolf 68, 97, 110–11, 117, 145, 169, 173, 180
Schnelle, Udo 58, 68, 76
Schofield, Ellwood Mearle 24, 26–7
Schrage, Wolfgang 132, 160
Schreiner, Thomas R. 73
Schürmann, Heinz 67
Schweitzer, Albert 4, 138, 151, 162–3, 184
Seitz, Christopher R. 88
Skeat, T. C. 25–6
Staats, Reinhart 69
Standhartinger, Angela 19
Stanton, Graham N. 50
Stendahl, Krister 52
Strawbridge, Jennifer R. 40
Sumney, Jerry L. 166
Sundberg, Albert C. 49–51

Tachau, Peter 98–9
Thielman, Frank 73

Thiselton, Anthony C. 157, 159–60
Thrall, Margaret E. 126–8
Ticciati, Susannah 113
Towner, P. H. 68
Trobisch, David 15, 21–2, 24–8, 30–3, 39, 46, 54–5, 88
Twelftree, Graham H. 69

Vegge, Ivar 125
Verheyden, Joseph 50
Vinzent, Markus 42, 46–8

Walker, William O. 19
Wall, Robert W. 5, 88, 142
Wallace, Daniel B. 116
Ward, Graham 154–5, 184
Watson, Francis 50–1, 63–4, 146, 157
Way, David 139–40
Weiss, Johannes 37, 157, 159, 163
White, Benjamin L. 57, 61, 81
Wilson, R. McL. 121, 166
Wood, Susan K. 154–5
Wright, N. T. 73

Yee, Tet-Lim N. 97, 100, 104, 110–11
Yorke, Gosnell L. O. R. 143–4, 170, 177

Zahn, Theodor 16–18, 22, 34, 39
Zuntz, Günther 17, 36

Index of Biblical References

Old Testament

Genesis
2	121
2.23-24	118, 179–82

Exodus
3.14	36–7
20.12	118
32.6	157–8

Leviticus
19.18	118

Numbers
11	157
14	158
16–17	157–8
21	157
25	157

Deuteronomy
32.21	158

Psalms
8.7	168–29
15	181
67.19	174–6
77.58	158
117.22	131

Isaiah
8.14-15	131
28.16	131
56.3-9	116
57.19	115–16, 118–19

Jeremiah
31.31-34	111

Hosea
2.25	116

Joel
2.32	101

New Testament

Matthew
5	181
6.32	175
21.42	131

Mark
12.10	131
14.58	104

Luke
15	109
20.17-18	131

John
12.28	176

Acts
2.21	37
2.25	181–2
4.11	131
7.48	104
17.24	104

Romans
1.1	27
1.7	35
1.15	35
1.20	100
2.17	123
2.23	123
2.25-29	104
3	79
3.9-23	98
3.21	116
3.24–4.2	96–103, 117, 123, 129, 135, 186
3.27	123
4	91, 123
4.1	103
4.2	123

4.13	112	3.9	138
5	121	3.9-17	129–32
5.1-2	115, 123	5	148
5.1-11	122–3	6	148–9
5.9-11	114, 122–5, 127–8	6.15	145
		6.17	115
5.12-13	127	7.11	125
5.12-21	172	7.19	103
6	91, 164–5, 167, 184	8–10	91, 117, 148, 156, 159
6.3-11	156	8.4-13	156
7–8	106	8.5-6	103
7.1-6	165	9.24-27	90
7.4	156, 164–7, 184	9.27	145, 148
7.6	156	10–11	164–5, 184
7.7-25	172	10.1-4	156–8, 163
8.3	106	10.1-30	156
8.11	150	10.4	110
8.24	101	10.5	161
9-11	108–14	10.6	157
9.3	111	10.10	158
9.4-5	108–14, 118	10.14-15	158
9.8	112	10.16-17	139, 143, 152, 156, 158–62, 165–6
9.12	99–100		
9.25	116		
9.33	131	10.18-22	158
10.1	111	11	148, 158–60
10.12	37	11.2-16	160
11.14	103, 111	11.17-34	156, 160–2
11.15	124, 127	11.24	166
11.26	111	11.25	111
11.28-29	112	11.29	152
12	86, 119, 143, 145, 175	12	86, 119, 143, 145, 150, 152, 158–60, 162–4, 166, 175–8, 183–4
12.4-8	156, 164–5		
13.14	128		
14	117		
14–15	91	12–14	159, 162
15.8	111	12.1-11	162–3
15.20	132	12.1-27	156
15.27	133	12.12-13	143, 162–4
		12.13	115
1 Corinthians		12.14-26	138
1.2	37	12.14-31	162
1.18	101	12.21	168
1.28-29	36–7	12.27-28	138, 143, 166
2.6-8	39	13.9-12	177–8
2.8	176	15	121
2.10	150	15.2	102

15.21-23	172	1.22-23	138, 145, 168–71, 173, 175, 177
15.40-44	150–2		
15.45	115		
15.53-54	127–8	2	168
16.10	27	2.1-10	4, 98, 108
		2.3	103, 105
2 Corinthians		2.5	78–9, 97, 100–2, 106, 135
1.1	37		
1.20	111	2.8-10	4, 64, 78–9, 96–102, 106–8, 129, 135
2.15	101		
3.5	99		
3.6	120		
4.7	99	2.11	102–8, 112, 135
5.1-2	104	2.12	103, 105, 108–14, 131, 173
5.14-17	125		
5.16	103	2.11-13	97–9
5.17	27	2.11-22	95, 106, 108, 121
5.17-20	114, 118, 122, 125–9		
		2.13-18	114–29, 173–5
6.1	128	2.14	105–6
6.2	102	2.14-16	170–3
7.5	103	2.15	99–100, 109, 135, 178, 182
8.13-14	134		
		2.16	145
Galatians		2.17	98, 171
1–2	90	2.18	171
1.2	37	2.19-22	116, 118, 129–34, 173–4
2.7-9	102–6		
2.20	103	3	90, 92
3.3	105	3.1-13	173, 181
3.16	111–12	3.5	132
3.27	128	3.6	173–4, 181
3.27-28	172	4–5	119, 121–2, 178–9
4	91		
4.22-31	105	4–6	124
4.24	108, 45	4.1-3	174, 178
5.3	104	4.1-6	177
5.6	103	4.1-16	74, 174
5.14	118	4.4	125, 171, 175
5.16-24	105	4.4-6	44, 102, 174–5
6.12-13	103, 105	4.7-10	175–6
6.15	103	4.9-16	173
		4.11	132, 169
Ephesians		4.11-16	176–8
1–2	173–4	4.13	172
1.1	35–6	4.15-16	145, 185
1.9	181	4.16	132, 134, 139
1.10	170, 181	4.17	175
1.11	173	4.17-20	106
1.18	173	4.17-24	130

Index of Biblical References

4.20-24	172, 178	3.10	127–8
4.24	127	3.11	103
4.25	177–8	4.16	16, 18, 36, 44, 47, 54, 77
4.30	74		
5.2	183	**1 Thessalonians**	
5.18	178	1–3	89
5.21-33	138, 143–6, 170, 178–83	1.8	37
5.21–6.9	179	3.3-4	89
5.28-32	172	5.28	24
5.31	118	**2 Thessalonians**	
5.31-32	153	2.1-12	59
6.2-3	118, 179	2.2	83, 89
6.19	181	2.15	83, 89–90
		3.10	89
Philippians		3.17	83
1.22-24	103		
2.12	102	**2 Timothy**	
2.12-13	100	1.9	107
3.2	104	4.6-8	86, 90–2
3.2–4.3	77		
3.12-14	91	**Titus**	
3.16-17	90	3.5	107
		Hebrews	
Colossians		7.6	111
1.15-18	166–7	8.8-9	111
1.16	127, 169, 172	9.11	104
1.18	172–3	9.24	104
1.19-23	114–15, 118–22, 124–5, 127–8, 167	13.12-13	25
		13.19-20	25
1.20	169	**James**	
1.22	172–3	2.14-26	100
1.24	166–7, 172–3		
2	91	**1 Peter**	
2.1	103	2.4-8	129–31
2.8-19	167	2.12	105
2.11-13	104	4.3	105, 175
2.14	125		
2.16-23	176–7	**2 Peter**	
2.19	167	3.15-16	16
3.18–4.1	179	**Revelation**	
3.9	115	2–3	36

Index of Subjects

Acts and the CP 18–19, 55, 60, 65, 76–7
Adamic Christology/corporate personality 118–19, 120–1, 127, 172–3, 177–8, 180–2
"Anthropos myth" *see* "gnostic"/"mythological" background to Pauline letters
authorship
  in canonical context 82–3, 134–5, 186–8
  conservative views 5–6, 64, 73, 144
  as a distorting preoccupation 6, 10–11, 73, 95, 100–2, 110, 113–14, 124, 129–30, 134–5, 144, 182
  recent alternative views 7–8, 80–1
  value of an agnostic approach 9–10, 78, 134–5
  see also pseudepigraphy
  see also under Ephesians, Pastoral letters, Thessalonian letters

body of Christ 137–84
  in 1 Corinthians 141–3, 145–53, 155–65, 168–9, 175–8, 183–4
  Christ as head 80, 132–3, 140, 143–6, 151, 153, 165–9, 177, 179, 183–4
  in Colossians 121–2, 140–1, 153, 165–73, 176–7, 179–80, 182, 184
  in Ephesians 80, 119–22, 125, 127, 140–6, 151–3, 155, 165–84
  eucharistic sense 139, 143, 148–9, 152–5, 158–63, 165–6, 170, 183–4
  marriage allegory 80, 143–6, 153, 165–6, 172, 178–84
  in Romans 143, 145, 156, 164–7, 175, 184
  social/organizational sense 139–40, 142–3, 148, 162–5, 169, 174–8
  and Spirit 139–40, 142, 147, 149–51, 156–7, 162–4, 171, 173–5, 183–4
  whether and how metaphorical 138–9, 142–8, 150–3, 155, 157, 159, 162, 166–7, 169–70, 174, 177, 179–80, 183

canon and reading community 1–2, 8–9, 92, 188
circumcision 97–8, 102–6, 112, 135

decadence schema of the CP 58–76, 138, 188
  in Baur 58–65
  enduring legacy 69–76, 80, 87–8
  in Käsemann 65–9, 140–3

early Catholicism *see Frühkatholizismus*
ecumenism and canon 63–4, 66–7, 141–2
Ephesians
  address/title 18–19, 21, 35–6, 54–5, 60, 77–8, 85, 87
  authorship 18–19, 59–64, 66–7, 71, 73, 77–8, 84, 109–10, 142–3
  ecclesiology 66–7, 69, 71–2, 75, 101, 127, 133, 138, 140–3, 152–3, 168–84
  eschatology 74, 101, 104, 124, 128–9, 133, 177–8
  incongruous grace 104–8, 110, 112–3, 135, 175
  integrating role within the CP 29–30, 134–5, 186–7
  mediating role within the NT 100, 105, 130–1, 135
  other views on its canonical role 84, 86–7
  with Colossians, marginalized or compromised as "intermediate" 71–2, 74–5, 87

Frühkatholizismus 61–75
  in Baur 61–5
  critical views 37, 67–9
  in Dunn 69–72
  and Ephesians 6, 64–7, 71, 75, 138
  in Käsemann 65–9, 71
  and the Pastorals 67–8, 71, 74–5

Index of Subjects

"gnostic"/"mythological" background to Pauline letters 101, 151, 164, 182
  in Baur 61–2
  in Käsemann 139–40, 142–3, 159
  in Schlier 140, 142

Hebrews
  ambiguous place in the CP 8–9, 16–17, 20–6, 28, 30–2, 40, 42, 46–56, 59, 186
  distinctive style and anonymity 55, 59, 64
history/philology *vis-à-vis* theology/exegesis
  in Baur 57–8, 61, 64, 78, 188
  confessional weighting 60–1, 68–9, 76
  constructive circularity 60–1, 78–9, 84
  critical views of their interrelation 3–6, 76–81
  integrated in canonical interpretation 8, 10, 15, 83–4, 88–9, 92, 187–9

independent circulation of letters 28, 35–7, 40–2, 54
institutionalization, early Christian 63, 68–75, 87, 142, 168
  in MacDonald 73–4
Israel 108–16, 118–19, 121, 124, 132–3, 135, 156–8, 161, 163

"Laodiceans" 2, 18, 35–6, 43–5, 47–8, 50–1, 77–8, 186
law 4, 48, 64, 66, 79, 97, 99–100, 102, 104, 106–8, 110–12, 116–18, 123, 135, 145, 165
literary dependency 129–30
  Colossians and earlier letters 122
  Colossians and Ephesians 10, 60–1, 121–2
  Pastoral letters 59
  Pauline letters generally 62–3, 78–9, 91
  and pseudonymity 78
Luther 57, 59, 60–1, 63–4, 68–9, 118

Marcion 1–2, 16–18, 20–1, 24, 34–6, 42–9, 51–5, 57, 62, 77, 85
Muratorian Fragment 2, 16–17, 34, 39, 44, 46, 49–54, 186
mythology *see* "gnostic"/"mythological" background to Pauline letters

order of letters within the CP
  chronological 10, 38, 46, 51, 76–9, 86–7, 125
  literary 10, 23–34, 38–9, 43–8, 51, 85–8

𝔓⁴⁶ 23–6, 28–32, 34–6, 46–7, 53, 108, 114, 178, 181
partition of letters 17, 19, 60, 77, 89
Pastoral letters
  authorship 5, 20, 24, 59–61, 71, 77, 84
  canonical role 20, 74–5, 84–8, 90–1, 153–4, 187
  eschatology 68–9, 71
  negative views 6–7, 58, 62–3, 67, 71–2, 80, 142
  when included in the CP 9, 16–17, 20, 24, 32–3, 40, 42, 46–50, 52–5, 185–6
Pauline school(s) 19–20, 74–5, 122, 134, 151
Paul's "seven churches" 18, 20, 33, 47–9, 51–3, 55
prologues, Latin or "Marcionite" 18, 35, 45–9, 52–3
pseudepigraphy 3–8
  as deceit 3–5
  less pejorative views 7–8, 57–8, 83–4, 188

reconciliation 114–29, 135
  in 2 Corinthians 114, 118, 122, 125–9
  in Colossians 114–15, 118–22, 124–5, 127–9, 171
  in Ephesians 103, 105–6, 108, 114–25, 127–9, 171
  in Romans 114, 122–5, 127–9
Romans as introduction to the CP 85–8, 187

stichometry 24, 31–2, 45–6, 54–5, 88
stylistic analysis 59, 76–7

Thessalonian letters
  authorship of 2 Thess. 59, 74, 77, 83–4, 90
  canonical role 83–4, 89–90

works, good or otherwise 4, 63–4, 78–9, 96–102, 107–8, 123, 135

www.ingramcontent.com/pod-product-compliance
Lightning Source LLC
Chambersburg PA
CBHW062222300426
44115CB00012BA/2176